FIRST
AMENDMENT
FELON

FIRST AMENDMENT FELON

The Story of Frank Wilkinson, His 132,000-page FBI File, and His Epic Fight for Civil Rights and Liberties

ROBERT SHERRILL

NATION BOOKS
NEW YORK

First Amendment Felon
The Story of Frank Wilkinson, His 132,000-page FBI File,
and His Epic Fight for Civil Rights and Liberties

Published by
Nation Books
An Imprint of Avalon Publishing Group Inc.
245 West 17th Street, 11th Floor
New York, NY 10011

AVALON
publishing group incorporated

Nation Books is a co-publishing venture of the Nation Institute
and Avalon Publishing Group Incorporated.

Library of Congress Cataloging-in-Publication Data is available.

ISBN: 1-56025-779-2
ISBN 13: 978-1-56025-779-0

9 8 7 6 5 4 3 2 1

Book design by India Amos

Printed in the United States of America
Distributed by Publishers Group West

This country was not built by men who were afraid
and it cannot be preserved by such men. . . . When
[the nation] begins to send its dissenters, such as
. . . Wilkinson, and now Braden, to jail, the liberties
indispensable to its existence must be fast disappearing.

JUSTICE BLACK, dissenting (*Wilkinson v. U.S.*
and *Braden v. U.S.*) 365 U.S., 399 and 431 (1961)

No account of the demise of the House Un-American
Activities Committee would be complete without a
notation of the extraordinary work done by the National
Committee Against Repressive Legislation—NCARL.
The work of this group, headed by Mr. Frank Wilkinson
. . . has been uniquely valuable to members of this
Congress who have sought to excise . . . that self-inflicted
wound called HUAC-HISC, which now after thirty or
more years will no longer be an embarrassment and
a disgrace to the Congress of the United States. . . .

Statement on the floor of the House by
REP. ROBERT DRINAN, the only liberal
member of HUAC, on January 14, 1975, the
day the committee was abolished

CONTENTS

Risk for risk, for myself I had rather take my chance
that some traitors will escape detection than spread
abroad a spirit of general suspicion and distrust. . . .

JUDGE LEARNED HAND

If fascism came to America, it would be
on a program of Americanism.

HUEY LONG

Congress shall make no law . . . abridging
the freedom of speech, or of the press; or the
right of the people peaceably to assemble.

FIRST AMENDMENT SEGMENT,

U.S. BILL OF RIGHTS

IF AT THIS moment you had in your hand the bicentennial issue of *Life* magazine that was published in the fall of 1991—an issue given over entirely to the "200-year history of the turbulence and triumph of the Bill of Rights"—you could turn to page sixty-seven and see a half-page picture of Frank Wilkinson. He is smiling grandly, as well he might. The text that accompanies the photo contains four factual errors, but the tone is totally admiring. And why not? After all, *Life* was featuring him as one of the greatest defenders of the First Amendment, and particularly of that portion of it that shaped his life: "Congress shall make no law . . . abridging the freedom of speech, or of the press; or the right of the people peaceably to assemble. . . ."

Actually, measured by what happened at various levels of the federal court system, Wilkinson lost that fight. But he wasn't alone. Of the twenty-one "political" First Amendment disputes mentioned in *Life*'s account of the twentieth century, more than half the defendants lost when they got to the Supreme Court.

Calvin Coolidge was right when he said: "This country is

no country for radicalism. I think it is really the most conservative country in the world."

Although Henry Luce's magazines sometimes had their liberal moments, generally they were marble monuments to conservatism, revered by patriots who followed that ideology. That makes *Life*'s tribute to Wilkinson such a delightful example of black humor that it deserves elaboration.

■

WILKINSON'S LONG BATTLE against the enemies of the First Amendment began in the early 1950s, when the Los Angeles City Council, the California State Anti-Subversive Committee and the U.S. House Un-American Activities Committee (HUAC) asked him, in serial hearings on public housing, to expound on his political activities. He refused to answer, in effect telling his inquisitors that the people he associated with, the kind of books he read, and the meetings he attended were none of their business. They let him get away with it—at first. But finally, in 1958, in Atlanta, HUAC cited him for contempt and he was convicted by a federal court in that town—where his long and close alliance with the civil rights movement made him an easy target.[1]

The Supreme Court refused, five to four, to overturn his conviction. Fittingly, the Court's decision was read by Justice Potter Stewart, who had been named to the Court on the recommendation of FBI director J. Edgar Hoover, Wilkinson's lifelong bête noire. So Wilkinson wound up in the Lewisburg federal penitentiary. He and his lawyers were disappointed, having nurtured a small hope based on a 1957 First Amendment case, but by 1961 the Court had slipped a notch.

But though Wilkinson was discouraged, he didn't show it. In his first press conference after the Court's decision, he said, "We will not save free speech if we are not prepared to go to jail for its defense. I am prepared to pay that price."

Wilkinson's close ally, Carl Braden, had the same luck with the Supreme Court and went off to prison with Wilkinson. Braden had already served time for what was then considered a heinous crime (in fact, it was considered an act of treason in Kentucky, where it was committed): helping a black man buy a house in a white neighborhood.

Shortly after Frank and Carl entered prison, a petition signed by two thousand liberal leaders was presented to the Justice Department—at that time ostensibly in the hands of reasonable Democrats—seeking clemency for Wilkinson and Braden. It was ignored. Those were tough days for rebels.

In the long run, though, Wilkinson's career must be considered a victory. A long-delayed victory, perhaps, but still a victory. Since 1953, shortly after he was fired as Los Angeles's premier public-housing advocate, he had been leading a national campaign to kill HUAC. The nine-month interim in prison (his one-year sentence was cut by three months for good behavior) only spurred him on to greater efforts.

From 1956 to 1975, Wilkinson traveled an average of one hundred days a year in thirty-five states to warn of the liberties being wiped out by the FBI and its marionettes. His objective was to organize opposition to HUAC in every congressional district in the country, and to organize noisy demonstrations wherever HUAC took its superpatriotic circus. He gave two or three speeches a day to civic and political and religious organizations; he met with reporters and editors; and he always made sure that his schedule included speeches and rallies on college campuses (he lost count of these after passing six hundred). He was enormously popular. Famously, when he stopped by the Berkeley campus on his way to prison, forty-five hundred students rallied to hear his speech and give him a rousing bon voyage ovation.

Indeed, it would be quite wrong to think that Wilkinson's crusade was a lonely one. He personally had the respect and often the affection—and his crusade had the unwavering support—of many hundreds of noted artists and writers and constitutional lawyers and educators. Yes, and even a few politicians—a very few.

A good sampling of the supporters behind Wilkinson can be found in the *Washington Post* of January 2, 1961, which carried a two-page petition to the 87th Congress urging the abolition of the House Un-American Activities Committee. Wilkinson and his team had had no trouble rounding up the four hundred signers. Some were old faithfuls like Eleanor Roosevelt and Martin Luther King Jr. Many of the names probably wouldn't register with readers of this generation, but in their day most were well known. They were the cream of the left-wing intellectuals, ranging from real iconoclasts and rebels to people who were simply sick and tired of all the right-wing bullying, including Harry Bridges, Aubrey Williams, Clifford Durr, Linus Pauling, Louis Untermeyer, Henry Steele Commager, Louis Jaffe, Harlow Shapley, Ben Shahn, William Carlos Williams, Helen and Melvyn Douglas, Lewis C. E. Ayres, J. Frank Dobie, George Kirstein, and William Kunstler.

By 1961, the bullying of HUAC had been going on for two decades, and although J. Edgar Hoover's allies in Congress and the right-wing press still made it somewhat risky to publicly accuse the witch-hunters of being nuts, many intellectuals weren't afraid to point out the obvious: HUAC had ruined the lives of thousands of patriotic Americans without giving one ounce of the promised national security in return.

It's safe to say that a very high percentage of the signers already had dossiers in the FBI files, and those who didn't have surely did as soon as J. Edgar Hoover saw that edition of the *Washington Post*.

How much credit can be given to Wilkinson's unflagging crusade is of course anyone's guess, but Congress, after spending hundreds of millions of dollars on HUAC's fruitless inquisition, finally decided in 1975 to withhold further financial oxygen, thereby killing its bastard offspring which, ever since 1938, while ostensibly hunting for subversives, was actually doing its best to erase the First Amendment, as well as the Fourth, the Fifth, and the Sixth Amendments of the Bill of Rights.

HUAC's end came three years too late to be considered a stinging victory over Hoover (who died in 1972), the bureaucrat Wilkinson considered his chief antagonist, but it *was* still a great symbolic victory. HUAC's decades-long inquisition had depended almost entirely on Hoover's assistance, and Hoover would not have had nearly as much power if the witch-hunters had not been out front doing much of his dirty work for him. In effect, Hoover and HUAC had been ideological twins, joined at the spleen.

Less important as a sign of Wilkinson's success, perhaps, but pleasing in a highly ironic fashion was the fact that he was being embraced by one of Henry Luce's magazines. Although by 1991 Henry Luce, founder of the *Time, Life, Fortune* empire was long dead, Wilkinson's appearance in what was once a centerpiece of the Lucean empire was enough to justify that smile in the photo. He must have been enjoying the thought that *Life* was celebrating him and his work although he stood for just about everything Luce hated.

W. A. Swanberg, Luce's biographer, has claimed for him "the function of founder and most effective long-term promoter of national anti-Communism and religious-moral superiority, having worked at it longer and harder and more influentially . . . week after week for twenty-nine years . . . than anyone else in sight."[2] Influential, he certainly was. As *Der Spiegel* pointed out with envy in the 1960s, "Every third U.S. family buys every week a Luce product; 94 percent of all Americans over 12 know *Time*."[3]

Luce came to his anti-Communism via a flirtation with fascism. His admiration for Mussolini and Hitler, and also for Francisco Franco, the fascist conqueror of democratic Spain, lasted almost to the eve of World War II.

It lasted as long as it did because those tyrants fiercely opposed "godless" Communism, a qualifying word Luce liked to use, as did J. Edgar Hoover. They considered themselves to be soldiers in God's army, and they talked of their crusade in militant terms. Take this, from Hoover, at a conference of Methodist ministers: "Communism is secularism on the march. . . . Either it will survive or Christianity will triumph because in this land of ours the two cannot live side by side."[4]

Both Hoover and Luce were Presbyterians, and although it is said that as a youth Hoover had planned to enter the ministry, in adulthood he seemed much less devout than Luce, and probably less demanding of God. "Luce's Presbyterianism . . . was so militant and aggressive that one could imagine him shouting his prayers at a God who might otherwise be inattentive and waste his time."[5] But alas, we'll never know if he actually shouted at God, because he never allowed anyone to travel with him on the thirty-six-floor elevator ride up to his office in the Time-Life Building on New York's Forty-eighth Street; he reserved that time for prayer. And at the end of each day he dropped to his knees for another conversation (as he called it) with God.

Obviously, Luce would have despised, yea loathed, Wilkinson, and it would have been a toss-up as to whether he would have loathed him more for his atheism or for his lifelong war against the FBI and HUAC. Taking them both together would surely have led Luce to identify Frank Wilkinson as a Communist.

But as Sam Rayburn, longtime and powerful Speaker of the House of Representatives, used to say, "What goes around, comes around." By 1991, the official end of the Cold War, the merry-go-round of history had dropped Luce into near-oblivion, but Frank Wilkinson, the First Amendment rebel, was still coming around—and enjoying the ride on the very presses Time Inc. had paid for.

Bobby Kennedy once said, "I was on the cover of *Time* and now Luce is turning over in his grave."[6]

It's easy to imagine that Luce was once again whirling in his grave in 1991 when *Life* ran its tribute to the men and women—some of them, like Wilkinson, considered extremely subversive in their day—who used the First Amendment to fight the government's oppressive nosiness. Luce certainly would not have called them, as the special edition of *Life* does, "some of our most courageous and principled citizens."

■

THIS BOOK IS about one such citizen in particular, and about his loyal cohorts and supporters, equally courageous and principled, as they joined his crusade to end the oppression of Hoover and his many minions—who were primarily responsible for unhinging the nation's psyche during the Cold War.

It was a lopsided struggle, a veritable David and Goliath fight. But Wilkinson, as I've said, had a great deal of support from many academics all across the country, from a small army of well-known writers and artists, and also important help from some of the feistier members of the bar.

Hoover waged his war from an entirely different strength. He had support—though sometimes only out of fear—from every one of the ten presidents he served under (especially, sad to say, from two of the most liberal, Franklin Roosevelt and Lyndon Johnson); from the top dogs of Congress; from most of the press—including those pure voices of reaction, Hearst and McCormick and Luce, of course; and from some of the wealthier patriotic organizations, such as the American Legion, the National Association of Manufacturers, and the U.S. Chamber of Commerce.

Perhaps the main reason Wilkinson had to fight such an uphill battle was that his public support was minuscule compared to Hoover's. A fabulously successful self-promotion campaign over many years had made Hoover a hero to most people, probably the most revered bureaucrat in history—the Great G-Man, the conqueror of car thieves, kidnappers, and interstate pimps (but, though it was rarely mentioned, a real pal to the Mafia). Flattering accounts of the FBI and Hoover had been written by the ton, but critical journalism about Hoover had been almost nonexistent, except in a few liberal publications.

Fred J. Cook wrote the first real exposé of Hoover for the *Nation* in 1958, but it took him six years to find a book publisher for his material, and then it happened only after Macmillan resisted heavy pressure from the FBI to reject it. In 1959 the *New York Post* assigned six reporters to spend a year putting together a fifteen-part series on Hoover, but in its public apology for the poor quality of the series, the *Post* explained that top officials all over the federal government "dried up in terror" at the thought of criticizing Hoover; none would speak on the record.[7]

If Hoover's status as a bureaucratic demigod hadn't been plain enough throughout most of his career, it certainly became evident at his death. Having had to put up with him for more than half a century, some on the left had begun to believe Hoover would never die, but he finally did, departing for the Great Witch-hunt in the Sky in 1972. The political establishment was plunged into grief: some of it was bogus, some of it was real. Congress voted permission for his body to lie in state in the Capitol Rotunda, a place usually reserved for former presidents and gold-braided military heroes. Politicians both Democratic and Republican, doubtless hoping their constituencies were noticing, lined up to praise his memory. President Nixon (who had once bitterly complained, "He's got files on *everybody*, goddamn it!") delivered the funeral eulogy. In it, he said, among other extravagancies, "The profound principles associated with his name will not fade away," a prediction that some must have found frightening.[8]

From Wilkinson's allies there came more candid and accurate appraisals. Dr. Benjamin Spock, the antiwar radical who was the People's Party candidate for president and got a great deal of attention from FBI agents over the years, called Hoover's death "a great relief."[9] The benediction of Gus Hall, secretary of the Communist Party USA, included an appraisal of Hoover as "a servant of racism, reaction, and repression" and a "political pervert whose masochistic passion drove him to savage assaults upon the principles of the Bill of Rights."

Gus, for once, was right on target (except that he must have meant "sadistic"). That's why the "political pervert" hated our troublesome defender of the First Amendment, Frank Wilkinson, so much—and, as you will see, there were 132,000 pages in the FBI files to prove it.

CHAPTER 1

Meet a Key Architect of the Cold War, Mr. Truman, and the Victim We're Primarily Interested In, Mr. Wilkinson

ABOUT A DOZEN years ago the BBC made a documentary called *The Un-Americans*. It dealt with the years of the Communist witch hunt in the United States.[1]

This book on the life and times of Frank Wilkinson, perhaps the nation's most successful First Amendment rebel, could open with nothing more instructive than the opening scenes of that BBC documentary. Patriotic parades in Washington show many flags flying, patriotic organizations and troops marching, and, fleetingly, a picture of President Harry Truman at his desk in the White House. Accompanying these scenes is Truman's voice, with an ironic message of assurance:

> My administration has been steadily and successfully fighting Communism. There is no doubt that Communists have tried to worm their way into the government service. So in 1947 I set up the Employment Loyalty Program. This was a real program to meet a real situation. I gave the FBI—the greatest counter-espionage organization in the world—complete charge of checking over two million employees. The FBI,

headed by J. Edgar Hoover [here the film shows Hoover pointing at a city map, probably of Washington, D.C.], is alert, vigorous, and skillful. It is watching the Communists, closely and systematically protecting our internal security. We have prosecuted and will prosecute subversive activities wherever we find them.

Before going on with the BBC program, it's useful to point out the political nature of Truman's remarks. First of all, Truman despised J. Edgar Hoover and the FBI. Many historians have underscored Truman's attitude by quoting from a letter he wrote to his wife, Bess: "If I can prevent it, there'll be no NKVD [Soviet Secret Police] or Gestapo in this country. Edgar Hoover's organization would make a good start toward a citizen spy system. Not for me . . ."

But Hoover already had been running a secret police in the U.S. for some time before Truman. Previous presidents couldn't stop him, or even encouraged him. Truman clearly couldn't stop him. So, how in the world did Hoover essentially become king of the FBI?

■ THE MAKINGS OF HOOVER

In 1917, the year the Bolsheviks successfully rebelled in Russia and began scaring the pants off oligarchs everywhere with their farfetched plans for leveling society, J. Edgar Hoover, then twenty-two years old, moved over from the Library of Congress to the Department of Justice so that he could get a draft deferment. He was smart and tireless and, with a shortage of labor because so many men were drafted, he got fast promotions.

Although there had been a labor shortage during World War I, by the end of 1919, 4 million workers in the U.S. were on strike, and some politicians were looking for scapegoats. An ambitious politician could exploit these troubles by persuading the public to stop thinking about fair wages and working conditions and to start worrying about an alien Communist conspiracy.

Attorney General Palmer, who not only wanted more money for his department but was hoping to run for president in 1920, warned that "the blaze of revolution is eating its way into the homes of American workmen, licking the altars of churches, leaping into the belfry of the school bell, crawling into the sacred corners of American homes, seeking to replace marriage vows with libertine laws, burning up the foundations of society."[2]

Attorney General Palmer did have one actual reason to be concerned. The war years spawned a very small domestic anarchist movement, again mostly made up of immigrants. In April and May of 1919, thirty-six bombs disguised as packages were dropped off at the New York post office. Twenty made it to their destinations, killing thirty-five persons and injuring two hundred. Then, on the night of June 2, 1919, a bomb exploded at Palmer's front door. Almost simultaneously, similar explosions went off in eight other cities.

General Palmer went to the U.S. Senate with the warning that he had almost certain knowledge that these attacks were part of a vast conspiracy to overthrow the government of the United States. From this moment, the Red Scare was officially under way, and Hoover, who had been promoted again, this time to head the recently organized General Intelligence Division (GID) of the Justice Department, was ready to do his part to keep it going. Fortunately for him, in August 1919 the American Communist Party was born. It was puny then, and it would remain puny, but a homegrown Communist Party of any size would be enough to keep Hoover and his supporters in business for three generations.

■ THE PALMER RAIDS COMETH

How was the United States to be saved? Simple: Deport as many of the alien troublemakers and homegrown radicals as Hoover and his bosses could lay their hands on. And never mind giving them their day in court, as "mere" deportations don't require full due process rights.

Thus were the infamous Palmer Raids conceived. Palmer should have shared credit for the raids with Anthony Caminetti, Immigration Commissioner. It was Caminetti who had the power to identify immigrants here illegally, and who thought to do mass raids and deportations.

The first raids took place in the early evening of November 7, 1919 in a dozen different cities. After rounding up more than two hundred possibly deportable aliens and supposed "anarchists" (that identification was mostly guesswork), Hoover, without supplying them with winter clothes, rushed them onto the rustbucket S.S. *Buford* (dubbed the *Soviet Ark*) that would carry them to Russia, sailing on December 21, 1919. Many left families that had depended on them for food money and had left wives who didn't even know their husbands had been kidnapped.

▪ NEXT, THE MONSTER RAID

That deportation fiasco was a practice run for truly massive raids that Hoover supervised on January 2, 1920 in thirty-three cities. The arrests were supposed to be of "radicals" only, but everyone in the path of these frenzied roundup agents was carried away. Most were arrested without warrants. Homes and offices were entered and searched without warrants. Teachers and students in night classes for immigrants were arrested. The raids were conducted in such a wild fashion that an accurate count of the arrests was never made—roughly ten thousand were arrested.

About four thousand of the suspects were released within a few hours because, as most were citizens, they were not deportable. But the remaining thousands were held—many for weeks, some for as long as eight months—without bail or for bail that was far beyond their means. Those arrested were not allowed to call an attorney. Many prisoners lost their jobs because they were held for so long. Some, having lost their jobs, then lost their homes, and their families were thrown on the dole.

The first days and weeks of their imprisonment were intolerable. In Detroit eight hundred men were held in a corridor on the top floor of the Federal Building. The corridor's total area was only 448 square feet—hardly enough to allow 800 men to stand up, much less sit or lie down in—and there were no outside windows, no light except through a dirty skylight, and the place was terribly hot. They were fed nothing for 24 hours. There was one drinking fountain and one (clogged) toilet. Sometimes there would be 40 to 50 men lined up awaiting their turn to use it.[3]

This time, Hoover and Caminetti had disastrously overreached themselves. An accurate account of the disposition of the cases of those not immediately released was lost in the cries of outrage that swept the nation almost at once. In time, hundreds of lawyers, clergymen, and civic groups protested the brutal treatment of the suspects.

When Attorney General Palmer was called before the House Rules Committee in June 1920 to defend himself against the charges of misconduct and abuse of power, Hoover sat at his side as the expert who knew all the facts. It was clear to everyone at the hearing that he had done most of the planning and supervision of the raids.

■

BY 1924, HOOVER was the assistant to the director of the FBI, William J. Burns. In that year, the new attorney general, Harlan F. Stone, faced the task of picking a replacement for Burns. As Burns's assistant, all Hoover had to do to get the job was impress Stone at an interview.

This called for what Frank Donner calls "Hoover's grand deception of 1924." William C. Sullivan, the FBI's number-three man and a very close observer of Hoover, told chronicler Ovid Demaris about his boss's talent for deceiving:

> Professionally, (Hoover) was a charmer. He'd charm anybody that came in there: ambassadors, admirals, generals. He could be all things to all people. If a liberal came in, the liberal would leave thinking, "My God, Hoover is a real liberal!" If a John

Bircher came in an hour later, he'd go out saying, "I'm convinced Hoover is a member of the John Birch Society, at heart."
He was a brilliant chameleon. Make no mistake . . . he had a
very cunning, crafty, shrewd mind and he could make fools
out of some of these people that I alluded to, he could make
fools out of some senators and congressmen. . . . He was one
of the greatest con men the country ever produced. . . .[4]

Hoover came out of the attorney general's office with the title of
acting FBI director. To get rid of that qualifying word, he would
have to perform one more con job.

▪ FOOLING BALDWIN

Roger Baldwin, a founder of the American Civil Liberties Union
and a good friend of the attorney general, wrote Stone to say he
thought that considering Hoover's record, it would be disastrous
to keep him around.

Stone got the two men together to see if they could work out
their differences, and Hoover assured Baldwin the Bureau would
never again investigate personal opinions or beliefs and that it
never had and never would investigate the ACLU. Baldwin then
wrote Stone, "I think we were wrong in our estimate of his attitude."
Hoover was eventually upgraded to permanent director.

In gratitude, Hoover sent Baldwin a note of such guile as would
have made even Iago in Shakespeare's *Othello* envious:

"If I can leave my desk each day with the knowledge that I have
in no way violated any of the rights of the citizens of this country
. . . then I shall feel satisfied."[5]

But vengeance was Hoover's middle name. "Having bent the
knee to Baldwin as the price of power," writes Donner, "he was
not the man to forget such humiliation when power came to
him." The FBI would continue to monitor the ACLU—members,
supporters, activists, officers—until Hoover died a half-century
later. "Ultimately, the FBI's files on the national ACLU and its field
affiliates totaled 40–50,000 pages."[6]

■ INCREASING HIS POWER

From the very first, Hoover had been violating his promise not to violate any rights of U.S. citizens, but he had done it on the sly. Well, not always on the sly. In the 1930s, with President Roosevelt's encouragement, Hoover had already done ad hoc digging for gossip about some of FDR's political enemies, and for the president's titillation had occasionally slipped him spicy items about his cabinet.

But on August 24, 1936, he officially became a thought policeman again. The president summoned Hoover to the White House and told him to start snooping on "subversives" and to give him a broad picture of what Fascists and Communists were up to. In his swift acceptance of the assignment, Hoover had little to say about fascism but much to say about his favorite topic, the Communist threat, which he said was huge and imminent: He implied that FDR had called on his assistance in the nick of time because Communists already controlled, or nearly so, the West Coast's longshoreman's union, the United Mine Workers Union, and the Newspaper Guild. If Communist control of those three unions became total, he warned, they could paralyze the country.

FDR was impressed. He asked Hoover to keep digging up that kind of stuff, especially as it affected the nation's economic and political welfare. Hoover, acting demure, is said to have pointed out "that no government agency was collecting this type of general intelligence, but that the FBI was empowered to investigate any matter referred to it by the Department of State." Taking the hint, FDR said he was reluctant to have a formal request come through State, because there were so many leaks, but that he would put a handwritten memo in his White House safe, instructing the secretary of state to request this information. "And so it was," writes Ted Morgan in his biography of Roosevelt, "that a decision that has affected the national life ever since, the collection of political intelligence by the FBI, was made by FDR in complete secrecy, with only a memo in his safe as written proof."[7]

In 1940, Roosevelt authorized wiretapping, in spite of Supreme Court decisions in 1937 and 1939. These decisions had held that the ban against wiretapping in the 1934 Communications Act applied to federal agencies and then their use of evidence obtained illegally would require dismissal or an indictment. FDR took this step because Hoover had persuaded him he "desperately" needed wiretaps and promised to use them only on suspected spies.

Roosevelt asked for wiretaps on presumed political enemies. From Morgan: "It was in this climate of twin threats from communism and fascism, magnified by Hoover, that FDR signed the Smith Act on July 1, 1940, which among other things, required 3.5 million aliens to register and be fingerprinted and fined or imprisoned for anything written or spoken that could subvert the armed forces."[7]

■ FAST-FORWARD TO TRUMAN

So by the Truman era, Hoover had for years been fanatically ferreting-out even the most comically-identified "subversives" in or out of government, and would continue to do so. When Truman became president, Hoover briefly lost his high level support for snooping. William C. Sullivan, former assistant director of the FBI, has written that when Truman came into office, he sent a message to Hoover that he had no intention of dealing with the FBI director personally and that "anytime I need the services of the FBI, I will ask for it through my attorney general." "From that time on," Sullivan recalled, "Hoover's hatred of Truman knew no bounds."[9] Sullivan recalls that in Truman's 1948 presidential campaign against Thomas Dewey, Hoover secretly supplied Dewey, an old friend, "everything we had that could hurt Truman, though there wasn't much."[10]

Then how to explain Truman's humbug admiration of Hoover on BBC? It was simply the kind of duplicity that was common in those dreadful times and beyond.

■

PERHAPS NO ONE could have done much better, but Truman was ill-equipped to cope with a maelstrom of postwar political changes.

When he became president on the death of President Roosevelt, on April 12, 1945, his entire previous service in the federal government totaled eight not very distinguished years in the U.S. Senate and three months as vice president. It wasn't much training for one confronted with the incredibly complex problems of ending World War II, guiding civilian activities from war to peace, and making postwar alliances. Roosevelt's political magic was not transferable, and besides, it had dramatically lost effectiveness. By the time he died in April 1945, the New Deal had almost disappeared. Major lifesaving programs that the underclass gratefully remembered by their initials—CCC, WPA, NYA (Civilian Conservation Corps, Works Progress Administration, and National Youth Administration, respectively)—were as dead as Roosevelt. They were killed by an increasingly conservative Congress. In only six years (from the 1936 to the 1942 elections), the Democratic majorities dropped from 242 to 10 in the House and from 60 to 21 in the Senate, and many of the remaining Democrats were southern renegades who, on civil liberty and international issues, sided with the most reactionary Republicans.

Truman was not a committed liberal; indeed, fervent liberals made him uncomfortable. Some, such as his vice presidential predecessor, Henry Wallace, an incorrigible idealist, he despised. What Truman was was an old-fashioned Democratic Party loyalist. He could take the passing of the New Deal without tremendous opposition, but he refused to let the Republicans win partisan supremacy without a bloody fight, fair or foul.

Round one was in foreign affairs. Saying that he was tired of "babying" the Soviets and tired of hearing right-wing Republicans say his efforts to deal with the Soviets constituted "appeasement," Truman went before Congress on March 12, 1947, and outlined what came to be known as the Truman Doctrine. Like the George W. Bush administration's reckless promise six decades later to fight terrorism anywhere in the world, the Truman Doctrine promised help for any country anywhere in the world that seemed to be having military problems with Communists. Whether or not the Truman Doctrine was "the most enduringly controversial speech made by a president in the twentieth century," as some have claimed,[11] it certainly proved to be a hollow, grandstanding promise that could not possibly be fulfilled. It raised false hopes and subsequent disillusionment in many oppressed nations. It rhetorically split the world into "free" versus "totalitarian" (meaning Communist) nations. And it had a devastating effect on U.S. foreign policy, leaving no room for compromise or moderation. Politicians were compelled to display only the most rigid, hard-line belligerence lest they be smeared as "Communist dupes."

The doctrine prompted Truman to send troops to butt into the quarrel between North and South Korea in 1950. This was done without congressional approval and in spite of the advice of some of his top military advisers, who argued that Korea "was of no value to the strategic position of the U.S. in the Far East."[12] Nevertheless, Truman felt it was "a 'testing ground' between democracy and Communism" and that we had to stay for prestige reasons, as "a symbol to the watching world" that we would stand firm.[13]

Cost of winning no more than a permanent truce: the lives of fifty-four thousand U.S. servicemen.

But the momentum of the Truman Doctrine was hard to stop, and less than ten years after the Korean fiasco, American troops were again in Asia, this time to stay for the longest "hot" war thus far in our history—Vietnam. Once again, we were defending a corrupt government in the name of anti-Communism, this time at a cost of fifty-eight thousand U.S. lives. Speaking in the middle of the Vietnam War, Senator William Fulbright, chairman of the Foreign Affairs Committee, made a judgment that, while perhaps too broad, was basically sound: "All American mistakes committed abroad since 1947 stem from the Truman Doctrine."[14]

■ MEANWHILE, ON THE HOME FRONT

Only nine days after launching the Truman Doctrine, the president struck again, this time signing Executive Order 9835, which created what Truman boasted of in his BBC speech—the Federal Employee Loyalty Program. This order established procedures, obviously, to investigate federal employee loyalty, including fingerprinting all employees.

Just as the Truman Doctrine was meant to silence GOP criticisms in foreign affairs, Executive Order 9835 was obviously meant to outmaneuver them in domestic politics. More exactly, it was a political ploy for the 1948 presidential election. The leading Republican presidential candidate, Thomas Dewey, along with other Republican politicians and particularly the House Un-American Activities Committee, were filling the air with hysterical accusations that Democrats were not only conspiring to let the Communists take over the government but had already surrendered the State Department to them. As White House aide Clark Clifford later admitted, the loyalty program was "manufactured" to silence the GOP. "We never had a serious discussion about a real loyalty problem," Clark says. "It was a political problem. Truman was going to run in '48, and that was it."[15] However, far from feeling outfoxed by Truman, the right-wingers were simply inspired to one-up Truman with even more oppressive security programs, both in his administration and in Eisenhower's.

■

ANY SENSIBLE APPRAISAL of Truman's loyalty program has to conclude that it was farcical, cruel, dangerous, and disgraceful. Also, it created something Washington certainly did not need: another enormous bureaucracy, this one with six thousand employees. Each government department and agency had a loyalty board: the post office had five, the army eighteen, the air force eighty-six, and the navy three hundred. Then there was a twenty-three-man Loyalty Review Board.[16] All were assisted by huge armies of clerks and supervisors and FBI investigators. Dismissal could be based merely on "reasonable grounds" for belief that the person was "disloyal," but the term "reasonable grounds" allowed for purely subjective judgments—and "disloyal" was never defined. Contrary to the guarantees of the Sixth Amendment of the Constitution, accused persons were not allowed to confront those who made charges against them; they were not even allowed to know what the charges were.

If it hadn't interrupted so many lives and cost so much, the program might have been an entertaining farce. In a bizarre fashion, the screening was democratic; that is, boiler attendants were given the same scrutiny as atomic scientists. After 2.5 million employees were fingerprinted and 10,368 given a full field investigation, only 102 were fired for being of questionable loyalty. These 102 employees were never told what they were guilty of, but the evidence against them must have been extremely slight, because no one was indicted and no evidence of espionage was found.[17] Apparently, several employees were dismissed because the review boards discovered they had read the Communist newspaper the *Daily Worker*. One who confessed to this apparently subversive activity may also have been fired for sarcasm. He complained to the board, "Now I'm afraid to read anything. Twenty years from now they'll be asking, 'Why did you read the *Wall Street Journal*?'"[18]

■ IMITATION EVERYWHERE

The madness quickly spread. Soon states were establishing their own witch-hunting apparatuses, and their victims sometimes took their harassment very seriously. After Massachusetts's "little HUAC" grilled the famous literary critic F. O. Matthiessen, he killed himself, leaving a note saying, "As a Christian and a Socialist believing in international peace, I find myself terribly oppressed by the present tension."[19] Indeed, "the present tension" was enough to make anyone feel oppressed. State and local governments, factories, schools, and trade unions were demanding loyalty oaths. Some were downright grotesque—such as the required oath of loyalty from professional wrestlers in Indiana and from amateur archers in California. The Mississippi legislature passed a series of fierce laws to fence in the Communist Party—and its single member in that state.[20]

From Truman's creation of the loyalty program in 1947 until 1956, forty-two states and more than two thousand county and municipal subgroups required affidavits of loyalty from teachers, lawyers, doctors, voters, and recipients of public welfare and housing.[21]

In private conversations with friends, Truman admitted that setting up the program that had helped launch all this was a bad mistake.

"Yes," he said, "it was terrible."[22]

■ MEANWHILE, THE FBI WAS VERY, VERY BUSY TAILING MR. WILKINSON

Let's now return to the BBC documentary and listen to Frank Wilkinson, one of the many and perhaps one of the longest targets of the era's hysteria.

The voice of Mr. Truman fades out, and the screen is taken over by a scene in which Wilkinson sits behind a table so large you can't see its edges even when the camera moves back. Covering the table completely are piles of what are obviously official reports of some kind. Wilkinson starts speaking:

I did not know that the FBI had been following me until eleven years ago when I was sixty-five years of age. When I got the first 4,500 pages of their surveillance [through the Freedom of Information Act], it seemed to deal entirely with my early work in integration and housing. With those first pages I went to the American Civil Liberties Union and asked if they were interested in filing a lawsuit on my behalf. They were.

In the second year of my lawsuit, the FBI came forward and said they had just found 35,000 *more* pages. We looked at those and they seemed to deal with my working for the abolition of the House Committee on Un-American Activities.

Then, two years later, the FBI said they had *just* found

70,000 more pages. At that point, the judge was quite upset. He ruled: No more of this 'just found' business. What is the bottom line?

The FBI then told the judge they had [a total of] *132,000* pages of surveillance on me over thirty-eight years. In fact, the files will show as many as eight agents a day, following me on shifts, day after day after day. Pages and pages of wiretaps. Every time I left Los Angeles on a field trip, you would have a memorandum from J. Edgar Hoover to all the agents in all the cities I was going to travel to: "Here is Wilkinson's travel schedule." It gave my time of departure, the flight, where I was going to speak. I have documents showing how the FBI was to disrupt my speaking engagements.

One memo reads, "Since Wilkinson speaks to many college audiences, the utmost discretion must be used to avoid any possibility that the FBI would appear to be interfering with academic freedom." At the very end of this file, it said, "Each SAC [FBI Special Agent in Charge] receiving this letter is instructed to have only those Agents assigned to the Counterintelligence program read this letter and after it has been thoroughly read, it should be personally destroyed [by the SAC] and I, Mr. Hoover, should be told it has been destroyed."

I think the greatest irony in reviewing these monstrous FBI files is that, to quote them, "It does not appear that Wilkinson has shown the willingness or capability of engaging in any act that would significantly interfere with or be a threat to the survival and effective operation of our government." That was their *own* judgment at a time [when] they were wasting millions of dollars on 132,000 pages of surveillance and disruption of my work.

The records you see on this table show that it all began with my work in housing. We had a dream that Los Angeles would become the first city in America free of slums. That entire dream was ended with this beautiful stadium.

The BBC documentary shows Wilkinson walking around the field in Dodger Stadium.

■ TWO PAGES FROM THOSE MONSTROUS FILES

On March 4, 1964, when Frank was out of jail and doing field organizing full tilt, he was almost assassinated. It remains unclear precisely who instigated it. We know the FBI was working hard to monitor his every movement, and to disrupt his activities, so they must have known of this? Yes, there is a two page FBI teletype marked "urgent" of the date, talking about the assassination. Five lines are blacked out and then "contacted by an undisclosed source to assist in an assassination attempt on Frank Wilkinson . . ." It notes he was to speak at a private home to an ACLU group in Los Angeles. It notes the FBI "will stake out residence. . . ." And "matter will be closely followed and pertinent developments promptly reported." A follow-up memo from shortly after, initialed by Hoover, notes "that no attempt has been made on the life of Wilkinson and there have been no further developments in this matter." Under orders from the Federal District Court, the FBI subsequently confirmed that house was staked out by the L.A. Police's Anti-Subversive division.

A few pertinent questions come to mind: Who instigated the assassination? To this day this is not confirmed. Were the L.A. police officers staking out the house to have done the act, or just watch someone else do it? We don't know. Did the FBI warn Wilkinson that he might be killed? No. Did the FBI ever tell Wilkinson his life had been or still might be in danger? No. Did the FBI know who was to do the assassination? We can't tell, but it sounds like it from the file. If the FBI didn't know the alleged assassin, did it try to find out? Not from record of the files. Did it prosecute or refer this for local law enforcement to prosecute? No.

This memo alone makes a laughingstock of any allegation that the FBI was tasked to protect citizens. It clearly assigned itself the job of spying on people engaged in dissent activity, without letting direct evidence of the worst kind of criminal conduct (i.e., assassination) get in the way of some important spying.

Frank found out about the assassination when the files came in from the litigation, almost two decades later. Even in the midst of thousands of pages of surveillance, this knocked the socks off Frank, his lawyers, and the rest of NCARL.

By 1983, when these files became public, activists were a little jaded from seeing the results of a civil suit against Chicago prosecutors and police proving that they, with active FBI assistance, had assassinated Black Panther Party activists Fred Hampton and Mark Clark in 1969. The guilt of law enforcement in that Chicago case also was upheld in February 1983 by the U.S. Supreme Court. And yet this evidence of related FBI behavior just a few years previously, against a white guy like Frank, showed a clear pattern of behavior.

Why would Frank be targeted? What was he doing that was so heinous? Welcome to the Cold War.

CHAPTER 2

Welcome to the Very Irrational, Very Cold War

TO APPRECIATE THE struggle Frank Wilkinson and thousands of other ordinary citizens went through in the Cold War to live their lives free of federal prying and federal retaliation for unorthodox beliefs, you have to remember how long this phase in our history actually lasted.

During and shortly after World War I and for three decades after World War II, the United States surrendered to those violent waves of fear that at intervals in a democracy inflame the public mind. The insanity around World War I was called the Red Scare. The much longer period after World War II, which primarily concerns us, was called the Cold War.

These periods of hysteria were largely created, and always exploited, by the American establishment—its politicians, businessmen, some of its clergy and some of its publishers—who acted as though they honestly feared Communism was imminently threatening to seize the electorate's heart and mind. This fear, whether real or contrived, was useful to those in power, for it gave them an excuse to denounce any liberal reformer, labor agitator, or civil rights leader as "communistic." Most reform movements that would upset the status quo had to run this gauntlet.

Like all wars, the Cold War had its heroes, its cowards, its quiet patriots, hysterical patriots, propagandists, opportunists, and madmen.

Although the term *Cold War* was meant to describe the relationship between the United States and the Soviet Union, it could as accurately have been applied to the relationship between segments of U.S. society. Those on the political right suspected that most left-wingers were either Communists or at least "fellow travelers" (a very small fraction were either), and those on or around the left thought the right-wingers were neofascists or political/religious nuts or political opportunists (most were).

To the right wing—J. Edgar Hoover's wing—*Communist* was a very elastic term. It could mean anything from real card-carrying Communists to old New Dealers, radicals, liberals, plain-vanilla socialists, civil libertarians, pacifists, feminists, hippies, practitioners of free love, people who admired longtime First Lady Eleanor Roosevelt's newspaper columns, and/or supporters of the United Nations. Viewed through the right wing's miasma, these people were identified as treacherous foes whose hearts really belonged to Joseph Stalin.

But here was the rub: how could homegrown Communists and Communist sympathizers be identified as "un-American"? Chief Justice Earl Warren, with properly modest puzzlement, had mused in one of his early First Amendment cases, "Who can define the meaning of 'un-American'?" Many otherwise seemingly intelligent people in powerful positions not only believed they could answer that question, but they believed that they alone could be the arbiters of "Americanism."

The confusion, the waste of time, the waste of money, the waste of temper, along with the groundless fears hanging like a swamp fog over the way Americans dealt with Americans in that era has been accurately re-created by many historians. Professor James David Barber writes:

> The response of the Red-hunters was so exaggerated, and in the end so ineffective, that the whole affair has come to stand

as a prime example of the madness that occasionally sweeps through American politics. Once the paranoid image of communism as a communicable disease caught hold, there could be no stopping the speedy logic by which those who inhaled the germs were as guilty as those who spread them. The spy stories fascinated and frightened people, and then offered a convenient explanation for every ill from Russian intransigence to high meat prices.[1]

And Michael Barson, in his book *Better Dead than Red: A Nostalgic Look at the Golden Years of Russiaphobia, Red-baiting, and Other Commie Madness*, writes:

> All those millions, billions, and trillions of dollars we spent trying to contain the voracious Soviet Bear . . . all the federal agencies dedicated to the proposition that, at any minute, America would be seized by the thousands of highly trained Red operatives lurking in the corridors of the State Department . . . all those dumb bomb drills and all the weekends spent stocking the bomb shelter with the best in canned goods and paperback novels . . . all those nights when we couldn't sleep for worrying about whether *our* ICBMs were quicker on the draw than *their* ICBMs . . . all of this, and so much more, and for what? . . . "Better Dead Than Red!" was a cry once proudly shared from sea to shining sea among all right-minded Americans. . . .
>
> The fact is, for twenty years or so [make that thirty], America lost its collective mind.[2]

■ PAIN IS NEVER IN THE ABSTRACT

But the results of the Cold War should not be thought of in the abstract. True, the fears and suspicions were permanently damaging to the spirit of the nation, but one should also remember the tremendously cruel things that actually happened to individuals: careers were ruined; jobs were lost and people were forced to sell their homes to get money to live on; embarrassment was heaped on the wives, husbands, and children of the accused; health and marriages were ruined by the stress of trying to maintain a defense against vague and unfounded charges.

Robert M. Hutchins, at that time chancellor of the University of Chicago, observed, "Every day in this country, men and women are being deprived of their livelihood, or at least their reputation, by unsubstantiated charges. . . . We do not throw people into jail. . . . We throw them out of work."[3] Actually, they were being thrown in both directions. Even out of house and home. And even into and out of cemeteries. The anti-Communist inquisitions in Hollywood, at the State Department, and at universities resulted in at least four fatal heart attacks and one suicide.[4] Many of the victims were famous. But as is proper in a democracy, the witch-hunting cruelties were handed out in an egalitarian way; indeed, the hunters were generous with their attention to the hoi polloi. Not even heroic ex-GIs were overlooked.

Consider, for example, what happened to James Kutcher. As an army rifleman fighting in Italy in World War II, his legs were so mangled by a mortar explosion that they had to be amputated at the knee. After three years of hospitalization and therapy, he was able to walk on artificial legs, helped along with two canes.

Thereupon he limped back to his hometown, Newark, New Jersey, and went to work as a clerk for the Veteran's Administration at thirty-eight dollars a week. Not wanting even the most humble suspect to slip through its anti-Commie net, the FBI looked over Kutcher's past and found that once upon a time, as a teenager, he had attended a summer camp for Trotskyites, where (somebody later said) he expressed the opinion that employers should share their wealth a little more generously with workers.

The FBI sounded the alarm to the Veterans Administration, and—as was common in "security" cases in 1948—it fired Kutcher. Although the VA was compassionate enough not to make him give back his artificial legs or canes, it did cut off his monthly $329 disability check.[5]

Not wanting to be outdone in terms of patriotism, the Newark

Housing Authority, without even giving Kutcher a hearing, evicted him and his parents as undesirables.

With the help of Joseph Rauh, a heavyweight lawyer in Washington's Democratic circles, and New York columnist Murray Kempton, enough attention was stirred up to shame the VA into giving back Kutcher's pension and (after a federal court order) returning him to his job, with back pay. But it took seven years to win this victory.[6]

Other heroic veterans were treated with similarly bizarre rudeness. In 1966, the Defense Department denied burial in Arlington Cemetery to Robert Thompson, even though he had won the Distinguished Service Cross for heroism in New Guinea in 1943. The Defense Department deemed Thompson unworthy of six feet of U.S. dirt because once upon a time he had been a Communist and had gone to prison for violating the Smith Act in 1949.[7]

■ THOUSANDS OF OTHER VICTIMS

In the intense years following World War II, dominated by J. Edgar Hoover and Joseph McCarthy, there's really no telling how many Americans lost their jobs—either by being fired or by being harassed into quitting—for similarly perverse "security" reasons, but some historians have estimated fifty thousand. That seems conservative, for according to those who specialize in such counting, there were at least four thousand seamen and waterfront workers fired as suspected Communists. No doubt many *were* Communists—that industry famously attracted radicals—and were all the better workmen for it. In the same period, an estimated ten thousand industrial workers were fired for being "security risks," and an estimated one hundred professors were fired for refusing to answer questions about their politics.[8]

There has never been an accurate count of how many were blacklisted in Hollywood, though there must have been several hundred. (Right-wing actors who ratted on them, such as Ronald Reagan and George Murphy, didn't like the use of the term *blacklist*. John Wayne said use of the term "was a lot of horseshit. The only thing our side did that was anywhere near blacklisting was just running a lot of people out of the business."[9]) An estimated five hundred state and municipal workers were fired for political reasons, and that doesn't include those souls who were constantly being required to swear loyalty, over and over, to Uncle Sam, or be fired.

In addition, sixteen thousand "suspects" were either fired or frightened into quitting the federal civil service, including some of the most competent foreign affairs officers in the State Department. Actually, the most valuable ones had been "guilty" of nothing more than serving in China when it was being taken over by the Communists and for accurately predicting that takeover—which their superiors back in Washington refused to believe was happening.

And we mustn't overlook the four hundred Americans who received the ultimate penalty, prison, for being thought to hold the wrong political beliefs; of these, 150 exhausted all legal remedies and served some or all of their sentences, including Frank Wilkinson. Some were indeed Communists, but that in itself wasn't against the law. None, not one, had been convicted of sabotage or spying. Most were sent to prison for "conspiring" to change our government at some vague time in the future, and "proof" of that "conspiracy" occasionally boiled down to the books FBI agents found in their homes—copies of which could be found in the local public library.

One of these suspects, Steve Nelson, chairman of the Communist Party in Pittsburgh, couldn't get an attorney to take his case, so he defended himself. He subpoenaed the librarian of the Carnegie Library, spread all the "conspiratorial books" in front of him, and asked the librarian to tell the jury if they were in the Carnegie Library, readily available to the public. Yes, the librarian said, they were. Some conspiracy. But Nelson was sentenced to twenty years in prison and a ten-thousand-dollar fine. Another "conspiratorial" reader was Wilkinson's friend Dorothy Healey, the beautiful "Red Queen of Los Angeles." For having dipped into the wrong books, she was sentenced to five years and a fifty-thousand-dollar fine. (A U.S. Supreme Court ruling finally rescued them but not before they served some time.)

There were also many victims of profiteering organizations like Red Channels, created by three former FBI agents, and Aware, Inc. Their racket was to issue long lists of "suspected subversives"—names supplied by the FBI and the HUAC of actors, writers, commentators, and producers who were employed in TV and radio and theater. You could get your name taken off the list if you swore you were, notwithstanding the contrived "rumors," a true-blue patriot—and if your employer paid a sufficient amount to have you "cleared."

William L. Shirer, the radio commentator and famed *Berlin Diary* author, was put on Red Channels' list. He refused to crawl, so he was blacklisted throughout the 1950s. At CBS, John Henry Faulk, the great Texas humorist, got on Aware's list of "possible subversives" very easily—by organizing his union to fight Aware. His bosses at CBS, he says, "urged me to write Aware and praise them for their good work, thank them for pointing out my errors, and promise to be a good little boy from now on. God almighty! If I had done that, I'd have felt like I was swimming through my own vomit."[10]

Instead, he fought back famously, suing Aware for racketeering. CBS, frightened, fired him. After a decade of unemployment, Faulk managed to get into court and won $3.5 million, but the appellate courts knocked that down to only enough money to pay his attorney fees (the great Louis Nizer did not come cheap) and repay the loans that had kept him alive. The networks never got over being spooked by the "subversive" smear. Faulk eventually was offered a well-paying job—appearing on the folksy *Hee Haw* television show in the 1970s.

No matter how much pain they inflicted on individuals, corporations could always find a way to profit from their Cold War perfidy. That was proven once again in 1975, when, eight years after CBS had banished Faulk, the network made itself a bundle of money by dramatizing *Fear on Trial*, the book Faulk wrote about his nightmare.

And then there was the case of Frank Wilkinson.

CHAPTER 3

The Real Beginning

FRANK WILKINSON WAS born on August 16, 1914, in a cottage behind the family's spacious house in Charlevoix, Michigan, a lovely resort town on Lake Michigan that offers a protected harbor for large yachts. Frank was one of four children—he had one brother, Alan, and two sisters, Hildegarde and Clara Marie. Alan and Hildegarde became physicians, like their father, Alan Marshall Wilkinson, whose family, of English stock, came to this country before the American Revolution. Their mother, Ada Marie Blodgett, was a Canadian of French bloodline.

When the United States entered World War I in 1917, Dr. Alan Wilkinson enlisted in the Army Medical Corps and was assigned to a camp in Douglas, Arizona. Apparently he liked the place, because after the war he took his family to Douglas and set up his medical practice there. Most people in Douglas worked for a copper smelter. Wilkinson also served Bisbee, a copper-mining town twenty-five miles away, and Agua Prieta, just across the border in Mexico. For most of the inhabitants of these three towns, income ranged from near-zero to middling. Dr. Wilkinson did a lot of charity work. He would continue to do charity work after they moved to California.

They lived in Douglas until Frank was ten. The stay there was memorable for his being bitten on the neck by a coyote (and being saved from rabies by being rushed to a clinic in St. Louis for six weeks of shots), dodging rattlesnakes in the desert, and dodging rocks thrown at him by Mexican children when he passed through their neighborhood going to and coming from his school.

Roads in Arizona in those days were a joke; long stretches were nothing but wood planks laid on top of sand. But Dr. Wilkinson liked to drive fast, and one very dark night, as he roared over the top of a sandy hill, he confronted a freight train without lights. The collision sent Frank and his mother hurtling through the car's canvas roof and up against the train. Frank came through without many injuries, but his mother had to wear a heavy body cast for years.

But she never lost her good spirits. Frank remembers his mother as being more fun to be with than his father, even when her mobility was severely restricted. "There was more laughter with my mother, although Dad told funny jokes occasionally. He wasn't stern. He could laugh. But I remember him as one who always wore a suit, a shirt with a two-inch-high collar, and a tie. He never sat around in a sweater."

Another powerful influence on Frank—almost that of a second mother—was his remarkable sister Hildegarde Roxanna June, twelve years his senior. She had finished her premed work at the University of California with a Phi Beta Kappa key and was ready to enter the Stanford University medical school—she was the first woman to be accepted there—but gave up that opportunity to stay home and care for her mother following the accident and, on the side, get a nurse's license. Finally, at the age of thirty-six—very old for that sort of thing in those days—she entered the University of California medical school in 1937 as the only woman accepted for that class. Graduating with highest honors in obstetrics and gynecology, she hung up her shingle to practice medicine at the hoary age of forty-two. Ultimately the doctors of the huge Glendale Memorial Hospital elected her chief of staff for the entire hospital; she was the first woman to hold that position. When Frank was imprisoned years later, was she embarrassed? On the contrary. One day in 1961, she opened all the loudspeaker lines at the hospital and declared: "This is Dr. Wilkinson speaking. I will be away from the hospital for approximately one week. I am going to visit my brother, who is in a federal penitentiary for exercising his First Amendment rights."

■

UNDER THE INFLUENCE of their father, family life was built around the Methodist Church. Sundays were consumed by Sunday school, followed by the main worship service, followed (often) by a very long midday meal with a visiting evangelist as guest, then the Epworth League, and finally evening church service. Every Wednesday was prayer-meeting night.

On one occasion there was a big three-day prayer revival, sponsored by all the Protestant churches (there were four) in Douglas. The revival's thrice-daily sermons would end with an invitation to sinners to come forward and accept Christ. Frank remembers that once he went forward three times in one day. His mother suggested that once was enough to be saved.

"Every morning of my life," says Wilkinson, "we had Bible reading and prayers at the breakfast table. It wasn't just saying grace. We got down on our knees and put our heads on the chairs. Isn't it funny that I still remember the smell of leather on the chair as these prayers were being said?"

Dr. Wilkinson opposed drinking, smoking, cursing, dancing, card playing, and gambling. (After Frank went to high school in Beverly Hills, he got his father to drop the dancing prohibition, and after Frank's sister, Hildegarde, went off to medical school, she got him to relent on the card-playing prohibition, so long as she played only bridge.) No one in the family was permitted to do any shopping on Sundays.

Dr. Wilkinson was an honorary member of the Women's Christian Temperance Union in Douglas, and nothing gave him more pleasure than accompanying the federal revenue agent for southern Arizona, who was also a Methodist, on long trips over sand and dirt roads to find and bust up whiskey stills (Prohibition was still in effect). Sometimes he would let Frank come along.

When Dr. Wilkinson moved his family in 1925—first for two years to Hollywood while their home was under construction in Beverly Hills—he became a lay leader in the Hollywood Methodist Church and, by expanding his moral crusade through a variety of important local organizations: anti-vice, anti-gambling, anti-liquor, something of a power in civic affairs. Often he was elected to a leadership position, and he was credited with influencing the election of some of Los Angeles's "reform" politicians, such as Mayor Fletcher Bowron, who served the city for fifteen years in an honest but not notably enlightened way.

Perhaps *naive* is a fair word to describe Dr. Wilkinson's political mind. There came a time when the gambling interests of Los Angeles set out to silence him, and to some degree they succeeded. One of the major figures in the Los Angeles underworld went to Dr. Wilkinson and convinced him that he had reformed and wanted to show he was no longer a sinner by contributing to one of the doctor's charities. A five-thousand-dollar check changed hands. When it was cashed, the fellow showed reporters a photographic copy of the cancelled check and said it had been a bribe. His trick made headlines. Not everyone believed the con man, but enough people did that Dr. Wilkinson's role as a reformer was weakened.

That one defeat, however, did not lessen his unwavering adherence to Christian teachings, especially the dictum that the first shall be last and the last shall be first. Who else in Beverly Hills insisted that their maid eat at the dinner table with the family and that nobody take a bite until she was seated for the saying of grace? That egalitarian gesture was typical. And his generosity in helping the down-and-out was so well known that when police encountered a penniless person who was injured or so hungry they were ill, they would often bring them to Dr. Wilkinson (Los

Angeles had no emergency hospitals in those days) and he would patch them up. If they were broke—and especially if they were young and broke—he sometimes brought them home, took care of them, got them on their feet, and tried to find jobs for them.

■ A VERY CUSHY LIFE

There were millions of Americans during Frank's youth and early manhood—which covered the 1930s Great Depression years—who would have considered him rich. The Wilkinsons' life was certainly very soft, but they weren't rich by local standards; indeed, their owning only three automobiles might have rated them almost as proletarian in some parts of Beverly Hills.

When the Depression hit in 1929, Frank was in his sophomore year at Beverly Hills High School, where the classes were smaller, the teachers were much better paid, and the laboratory equipment much newer than in the Los Angeles school system. It was, in fact, much like a prep school. All graduates went to college if they wanted to. Wilkinson recalls that the fathers of some of his schoolmates were film celebrities, actors as well as producers such as Ernst Lubitsch. Eddie Cantor's daughters were there. Joe E. Brown's son Don was one of Frank's closest friends.

However, until Wilkinson graduated from the University of California at Los Angeles in 1936, and began traveling and visiting the most deprived neighborhoods here and abroad, the Depression simply did not exist for him. He had never even traveled across town to see Watts, or downtown to see the rattier sections of Main Street.

He had seen individual poor people but not slums. Frank recalls his isolation from want:

> I don't remember people losing jobs at all. I never saw unemployed people. I never saw begging. I never saw soup kitchens. The only hint I had that hunger existed in America was the annual assemblies at Beverly Hills High School where we would bring a can of food, and that was to go to some poor

kids that lived somewhere in L.A. It was sort of a headache to carry a can of beans, or whatever, to school on that day, but you wanted to go to the assembly because there'd be all these motion picture stars to entertain us, and so you would do it.

I was not touched by the Depression. I was wearing tuxedos to the Bel-Air Cotillion, and the most important thing was to have a better corsage for your girlfriend than anyone else would have. I was doing this at least once a month up there at the women's clubs. I went to parties at places like my good friend Eddie Janss's home, a twenty-acre estate on Sunset Boulevard, where the swimming pool and recreation area was a hundred yards from the house.

And when I was in UCLA, a group of my fraternity brothers and I would go dancing almost every Friday night, the preferred venue being the movie stars' hangout, the Coconut Grove in the Ambassador Hotel. (My friends knew my scruples and thought it great fun when I toasted them only with milk on those occasions.) I just floated through the Depression oblivious to what was going on around me, focusing on my own social development, my own social life, my own ego needs of popularity.

■ THE INVISIBLE BLACKS

There came a time much later when, with good reason, Fannie Lou Hamer, the famed militant of the Mississippi Delta, called Frank "the blackest white man I know." But for the first quarter of his life, blacks were virtually invisible to him. There were no poor blacks in Beverly Hills, nor blacks of any other kind—not as residents. Blacks were forbidden by law to buy property there, as elsewhere. He recalls that in his high school of twelve hundred students, only three were black; they were brought in from the "outside" to integrate it, with some self-congratulatory fanfare by the school administration. When he went to UCLA, the racial proportions were similar, but Frank did manage to make friends with one black student, Jimmy La Valle, an Olympian athlete. Naturally, this being the 1930s, there were no blacks in Frank's fraternity (nor any Jews, for that matter). His "brothers" refused to let Frank invite La Valle and his date to the frat's Thanksgiving ball, so Frank went with them elsewhere, which he did more from a feeling of fair play than from any civil rights militancy. That would come later, in his radical adulthood.

■ FATHER'S POLITICAL INFLUENCE

Frank's father was the most important influence in his life. In 1932, Alan Wilkinson made speeches all over town trying to protect the Eighteenth Amendment (Prohibition).

> My brother and I would go along with him and would speak. We also came up with the idea to make a little metal plate that you could attach to your license plate—Keep the 18th Amendment—and we sold hundreds and hundreds of them, but it was all part of the Youth for Herbert Hoover–type activity. My last year in Beverly Hills High School, I was head of that. Hoover was *the* important person. He must be elected. He will keep the Eighteenth Amendment; he'll stop alcohol. Roosevelt was some very foreign guy, strange, not like us, but most of all he was a *wet* [term of the day for a person with an anti-Prohibition position]. It wasn't the economic issue facing the nation we were concerned about. It was Christian sobriety. I emphasize the word *Christian*.

And two years later, the Wilkinson family actively crusaded against the writer Upton Sinclair, a socialist-leaning Democrat who was running against Republican governor Frank Merriam, a total incompetent, whom *Time* magazine described as "a small-bore Iowa-born politician . . . lacking personality or popularity," a stooge for "big industrialists."[1] Even Herbert Hoover labeled Merriam an "ultra-conservative."[2]

Being Republican was a tradition for the Wilkinsons, but if

they had needed any assurance as to the rightness of their decision to oppose Sinclair in 1934, they got plenty from the horrendous anti-Sinclair publicity pumped out by the establishment. The California Real Estate Association warned wealthy property owners that if Sinclair won, their holdings would be worthless and the rabble would seize their swimming pools. Owners of Hollywood's studios threatened to move to Florida if Sinclair won.[3]

Those fearful predictions were impressive, but Frank remembers that he and the rest of his family were primarily convinced Sinclair was "very bad, evil, because he didn't believe in God. He was an atheist."

■

IF IT HADN'T been for the virtually total opposition from the California press and the business world, Sinclair just might have won. As it was, running on the EPIC (End Poverty in California) ticket, he got more votes than his eight Democratic rivals combined.[4] And in the general election, Sinclair won 900,000 votes to Merriam's 1,100,000, with the spoiler, Ray Haight, creaming off 300,000.

The revolutionary excitement of that campaign was completely lost on the Wilkinson family because Alan Wilkinson's political persuasions all stemmed from the moral point of view. "He knew nothing of economics, to my knowledge," says Frank. "He wouldn't have known the economic arguments of Herbert Hoover versus Roosevelt or Warren G. Harding versus Bob La Follette. He knew very little about the progressives, I'm sure."

But despite Dr. Wilkinson's politics, he was a well-meaning father who led a disciplined life, and transferred some of that discipline to his children. He would wake up Frank and his brother and sisters at 7 A.M. on the dot and drive them down to Santa Monica beach, where they would take a swim in the ocean—even on cold days—and run a mile on the beach. Then, home for breakfast and prayers.

Frank always claimed, "His values were my values."

■ THE FRONTIER ATTITUDE

Before coming to California in 1924, Wilkinson had lived in Arizona, the last of the lower forty-eight states to enter the Union. It was still very much a frontier when Frank and his family lived there, but it would be absurd to suggest that those few years could have had much influence on his character. And the part of California in which Wilkinson grew up from the age of ten can hardly be considered a frontier of the Old West sort, although one might jokingly point out that his neighbor, three doors down from his first home in Hollywood, was a "cowboy"—movie star Tom Mix. Frank's second home, in Beverly Hills, put him within rifle shot of the four-hundred-acre in-town "ranch" owned by E. L. Doheny, a real pioneer, who had brought in the Southland's first oil well in 1884 using only shovels and the sharpened trunk of a eucalyptus tree for a "drill." Los Angeles in 1884 was a town of just twelve thousand. Two years later, the population was one hundred thousand. The explosion continued, and by the 1920s, more than a million people had moved into Southern California, making it the largest internal migration in U.S. history.

The Wilkinsons were part of that stampede, and if Los Angeles wasn't a frontier outpost anymore, it certainly had the mentality and the atmosphere of one. Roger Morris has written that Los Angeles in that decade "far exceeded the national average in divorces and suicides, and led the country in embezzlement, bank robberies, narcotics addiction and society murders."[5]

Also arriving in the 1920s was a man who, nearly four decades later, would help recruit Wilkinson into his first national effort to kill HUAC. This newcomer was Carey McWilliams, whose father had once presided over a politico-ranching empire in northwestern Colorado, running seventeen thousand cattle one year; the crash of the cattle market after World War I had wiped him out, and some of the McWilliamses—like thousands of others in hard times—headed west. Carey, who became a noted chronicler of California life (and ultimately editor of the *Nation*), recalls Los Angeles in the mid-1920s as "a village in outlook, civic feeling, and even appearance. Westwood was yet to be; in the spring, after the rains, the area between La Brea and Beverly Hills would be ablaze with wild mustard growing in what were then open fields. Hollywood was still a village. . . . On my first night in Los Angeles I attended a benefit concert staged by motion picture stars in a circus tent on a vacant lot at Sunset and Vine."[6]

By 1930, when Frank was still in high school, the city had boomed into a population of 1,470,516—tripling its population in ten years and making it the fifth-largest city in the nation.

Frank lived in a posh corner of the city untouched by some of the darker forces in Los Angeles, and he was an extraordinarily sociable person; nonetheless he was a latter-day frontiersman in at least one respect: the degree to which he swore by the code that forbade unnecessary snooping into a person's private life.

If that attitude was a mark of the nation's youth, then the twentieth century clearly showed that the nation had reached late middle age. It had become painfully evident that privacy—or what Justice Louis Brandeis called "the most comprehensive of rights and the right most valued by civilized men," which is "the right to be let alone"—would henceforth be virtually unobtainable.

The change came about in part, of course, from so many Americans packing into urban areas elbow to elbow. But the most invidious intrusion into the life of the individual came from government and business investigators cooperating to build what the late Senator Sam J. Ervin Jr. accurately called "a dossier society." Skeletons (or even just a few bone chips) that used to be in closets were now in files, millions of them, officially indexed.

Because nobody in the twentieth century did more to create the dossier society than the bureaucrat who ordered the 132,000 pages of surveillance kept on him, Frank always tried to return the favor by persuading anyone who would listen that the twentieth century, in terms of ideological terrorism, should be named "the Age of J. Edgar Hoover."

CHAPTER 4

How the Playboy "Scholar" Almost Wins the UCLA Student Body Presidency

WHEN FRANK ENROLLED at the University of California at Los Angeles, he had no intention of trying to win a Rhodes scholarship. One thing he was not, nor wanted to be, was a bookworm. "You must understand that I was a lightweight in terms of reading knowledge, or in terms of my scholarship," he admits, though he hastens to add that he made perfect grades in public speaking and physical education. "However, I respected scholarship. I wanted to associate with scholarship the same way that I wanted to associate with people of means and political power. But I was not a good student, and that relates as I see it now, to my hearing problem." His hearing deficiency was about 80 percent. He jokes, "The reason I wasn't hurt by UCLA was that I couldn't hear the lectures."

Although it was against the rules to a pledge a fraternity before enrolling, in fact Sigma Alpha Epsilon let him know he was a de facto member even before he left high school. The value of this immediate connection to the fraternity became clear when one of his fraternity brothers, who had become manager of the Los Angeles Municipal Coliseum, hired Frank as an usher for the 1932 Summer

Olympics games—a plum job. This meant that he could have a seat on the fifty-yard line for all the games—and be paid for it.

UCLA especially appealed to Frank because it was just beginning to blossom, at least physically. Much of it was brand-new. The men's and women's gymnasiums and other major buildings were just being completed. Westwood Village, which surrounded UCLA, was brand-new.

"We were all very conscious of creating a new university," he recalls.

> If anyone pinned me down and asked why I was thrilled to be at UCLA, I would have said it was to get an education. But that was really secondary, in the back of my mind. Classes were an avoidable diversion from the main goal in life, which was to rally round the bonfire and beat USC. I was going for the whole social life found at a grand university and to immediately get involved in campus politics, all of the things that were organized by fraternities and sororities.

That was inevitable, for even before he stepped on the UCLA campus, Sigma Alpha Epsilon had decided to groom him to become student body president in his senior year. It wasn't difficult to develop Frank for the top position. He was into everything at UCLA; he was a very friendly, popular guy. He was a joiner and a doer. He was in charge of the March of Dimes on campus, a member of the freshman eight-man crew team, president of the Freshman Council. He was in charge of getting celebrities (mostly Hollywood stars) to judge the homecoming parade, and in charge of building the pre-game bonfire for the 1934 homecoming game. He was involved in the University Religious Conference, and he was elected to the honorary Blue Key Society in his sophomore year (usually, a student had to be a senior). And, he claimed, probably correctly, that he knew the first names of two thousand of his college mates.

"You built a record until, finally, by your senior year, you're the only one that's logical to be student body president," he says, and anyway, "it's already preordained that you will be student body president. I had the mandate from the fraternities and sororities to be their candidate—that was in the bag. That was promised and committed."

In the bag? How could that be? Because the Greek associations had always controlled political life at UCLA, passing around the various campus political posts, negotiating among themselves as to who, for example, would be student body president year by year. The fraternities and sororities had the power because *only* students who belonged to the Associated Students of the University of California (ASUC) had the right to vote. You didn't *have* to join the ASUC, but inasmuch as it cost ten dollars to join—which in those Depression days was like a hundred dollars today—very few non-organization students did join. On the other hand, to be in a fraternity or sorority you had to have money and you had to join the ASUC, which meant that only a couple of thousand students out of seven thousand could actually vote.

The fraternities had agreed that Frank Wilkinson would be given the student body presidency in 1935–1936, an arrangement that would repeat itself several times in Wilkinson's life—that of being elected to a position for which somebody else was calling the shots.

This time, however, he was spared that indignity. The "inevitability" of his being given the presidency was torpedoed when the UCLA administration was momentarily overcome by a desire to embrace democracy. It decreed in 1934 that tuition alone covered the right to vote, which transformed the election process. Now the non-organization students overwhelmingly—more than two to one—held the balance of power.

With that change, Wilkinson's chances died.

Or so it seemed, until UCLA provost Ernest C. Moore's nephew sought out Frank privately and confided that his uncle wanted him to stay in the race and not be discouraged. It seems that Moore had an underhanded scheme in mind.

▪

THE SCHEME WAS born of Provost Moore's hysterical fear of Communism. In 1934, San Francisco longshoremen pulled a strike that other unions joined and that resulted in a citywide shutdown. On July 5 there was a battle—"Bloody Thursday"—between the longshoremen and police and National Guardsmen. There was one death and hundreds of serious injuries.

Moore confided to his diary that the San Francisco strike "may be the beginning of the Revolution." In that dark mood, he wrote UC Berkeley president Robert Sproul that he had been "brooding" over the Communist effort to "undermine and destroy the public school system," a fear that was heightened when the head of the California State Police warned that "Communists . . . have orders . . . to center their efforts in the U.S. on two universities," meaning UCLA and UC Berkeley.[1] Sproul could believe it. After all, some of the left-wing students at his own university had crossed the bay and joined the longshoremen's picket line. What was the world coming to?

Indeed, many university and college administrators, and many industrialists and politicians, were asking the same question. That year, 1934, was also the year a strike encompassing the entire textile industry broke out. Troops with fixed bayonets began charging pickets outside mills in North Carolina and Georgia. Fourteen workers were killed. Also that year, truck drivers trying to establish a union in Minneapolis fought police and troops for two days; one person was killed and scores were seriously wounded on both sides, and the union temporarily controlled the city. That was also the year unions struck Goodyear, Firestone, and Goodrich plants, and steelworkers got ready to strike many plants.

Right smack in the middle of the Great Depression, 1934 was, to put it mildly, a year of unrest.

On campuses across the nation, left-wing students were also on the march. Nowhere was this more dramatically to be seen than at the City College of New York, which (as one writer put it) "produced student radical leaders at about the rate that Notre Dame churned out college football stars."[2] CCNY was tuition-free, thereby attracting hordes of students from the city's ghettos, full of Eastern European immigrants who leaned to the left sharply enough to comfortably include socialism.

CCNY's president, Frederick B. Robinson, and his subordinates, according to Robert Cohen, one of the best historians of this period, "violated student free speech rights more frequently than any other college administration in Depression America."[3] In October 1934 he went too far. Obviously taunting his heavily radical student body, Robinson invited a delegation of Italian fascist students to be honored at a special assembly.

The student chosen to introduce the visitors was told to be polite, but he rebelled and called them "tricked, enslaved students." A professor grabbed the mike away from him and members of the school's Italian Club jumped on stage and began to beat him. That triggered a full-scale riot, with dozens of antifascist students leaping on the stage to do battle with a wave of antiradical students that Robinson had organized for just such an occasion.

Later, thousands of students participated in an "Oust Robinson Week," burned Robinson's and Mussolini's effigies, and marched on city hall to demand that Robinson be fired.

Robinson expelled twenty-one students. All were leftists.

Such tactics were not unusual. On many campuses, administrators covertly encouraged—or refused to punish—frat members and school athletes who physically attacked "radical" students.

■ THE SCHEME TO ELECT WILKINSON UNFOLDS

UCLA's provost Moore wrote a letter to Robinson praising him for showing "backbone" in the "splendid bit of housecleaning you have done." Moore was about to do some "housecleaning" of his own and thereby provoke what historian Robert Cohen calls one of "the largest campus free speech protests on the West Coast during the 1930s."[4]

His scheme to free campus politics of radicalism unrolled as follows.

In October 1934, John Burnside, president of the student council, asked Moore to allow the students to run open forums themselves, without having faculty members present to supervise them and decide what topics could be discussed and what speakers could be invited. Peace movements were gathering strength. Hitler had seized power in Germany. Mussolini was expanding his power; Franco was gearing up in Spain. Fearing another war was in the offing, many students were holding antiwar rallies on campuses across the country. UCLA wanted to discuss the dangers of war, too—without faculty supervision.[5]

Moore ruled that there would be no open forums—and that Burnside should stop asking for them.

Burnside responded by holding a forum anyway, without permission. Frank Wilkinson not only attended the forum, he gave a speech on peace and social justice—after which, he went immediately to inform Moore that the bootleg forum had been held.

What? Was this the man who would make the First Amendment his lifelong crusade? Would this fanatical lover of free speech and free association—who even went to prison to protect those things—actually rat on his schoolmates for exercising these freedoms?

Yes. But we are dealing here with a young man who had never read, and probably never heard of, the Bill of Rights, and whose social calendar—this is "Good-Time Frankie" we're talking about—scarcely left any time for reading it, even if he'd wanted to. Besides, his ambitions in campus politics had corrupted him. Many years later, he would review that moment in his life: "I got involved because the administration always wanted to have things calm and peaceful and noncontroversial at UCLA, to protect our annual budget at the state legislature. The administration always wanted stable students to be elected so that the legislature would see that UCLA was turning out good American business types. I was always on the side of the administration and against the controversial things. This is a very good example of my bad civil liberties at that time, because I was going really blindly. If Ernest Carroll Moore said 'Jump!' I jumped."

That would fit in with his later confession of catering to people at the top, including Provost Moore. "God, how I sought out people

ROBERT SHERRILL

who were in elevated positions, or the fastest athletes, or the most beautiful women."

Wilkinson had two reasons for informing on his friends. He did it partly out of loyalty to the administration, but mostly he hoped it would result in his election as student body president. Now that the nonorganized students had the vote, their nominee—Tom Lambert—would undoubtedly win.

Moore's nephew had assured Wilkinson that he would get help from his uncle. Now he got it. Moore suspended five students as leaders of the illegal meeting—among them Tom Lambert, who was the only one Moore really wanted to get rid of. If his suspension was turned into an expulsion, Wilkinson's election was a certainty.[6]

The suspension of Lambert alone might not have roused the student body. But the leader of the suspended group, John Burnside, was one of the most popular men on campus, not only because of his personality but because he was an amazing stunt-creating cheerleader at the football games, and football was as important as war at UCLA (even though its team was pretty lousy, having lost its last game to archrival USC by a score of seventy-three to three). It is probably cynical to harbor the thought, but it's possible that the outcry following the suspension was prompted as much by the student body's fear of losing a great cheerleader as by its fear of losing free speech.

Moore's singling out of some of the school's outstanding mainstream students for heavy punishment prompted a protest rally of three thousand students—the largest political turnout ever seen at UCLA. Those who opposed the suspensions were assaulted by athletes and frat men recruited by the administration. The result was a full-scale riot.

Meanwhile, up at UC Berkeley, there was another riot, as the thousands who turned out in sympathy for the suspended UCLA students were attacked by some of Sproul's student vigilantes, who hurled literally truckloads of eggs and tomatoes at the rally's speakers.

Totally embarrassed, and under pressure from the board of

regents to quiet things down, Sproul—although he hated "radicals" just as much as Moore did—overrode the suspensions. And Wilkinson lost the election to Lambert. His consolation was that he lost by only five votes.

In the somewhat distant future, there would be two pleasantly ironic twists to this imbroglio.

One of the key organizers of the huge rally in Berkeley demanding that Moore reverse the suspensions was Richard Criley, a PhD student whom Sproul correctly suspected of being a Communist. At the moment, Criley and Wilkinson seemed to be going in irreversibly opposite directions. But years later, Criley would become probably Wilkinson's most useful and most militant lieutenant in his long effort to dismantle the House Un-American Activities Committee.

The other irony occurred when the paths of Wilkinson and John Burnside crossed years later. Wilkinson was on his way to prison for refusing to answer HUAC's questions when he encountered Burnside in Washington, D.C. During his distinguished career in the army, Burnside had reached the rank of general and was then commandant of the Army War College in Washington.

The FBI agents must have had some weird theories as to why a pillar of the establishment like Burnside would seem so happy and friendly as he walked away to lunch with that notoriously subversive Frank Wilkinson.

■ WIDENING FRANK'S CIRCLE

Even though Frank lost the election, his senior year would be fortuitous in ways he could not have foreseen. Before college, few Jews had ever played any noticeable role in Frank's life, except for early schoolmates who were children of Hollywood's actors and moguls. This changed at UCLA, and although his fraternity did not accept Jews for membership, by his senior year, Frank had made friends with Maury Grossman, his campaign manager for student body president, and Bernie Levin, head of the student

Rally Committee and son of the owner of the Kelly Pipe Company in Los Angeles's south-central ghetto area. Levin gave Frank a job when he sorely needed one, and long after Frank became a notorious radical and ex-convict, Levin kept giving financially to his civil rights work.

Not nearly so loyal, but far more important to Frank, was Gilbert Harrison, the first Jew he really knew intimately. Their friendship was extremely close at UCLA and for a few years thereafter. Harrison was an excellent student, well read, an editor of the student newspaper the *Bruin*. He was the most important of Frank's non-fraternity friends. On the afternoon of Frank's graduation from UCLA, Harrison met him halfway between the library and Royce Hall and gave him a watch. Frank was impressed—Harrison was generally broke, and would not have had a watch to give had his father not been an itinerant jewelry salesman. The back of the watch was inscribed: "If this watch lasts as long as our friendship, it will be a better watch than I think it is."

(The watch often came in handy on his post-college European trip, spending time in hock shops when Frank went broke.)

While their close friendship lasted, and it did last more than a decade, Frank greatly benefited from it. During that last year at UCLA and for a few years after he returned from his European adventure, he credits Harrison with "accelerating my growth. I wanted to open my mind and fly, and Gil's relationship with an intellectual world and a more sophisticated world encouraged my thinking. But it wasn't directly from sitting down with Gil and having conversations. I don't think I was equal to a real debating conversation with him, but I enjoyed a one-sided conversation, hearing what he was doing, and then dwelling upon that privately."

Among the things they shared was a love for Jean Benson. Both men dated her in college, and in 1939 Frank married her. Ultimately Harrison would marry an heiress to the McCormick fortune, which enabled him to purchase the *New Republic* magazine, become a frequent guest at the White House, and mingle with the Democratic Party elite.

CHAPTER 5

Frank Begins His Real Education

SINCE FRANK HAD essentially majored in fun, he did not leave UCLA in 1936 equipped to begin a promising career. When people asked him what he intended to do next, he told them he was going to travel, then return and begin studies at Union Theological Seminary to prepare for the ministry. Given his lifelong immersion in Methodism, the second part of that answer sounded reasonable, but in fact, he considered it no more than "a good answer" to give curious people.

As for traveling, however, he really meant that. His uncle had died and left him $250, and he intended to use the money for an extended pilgrimage through Europe and the Holy Land. That amount of money wouldn't be enough to buy a one-way ticket to Europe these days, much less travel for weeks (as he would do), but we're talking about 1936, when millions of Americans would have been deliriously happy to earn $250 for three months' work—if they could get work at all. Besides, Frank's father would send additional funds as needed and, once abroad, Frank intended to live on no more than a dollar a day—which, for the most part, he did: traveling by bike or hitchhiking, spending nights in a sleeping bag.

At a Baptist seminar in northern California the year before, he had heard a lecture about Jane Addams, and now he wanted to know more. Addams was the radical head of Hull House, a huge settlement house in Chicago where people could get help in the form of emergency clothing and food, training in sewing (for immigrant women forced to work in the needle trades), and tutoring in the English language—no small matter for the many, many foreign residents in that city. Perhaps her most practical touch was building five bathrooms in Hull House and making them available to people in the neighboring tenements, where plumbing was rare. In one July, she recorded 980 baths taken.

Jane Addams's life and philosophy were a fascinating amalgam. She was a pacifist anarchist who'd seconded the nomination of Theodore Roosevelt at the Progressive Party convention in 1912 and voted once for the Socialists' presidential candidate, Eugene Debs, and twice for Herbert Hoover—prompted mainly by his good work in feeding Europe after World War I. She was publicly reviled for opposing the U.S. entry into World War I but adored for winning the Nobel Peace Prize in 1931, and was reputed to be the most famous woman in the world, next to the Queen of England. Like Frank, she had been reared in great comfort and saved herself by working for the poor, although she certainly was no apologist for the defects of the underdog's character.

Frank made Chicago his first stopover; he wanted to visit Hull House. That's how he encountered Maxwell Street, which was, he says, "one of the real turning points in my life because I had never seen poverty before." On Maxwell Street there was a market area for the poor. "There were thousands of people trading and bartering and buying in this area, and they were terribly poor. Raggedy clothes were being traded. The vegetables being sold were rotten. They had probably been retrieved at stores that were throwing them away.

"I just walked into this, sat down, and watched a whole new dimension of American life, thousands of people desperately hungry. I watched people eating out of garbage cans for the first time in my life."[1]

Frank says he watched this "until I was revolted, knowing that if they went around to the front of the café, they could get a full meal for a dime. And I had money with me, so I began feeding people. I'd say to a person eating from a garbage can, 'Come with me,' and take them around from the alley in back of the restaurant to the front and take them in, introduce them to somebody inside, give them a dime and say, 'Feed this person.'

"I kept doing that until, literally, all the money I planned on spending in the first three months was gone. It was not till then that I realized I was not making much of a dent in the economic crisis in Chicago." He continued his futile efforts a little longer by going to places like the spiffy Edgewater Beach hotel and asking for money from baffled people with the question, "Do you know about the hunger down on Maxwell Street?" Then back he would go to buy more ten-cent meals for his new wards.[2]

Frank describes another scene from Maxwell Street: "The one experience that I shall *never* forget was sitting in the middle of this unbelievable poverty and filth and hunger of hundreds and hundreds of people—they were almost entirely white poor—with wagons being pulled by horses, and the horse dung just adding to the mess of rotten garbage. I saw a little child, about six years old, in the middle of this, and underneath all of these rotten vegetables and horse manure, she spots a little dead puppy. It was not a mess; it was just dead; it had died there. She picked it up and I watched her as she rubbed the fur of this dead dog against her cheek. Then other children came up, and they all wanted to pet this little dead dog.

> Then it suddenly occurred to them to play a game of tag. The girl took the dog and threw it at another child. Then that child picked up the dog and would chase others and throw it. The dead dog was getting to be more and more of a bloody, ugly mess, as the children played tag with it, dashing in and around and under things.
>
> Then, up that street came another horse-drawn wagon. It was empty, except on the back of the wagon was a box of

overly ripe tomatoes. A bump in the street caused that box to flip upside-down as it fell off the wagon. I watched these kids drop their game of tag and pile into that box of rotten tomatoes in the middle of the street. As fast as they could, they were shoving tomatoes into their faces, along with dirt and everything else.

Within a matter of a minute—there were lots of kids involved—there was just a clean, smudged area in the middle of the rotten vegetables and the horse manure on the street. Then the kids walked over and picked up the little dead dog and the game went on.

I had just seen a part of America that I had never, never known existed. At that moment, my notion of making my trip a Richard Halliburton sort of thing—doing the clever things, the voyager, the adventure type of things—was gone. My focus, from that time on, was determination to really *see* what America was like, and then what the world was like, and to simulate the living conditions of the lowest-income classes.[3]

Maxwell Street was the beginning of my new world, my new life.[4]

Frank got another glimpse of what the underbelly of society was like when he arrived in New York City and checked into a Bowery flophouse that had four toilet stalls and two showers for a hundred men. The men were roused before daylight and pushed out on the street immediately, to repeat the cycle of begging. He saw beggars who hadn't eaten a recent meal but, given a nickel, would immediately retire to a bar to buy a glass of wine. (In some low dives, you could get a glass of beer for a penny.) Frank was no beggar. His personal fortune, so to speak, allowed him to live on fifteen cents a day, buying hot dogs. To get a feeling for how the penniless lived, he dressed, ate, and lived like one.

But he could have ended the experiment any time he wanted, for inside his sleeping bag he had letters of introduction from California governor Frank Merriam, Los Angeles mayor Frank Shaw, Los Angeles County sheriff Eugene Biscailuz, and, most useful of all, a letter of credit to the Bank of America from his father indicating a cable address where there were thousands of dollars available on call.

■

NEITHER MAXWELL STREET, nor the Bowery, nor any other slum in the United States could begin to compare with the unspeakable filth, poverty, disease, and hunger Frank would encounter when he got to the countries of North Africa and to Palestine and Jerusalem.

In many of those places, it was commonplace for the residents to defecate and urinate, in broad daylight, in the middle of the street where they lived. On one occasion in Tunis, assaulted suddenly by diarrhea, Frank was forced to drop his pants and follow this local custom.

In countries where the roads permitted, he usually traveled by bicycle or hitchhiked. But when he had to travel by ship or train, he always traveled the lowest fare, fourth class. This meant no toilet, no water, no beds, and often not even a bench to sit or sleep on. And inevitably, the space was packed with bodies. On one train, to his surprise, he found space to sit next to a sleeping Arab. It was bitterly cold, and he pressed close to the Arab for warmth. The next morning he discovered the reason other passengers had left the space vacant: the Arab was a leper.

On one occasion Frank missed his train, so he slept under a bridge. Numerous Arabs were also sleeping there. The next morning he awoke to find that they had stolen everything except what he had crammed into his sleeping bag. He calmly accepted robbery as part of the life he had set out to investigate and be a part of.

He arrived in Bethlehem in time for the crush of Christmas tourists. They were accompanied by hundreds of beggars. The area in front of the Church of the Nativity was so packed with beggars he couldn't get inside, until he found a convenient window to climb through.

Frank wasn't exactly dressed like a swell: Keds, blue jeans, an

old shirt, and, for warmth, a trench coat he had picked up somewhere in Philadelphia for three dollars. But he looked rich to the
beggars, and a sea of hands was thrust at him everywhere he went.
Most of the beggars were barefoot, despite the snowy night, and
wore clothing that looked like gunnysacks. The one that stuck in
his memory was

> this one child, I would guess sixteen, seventeen—how can
> you tell the age of a poverty-stricken girl?—who came up to
> me begging. She was nursing two babies through her gunny-
> sack, her breasts open and nursing two babies. Her body
> was filthy, grimy dirty. Her eyes had trachoma[5] to the extent
> that they were running sores. The dripping of the trachoma
> infection was running down her cheeks, literally dripping
> down right into the faces of her babies, and she's reaching
> around them saying, "*Baksheesh! baksheesh!*"—the historic
> call for alms. The coin she was asking for was the equivalent
> of one-tenth of one penny.

Frank says he went back to the Church of the Nativity many times,
though it is difficult to understand why—unless he was fascinated
by the warring religious sects: "I came there one time when the
Greeks [Greek Orthodox] and the Coptics [black Christians from
Ethiopia] were simultaneously celebrating their Christmas. The
hostility between the groups was enormous. When the Greeks
were praying, the Coptics would come near them and rattle little
tin cymbals so loudly the Greeks couldn't hear their own prayers.
And when the Coptics prayed, the Greeks shouted and sang so
loudly the Coptics couldn't hear theirs. And in the middle of this
uproar, there was constant fighting between the priests. Then into
the church came a hundred British soldiers with full military gear,
including bayonets on their rifles, and they formed a cordon right
straight across the center of the church to separate the two groups.
I watched for hours as the British troops kept these Christian
priests from fighting each other, right there where Christ supposedly had been born."

But Christians weren't the only ones he witnessed having spiritual encounters. The second-most-important mosque in all of Islam is at the Dome of the Rock in the old city of Jerusalem. However, this is also the site of the King David Temple, where, Jews believe, Abraham considered sacrificing Isaac to satisfy God. Muslims controlled the area, but nearby—bordering it and as close as the Jews could get to their temple—was their wailing wall, where they would pray. Bear in mind that Jews and Arabs were killing each other just as enthusiastically in those days as they are today. So when Jews went to the wall to pray, Arab snipers would try to pick them off with rifles—unless British soldiers happened to be on hand to kill the snipers first.

Until the wall was built high enough to stop them, Arabs had regularly taken garbage out of the main Muslim mosque and thrown it over the wall onto the heads of the Jews as they prayed there.

These experiences deepened Frank's understanding of the anti-Semitism he had encountered in Germany, where Jews could sit only on yellow park benches and the sign No Jews or Dogs was stuck in many a store window; Poland and Romania were even worse. Not surprisingly, the intensity of his revulsion to these practices reflected the friendship he'd started at UCLA with Gilbert Harrison. "Having known Gil as my closest friend, and Gil being the first Jew that I really knew intimately, I always sort of juxtaposed: anti-Semitism is anti–Gil Harrison. For that reason, in all my travels if I saw anti-Semitism in Morocco, or in Poland or Romania or anywhere—Germany, of course—it was as though somebody was attacking Gilbert Harrison."

■ HOW FRANK LOSES HIS FAITH AND LEARNS HE ISN'T THE FIRST TO DO SO

After Frank had been in the modern part of Jerusalem long enough to be fed up with its backwardness, he got the urge once more to experience slum life at its lowest, so he went to the old part of the city. There, with the help of an English-speaking cop, he was introduced to a landlord who rented him space in a windowless room also occupied by eight Arab beggars. The rent was fifteen cents a day, room and board. Just off the room there was a little courtyard, in which a hole in the ground served as the toilet. Urinating was done in the middle of the street, with the flow eventually reaching a catch-basin gutter.

His roommates were suspicious of Frank. Obviously he wasn't an Arab. So are you a Jew? they asked. No. Are you British? No. What are you? American. From the United States. They had never heard those words. Finally he scored: Hollywood! Ah, yes, well, okay, they knew that word.

From then on, one of the beggars adopted Frank and accompanied him everywhere; when they passed groups that looked hostile, his guardian would shout out assurances that Frank was not a Jew. Whatever other reasons he might have had for protecting Frank, hunger was one of them. It turned out that the fifteen cents Frank paid daily for room and board was in fact enough to feed all nine in the room—sharing a large plate of beans and a loaf of bread, with sometimes fat from a sheep's head thrown in.[6] While Frank was in Jerusalem, he too came down with trachoma, but Arabs he had befriended guided him—he was temporarily blind—to the British hospital.

■

BY NOW, WILKINSON—ONCE the consummate believer in Protestantism, and particularly in Methodism, with all its faith in the Trinitarian miracles—was rapidly becoming something he never would have thought possible: an atheist.

Roughing it through North Africa, the Middle East, and Europe had changed Frank's ministerial ambitions—if in fact they had ever really existed—and changed him in other ways as well. The coarseness of life—going days without a bath (he arrived in Paris so filthy that he took off his clothes right in the middle of the city, lathered up with his bar of soap, and dived into the Seine); wearing dirty clothes; eating food he could hardly bear to look at; sleeping in beds so full of bedbugs that his sheet was wet with his blood the next morning; missing meals several days in a row; waking up to find homosexual natives trying to crawl into his sleeping bag with him—all that became commonplace. He almost enjoyed it—as an adventure. It was what he had set out to discover: life at levels he had never imagined.

Not that it was all like that. He spent many days in places like the Vatican Museum, soaking up the paintings and archeological findings. Yes, he lived in the souks with the poorest of Arabs in one part of Jerusalem, but he also struck up friendships with middle-class Arabs. He met a young Arab woman who knew English and desperately wanted to see *Romeo and Juliet*, then playing in a Jewish theater. She was forbidden to go to such a theater, but Frank sneaked her in. He knew nothing about opera, but he hankered to see one in Rome, so he made friends with an American musician playing in a hotel orchestra and borrowed his clothes several times. "I'd come in filthy from my day in the slums of Rome, or the catacombs where I'd been studying the persecution of the early Jews, come to the hotel, go to his room for a shower, get dressed up [in the musician's clothes]—top hat, tails, white tie, gloves—and then meet these women from Germantown, Pennsylvania [who had the tickets]." Frank made friends easily, and wasn't modest about accepting their largesse, just as he wasn't stingy about sharing his own—when he had something to share.

But for the most part, Frank experienced the underside of the world in his travels. And there he discovered that Calvinist standards are profane compared to humanism and compassion, and that the "dirty" words that were forbidden in his youth are ridiculously inconsequential compared to the real filth in which huge masses of people have to live.

■

FRANK'S FAITH WAS being whittled away by all the astonishing practices he was being exposed to for the first time. Before he reached Jerusalem, the most stunning he saw was the one saturating Kairouan, Tunisia. "What I saw there," he says, "was one of the real changing points in my life.

It didn't touch me as affecting Christianity, but in terms of the superstition and ignorance of the Muslim faith. In Kairouan they have three hairs, seven hairs—some number of hairs—from Muhammad's beard, and they are in a sacred gold shrine, which is inside another gold shrine and a huge mosque.

According to the Muslim faith, if in your lifetime you can make one trip to Mecca or Messina, then you are guaranteed a chance for an afterlife in paradise. But if you are poor and cannot go on that long trip to Saudi Arabia, then you can make seven trips to Kairouan and pray before the hairs of Muhammad's beard, and you'd have the same chance of going to paradise as if you'd gone to Mecca once.

I saw these Arab peasants, barefoot, walking for miles to get to Kairouan, hungry and sometimes in pain, but full of ecstasy when they got there and knelt on their prayer rugs. Inside the mosque you would find hundreds and hundreds of people praying before the hairs of Muhammad's body. It struck me as pitifully ridiculous, and I was beginning to question the foundations of the mythology of our Western religions. Of *any* religion.

■ THE FINAL CUT TO HIS RELIGIOUS UMBILICAL CORD

During the time Frank was living in the one-room hovel in Jerusalem with eight Arab beggars, he took two excursions that put the finishing touches on his atheism.

One was to the Church of the Holy Sepulcher, built where the faithful believe Jesus was crucified and buried. Late one night when Frank was there, a priest entered. He was wearing extraordinarily elaborate robes sewn with gold thread and a giant Greek Orthodox or Russian Orthodox hat with jewels in it.

Shortly thereafter, a barefoot, gunnysacked peasant woman came in. Her trachoma-infected eyes were leaking. She fell at the feet of the priest and rubbed her face in his robe. He did the incense cross over her. She jumped to her feet and ran out of the church and down the alleyway shouting her assurance (Frank assumed) that God would now cure her near-blindness.

To Frank, such religious hallucinations were highly offensive.

At Hebron, under a tomb made from giant chiseled stones, is the place where Abraham and Isaac and Sarah are buried. Christians, Muslims, and Jews all revere the place. "They believe that Sarah, who produced Isaac in her ninety-first year (according to the Bible), can bestow fertility on petitioners," says Frank.

If she could produce a child at ninety-one, she must be something special to God. So, when I was there (I don't know if they are still doing it), barefoot, gunnysack women who were barren would come great distances to Hebron. When they got there, they stood outside the temple at a place where they could see down through the cracks. And they would take a rag of any kind, pull up their garments, wipe it on their vagina, and push the rag down through the cracks, hoping it would fall onto the tomb of Sarah. Having done that, they went away shouting hallelujah, exclamations of joy, for now they were certain they would have a child.

I watched this happen and I said, "My God, any woman who is totally illiterate and has a child after doing that is going to believe it came not from her husband but from God because she never had a child until she visited the tomb of Sarah."

And then it dawned on me: here we are in the twentieth century and ignorant women come to the conclusion they have been impregnated by God. That's Immaculate Conception. Two thousand years ago, what about Mary? What about Joseph? What about their ignorance? They still thought the world was flat. What education did they have? And I suddenly began to see that if some women in the twentieth century could deceive themselves in that way, they could certainly have deceived themselves in Mary's day. So for the first time I challenged the basic part of the Christian credo of the Immaculate Conception.[7]

That did it. For Frank, God was now dead.

Looking back on his early revelations, Frank recognized his own naiveté: "I thought I was the first person that had ever questioned the existence of God."

He even spent a day in the library at the American University in Beirut seeking proof of his singularity. He believed it so firmly that he wrote UC Berkeley president Robert Sproul, whom he considered a friend: "Dear Bob, There is no God. Do you realize I have been around Palestine for some weeks now and I have learned that there's no evidence of his existence. The evidence is all to the contrary. There is no God. Christ is not immortal. A belief in God is a misunderstanding of the unknown."

The revelation of this epiphany must have stunned President Sproul, although not in the way Wilkinson would have liked.

■

BUT AT LEAST Frank—who had once lived by the mantra "My father's faith is my faith"—deserves credit for the courage it must have taken to tell his father of this change of heart. Actually, he had been alerting his parents to the change bit by bit, throughout his travels. Except where postal service was out of the question, he wrote them twice a day, telling them of all his experiences and of his reactions to them, hiding nothing. So when he alerted them to the final break with Methodism and the ancient Apostles' Creed, it did not come as a stunning blow.

Fifteen years later, in 1952, when Frank was fired from the Los Angeles Housing Authority and made to appear a dangerous subversive for refusing to answer questions about his political beliefs, this period was resurrected to smear him further. City Councilman Earle D. Baker decided to add the crime of patricide to Frank's reputation. Claiming that Dr. Wilkinson was "my most intimate friend" (a claim that surprised the Wilkinsons), he told the Hearst newspapers *Herald-Express* and *Examiner* that shortly after Frank returned from abroad, Dr. Wilkinson had confided, "Earle, this American boy I have raised has returned to me with a completely changed philosophy and outlook. I've lost my boy. My heart is broken." Baker added that Dr. Wilkinson "died a week or two later of a broken heart."

The *Herald-Express* memorialized this revelation on September 3, 1952, with a four-column front-page headline:

FATHER'S BROKEN HEART DEATH
TOLD IN WILKINSON'S CHANGE??

There were a couple of fairly important things wrong with Baker's sad little tale, as the Hearst papers would have known if they had bothered to check their obituary files. First, Dr. Wilkinson did not die "a week or two" after Frank's return at the end of 1937. He died more than *two years* later, in 1940. And second, he did not die of a broken heart but of devotion to his calling. After working straight through seventy-two hours of caring for patients in a flu epidemic, he was so exhausted that he contracted a fatal case of the disease himself.

■

ACTUALLY, FRANK SAYS, his father took the news of his atheism rather nonchalantly, and that's easy to believe because he must have known his son would never change in essentials. It was a sound conclusion. Frank continued to believe wholeheartedly in the teachings of Christ.

And his love never lessened for the physical church he'd grown up attending:

> I used to come back to the Hollywood Methodist Church
> in the middle of the forties. I'd come in there at night—it

would be open—and I liked to go down and sit in the family pew, just sit there. No one around, just reliving, rethinking where I'd come from. I think it's a healthy thing that I didn't go from being very religious to being a person that wanted to destroy everything religious in my background.

I came to appreciate that there were some emotional ties to goodness in my life, which, I think objectively, were related to my Methodist upbringing. Somehow, when I got in deep trouble here in Los Angeles in terms of my politics—that is, in 1952 when I had been blacklisted out of my work with housing—I still liked to go back there alone, and sit in the family pew, and think of my family's life in the church, and of the ministers and the others. To this day, I still feel that whatever has been good in my life came out of the Methodist Church and the family upbringing.[8]

But sentiment was secondary to his new faith. "The moment I mailed that letter to President Sproul, it was like suddenly my mind was open, just blown open. I had committed myself. My drive toward building my ideals on the Christian gospel, or social concern, or building the Kingdom of God—as my family would have said—was still completely there. I wanted, in every way, to build a better world, but not what I would then call a 'Kingdom of God on Earth.' I wanted to build a better *world* on earth. From then on, with my mind open, everything was seen through a new perspective, and I changed and I grew every day from that day forward, all, I think, for the better in terms of my social concerns."

▪ PIOUS FOLK HAD ONE FINAL LESSON TO TEACH FRANK

Before he bade adieu to Europe's orthodox religious world, he did have one highly instructive encounter from which he learned—if he didn't already know it—that you can't judge even the holiest-seeming persons by their cover. Fittingly, it happened in Paris.

He obtained permission from the mother superior of a Catholic nunnery to put down his sleeping bag in the garden.

He was asleep when it began to rain gently, and he was awakened by one of the nuns, who motioned for him to come inside. She led him up to the second floor, where the nuns had their living cubicles. "I was," Frank tells us, "half awake and glad to have shelter from the rain. I go into her cubicle and I turn to thank her and, at that point, she totally disrobes and stands nude in front of me. Well, I was absolutely shocked. I was twenty-three and I had never seen a nude woman in my life. She reaches out and takes me into her arms, and then takes me down on the bed. This is where I became something of a hypocrite, because I am sure I could have stopped right then and said, 'Please, I don't want this. Leave!' But—I don't know, maybe it lasted five minutes—I continued to lie there with this nude woman. We did not have sex; that I know. But I was very excited. I let her lie there and I enjoyed it. But I was just overwhelmed with guilt."

Shocked and remorseful he may have been, but the nun's offer—albeit quickly declined—set him to thinking. One thing he thought about was that, as he left home, his father's only admonition had been, "My son, do not let alcoholic beverages touch your lips." He had said nothing about sex. Perhaps hoping a confession would help expunge some of the guilt he felt for having gotten so excited by the nun, Frank wrote a girlfriend back in Beverly Hills all the details of his strange encounter. Her sympathetic response was only a brief note, quoting something of Goethe's. It arrived when Frank was in Germany, so a translation was easy to obtain: "Sleep in many beds, enjoy, and when you find mine sweeter, return again to me."

Soon after that, in Nuremberg, he met a young woman from Long Island who was a good conversationalist—always his first consideration in choosing companions. Indeed, Frank recalls just how important conversation was in breaching the wall of chastity: "I remember so well in the ruins of the old, old, old city of Nuremberg, of walking around and talking with her, and talking with her, and talking with her. I'm sure I must have told her all my life story. It was only after I had talked for hours that we reached the point where we wanted to go to her apartment and make love. I don't know what she was thinking of this; I'm sure she'd never met a man my age who approached it almost conversationally." But with Goethe's advice in mind, Frank ultimately found it convenient to guide her, or let her guide him, beyond conversation. He was, after all, twenty-three.

In the same way that he had written a full account, step by step, of his passage through and out of Christianity, Frank regaled his family with the minutiae of his trip through and out of chastity. He never held anything back from them, whether they wanted to know all the details or not.

∎

FRANK'S VISIT TO the Soviet Union in 1937 was so brief and circumscribed that he learned few of the truths about that nation. He learned nothing about Stalin's great purges of the early 1930s that were crippling the government and the military. He learned nothing about the millions who had starved and continued to starve as a result of Stalin's disastrous agricultural "reforms." But he did see enough of the USSR to sense that it was on the cusp of an industrial renaissance that, by the end of the decade, would eclipse the industrial output of France, Japan, and Italy.[9]

Frank says, "I saw plenty of poverty, but unlike some of the other countries I'd visited, it wasn't accompanied by filth. I saw child-care centers for the workers in every factory. I learned that every worker had total medical care, cradle to grave. Yes, I saw backwardness. But I saw a country coming out of feudalism, out of total illiteracy, and gradually building something promising— and the progress was astonishing, for this was only twenty years after the revolution."[10]

Frank's experiences abroad had a deep and lasting, if sometimes distorted, effect on his view of the world. He was never a "tourist." He used the world as a classroom with a much more earnest sense of purpose than he had ever used the classrooms of UCLA.

CHAPTER 6

Robert Frost Was Right: "Home Is the Place Where, When You've Got to Go There, They Have to Take You In."

DECEMBER 1937: HOME again. If Frank supposed that he would be greeted by friends and family as the bearer of golden truths, he was severely disappointed. To be sure, his family treated him with loving tolerance, but as he continued to talk about the nonexistence of God, he noticed that a few of his old friends began to shun him. Did his atheism really offend them so much? Or did they just get tired of hearing him talk about his epiphany?

For the most part, however, his friends were more curious than critical and gave him a warm, if somewhat tentative, reception. It seemed that everyone had heard wild stories about his physical and spiritual adventures. Because they considered some of the material too shocking, his parents had concealed those letters in which he had freely written about the political, religious, and sexual transformations in his mind; but, in their worried state, they had passed along some of the details to the Hollywood Methodist Church hierarchy, from which gossip, increasingly elaborate, quickly spread. And besides, Frank had also written to a few close friends who considered the stories and musings that came in the mail interesting enough to pass along to others in his circle.

"My family," Frank recalls, "was very hopeful that I could be reconciled with the church."

> I don't remember them sitting down and worrying with me about this. I do remember that my father, who was an important member of the church, listened to me and then asked in disbelief, "Frank, you mean you don't believe in the Apostles' Creed?" And I said, "No, I don't." That didn't bring him to tears. But it was hard for my mother and father to grasp and understand what I really was saying. Their son, who had been their hope in terms of being a religious leader, actually had returned to them after a year and a half as an atheist.

Frank remembers that on his first visit back to the Hollywood Methodist Church, the minister patted him on the back with a hearty, "Hello, Frank. Glad you're home." Then, he recalls, he overheard the minister say to his father and mother, 'Don't worry about Frank. He'll be all right. Anyone with his background will be all right.'" The suggestion that he wasn't "all right" irritated Frank then, and years later he was still complaining about it. After all, he *had* spent months abroad, "having real, real experiences in the Holy Land and across North Africa and Europe and had observed how all religions were reduced to superstition and inhumanity of various sorts." What evidence did this minister—or any minister—have to counteract his findings? *They*, he argued, had not seen what *he* had seen. Frank states today at ninety, "Even now, as I repeat their remarks more than half a century later, I still resent it and I still am not 'all right,'" as these folks would describe his now lifelong atheism.

However, part of Frank's resentment toward the minister, and others like him, probably came from an abiding envy that they still had something that his "enlightenment" had deprived him of forever: a guaranteed rationale for doing good. The desire to do good to please God had gone out the window when God went out. So where would his motivation come from now? This question—which launched a period of restless adjustment to his atheistic mind-set—struck him, oddly enough, in the middle of an activity that probably hasn't sparked many ethical musings over the years: he was mowing the lawn.

Frank recalls:

> It suddenly dawned on me to question all of my actions. "Why are you cutting the lawn? Why do you wash the car? Why do you want to make a better world? Why?" And I just stopped that lawn-cutting right in the middle of the process and came inside and sat down and thought about it for hours. Indeed, for months the question plagued me. I had never thought about what I would replace Christianity with, when I dropped it. What do you do if you have no religion? What is the basis of your ethics?

Perhaps this last question struck a particular chord, as it was something Gil Harrison had often faulted him for: "Frank, you have no base for your ethics. You've got to have a base!"

"I certainly had no political base. My move toward socialism or toward Communism, or whatever my future direction was going to be, was not there."

But such worries were a waste of time. He was more comfortable exploring practical thoughts and real-life situations than metaphysical abstractions, or seeking deductive proofs. "Finally I got tired of thinking, got tired of saying there's no basis for my ethics, and I just decided that doing useful things and having good human relations made me happy, and that was enough ethics for me. I told myself that fighting for programs to get rid of crime and disease, fighting for integration, fighting for civil liberties, would be smart things to do because they would make a happier, safer world for *me* to live in. Self-interest became my new ethics. But that argument, though I believed it, was a jolt to me because somehow it seemed more selfish than I wanted to be. I still wanted to do good just for the satisfaction of doing it for others."

He may have stopped worrying about it, but for years, at odd moments, the dilemma would pop back into his mind.

▪

THERE IS REASON to think that Dr. Wilkinson, far from being ashamed of the change in Frank, was quietly proud of his son's rough adventures and independence of mind. After all, for one of Frank's first breakfasts at home, Dr. Wilkinson invited his closest friend, Los Angeles County supervisor John Anson Ford, to come over and hear what Frank had to say about his journeys. It was a visit whose consequences would shape much of Frank's life for the next two years. He started talking around 9 A.M. at the breakfast table, and five hours later he was still talking, because Ford, fascinated, kept asking questions. At the end he said, "More people should hear about this," and invited Frank to speak at one of Ford's regular Saturday-morning breakfast get-togethers for about fifty of his political supporters. He brought back Frank for a second lecture, and then a third. Frank's lecturing career was launched.

Word got around, and the invitations began pouring in from every conceivable forum. The standing title of his lecture (which included details of his stopover in Chicago's Maxwell Street and New York's Bowery) was "The Social Conditions of the Lower-Income Classes in North Africa, the Near East, and Europe."

Lecturing would have been impossible if he had not, immediately upon returning home, asked his father to buy him a hearing aid. All his life he had been 80 percent deaf, but as newer technology was now available, he knew that he didn't have to live with the deafness anymore. He was tired of having to stop conversations and ask people to repeat themselves, louder. The instrument he got certainly wasn't discreet. It was two inches high, four inches wide, and ten inches long and contained large, heavy batteries. He carried it by a strap over his shoulder. The wire coming out of it was attached to a metal band going over the top of his head and coming down on the bone behind his ear.

His whole life changed immediately. Suddenly he began to experience the world anew, with childlike wonder. The Wilkinson house had a roof garden. He would go up there with his hearing aid and sit by the flowers, put a little syrup or honey on his hearing aid's microphone, and listen to the flies and bees that dropped by. For the first time in his life he could go to a concert at the Hollywood Bowl, sit in the fortieth row, and hear the violins as well as if he were sitting on the stage.

Another immediate effect of having his hearing restored was that he could, for the first time in his life, really hear *himself*, which prompted an instinctive change in the projection of his voice; it dropped a full octave. He became a baritone with an appealing timbre that greatly contributed to his success as a speaker.

Frank counted some six hundred lectures given between 1938 and 1941. And although he held several jobs during that period, he was always able to squeeze in time for lecturing. "I think I probably spoke to every Rotary, Kiwanis, Optimists, and Lions club in Southern California at that time, at least once and sometimes on several occasions. I wanted to share what I had learned, but it also became a source of income for me. In today's money it may sound ridiculous, but five dollars was the going rate to speak to a service club, and in the 1930s five dollars for a half-hour talk at a luncheon was pretty good money."

Once he got fifty dollars for speaking to the Los Angeles Rotary in the Biltmore Bowl, and out of that came other fifty-dollar invitations from corporate executives. They were eager to have him tell their employees about the dictatorships of Europe, apparently as a way of reminding them that even if they were getting pitifully low wages, things could be worse. A dozen years later, when the smog of Communist suspicions descended on his life, nobody would remember that Frank Wilkinson had once indirectly served as a pitchman for patriotic capitalists.

■

IT'S HARD TO say whether Frank's homecoming was more difficult for him or for his family. One small adjustment required of Frank involved his bed. It was much too soft. He was used to his sleeping bag, spread on everything from pavement to hard ground to cobblestones. It took him two weeks to get used to the bed's softness. In the meantime, he slept on the floor in his trusty sleeping bag.

More significant were the offbeat activities Frank restlessly engaged in, which indicated that he not only had become something of a rebel, but wanted to be identified as such.

Why else did he bring a few blacks to Sunday service at the Hollywood Methodist Church, where they were about as welcome as Franklin Roosevelt would have been at a GOP convention?

Why did he chuck his desultory plans to go back to UCLA for an advanced degree in social psychology and instead persuade his old college chum Bernie Levin to give him a short-term job in Levin's pipe company? Frank was the only Anglo in a crew of twenty blacks and Mexicans. They sorted and stacked and then loaded onto trucks heavy drilling pipes, filthy with oil and grease. In Frank's memory, "It was muscular work, stripped to the waist, sweaty, dirty. By the time noon came around you could not tell me from a Mexican or from a lighter-skinned black person. I was just one of the people. If there was a toilet, I don't remember it. For a wash-up, there was no sink, no soap, no towels. There was nothing but a faucet and some old newspapers to wipe off the heavier layer of dirt. I loved it."

And when he was arrested for speeding, why did he refuse to pay his fine and insist on going to jail instead? He told the judge he had seen some of the jails in Europe and wanted to see what they were like in this country. Nice try, but it was hard to be a rebel in Beverly Hills if you were the son of Dr. Wilkinson. The judge, who was among the doctor's multitude of friends, airily ruled—after phoning the doctor to get his advice—that Frank would only have to come back and spend the weekend in jail. When our rebel said he had tickets for a concert that Saturday evening, the judge said okay, he could check himself into jail when the concert was over, or whenever it was convenient.

Why else but as a "rebel" did he briefly join the picket line of strikers at the *Hollywood Citizen-News*? Admittedly, the atmosphere of the strike was a far cry from the head-cracking confrontations at Ford's Dearborn plant six years earlier. As Carey

McWilliams, who was the newspaper union's lawyer, recalls, "Since the locale was Hollywood, the strike promptly assumed show-biz aspects. Prominent stars paraded on the picket lines and signed autographs. Tea was served. Mannequins twirling parasols pirouetted in fancy gowns. For several weeks the picket lines were the best show in town."[1]

Nevertheless, it was a bold and brassy move on Frank's part, because the newspaper's publisher was Judge Harlan G. Palmer, a close friend of his father's and, like him, a leading figure in the local "reform" movement: a man of integrity, piety, and "liberal" views—on most issues. He just didn't want to deal with a union.

The paper's business manager had been Sunday school superintendent at Frank's church, and he promptly conveyed to Frank's father the horror he felt at seeing his son parading with those radicals.

The route by which Frank arrived at the picket line was a portent of his future.

He had seen a newspaper ad of Labor's Non-Partisan League (LNPL) asking for volunteers. Frank knew absolutely nothing about the world of labor, but the idea of workers forming unions appealed both to his newfound rebelliousness and to his interest in the rights of the underdog. So he caught a bus downtown, walked into the LNPL's office, and asked what he could do to help. He was directed to the newspaper's strike line.

Although he didn't know it at the time, the person giving him those directions—the charming, very militant Dorothy Healey, director of the LNPL and wife of Philip M. "Slim" Connelly, head of the local newspaper guild and a powerful official in the Southern California Congress of Industrial Organizations (CIO)—was a Communist. She was the first person of that persuasion to have even a passing influence on his life.

■ LEFTWARD, HO!

Since the FBI had for years been keeping a close eye on Dorothy Healey and on anyone who had anything to do with her, this innocent meeting would seem to have been the likely point at which the FBI opened its 132,000-page file on Frank Wilkinson. But in fact, it neglected this "subversive meeting" and did not open a file on Frank until 1942.

Although the signs were faint to begin with, Frank Wilkinson was indeed drifting leftward. Part of that drift could be seen in his casting off, hippie-like, the capitalist comforts he had grown up with. The marriage certificate issued on September 9, 1939, was to "Jean Benson, teacher" and "Frank Wilkinson, manual laborer"—a designation based on his work at the pipe factory, work that he relished but was about to give up. Even at only nineteen dollars a month, the rent on their first home (a garage apartment in Santa Monica at Nineteenth and Wilshire Boulevard) required a job that paid more.

He was hired as a social worker with the state relief agency. The nation was still drowning in the Great Depression, and waves of its castoffs—homeless, jobless, often penniless families and single men—were washing up on the streets of Los Angeles. Frank was given a caseload of one hundred single men to help in finding housing, clothing, food, and jobs. He immediately joined the small State, County Municipal Workers Union. He hadn't been a member long before he was elected president of the single men's division. Looking back on it, he thinks most of his fellow members were Communists. Caught up by their enthusiastic radicalism, he became so gung ho that six months later, when Governor Culbert Olson cut funds for the state relief agencies, Frank organized a protest movement—placards and all, like the ones he had carried in front of the *Hollywood Citizen-News*—and marched his followers down to Governor Olson's Los Angeles office.

He was promptly fired.

Now Frank was in a perilous financial condition in the middle of the Depression. True, as a Wilkinson, he could have easily rescued himself in the stagnant white-collar job market; because of his father's civic and church reputation, his name would have garnered him a job in and around Beverly Hills and in much of Los Angeles. But Frank didn't even consider taking that route. He had tasted the liquor of social activism, and he wanted more.

He would soon become an addict and then a peddler of it. And it would happen because of his most unlikely ally—a Catholic priest—and because of another picket line.

The priest was Monsignor Thomas J. O'Dwyer of the St. Mary's Parish at Fourth Street and Chicago Street. He was archdiocesan director of hospitals and charities and a never-flagging battler for the poor in Los Angeles. And in particular, he battled for better housing for them.

Frank's association with Father O'Dwyer led to a major turning point in his life, along with his new marriage to Jean, of course.

In 1939 O'Dwyer had founded an organization called the Citizens Housing Council of Los Angeles to promote public housing. It was a very small council, almost insignificant, made up mostly of builders who hoped to profit from any public funds that were pumped into it, and by a few idealistic women leaders from organizations like the Catholic Women's Club and the League of Women Voters. A small operation it may have been, but O'Dwyer needed a secretary to help him keep things from falling apart.

He had heard of Frank's lecturing on the world's slums, and he had heard of Frank's low opinion of organized religion. He had also heard that Frank was restless, looking for some work that would—at his age, what else?—"improve the world."

So he knocked on Frank's door, was invited in despite his priestly garb, and quickly disarmed Frank with his offer. "Come with me," he said, "and I'll show you slums as bad as any you saw in Europe or North Africa or the Middle East. And if they make you angry, I've got a job for you."

They did make him angry, and he took the job as O'Dwyer's secretary—or, more accurately, as his chief agitator and scheming confidant—for a saintly fifteen dollars a week, a *cut* in salary from his previous near-starvation wages.

They were an odd couple. They violently disagreed on women's rights, on abortion rights, on the proper separation of church and state, on the validity of priestly powers, and on the existence of God and Satan. O'Dwyer tried in vain to defend the Catholic Church, but Frank—having seen its support of Franco in Spain, of

Mussolini in Italy, of Metaxas in Greece, of Hitler in Germany; having seen its inbred anti-Semitism in Catholic Poland and Catholic Romania—never let O'Dwyer forget that he considered it, of all religions, to be the worst, the cruelest, the most hypocritical.

But in fighting for decent, integrated housing, they were in total, militant agreement—soul mates—and would remain so for a decade (at which time the Catholic Church transferred O'Dwyer to save him from further contamination by Wilkinson's radicalism).

Their first objectives were to end public-housing segregation and force the city to stop building slums. The Los Angeles Housing Authority (LAHA), which always looked for noncontroversial sites for projects, had a habit of throwing them up in areas that had been cleared but were bordered by railroad tracks on one side and dirty industries on the other. In plots that should have been left for industrial truckers, the city built housing for the poor. That had to stop.

Frank and Father O'Dwyer began their collaboration in deeply segregated 1939, nine years before *Shelley v. Kraemer* outlawed restrictive covenants and fifteen years before *Brown v. Board of Education* demanded integration.

So when LAHA built Hacienda Heights, it was segregated. Wilkinson and Father O'Dwyer and a few allies set up a little picket line in protest. LAHA boss Howard Holtzendorff was furious at this impertinent criticism from the runty, rival organization. But to avoid a fight and the resulting bad publicity, he and the LAHA board of directors integrated the project—a first for L.A.—and sent an emissary out to the picket line to tell Wilkinson, "Since you like n*****s so much, maybe you'd like to manage the project." Wilkinson accepted the position working for Holtzendorff at the LAHA in 1942, and, he says, "I put the zeal into my job that I would have put into the Methodist Church in trying to make that project not only an integrated project but a garden where people of all colors and nationalities could live together as sisters and brothers." Yes, when talking about his role in public housing, he could become a bit florid. But he must have done a good job, because it wasn't long before Holtzendorff made him manager of two other projects.

CHAPTER 7

Integrated Public Housing— a Most Effective Scandal

THE LAHA WAS the first housing project in California and certainly one of the nation's biggest, financed by the federal treasury up to that time—a $110 million share of the Congressional Housing Act of 1949. That would equate to a billion dollars in today's economy.

Some 7 million men and women in the armed services had passed through Los Angeles during the war, and a great many came back to make it home. Returning veterans at the end of World War II continued to overwhelm the existing housing stock. People who had come to work in L.A.'s war factories intended to stay. Thousands of Japanese citizens who had been held in detention camps now returned to find homes. About 162,000 families, including 50,000 veterans, were living in tents, garages, trailers, even in chicken coops; or were doubled- and tripled-up in existing homes. In 1945, Mayor Fletcher Bowron appealed to President Roosevelt for help, noting that the housing shortage was so critical that the LAHA had over 100,000 applications for rental dwellings that couldn't be filled.

■

ONE OF FRANK'S first tasks at his first job at the LAHA was to act as referee in the frequent squabbles between tenants and management. At the middle of some of the fusses were Communists, who were voluntarily taking charge to see that the neighborhoods were shipshape and sanitary (an assumption of leadership that irritated some of the residents). Holtzendorff designated Wilkinson to be the liaison with the Communists, too. Frank admired their energy, and the feeling was mutual.

And just to make sure that he knew what the public housing people had to put up with—too much noise, too much crowding, few places for their kids to play—he and his family always lived in one of the projects.

Then, as he was wont to do, Wilkinson outraged his boss, Howard Holtzendorff. In 1944, at the regional meeting in Las Vegas of two hundred members of the National Association of Housing Officials (NAHO), the attendees were to be integrated by day but segregated at night. Whites were assigned rooms in the Frontier Hotel. Black delegates were sent to a temporary housing project fourteen miles out on the road to Boulder Dam. Wilkinson would have none of it. He recruited other liberal whites at the meeting, including a Catholic priest from Phoenix, to join him at the blacks' quarters.

At the meeting in the main ballroom of the Frontier Hotel the next day, he made a motion that hereafter no convention of the NAHO would be held in a segregated facility.

Holtzendorff turned red with rage and embarrassment. The chairman of the meeting hesitated in putting the motion to a vote. Wilkinson repeated his motion. Silence. He went to the podium and repeated it again. Still silence. So Wilkinson took the gavel away from the chairman, seconded his own motion, asked for ayes (there were about ten) and ruled that it had passed.

Holtzendorff did not speak to his rebellious aide on the way back to Los Angeles, but sent a management supervisor to tell Wilkinson that although his boss doubted his emotional stability, he would, out of fairness, wait two weeks before firing him, to see if he might recover his sanity in the meantime.

Their meeting at the end of those two weeks once again showed Holtzendorff's pragmatism. First he was full of bombast about Wilkinson's having embarrassed him and the city of Los Angeles before all those folks in Las Vegas by raising such an inconsequential issue as racism. That was followed with peevish, self-pitying questions about Wilkinson's intentions ("What are you after, Frank? You want to be executive director? Do you want my job?"). It ended with a typical Holtzendorff reversal and peppy offer for a higher position: "Well, Frank, how would you like to be my assistant, work with me, and promote the new housing program?" Frank accepted this new job, which greatly expanded his role in creating and gaining general acceptance for public housing.

■

FRANK BROUGHT TO the LAHA a critical upswing in the development and promotion of public housing in Los Angeles. He became the liaison with the architects on the new projects; the liaison with all the political parties; the liaison with all the churches and all the community groups. He also faced conflicts with the city's influential realty developers.

Realty developers loathed the idea of spending federal money helping the poor to get shelter and tried to play down the shortage of low-cost housing. The *Los Angeles Times*, which in those days was considered by many journalists to be perhaps the most irresponsible major newspaper in the nation, appraised the public housing program as "creeping socialism." Editorially, it asked repeatedly, "Where's the housing shortage?"

The enemies of public housing would have loved to persuade the public that the Federal Housing Act was a central part of a Communist plot, but that was impossible to do, since two of its chief authors were Senator Robert ("Mr. Republican") Taft and Senator Allen J. Ellender, Louisiana's vertebra in Dixie's backbone of conservatism. Furthermore, it had been supported by such feverishly anti-Communist stalwarts as Senators William Jenner of Indiana and Bourke Hickenlooper of Iowa.

Wilkinson's most powerful weapon against the real estate lobby was knowledge. He had to have it, because he was responsible for developing all the material for the city council presentations. He did all the site-selection work for the city health and planning departments. For weeks, he and Si Eisner of the planning department, and Joe Sollins of the health department, canvassed every block of Los Angeles by automobile and then by Goodyear blimp, mapping the entire city as to standard and substandard conditions. He became the liaison with the U.S. Census Bureau and was sent to Washington, D.C. to work with the bureau to define where and how widespread the bad housing was.[1]

Selling and reselling the housing program to the public was essential, because the *Los Angeles Times* and the real estate lobby were conducting a constant heavyweight campaign against public housing, trying to get the program outlawed, either through referenda or court decisions or by reversing the city council's support.

Wilkinson knew that most people on the west side of Los Angeles were totally slum-dumb; that was the snooty side of town he had grown up in, and he had grown up knowing absolutely nothing about the slums. So over a period of five years he organized countless tours, sometimes five or six a week, bringing seven hundred schoolteachers and an estimated ten thousand other residents of the west side by automobile caravan and Greyhound bus to see the seedy neighborhoods and learn about what the Housing Authority was trying to do.

Even with his best efforts at educating the outside world through tours of the slums, he couldn't reach as many people as he wanted to. How could he bridge the rest of the gap? By a stroke of great luck, Wilkinson got the answer. The luck came when he was approached by two graduate students at USC who were doing their graduate thesis in cinema. They asked if he had any good ideas for a film theme. Did he ever! "I realized at once that if we could turn a slum tour into a film and take twenty prints of that film to the west side of L.A., we could reach hundreds of thousands of people, and stop invading the privacy of slum dwellers with our constant motorcades."

I spent a year with these two students—Eugene Peterson and Al Walker—helping them maneuver around the landlord problem. We'd get a hundred, two hundred feet of cable—we had to have electricity for lights—and we'd get into somebody's house where they'd agree to let us plug in briefly, drag the cable over fences, into alleyways, up into the inside of these wretched apartments to take a quick picture before the landlord would come in to drive us off. Everything I'd been showing people got covered by this film.

USC did the laboratory work on the film. Wilkinson persuaded Chet Huntley, then a prominent CBS commentator, to do the narration, and he got MGM to contribute a musical score and sound effects, which the studio's experts cut from old movies and dubbed into the housing film for free. There was a factory in the slums where violin bows were made; the workers put up with the constant stink of rotting horse tails. For a touch of realism, MGM spliced in a piece from an old flick of flies buzzing.

Perhaps the most impressive part of the film featured the shack (and the overflowing outhouse) that had been home to David Gonzalez, the first Chicano to be killed in the South Pacific in World War II. He was awarded the Medal of Honor posthumously; the medal was going to be given to his mother. Finding one's way through that part of the slum required a guide who had been there before, so Wilkinson was assigned to accompany the U.S. Army officers for the ceremony.

They came in their spit-and-polish and fancy cars, parking outside the structure where David Gonzalez had lived with eleven brothers and sisters. Actually, by then it was considered too dangerous to live in, so the Gonzalez family had been evicted. The mother was living next door in a tent, with no running water, no nothing. When she took the medal, crying, the only thing she said was, "My son was born here."

Sadly, this remarkable documentary was buried and then lost for decades in the scandal that ensued.[2]

■ THE RESIDENTS WERE UNDERSTANDABLY SUSPICIOUS

During his time at the LAHA, Wilkinson also had to sell the housing program to the people living in Chavez Ravine, which was the main target—or hope—for the LAHA in terms of wiping out what it considered to be slums and replacing them with better homes and neighborhoods.

The villages of La Loma, Bishop, and Palo Verde—spread across the Chavez Ravine—were, as Mike Boehm of the *Los Angeles Times* later wrote, "home to some 1,100 mainly poor, mainly Mexican American families. The terrain was rough and steep, the views picturesque, the community tradition-steeped and tightly knit as it lived in sight of city hall's tower yet a world apart"—a poor man's Shangri-la, as some called it.[3]

Not only were their dwellings better than no homes at all, they were really *home* to these people. They didn't feel they were living in shacks; maybe the structures needed renovation, lots of it, but they weren't shacks. So they were frightened by the thought that they would be torn down. For what? For fancy apartments for rich people? Wilkinson talked to them in groups, and sometimes went door to door, to explain that they would be guaranteed—in writing—a place in the new projects; there would be homes with enough bedrooms for everyone, and the homes would be low rent and fully integrated, with playgrounds and adequate child-care facilities.

■ THE TUMULTUOUS END TO HIS HOUSING CAREER: AUGUST 29, 1952

One of Wilkinson's various assignments was to work with lawyers to persuade superior court judges to force slum landlords to sell their property to the LAHA under the law of eminent domain, as a way of clearing the area for new housing that would hopefully be free of rats, disease, delinquency, and crime.

Since Wilkinson had been working in the slums since 1942, he was the LAHA's expert witness. He knew all about rat infestation and the threat of another bubonic plague outbreak, which had occurred in Los Angeles not long before. He had given similar testimony at nine previous eminent-domain hearings. He was at this hearing to give humanitarian reasons why the court should condemn twenty-eight acres for public housing in Chavez Ravine, a choice location near downtown Los Angeles. He had been testifying for two days at this hearing with no trouble.

But the tenth superior court hearing, on August 29, 1952, was doomsday for Wilkinson—and the public housing program. He was answering questions from Felix H. McGinnis, attorney for two of the biggest development companies at the time. As Frank was in the middle of his usual spiel, suddenly McGinnis seemed to lose interest in rats and bubonic plagues. While Wilkinson was talking, McGinnis reached into his briefcase and brought out a dossier the FBI had put together on Wilkinson and some other LAHA employees. It had been given to Los Angeles Police Chief William Parker, who in turn had passed along the dossier's juicier details to the leaders of the realty lobby.

Out of the blue, McGinnis asked Wilkinson to name all the organizations he had belonged to since his last year at Beverly Hills High School.

Though he was somewhat taken aback by a question that was no more relevant to housing than a question about his cholesterol level, Wilkinson, always polite, started with his leadership role in Youth for Herbert Hoover and kept naming religious, civic, fraternal, and university organizations he had belonged to—and he had been quite a joiner. When at last he stopped, the lawyer asked, "Is that all? What about political organizations?" Frank, sensing he was being set up, conceded he might have belonged to other organizations. Pushed to name them, he refused, as a "matter of personal conscience. And if necessary I would hold that to answer such a question might in some way incriminate me."

He was taking the disreputable Fifth.

■

WHAT FRANK COULD not have known at the time was that Chavez Ravine was slated to become Dodger Stadium, and that he was the mechanism by which the powers that be planned to see their project to fruition.

Frank's dream of integrated, state-of-the-art public housing ended in 1952, when he refused to answer the real estate lawyer's question about the political organizations he had belonged to. He was fired, with the Los Angeles press screaming "Communist" in his wake.

Wilkinson recalls from information retrieved from the FBI files: "The program was attacked, first of all by the people who owned the slum, and then there was a teamwork between the FBI, the Los Angeles Police department's chief, and others to try to discredit the housing program and to discredit it through me . . ."

The way to succeed in discrediting Frank, and thereby gain that huge parcel of land, was to create a scandal, and in the early 1950s the most effective scandal was anything that had to do with Communism—real or imagined. Was Frank Wilkinson a Communist? Whether he was or not, he was the logical one to target. Indeed, if the real estate lobby were able to bring him down, it would bring down public housing in that city. To the extent that one bureaucrat—through energy and willpower and imagination—can embody a whole program, even a billion-dollar program, Wilkinson certainly did.

Since 1942, Wilkinson had been a leader, perhaps it's accurate to say *the* leader, in public housing, first with the small, private Los Angeles Citizens Housing Council and then with the ponderous, official Los Angeles Housing Authority. Howard Holtzendorff had been executive director of the LAHA since its inception in 1938. He was an able bureaucrat, but aside from a streak of deviousness, he had little imagination. He was, however, smart enough to recruit Wilkinson from the Housing Council and then promote him to de facto director of the LAHA. In military terms, Wilkinson became the field marshal, which made him the natural target of the *Los Angeles Times* and the real estate lobby.

Rating the public-housing activists in every major city, Dana Cuff, professor of architecture and urban design at UCLA, wrote in a recent retrospective: "In Los Angeles, Frank Wilkinson was in a class of his own."[4]

CHAPTER 8

Why Join the Party?

WHY, IF FRANK knew that joining the Communist Party might be a liability in his future career, did he join the Party in 1942? It is perhaps significant that Frank became a party member only a few months after the United States entered World War II. He probably would not have done so a year earlier, because when Stalin entered a nonaggression pact with Hitler in 1939 and U.S. Communist leaders began supporting this sellout to the Nazis, so many thousands of members deserted the party that there wasn't much of a party left to join. But by 1941, membership was rebounding, thanks to the Soviet role in World War II.

In those three Hitler–Stalin nonaggression years, the American Communist Party was antiwar and its leaders preached that the United States government should not interfere with strikes at U.S. defense plants simply to help England and France "save the crumbling capitalist system."[1] Ironically, this antiwar position also reflected the majority of Americans at that time. The first wartime Roper poll, taken in September 1939, gave eloquent testimony to the nation's basic isolationist mood. Only 2.5 percent of those polled said they thought we should enter the war on the side of

England, France, and Poland. Two other notable responses: 37.5 percent said "stay out of the war entirely, but offer to sell to anyone on a cash-and-carry basis" and 29.9 percent voted to "have nothing to do with any warring country—don't even trade with them for cash."[2]

So, whether he was proving himself to be a typical American or a loyal Communist-to-be, while the war was strictly England and France against Germany, Frank was a conscientious objector. He saw that war, he says, as a war between greedy capitalists, "a competition between the major world powers over economic colonies." But when German troops invaded the Soviet Union on June 22, 1941, the CPUSA began clamoring for U.S. defense production to be sped up to help Mother Russia. And Frank now saw it as "truly a war for the survival of democracy." After the Japanese attack on Pearl Harbor on December 7, 1941, he tried to be drafted into the Army; his hearing difficulties, of course, prevented that.

As soon as the United States entered the war, the country's previous attitude toward the Soviet Union—full-fledged suspicion and distaste on the part of most citizens—changed, too. By then, the Soviet Army was proving to be the kind of gutsy underdog that would appeal to the American people, press, and politicians. The war was just starting, and already, in the second half of 1941, the Red Army had suffered huge losses—at least 5 million casualties, 3 million prisoners, twenty thousand tanks and thirty thousand big guns. All gone. And yet it was holding out with heroic stubbornness.[3]

All of a sudden, adopting the philosophy that the enemy of one's enemy is one's friend, the press and many in the government began telling Americans about virtues in the Soviet Union that nobody—understandably—had noticed before. The results were sometimes absurd. Hollywood, encouraged by the government, began turning out overwrought pro-Soviet films. One was *Mission to Moscow*, vaguely based on the career of Joseph Davies, former U.S. ambassador to the Soviet Union. Walter Huston, playing the role of Davies, tells Stalin (who in real life had by that time committed at least several million political murders), "I believe, sir, that history will record you as a great benefactor of mankind."[4]

Not to be outdone by Hollywood, national magazines joined the chorus. Even the renowned Communist-hater Henry Luce allowed his *Life* magazine in a March 1943 issue to muse in tones of grumpy admiration, "When we take account of what the U.S.S.R. has accomplished in the 20 years of its existence we can make allowances for certain shortcomings, however deplorable. . . ."

Former Ambassador Davies continued the gushing of his movie self in *Look* magazine of April 7, 1942, under the title "Meet the Real Stalin": "What sort of human being is Joseph Stalin? He impressed me as quiet and kindly. . . . From what I could learn, Stalin himself has a real affection for people as individuals. . . . His personality is exactly the opposite of what rabid anti-Stalinists conceive."[5]

Look's second cadenza came in June 1944, under an even friendlier title ("A Guy Named Joe"), with Moscow correspondent Ralph Parker telling the magazine's readers, "In addition to his trenchant speech, indomitable will and extraordinary mental capacity, there is another Stalin—a lover of literature . . . a Stalin who at the age of 16 was writing poetry; who—even during the war—is deeply concerned with the work of younger poets, playwrights, novelists, eager that they should express the new Russian Soul."[6]

■THE PERSUASION OF BREAKFAST FRIENDS

The nation's new attitude toward the Reds helped revive the virtually dead American Communist Party. Between 1941 and 1944, its membership was estimated to have doubled. And this general wave of admiration undoubtedly shaped the conversations Wilkinson had during what he describes as "breakfast after breakfast on the porch of an architect friend, with those wonderful people who were in the Communist Party." They were all trying to persuade Wilkinson to join. He hesitated, he says, because he didn't want to be bossed around by any organization; he wanted to be totally independent.

Oh, absolutely, you *can* be independent, they assured him over and over. So, finally, he gave in. Frank would remain a member of the party for thirty-one years, leaving it in 1973.[7]

Joining the Communist Party, says Wilkinson, seemed so natural, so normal; these friends (of course he does not name them, for some are still alive), were "people in high places in Los Angeles, in the community, in churches, in trade unions," and they were "committed to the highest traditions of American patriotism and respect for our own country, working for social justice in our country, for a better world generally, and none of them ever did anything illegal."

For Charles Nusser, a mail-room supervisor and the Education Director of the Communist Party in New Jersey for fourteen years, "The appeal of the Communist Party wasn't what they said, and they said plenty. It was what they *did*. People were being thrown out with their furniture onto the sidewalk. The Communist Party organized people to put them and their furniture back in. They organized people to go to the relief office and file for relief and for unemployment insurance. That was the appeal of the Communist Party."[8]

That's easy to believe. But Frank's friends in Los Angeles were nevertheless members, as he would now be a member, of an organization that had occupied a uniquely despised and feared position in the American psyche for more than a generation, and, once the war was over, would revert to being despised and feared—even more so than before.

Years later, J. Edgar Hoover would deliver before a Congressional committee what had become his mantra against Communism: "Communism in reality is not a political party. It is a way of life, an evil and malignant way of life. It reveals a condition akin to disease that spreads like an epidemic and, like an epidemic, a quarantine is necessary to keep it from infecting the nation."

Some of Frank's "breakfast club" friends may also have been sincerely ignorant when they assured him that the party was tolerant toward independent-minded members; after all, most of his friends were probably what Hoover would have called "Parlor

Pinks," mere dabblers in radicalism. But if Dorothy Healey was among them—and it's a good guess she was—a few words from her could have cleared the air of pretended independence. For decades she was Southern California chairman for the Communist Party—a beautiful agitator better known in Hearst headlines as "The Red Queen."

Films of Healey in action, all four feet eleven inches of her, show just how charming and persuasive she was, and apparently had been since her teen years, when she followed her mother (reportedly even more charming and persuasive) into a life of social agitation. A typical story is that in 1931, at the age of seventeen, in the course of addressing a skid-row throng in Oakland on International Hunger Day, she was arrested and put in a juvenile detention home (the first of several jails she became acquainted with). But the authorities quickly released her—she had started teaching other inmates Communist songs. As she left, her "recruits" stood at the windows serenading her with "The Internationale."

At the time Frank joined the party, this is how Healey was describing the "independence" expected from party members: "You accept things that are sometimes quite stupid things, because in the end the important thing is not the individual but the Party. The individual can be wrong, the Party is never wrong. After all, the Party understood all the niceties of Marxism and Leninism. I mean it was the *leadership* that understood those things so perfectly—and there was an infallibility that came along with that and you inherited that [infallibility] and it became a part of your legacy as well, because you were part of that organization."[9]

That was party dogma. And for the first three decades of her life as a Communist, Healey went along with it. She says, "Let me be very blunt. I thought Stalin knew what he was doing. I thought he was doing what was best for his country and for the workers of the world. Stalin was the personification of all that one believed in. He, in one man, represented the authority of wisdom, of honor, of compassion, of realism."

When Stalin died on March 5, 1953, Healey wept.

But she wept again, for quite another reason—"convulsed with tears," she says—at a meeting of CPUSA's National Committee on April 28, 1956, when she and other committee members heard a reading of the text of Khrushchev's "secret speech" detailing the horrors of the years of Stalin's leadership. She was devastated because "we had marched for so many years with the purity of the Soviet Union as our banner. . . . And here we were, after all these years, sitting in a meeting of the Party's leaders and being told by no less an authority than the First Secretary of the Soviet Communist Party that . . . wretched bloody crimes had been committed in the name of defending socialism."[10]

At the same time, she felt liberated, she says, because Khrushchev's speech "severed the bonds that kept us in subordination to the Soviet Communist leaders all those years. Just as the rank-and-file members of our own party looked to American Communist leaders as perfect beings incapable of error, we had taken the same attitude to the Soviet leaders." It was, she says, "the most significant day of my life," because it convinced her of the absolute necessity of subjecting everything that came from the party to her independent criticism.

After that, no one was more of an insider rebel than Healey.

An FBI agent's memo to J. Edgar Hoover, dated August 6, 1969, notes that "for several years, Healey has openly manifested serious and organized political opposition to the policies of Gus Hall [the general secretary of the CPUSA]."[11]

Indeed, although for years she had sat on the national board of the CPUSA and run the party's largest operation on the West Coast, she had now become extremely rebellious, at one point accusing Communist leaders in the United States of playing "a servile role in promoting every lie and calumny being spread by the Soviets."[12] For her, the Soviet occupation of Czechoslovakia in 1968 (coming after its intervention in Hungary in 1956), and Gus Hall's support of it, was the last straw. He of course could not let her open contempt be displayed forever without reprisal, so at the party's national convention in 1969 he announced that Healey had been "released" from her duties "so that she can spend a year's sabbatical leave for study."[13]

It was the beginning of the end of her very long and distinguished membership. That is, *official* membership. She remained a Communist in her bones forever. And from her, Frank Wilkinson would get encouragement for some of his own rebellions; not that he needed it—rebel was a role that he took on easily. He had never considered himself a Soviet-copy Communist—quite the contrary, in fact.

His first rebellion came when local party officials (not including Healey) tried to tell him how to allot public housing.

Frank had been instrumental in making the LAHA integrate its public-housing program in the early 1940s—it was the first integrated housing in the city. Numerically, it had been easy to do. But by 1948, it had gotten a lot harder. The racial makeup of Los Angeles had gone through enormous changes. Thousands of blacks had come to L.A. during the war to work in the defense plants, and when the war ended, they didn't particularly want to go back to the glories of racist Mississippi and the grandeur of segregated Alabama. Ditto the thousands of black war veterans who had passed through the city and decided it was a swell place to come back to. And Japanese residents who had been moved elsewhere during the war as "security risks" returned to reclaim their homes—evicting blacks who had taken them over. And, of course, the migration from Mexico, always significant, had increased during the war.

So by 1948, Frank's public-housing program had a waiting list of many thousands, and the great majority were blacks.

At that point he decided that the integration he had launched in the early 1940s and held so dear had to be given up. He recalls:

Top Communist Party leaders came to me and said, "Now, Frank, we know how you're feeling about this, but we think we should hang on to integration."

I said, "Can't you see what's happening all over this city? Look, there's a place down at Hewitt and Fourth Street that's four stories high, with two outdoor toilets for every floor. There are 160 people living on each floor. They're all black.

You think I'm going to tell a black single mother with five kids living in one room on the fourth floor down there, 'You're really next in line for housing assistance but we can't give it to you because there's a white family whose needs are not as great as yours, but we must put them in the public housing projects in order to maintain integration'? I won't do it."

The Communist spokesmen kept at me. "Frank, you're going to integrate these projects." And I answered, "Well, the projects are not the answer to the nation's or the city's racial problem. The projects are just projects. They are emergency-type housing for people of low income. If you adhere to strict integration—this percentage of blacks or Chicanos and that percentage of whites—you're going to deny some people with the greatest need, and need is the only correct way to do it." Some of the CP leaders brought great pressure on me to change, but I said, "No way, no way. You're wrong." I refused to budge.

Frank didn't back down to the Communist Party when he thought he knew best about L.A. public housing. And after some early fudging on forms, he didn't back down at the eminent-domain hearing in 1952. Not even when it cost him his job and his career in public housing—not to mention his wife Jean's teaching job.

CHAPTER 9

A Moment of Ominous Silence— the Impact of the Fifth

PERSONAL CONSCIENCE OR not, when Frank claimed his Fifth Amendment right not to incriminate himself, it didn't sound so good. Not in those days. The Communist-hunters in state and federal governments were having a field day. Senator Joseph McCarthy was in full voice. The U. S. Chamber of Commerce had recently distributed four hundred thousand copies of *Communist Infiltration in the United States*. Alger Hiss, whom the press had portrayed as a dangerous spy, was in the middle of a four-year prison term for something he had or hadn't done at the State Department *eleven years* earlier (actually, he was in prison for denying he had given State Department documents to Whittaker Chambers, a former Communist, in 1938).

Talk about field days. California's loudest anti-Communist, Richard Nixon, was really having one. He had won a seat in the House of Representatives by accusing Jerry Voorhis, a congressman from California's Twelfth (who hated Communism), of being a Communist. (Much later, Nixon admitted, "Of course I knew Jerry Voorhis wasn't a Communist. . . . The important thing is to win."[1]) As a member of the House Un-American Activities Committee, Nixon played a key role in sending Hiss to prison.

In 1950 he had taken Helen Gahagan Douglas's seat in the Senate by implying that she was a Communist, endlessly referring to her as the "The Pink Lady, right down to her underwear" while his political organization distributed five hundred thousand attacks printed on pink paper. And in an off-screen spectacle equal to *Ben-Hur*, Hollywood's patriotic producers had helped HUAC railroad "The Hollywood Ten"—nine screenwriters and a director accused of being Communists—into prison for refusing to answer questions about their political beliefs.

Obviously, California of all states, and Los Angeles of all cities (its largest newspapers were ferociously against left-wingers) was not the place to refuse to be silent "as a matter of conscience" in a star chamber inquisition.

■ L.A. BLOWS ITS LID OVER FRANK

The FBI, the behind-the-scenes stimulus of the anti-Red frenzy sweeping the country, had obviously supplied the establishment's superpatriotic hounds with enough material to chase Wilkinson up a tree. Actually, the only publicized evidence of radicalism on Frank's part was that he had been caught reading the *People's World*, a CPUSA publication, and subscribed to the *Nation* and other liberal magazines. It wasn't much, but it was enough.

The next day, August 30, 1952, the *Los Angeles Times* stripped across the top of its front page in type two inches high:

LID BLOWS OFF HOUSING;
TOP OFFICIAL SUSPENDED
Red Probe Asked by Council as
Wilkinson Refuses Data on Ties

And Hearst's *Examiner*, never to be outdone in such matters, greeted the day with:

SUSPEND L.A. HOUSING AIDE
AS RED PROBE DEMANDED

Wilkinson Refusal to Answer Blasted
CHA Aide Balks on Replies During Condemnation Suit

■

WILKINSON WAS IMMEDIATELY suspended from his job, and he would be in for more high-decibel accusations when the city council met shortly thereafter. At that session, Mayor Fletcher Bowron (a supporter of Wilkinson—understandably, since Wilkinson's father had helped him get elected) slugged a heckler for calling him "a servant of Stalin." The furor at city hall would continue for months.

That was outside the council chambers. Inside, Councilman Ed Davenport, who was anti-housing, began acting so odd that the council's chairman summoned a squad of homicide officers and two doctors for help—nevertheless, Davenport continued stalking the council chambers in "an incoherent, bellowing, frothing rage" for forty minutes (according to the newspaper description). When Councilman Edward R. Roybal offered, "I'll sit him down if you want me to," Davenport screamed, "He's threatening me with a knife!"[2] Finally Davenport's colleagues gave up and walked out, leaving him to continue screaming without an audience for another twenty minutes.

Indeed, some members of the council had been acting oddly for months. Why, after voting *unanimously* in favor of the housing project, did the council then vote eight to seven to kill the program? Was it possible that somebody, gulp, had been bribed? At least one somebody had been: Ed Davenport. After previously voting, consistently, to support public housing, he had cast the decisive vote to kill the program. Why the change of heart? Suspicions of bribery, writes one historian, blossomed when Davenport's wife "described $50,000 found in his wall safe upon his death as 'gifts' from the real estate lobby."[3] Another historian flatly states that Davenport "had received $50,000 in bribes from the real estate lobby to round out the mere $7,500 he received in councilman's salary."[4]

■ THE STATE'S OWN WITCH-HUNTERS ENTER THE GAME

A few days after Davenport's outburst, the melodrama reached new heights: California's Senate Un-American Activities Committee (SUAC) hit town, under the guidance of State Senator Hugh Burns, a Fresno undertaker. The committee was mainly there to pounce on Wilkinson, but he disappointed them by being in the hospital for a knee operation. Not to be delayed more than necessary, two officials of the SUAC followed Frank's gurney out of the operating room and into the recovery room, where they tried to shake him back to consciousness. Screams from nurses stopped that effort, so they settled for pinning a subpoena to his gown. Ten days later, Frank was on the stand, again refusing to answer questions about his politics. And on October 28, 1952, Frank Wilkinson, the man identified by the *Los Angeles Times*—with its usual ounce of objectivity—as "the chief propagandist for Los Angeles's unwanted $110,000,000 federal public housing scheme," was fired.

It seemed that the reverberations would never end. The *Los Angeles Examiner* warned with billboard-size headlines that state investigators had uncovered "evidence of a Communist plot . . . apparently headed by Frank Wilkinson, to recruit thousands of teachers and other county and city employees to literally take over Los Angeles."

HUGE RED PLOT TO CONTROL PUBLIC WORKERS HERE BARED

When that came to nothing, the *Los Angeles Mirror*, the sister publication of the *Times*, reported that the State Un-American Activities Committee was going to name six hundred Los Angeles school employees believed to have "connections" to the Communist Party. That fizzled out when School Superintendent Alexander J. Stoddard said that his administration had dutifully compiled a record of every tip or innuendo or rumor that came its way, including those from the FBI, and said that if all those accused by these nebulous sources really were guilty of radicalism (whatever that meant), they would still number fewer than hundred—out of about thirty thousand school employees.

•

AT THE END of this yearlong uproar, five members of the LAHA (including Frank Wilkinson) and five school employees (including his wife, Jean) had been fired, not for anything they had done, but for what they hadn't done: answer a question about their political beliefs. Frank and Jean and the now three kids went from being solidly middle-class and respected in the community to being jobless, notorious—even the kids—and poor. It was a horrible shock to them all.[5]

Because he had supported Wilkinson longer than was politically wise—and because he refused to take orders from the *Los Angeles Times*—Mayor Bowron was defeated in his next election and replaced in 1953 by Norris Poulson, who never said "nay" to the *Times* or to the Los Angeles real estate lobby, which was led by Fred B. Burns (no kin to the state Un-American Activities Committee chairman), the most powerful builder in Southern California and head of the Committee Against Socialist Housing (with its perfect acronym: CASH).

In the midst of the housing uproar, Burns was designated "Builder of the Year" by the Los Angeles chapter of the Building Contractors Association of California in a circuslike celebration at which, as the *Herald* reported, "Speaker after speaker emphasized Burns's effective leadership in helping to checkmate the spread of socialized housing in Southern California."[6]

With a Republican moving into the White House and Republicans controlling Congress, Burns and some of his friends headed for Washington to help rewrite history. In those seemingly forgotten days when Los Angeles had received its federal housing grant, the city had promised that the land it acquired would indeed be used for public housing, or at least for some public purpose. Burns et al. wanted that agreement cancelled.

They got what they wanted.

By 1956, Poulson, the *Times*, the Burns group, and Brooklyn

Dodgers owner Walter O'Malley were deep in negotiations. *Frontier*, the feisty little magazine that helped keep Southern California liberals breathing, put it this way:

> The enticement Poulson dangles before the covetous eyes of the Dodgers' Walter O'Malley is 185 acres of unoccupied city-owned land lying between the Hollywood Freeway and the Pasadena Freeway, only three minutes by automobile from downtown Los Angeles. This area, known as Chavez Ravine, is touted as a superb site for a baseball stadium.
>
> Why this huge piece of land in the heart of the city remains vacant while builders uproot orange groves 50 miles distant for housing tracts might puzzle newcomers to Los Angeles. And how this particular plot of real estate happens to be owned by the city is a strange page in the history of Los Angeles. If Chavez Ravine is made available to the Brooklyn Dodgers, several thousand persons evicted from the area will not share in the predicted general enthusiasm. They are the people who were promised, in writing, first choice on new low-rent houses once planned for the site.
>
> From public housing to a baseball stadium is a curious turnabout, and if the Dodgers are lured to Los Angeles, what of the evicted people of Chavez Ravine? Were they pushed off their land under the power of eminent domain to make way for a baseball stadium?

Well, yes, as a matter of fact, it seems that they were. By what is quaintly described as "a strange series of machinations"[7]—a process in which the *Los Angeles Times* and Burns had powerful roles—O'Malley and the Dodgers were virtually given the Chavez Ravine land on which the privately built and privately owned fifty-six-thousand-seat stadium now stands.

Capitalism had squelched socialism once again.

■

THE DEMOLITION OF public housing in Los Angeles was the epicenter of a quake that rippled across the nation, as many other cities, following the pattern set by L.A., backed out of their federal public-housing programs. As a portent of things to come, Eisenhower had won the GOP nomination in 1952 by defeating Robert Taft, one of the architects of the Housing Act of 1949.

James T. Keane has noted, "Eisenhower's election was a triumph for the real estate and building trades, particularly on the issue of public housing. Eisenhower asked Congress for an allocation of only 35,000 units of new public housing in his first term; in the second, he asked for none at all. He also refused to execute contracts for housing that had already been approved as part of the Housing Act."[8]

Looking back from a distance of half a century, Frank Wilkinson said of the people living in Chavez Ravine:

> It was a wonderful little community, but there were problems in terms of health and safety. A good strong fire would have taken the whole place out, like a tinderbox. The rat infestation was the heaviest in town. If the residents had a choice of having the project built or not, they would have said No, no question about it. But I don't think I ever had a second thought; I don't think anyone in the field of health or housing or planning did. It was a place that had to go.
>
> Every family living in Chavez Ravine got a statement in writing guaranteeing they would be the first occupants when the project was built. So I felt horrible that people's homes were destroyed and the project was taken over by a ballpark. These people had a piece of paper in their hands, guaranteeing their rights, and then it falls apart. I was the one who made the promises to the people; I discovered the site, recommended the site, and knew it was correct from every standpoint, moral and social. I did the right thing, but to this day I have a certain sense of guilt. I hurt people really badly."[9]

CHAPTER 10

Wilkinson Takes On a New Role: Pariah

COMPARED TO THE disaster facing low-income people who needed housing, Wilkinson's own fate wasn't very significant. But he was suddenly an untouchable. Many people who had once greatly admired him—especially those in the state and local governments who had worked closely with him on housing—now detested him. Many refused even to speak to him. They felt, and rightly, that his political contretemps had devastated the housing program. All the work he had done and that various officials had done with him was wiped out—all the hundreds of studies he had supervised, all the papers correlating disease and delinquency to bad housing, everything he and his colleagues had touched was ordered destroyed by the LAHA the first week he was gone. City Councilman Edward R. Roybal gave voice to the suspicious feelings of a large group when he bitterly denounced Frank as "typical of Communists who work their way into leadership of good programs, knowing that ultimately they would be revealed and that this revelation would destroy the things they were ostensibly supporting."

There were some strange deserters from his circle, such as the young woman he had rescued back in 1943—one of the 110,000

Japanese Americans (of whom 72,000 were citizens by birth) who had been snatched from their homes and dumped in relocation camps for "national security," even though they had not been found to have any links to espionage. Wilkinson had gotten the LAHA to let him hire her. Then, fearing that if she rode public transportation during the war she might be manhandled by an outraged patriot, he picked her up at her home every morning and took her home every night until the war was over. She worked for him until his downfall in 1952.

The day Frank was suspended, she stopped talking to him.

■

WILKINSON'S FAMILY DISCOVERED—as did many others who fell through the antiradical trapdoor—that friends and family would also be bruised by the fall. One example was Frank's sister Mrs. Clara Marie Evans, who lived in Berkeley, California. When things got hectic for Frank and Jean, Mrs. Evans came down for a week to babysit their three children, Jeffry, Tony, and Jo. The children were in grade school by this time. When Mrs. Evans got back to Berkeley, she was called into a special meeting of the very upscale Berkeley Women's City Club, whose members had nominated her for the position of vice-chair that year. They asked why she had gone to Los Angeles, already knowing the answer, which she promptly gave: to help brother Frank. The spokesperson for the fifteen women present said, "We know your brother's ideas, what he stands for. We want to know, Betty, if you share those ideas." She answered, "I will not answer that question. You know me. You know my work."

They threw her out of the club.

At Glendale Memorial Hospital, where sister Hildegarde and brother Alan were both physicians, they were visited by a group of doctors who in effect said, "Disown Frank or expect no further medical referrals." Apparently, in this case, the threat went unfulfilled. However, the ripple effect of blacklisting often seriously affected uninvolved siblings, as it did with Frank's family.

■ AFTER THE STORM, MORE SUNSHINE THAN HE HAD ANTICIPATED

If Frank was discovering just how fickle and foolishly frightened people could be, he also discovered that in his banishment he was going to have some great supporters—all of them gutsy, many of them brilliant, some so generous they made Frank literally weep with gratitude.

At the eminent-domain hearing in superior court in 1952, when Frank first refused to answer the question about his political memberships, Judge Otto Emme (hardly an enemy, since he had been put in office by the Red-tinged CIO) leaned over the bench and gently advised, "Young man, you need a lawyer." Of course Frank already had a LAHA lawyer right at his side, but the judge meant a *real* lawyer. And Frank would need one who could write a brief by the next morning. The court had ordered it.

Finding an attorney willing to act with that speed would take far more money than Frank had. Not to worry, said his loyal housing compadre of a dozen years, Monsignor Thomas J. O'Dwyer, who dipped into the parish till for fifteen thousand dollars and tried to hire the celebrated criminal defense attorney Jerry Giesler. "Sorry," said Giesler. "I would be happy to handle his case if he were a murderer, but not as a Commie suspect." Frank's efforts to get help from old college chums who had become lawyers came to nothing. It was part of a frightening trend from coast to coast: many lawyers were ducking, having seen that those who defended Communists or suspected Communists could get in serious trouble with judges or with the bar.

As Frank was leaving the LAHA offices to hunt for a lawyer, Holtzendorff had urged him, "Please do *not* hire a Communist." Frank asked what he meant, and Holtzendorff said, "Well, don't get Bob Kenny. Don't get Bob Morris. And don't get Dan Marshall." He was referring to Robert W. Kenny, former California attorney general, who had been a key defense lawyer for the "Hollywood Ten," and his law partner, Robert S. Morris Jr., and Daniel G. Marshall, head of the Catholic Legal Society. For years they had been and would continue to be part of the West Coast's suicide squad of civil-libertarian lawyers who refused to be frightened out of court.

As the day evaporated, Frank was desperate. He finally ignored Holtzendorff's advice and went to Kenny's office. There he found the three "Communists" drafting the brief he needed for the next morning. Kenny said, "We knew you'd have to have something, so we met to prepare this for you. And by the way, Frank, the way you handled yourself in court today—you couldn't have done better if I'd been there with you."

Frank was so relieved, so overwhelmed by this sudden, unexpected bonanza of kindness that when he got back into his car he began crying, and he cried all the way to the home of sister Hildegarde and brother Alan in Glendale. The two doctors knew just what to do: they draped him over the car's fender, gave him a suitably heavy shot of morphine in the rump, then literally carried him into the house and put him to bed.

▪

A YEAR LATER, in 1953, many people were still shunning Frank. For example, he was informed that, while his children would still be welcomed at the YMCA summer camp they had regularly attended, he and his wife would not be permitted to visit them while they were there.

Into this state of affairs came Robert Hutchins (the former chancellor of the University of Chicago, who had recently set up the Center for the Study of Democratic Institutions in Santa Barbara) and Alec Hoffman (of the American Friends Service Committee), offering a welcome to all the Wilkinsons at the Quakers' free family camp.

Hutchins and the Quakers were among the many heroes—and having an open friendship with suspected subversives did make one a sort of hero during the Cold War—that Wilkinson would luck into. The bleakness of those years is so often stressed that one tends to forget that while the good guys were in the minority, there were plenty of them and they were usually fearless in the face of horrendous negative publicity. Hutchins was like that, and his kindness, along with that of others, helped keep Frank and his family going.

CHAPTER 11

Finally, Real Employment

FRANK WAS SO thoroughly blackballed in L.A. that he could not find a job for ten months; finally, he was hired by a sympathetic Quaker who owned a three-story department store in Pasadena. For a dollar an hour, Frank would daily clean sixteen toilets and all the showcases.

His new employer politely requested, however, that Mr. Wilkinson come and go after dark.

Jean had been fired as a regular teacher late in 1952 and since then was picking up only part-time work. Frank's janitorial work gave him little income, no incentive, and no hope. He desperately needed to do something that mattered.

It was at this juncture that those who'd rallied to his support—mostly lawyers—rescued him from financial and emotional poverty and began to direct him toward his new career. HUAC had come back to Hollywood in 1952 to see if it could duplicate the headlined success of its rowdy "Hollywood Ten" hearings of 1947. It failed, partly because this time, instead of focusing only on the film colony, it was poised to abuse doctors and lawyers and other professionals—and this was a crowd that would really fight back. This was also the crowd that told Frank he should help organize that fight.

After many years as a director of the ACLU, Reverend A. A. Heist had retired and formed the Citizens Committee to Preserve American Freedoms (CCPAF) to counteract HUAC's 1952 invasion. The leadership was made up of about twenty aggressive liberals in the Los Angeles area. Its goal was to defend all victims of the un-American activities committees, state and federal—including Senator James Eastland's Senate Internal Security Subcommittee (SISS), which got fewer headlines than HUAC but was just as brutal.

Inquisitorial committees were coming constantly to Los Angeles through the 1950s. And when the CCPAF wasn't girding up to battle them, it was combating some of the more outrageous bills spilling out of the legislature in Sacramento. One of the bills proposed that the state refuse to license any person who exercised the Fifth Amendment in a state or federal hearing. The bill covered 107 professions then being licensed by the state—everything from doctors to yacht brokers to boxing managers to dozens of etceteras—and put their livelihood at the mercy of political patriots. The CCPAF played a big part in blocking it.

One day Frank dropped in to see Eason Monroe, who had been a professor of English at San Francisco State University (then College) but was fired when he refused to sign the state's loyalty oath. It took Eason fifteen years to get his job back; meanwhile, he'd become an executive of the ACLU. Frank mentioned that he had been reading papers and magazines to find examples of witch-hunt victims who had fought back successfully, and had found quite a few.

"That's it!" Frank remembers Eason exclaiming. "We need a constant drumbeat of encouragement for our people. Why don't you become an official ACLU observer? You read everything you can get your hands on to find stuff like that and then in every issue of *Open Forum* we'll have a column called 'The Changing Tide,' with your byline."

The job paid nothing, but Frank was given fifty dollars a

month, enough to buy thirty publications for research. It kept him from going bonkers while working as a janitor at night, and when a spot in the CCPAF's hierarchy opened in the early fall of 1953, he was recruited for it. Though he longed to take the job, at first he resisted, arguing that being "totally pariah in this community, totally anathema, I'm the last person that should lead the defenders of the victims."

His excuse was brushed aside. Rev. Heist, Eason, key lawyers whom the press had headlined as villains in recent L.A. civil liberties fights, renowned doctors whose practices had been critically damaged by political innuendoes, and others who were fed up told Frank, in effect, "Don't be stupid. Your experience in being kicked around and the survival skills you've learned from it are exactly what's needed to defend the victims."

His salary was one-fourth what he had earned at the LAHA, but he didn't care. He was somebody again, and he was busting to fight back. (J. Edgar Hoover was watching with a frown. In a memo sent to HUAC, he identified the CCPAF as Communist-funded and Frank Wilkinson as its "brains and energy.")[1] "I think the growth of the organization was prophetic," says Frank, looking back. "I mean, when an off-the-wall congressional committee subpoenas a brilliant group of lawyers, doctors, and other professional people for the purpose of smearing them, they don't just lie back. They organize a fight-back. They thought they were organizing for only that one hearing in '52. But once it was created, it became obvious that the organization should be kept intact. It developed a lasting momentum. From that time forward, until we went national and formed the National Committee to Abolish the House Un-American Activities Committee, we were never without a program and focus."

CHAPTER 12

The Smith Act— and Taking Down CP Leadership in Court

WHY HAD ORGANIZATIONAL membership become such a hot-button issue? By whose authority was it relevant to ask people about their associations, anyway?

In 1940, the Alien Registration Act, better known as the Smith Act, was passed and became the main authority for this line of attack. Appropriately, the bill was named for its chief sponsor, Rep. Howard W. Smith of Virginia, one of the most powerful enemies of democracy ever to serve in Congress. If he didn't like a piece of legislation (he disliked bills that, for instance, sponsored public housing or raised minimum wages), he would literally disappear for days, and since he was chairman of the House Rules Committee, through which all bills had to pass, his disappearance would usually kill the legislation. This tyranny went on for a decade, and the coalition of Republicans and southern Democrats he led were responsible for paralyzing the last years of the New Deal.

The Smith Act, written with Congress's usual splurge of words, made it a crime "to knowingly abet, advise or teach the duty, necessity, desirability or propriety of overthrowing or destroying any government in the United States by force or violence" or "be a member of, or affiliate with" any group that advocated such action—thereby making it, in the words of free speech authority Professor Zechariah Chafee Jr., "the most drastic restriction on freedom of speech ever enacted in the United States during peace"[1] and the first federal law to sanction guilt by association. It was, in fact, the first peacetime sedition statute since 1798.

The only good thing about the Smith Act was that it was virtually ignored for a decade after its passage. It was used successfully only once, by President Roosevelt, to get rid of Trotskyite Teamster officials who were bothering his political supporters in Minnesota; it was attempted a second time in a trial involving right-wing activists but was aborted with the death of the presiding judge.[2]

But as early as 1945, J. Edgar Hoover saw the possibilities of using the Smith Act to wipe out the Communist Party USA, and within two years he had put together a legal brief of nearly two thousand pages and eight hundred exhibits. Lobbied by Hoover and members of HUAC, the U.S. attorney in New York City, John F. X. McGohey, took that material to a grand jury and on July 20, 1947, it returned a true bill against eleven national leaders of the Communist Party.

The New York trial, which quickly came to be known as "The Battle of Foley Square," dragged through nine months of vituperative wrangling between Judge Harold Medina and the six defense attorneys (counting Communist Party General Secretary Eugene Dennis, who acted as his own attorney).

All six were members of the National Lawyers Guild, one of the only legal groups who would stand up to HUAC's attacks.

The case against the Communists was built around some very strange testimony. No evidence was introduced to show that any of the defendants had lifted a finger to overthrow the government by violence, or even recommend that it be done. As Victor Navasky has written in *Naming Names*, "One hundred percent of the government's 'evidence' . . . was provided by thirteen ex-Communist informers and FBI informants. . . . And 90 percent of the evidence had nothing to do with Dennis or his co-defendants but, rather, related to the meaning of Marxist-Leninist classics."[3] The key prosecution witness was Louis F. Budenz, an ex-Communist and former editor of the *Daily Worker*, who quit the party, rejoined the Catholic Church, became a professor of economics at Fordham University, and also became a commercial "regular" on the informer circuit—making well-paid rounds to testify at anti-Communist hearings and trials.

His specialty was laying out in long-winded and disjointed details what he said was the "conspiratorial apparatus" behind the Communist Party organization. Inevitably this led to his exegesis of the deeper meanings of Marxism and Leninism—a subject about which few could argue with him, since few (if any), even among the CPUSA leadership, had ever wasted much time trying to plumb the muddy waters of Hegelian dialectic and the surplus value of labor.

Simply put, Budenz's argument began by quoting the first sentence of the CPUSA constitution: "The Communist Party of the United States is the political party of the American working class, basing itself upon the principles of scientific socialism, Marxism-Leninism."

And then, in a "gotcha!" tone, Budenz went on to say that since Marx and Lenin believed in overthrowing "the capitalist state" by force and replacing it with "a dictatorship of the proletariat," the CPUSA's reliance on the "principles" of Marxism-Leninism could only mean it hoped to bring about the same thing by force in this country. And if that was the party's official line, it must be party members' beliefs, too; therefore, they were violating the Smith Act.

The eleven Communists were convicted on October 14, 1949, by a jury that deliberated less than seven hours. The trial and circus surrounding it were grist for national news and laid down the pattern for years to come. Los Angeles was watching closely.

■ AND NOW, KILL THE LAWYERS

Having received the jury's verdict, Judge Medina, with obvious relish, declared, "Now I turn to some unfinished business"—meaning a recitation of forty reasons he was going to hold the six lawyers in contempt.

Medina had often interrupted the trial to accuse the defense attorneys of conspiring to destroy his health by acting mean and ugly.[4] Indeed, they had sometimes been a bit ugly, but their primary offense was serving their clients badly. By allowing the prosecution to channel the trial into a meaningless debate over Communist Party beliefs rather than insisting that the emphasis of the trial be on the constitutional civil liberties of individual party members, the defense attorneys let the trial fall apart like dunked toast. And in the process of designing their own defeat, the defense was often boisterous and rude—but no ruder to the judge than he had been to them. In any event, it could certainly be argued that they did nothing outside the Canons of Professional Ethics, which states "The lawyer owes entire 'devotion to the interest of his client, warm zeal in the maintenance and defense of his rights and the exertion of his utmost learning and ability. . . .' No fear of judicial disfavor or public unpopularity should restrain him from the full discharge of his duty."[5]

If the defense attorneys had acted with "no fear of judicial disfavor," they now learned it might have been smarter to act with at least a little fear. Medina's stored-up fury spilled out in an exaggerated description of what he considered their "cold and calculated, deliberate, premeditated conspiracy to obstruct the trial by attacking him, the jury system, the Department of Justice, the President, the police, and the press."[6]

The lawyers' contempt punishment ranged from thirty days to six months in prison, but the government had ways of dragging out and intensifying those sentences. Richard Gladstein of San Francisco, famous in that city for his successful defense of the longshoremen's leader Harry Bridges, asked to be allowed to serve his six months on McNeil Island in Washington, in order to be closer to his family and friends. "Instead," writes Stanley Kutler, "he was sent to Texarkana, Texas, hardly one of the 'country club' institutions. Nor did he travel first-class; he was driven cross-country for nearly seven weeks, manacled and in leg irons.

He was held incommunicado in seven jails en route to Texas and deprived of normal prisoner privileges."[7]

Never before had a group of lawyers been subjected to such punishment. And the worst was still to come. The careers of all six were at a standstill for years as they fought off disbarment efforts by local, state, and the American Bar Association (ABA). Those who were disbarred went through agonizing, hugely expensive years fighting to clear their names.

All over the nation, Attorney General Tom Clark's 1946 call to action against radical attorneys was bearing rotten fruit. Well into the 1950s, the ABA urged local affiliates to disbar all Communists and make life hell for lawyers who dared defend clients who were no more than suspiciously left-wing. New Mexico's bar refused to give a license exam to an applicant who had belonged to the Communist Party twenty years earlier. For doing no more than make critical comments about the outcome of Julius and Ethel Rosenberg's spy trial, two Michigan attorneys were given a going-over by the state bar's Committee on Professional Ethics.

■

WHEN THE U.S. Supreme Court in 1951 upheld the conviction of the 11 "Foley Square" Communists, thereby giving its imprimatur of legality to the Smith Act, the Justice Department was off and running. The government quickly indicted 52 second-level Communist leaders in New York, California, Baltimore, Pittsburgh, and Honolulu. Over the next few years it won indictments of 126 other Communist Party officials, and in trials across the country it won convictions on all but 10.

Such was the atmosphere of the era; they probably would have been convicted even with the best and most aggressive defense lawyers on their side. But for obvious reasons, it had been extremely difficult to hire lawyers of that type. Indeed, extremely difficult to hire lawyers of *any* worth. And that, of course, was the government's goal. For the second round of Smith Act trials in New York, more than two hundred lawyers refused to be hired by the seventeen accused Communists. Four members of the National Lawyers Guild (NLG), including its president, Thomas L. Emerson, stepped forward to do the job and risk the usual professional harassment.

▪ CALIFORNIA'S REBELS DID IT RIGHT

Right about the same time that Frank, as an official of the LAHA, was being called to testify about his memberships, a second nationally watched prosecution of Communist Party leadership was going on in Los Angeles. In California's 1952 Smith Act trial, things were very different from the New York trial. Although, once again, most of the lawyers were members of the NLG, the accused enjoyed the luxury of being able to choose from among a large number of lawyers eager to take their case—though some would suffer as a result: for defending the Communists, Alex Schulman lost his job as attorney for the Los Angeles American Federation of Labor (AFL) council, and Daniel G. Marshall, lawyer for the Catholic diocese in Los Angeles, lost the diocese as a client because he represented one of the accused in his bail appeal.[8]

True to the maverick history of the state, the California Communists brought to their trial a different idea of how to handle themselves.

Ben Margolis, who led the defense team in California, recalls the New York defense's mistake as "turning it into a trial of the Party instead of a trial of people."

> Our position, which was taken over the objection of the Party in the East, was that the government had to prove separately the guilt or innocence of each person. Under American law you couldn't have guilt by association. We also took the position, factually, that the New York defendants in both the first and second Smith Act trials were unwilling to take, and that is that members of the Communist Party did not agree on everything. There were differences of opinion, there

were arguments. . . . That was our position, and that was what
won the case for us before the Supreme Court.[9]

(When it finally got there, five years later, in 1957.)

Unlike the New York defenders, the California lawyers went
through the standard routine of challenging and cross-examining
prosecution witnesses (most of whom were FBI informers). It often
paid off. For instance, an informer claimed he had been given a
book by two of the accused that contained a top-secret outline of
a coming revolution and that the book had been smuggled into
the United States by Russian sailors. Defense attorneys thereupon
submitted to the court three copies of the same book from the
Los Angeles public library, with evidence showing it had been
publicly distributed in this country by a New York publisher for
the past five years.

Treating the jury with respect by offering evidence and
counterevidence—instead of ideological tantrums, as had been
offered in New York—did not win the case for the California Communists, but at least the jury responded with what might be called
a quantum of similar respect by deliberating six days (unlike the
seven hours in New York) before coming in with a guilty verdict
for them all, on July 31, 1952.

A month later they were released on bail and started a five-year
wait for their appeal to slog its way to the Supreme Court.

Refusal to let their ideology be seen as setting them wide of
the political mainstream was one of the virtues of the California
Communists, and it was probably what made them among the
most successful in being tolerated by a surprisingly large fraction
of the general public in California, if one can make that assumption from such samplings as the political careers of three of the
accused. When Henry Steinberg, a well-known Communist community leader in east Los Angeles, ran for the board of education
in 1951, he got almost 40,000 votes. Oleta O'Connor Yates, who
had been well known as chairman of the San Francisco party since
World War II, ran for mayor of that city and got 40,000 votes. And
Dorothy Healey won 86,149 votes—more even than Earl Browder

won when he ran nationally as the Communist Party's presidential candidate in 1936—when she ran for Los Angeles County tax assessor in 1966.[10] But by that time she had flaunted her Communist Party affiliation so long and openly, and had worked with so many left-wing organizations, that the locals probably thought of her not with a party label but simply as a hometown troublemaker.

The defense attorneys in the 1952 California trial were also levelheaded in their belief that, however mean the government might be getting, it wasn't the end of the world. And their refusal to collapse into hysteria prompted an equally levelheaded response from the California bar, which refused to go along with the national ABA's advice to "excommunicate" or disbar lawyers who were allegedly Communists.

Far from huddling in despair, the defendants organized what they called the California Emergency Defense Committee (CEDC) to mobilize public support. It sent speakers to churches, unions, and community organizations to tell its side of the story. It published pamphlets. It asked people to sign petitions as "friends of the court," challenging the indictments. To make sure that the court was aware of the public concern that they had drummed up, they organized groups to fill the courtroom every day—and fill it they did, with Quakers, union members, ACLU members, members of race organizations. "We couldn't sway the jury or the court's decision in the case," says Healey, "but at least we could see to it that in areas of public opinion important to us the government's case would be understood for the frame-up it was."[11]

Frank would borrow heavily from that organizational strategy and work with many of the folks in Los Angeles who were already energetically beating back these constitutional abusers by the time he was fired from the LAHA.

CHAPTER 13

Sorry, But Frank Was Not Issued Cloak and Dagger

BIOGRAPHIES BENEFIT FROM all the spices one can find to make them tastier, so unfortunately for that purpose Frank Wilkinson was not a spy of any sort—neither one who came in from the cold, nor one who stayed out in the cold. He was not a saboteur, a foreign agent, or a collaborator. It's a pity, but it must be admitted that his experience as a Communist came very close to resembling that of a Rotarian or a YMCA counselor.

Frank's activities were unobtrusive enough that even his daughter Jo didn't know her father was a member of the Communist Party until she was eighteen. She recalls, "I found out through friends of mine who were young people, and were members themselves. I think it came up because I had walked in on a discussion they were having, in my family's living room, about some inner-party conflict. I didn't know, at the time, that any of these people were members of the party. But they included me in the conversation, and through their political debate, I was informed of my father's party membership."[1]

Usually, members of the Communist Party—at least, Frank

says, this was true in Los Angeles—were assigned to small study groups or "clubs" (nationally, the CPUSA in 1920 had officially abandoned the term "cell") made up of people with similar professional interests. They met in each other's homes. There were schoolteacher groups (Frank's wife, Jean, was in one). There were journalist groups. Arts and motion-picture groups. Labor union groups. The other people in Frank's group of about fifteen who got together every week or so were professional social workers. Frank says they gave each other useful ideas on how to do their work better, and that outsiders would surely have found their exchange of tips on "serving the public" boringly devoid of revolutionary spirit.

During World War II, sympathy for socialism wasn't all that scandalous. In fact, in some circles, it was considered a kind of sub rosa patriotism. Of course, if a person worked for the government, or for any sort of establishment that clearly wanted no one on the payroll who'd rock the boat, the person knew it'd be smarter not to mention these sympathies.

But many people, from independent professionals down to day laborers, made no secret of their membership—and got away with it. Frank recalls that in the early 1940s, there were open Communist Party clubs all over town, and in eastern Los Angeles, where many day laborers lived, the Communist Party had an office and a public meeting room with a sign out front and a standing invitation to the public to drop by for literature and to hear speeches.

Frank was such an enthusiastic member that, as the Cold War got colder and his "club" kept thinning out—until only one other member was still attending the meetings—it didn't occur to him that just maybe there was something fishy about the other member's party loyalty. From evidence presented at a 1962 HUAC hearing, he learned that, indeed, the other member had been the FBI's key informer against him.

At times Wilkinson did take precautions against being caught. Shortly after he joined, he was nervous enough to burn his Communist Party card because "I didn't want it accidentally to fall into somebody's hands." The party became nervous enough, too, that it stopped issuing cards in around 1943 or 1944.

And in the late 1940s and early 1950s, he got downright panicky—as did a great many members of the CPUSA—because the feds were really cracking down, arresting and convicting Communists by the score under the Smith Act. And one part of the Internal Security Act (the McCarran Act) of 1950 called for setting up concentration camps to hold subversives.

"We got to the point that we actually expected all Communists to be rounded up and put in those concentration camps," says Frank.

We had a wonderful library in our home of all kinds of books, many of them published by the Communist Party. I remember around two o'clock one morning making contact with a neighbor living across the street. He was in the party. We boxed up all the books that had anything to do with the Communist Party and carried them over to hide them under the beds in their house for protection.

I remember another occasion when Jean and I drove up to Canada. We took with us a book—*History of the Communist Party in the Soviet Union*. We'd never read the darned thing and thought maybe we could read it on the trip. Well, as we approached the border, we got paranoid because by that time the Walter-McCarran Act had passed and there were all sorts of immigration controls on people and we were afraid when we got to the border they would search our belongings and find the book.

We stayed in a motel and tried to figure out how to get rid of it. We were afraid to throw it away because maybe our fingerprints would be found on it. While Jean talked to the manager in the office at the front of the motel, I tore the book apart, a few pages at a time, and threw it into an incinerator at the back of the motel. Silly maybe, but that was the kind of fear we had at that time.

But for several years prior to that, Wilkinson had probably been too bold for his own good. He was, in fact, an active recruiter for the party "because I believed in it. I thought the party was an important and valuable political organization working in the right direction. I tried to be just as open as I could about my membership. I tried to socialize and maintain an organizational liaison with members of the Communist Party leadership, just the same as I would with the Methodist Church or the Democratic Party."

He would meet publicly with Healey (not a smart thing to do, since Healey's face was known to every FBI agent in the region) "to ask for party information and pay her my dues—tithing, you know, just as I did in the Methodist Church."

∎ CALIFORNIA'S "LITTLE HUAC"

Without question, Frank's immediate superiors in the LAHA knew he was, if not a Communist, then close to being one, but because he was so valuable they helped him cover it up. This was evident in the way they handled the California Senate Un-American Activities Committee or "Little HUAC," as some called it. The two committees were alike in their lunacy, but the California committee was even more corrupt than its big brother.

To most Californians who followed state politics, the committee was known simply as "the Tenney Committee," because under Jack B. Tenney it had developed its unique and abiding character. He controlled it first as an assemblyman and then as a state senator, from its founding in 1941 until 1949. Tenney, a spectacular chameleon, had not always been savagely anti-Communist. In fact, he began his political career as a very loud and aggressive liberal, to the point that he was considered by some to be unquestionably, yes, a Communist.

In 1936, after law school, Tenney went for an interview with Art Samish, the most powerful lobbyist in the state, who could "select and elect" politicians at all levels. Samish liked Tenney and got him elected, and he was a good legislator—for a while. At least he was certainly a very left-wing one. And in 1937, his first year as legislator, he was also elected president of Local 47, the American Federation of Musicians, a union that was supporting just about every left-wing movement and every labor-union action in the area.

When several union men were convicted of plotting to dynamite a Standard Oil plant in Modesto, Tenney ridiculed their prosecutor as "a man who believes that Communists are lurking behind every pillar and post and that 'Red' armies are apt to materialize out of thin air at any minute to destroy the government."

But then something happened—something that led to what veteran political observers in California declared was the most dramatic flip-flop they had ever seen. The musician's local that had elected him president in 1937 overwhelmingly defeated him for reelection in 1939. Blaming his defeat on "communistic" elements within the union, Tenney shed his liberalism with breathtaking suddenness.

When California's "Little HUAC" was established in 1941, he became its leader, banners flying, as the most rabid anti-Communist west of the Rockies.

Tenney led the committee through what were virtually one-man "investigations" whose alleged goal was to expose communism in unions, in relief organizations, in religious and racial organizations, in classrooms (especially those teaching sex education), and in "subversive" organizations like the ACLU and the National Sharecroppers Fund.

His committee issued a list of two hundred organizations and several thousand individuals that patriotic Americans should be leery of—although very few had been given a hearing before his committee. The blacklist had its minor-league effect. Author Carey McWilliams, for example, had been scheduled to give two speeches to Riverside County teachers, but the school department cancelled them when the American Legion protested that he had been named forty-seven times in the latest Tenney committee report.[2]

By 1949, Tenney had become so clearly out of control and such an embarrassment to the legislature and to the political establishment in general that lobbyist Art Samish joined other lobbyists to dislodge him from the chairmanship of the committee.

Fittingly, when last seen, Tenney was disappearing into the mud of history with plans to become the running-mate of the United States' premier anti-Semite, Gerald L. K. Smith, in some preposterous try for the presidency.

■ USEFULNESS GAVE IMMUNITY

This brings us to Frank's strange relationship with the California Senate Un-American Activities Committee. As noted above, it was taken over in 1950 by Senator Hugh Burns, a mortician from Fresno. Burns was a smoothie. He did not abuse witnesses, but he made every effort to appear terribly worried about Communists taking over important parts of the government. That's why one of Burns's first investigations—which came to nothing—was into the career of perpetual suspect Dr. J. Robert Oppenheimer.

Oppenheimer was a legendary example of someone who was— as Frank Wilkinson had once been—so valuable that his superiors protected him from witch-hunters. He ran the Los Alamos laboratory in New Mexico where the first atomic bomb—the most closely guarded secret of World War II—was being put together. Col. John Lansdale, head of security at Los Alamos, was convinced, after probing their background, that Oppenheimer's wife, brother, and sister-in-law were probably Communists, in addition to many of his friends. Throughout the 1930s, Oppenheimer himself had attended pro-Communist gatherings and made regular contributions to Communist-supported causes.[3]

Although J. Edgar Hoover was horrified, General Leslie Groves, head of the entire Manhattan Project (as the atomic bomb was called), insisted on leaving him in charge at Los Alamos despite his background because he considered Oppenheimer essential to the bomb's development.

Oppenheimer's immunity was also evident when a number of witnesses—mostly ex-Communists—brought their tales to California's "Little HUAC." Chairman Burns tried to implicate

Oppenheimer as at least a fellow traveler in the prewar past, but Oppenheimer readily admitted that he had once been a radical. However, he said, he had long ago renounced it: "I became a real left-winger, joined the Teachers' Union, had lots of Communist friends. It was what most people do in college or late high school. . . . Most of what I believed then now seems complete nonsense."[4] Burns's plan fizzled.

Witnesses with much better excuses for their suspicious conduct had been hazed for hours, but Senator Burns seemed to have no inclination to probe behind Oppenheimer's rather glib explanation, just as he seemed to have no inclination to target Frank Wilkinson's past. Perhaps he was just being pragmatic. That is to say, a politician with the power to ruin careers obviously knows he or she can be rewarded with headlines either way; the same politician also knows that to occasionally refrain from using this power may also bring other rewards.

For example, money. Maybe money had nothing to do with Oppenheimer's easy out. But it certainly had something to do with Frank's.

As mentioned earlier, Frank was in the hospital having a knee operation when the California Senate Un-American Activities Committee's circus hit town (and pinned that subpoena to his hospital gown) in late September 1952. But a month later he was able to attend the hearing, which came to nothing more than a quiet display of Frank's stubbornness. Holtzendorff told him on October 29, 1952, that he was no longer suspended; he was officially fired.

The strange thing is that Frank had never before been forced to face an inquisition from the "Little HUAC." Senator Tenney, who seemed willing to haul anyone and everyone into a hearing to be harassed and labeled a Communist, surely must have been suspicious of housing officials. What could be more socialistic than housing for the poor? And wouldn't Senator Burns have felt the same? And yet, for more than a decade, both Tenney and Burns ignored the LAHA and its most aggressively socialistic executive, Frank Wilkinson.

That was especially curious in light of the eight-column, double-layered headline stripped across the front page of the *Herald-Express* on September 26, 1952:

HEARD REDS ON STAFF SINCE 1941, HOUSING CHIEF ADMITS

The headline was referring to Frank's boss, Holtzendorff, and to his response when "Little HUAC's" counsel, Richard Combs, asked him:

"Have you ever received any report of subversive activities on the part of Los Angeles City Housing Authority employees?"

Holtzendorff answered: "Yes."

"For how long?"

"Almost ever since I came to the authority in 1941."

If Holtzendorff had been hearing such reports for so long, surely rumors of the same thing would have reached the hospitable ears of those great witch-hunters Tenney and Burns. And yet for over a decade they had not made a single effort to root out the L.A. Housing Authority's suspicious employees. Why not?

Years later, Frank reveals:

Holtzendorff had secretly developed a protective relationship with the California Senate Un-American Activities Committee.

Holtzendorff was a very important man to Los Angeles and a very interesting man, because I don't think he had any heart for the slum problem, for housing conditions, for the people. I think he feigned a great care about the people in the slums and doing something about it, but I never believed his sincerity in that. He was just a totally committed and effective bureaucrat. Once he got the job of building housing, he did whatever was necessary to achieve his goal, including working intimately with people like me, even though, I'm sure, he had every reason to believe that if I was not a Communist, I was close to the Communist Party.

Once I said to him, "Do you want to know if I'm a Communist? Ask me, and I'll answer you." He said, "No, Frank, I don't want to." (Frank laughs.) He needed me.

He would do everything that needed to be done to fight for housing in a sick society, and that would include electing members of the city council who support you, electing members of the state Senate Un-American Activities Committee with the understanding that they wouldn't interfere. Holtzendorff was a pragmatist. You've got a Cold War; you've got witch-hunters around; everybody has a price, so you buy them. I was told it took substantial amounts, thousands of dollars a year. I was told, "How do you suppose we kept the Un-American Activities Committee out of all this up to this time if we hadn't been helping them?"

Not exactly bribes, says Frank, but very generous "campaign contributions." But as the very corruptible U.S. senator Russell Long used to say, "There's only a very thin line between the two."

During the early part of Frank's career at the LAHA, it would have been unthinkable for the state's inquisitors to pick on him—campaign contributions or not—because he was such an ostentatiously good patriot. He enthusiastically went through the loyalty rigmarole every year. State and local government employees were required to take the Levering oath—swearing that they did not advocate overthrowing the government by force or violence. It was an oath Frank could honestly swear.

Moreover, he did it with flair. As the LAHA's liaison with all the major veterans' groups, he invited their representatives—decked out in medals and symbolic veterans' caps—to come each year to the LAHA's conference room to join the mayor, or judge, or both, and stand in front of a row of flags to have their photo taken. The L.A. papers would routinely carry the photo with the boilerplate heading, "Housing Authority Repeats Levering Oath."

Only toward the end of his years at the housing authority did Frank become uncomfortable going through this ritual. Why the hell would an American think it necessary—or in good taste—to make a publicity stunt out of professing loyalty? Ah, but that question didn't hit him forcefully until after he had been fired. His basic motives while employed were less libertarian that bureaucratic.

"The development of my civil liberties," he says, "was slow in coming. I don't think I had much commitment to civil liberties until the late 1940s. As the Cold War came on and the Un-American Activities committees held hearings, I did not speak out against those committees or about their harassments."

Why not? Because he wasn't personally endangered. He was smug. "I was in a place of great security. I was assistant to the director of the housing authority. I had taken all of those loyalty oaths. I was very much respected. I came from a strong Republican-Methodist background. I was in daily association with the Catholic archdiocesan director of hospitals and charities. So I was protected."

Well, yes, but not forever. When the FBI and HUAC began stripping away that protection, his interest in civil liberties accelerated with remarkable speed, and all those showy loyalty-program events he had orchestrated became an embarrassing memory.

CHAPTER 14

"Human Rights Shall Be More Highly Regarded Than Property Rights": Obviously, the NLG Was Subversive

IN ANY DESCRIPTION of the evolution of the Cold War and HUAC, it's critical to understand the story of the National Lawyers Guild (NLG)—its activities and the attacks against it, which provides a window into how other groups survived the Cold War and HUAC. It also helps explain the strong bond that developed between the NLG and Frank that would last his whole life.

The NLG was founded in 1937, smack in the middle of the Great Depression, and its founders, like many who were energized by the New Deal's social reforms, hoped to inject a sense of real justice and humanity into a profession that heretofore had lacked it.

The appeal of the NLG's charter, vowing that "human rights shall be regarded as more sacred than property rights," was strong enough that a few governors and U.S. senators, as well as many government lawyers in the Roosevelt administration, became members. They were mostly liberals, with the usual 1930s-type smattering of Socialists thrown in; a few Communist lawyers belonged to it, too, and though they certainly did not flaunt their ideology, their existence was suspected, and appreciated, because they were among the most enthusiastic organizers and recruiters for the NLG (as they were for any organization they were part of).

By the late 1940s, the guild had become, as one of its historians has written, "a last outpost of the prewar liberal-radical alliance ... an embattled and declining 'progressive' minority."[1]

Needless to say, J. Edgar Hoover hated the organization and did everything in his power to undermine it. The hatred was mutual. The guild was one of the first professional organizations to do outright battle with the FBI. Up to then, the FBI had been treated by virtually every professional organization and certainly by most politicians as beyond reproach—or too powerful to risk offending.

Perhaps the guild's most successful public attack on the FBI was in 1950, when it released a documented account of FBI wiretappings, burglaries, and unauthorized surveillance.[2]

Hoover's counterattack was awesome. The FBI put together a fifty-page *Report on the National Lawyers Guild: Legal Bulwark of the Communist Party*, which was released through HUAC in the guise of the committee's own investigation. Among its many "findings" was the charge that 6.6 percent (a nicely scientific number) of the guild's members were outright Communists and that another 25 percent were Communist sympathizers.[3]

Using material it acquired through wiretappings and burglaries of guild offices, the FBI continually planted negative stories with its most devoted reporters, who invariably described the guild as "a left-wing organization already suspected as a Communist front."[4]

This constantly repeated refrain began to seriously erode guild membership, and in 1951 it had to close its Washington office for lack of funds.

But smearing was not enough to destroy the guild. What its enemies needed was an official rating of disloyalty, and since 1947 the obvious way to get that was via the Attorney General's List.

■

WHEN PRESIDENT TRUMAN launched his loyalty program in 1947, one of its most important weapons was the "Attorney General's List" of "totalitarian, fascist, Communist, or subversive" groups. Because the list was open to public inspection, people and organizations placed on it could be seriously discredited or even professionally ruined. Hoover wanted Attorney General Tom Clark to put the NLG on the list, so he again sent FBI agents to burglarize its offices and steal any documents that looked "subversive" enough to persuade Clark to take that action.

The plan failed. As Clark explained to Hoover, "I have many friends in the guild." He understood the plight of "many friends," now in high political places, who had joined the NLG back in the 1930s whose past might return to ruin them. The 1930s had been the height of the Depression, when the economy was a wreck, and it was normal for young lawyers to have liberal impulses for reform, or at least pretend to have such impulses if they wanted to be hired by the Roosevelt administration. Among the early members of the NLG were at least two state governors, several U.S. senators, and many government lawyers—all the way to the top of the bureaucracy. For instance, Democratic congressman Francis Walter of Pennsylvania—who had climbed to the chairmanship of HUAC and perched there for eight years, sponsoring many "security" bills—would certainly have blushed if it had become known that he had joined the guild in 1939.

■

LEARNING THAT THE NLG was putting together an extensive bill of particulars about the FBI's illegal actions, Hoover ordered a counterattack. The three-hundred-page report pointed out a vast range of NLG sins, including urging the abolition of HUAC, "favoring legislation beneficial to labor," urging "an extension of social welfare measures," and advocating "lower taxes for lower income groups and higher taxes on higher income groups and corporations."[5]

The guild's reputation among "nice" people was already bad enough. After all, here was an organization that opposed Truman's loyalty program, that felt the Marshall Plan and NATO were unwisely provocative vis-à-vis the Soviet Union, and that counted among its proud but shrinking membership such liberal/radical fellows as Clifford Durr, who refused reappointment to the Federal Communications Commission (FCC) because he opposed Truman's loyalty program, and the combative civil libertarian and Yale law professor Thomas I. Emerson.

Emerson was judged by the FBI to be an especially dangerous and elusive adversary. His elusiveness was particularly irritating to Hoover because it was the result of the fact that Emerson traveled in the right circles. In a 1953 memorandum, Hoover griped that "it has been impossible up to the present time to have Emerson called before any committee because of the intercession on his behalf of Senator Taft, who is on the Board of Trustees of Yale University."[6] To compensate for that failure, the FBI kept Emerson under constant investigation for three decades, resulting in a file of more than fifteen hundred pages. His office was often wiretapped and was burglarized at least twice so that his private papers could be photographed. His name was placed on a list of persons to be seized and held in a concentration camp in case of a national emergency. Much of the information FBI agents placed in his file was false. For example, one entry stated that for over a decade Emerson had been a member of a Communist cell on the University of Washington campus, when in fact he had neither been on the campus nor in the state of Washington at all during that period.[7]

Among the many other notable NLG members who refused to be intimidated by the FBI's campaign of slander were Supreme Court justice-to-be Thurgood Marshall and Robert W. Kenny. Kenny was elected California's attorney general in 1942; he not only once served as the guild's president (as did both Durr and Emerson) but he also represented it at the founding convention of the United Nations. Like Emerson, these men would play important roles in Frank Wilkinson's efforts to fight HUAC.

CHAPTER 15

Organizing to Repel the Storm

BY THE TIME Frank was hired to head up the CCPAF in 1953, much of the fireworks from both Frank's hearing and the Communist Party–leadership prosecutions had died down in Los Angeles. In 1952 Healey and her confederates had been convicted. Also, in September of that year, twenty-four Los Angeles Lawyers Guild attorneys had been called to appear before HUAC for the usual questions about their politics and had given the usual defiant answers. And also that year, a separate HUAC inquisition of some of Los Angeles's most prominent lawyers and doctors had come and gone, with nothing to show for it except some surreptitiously taped recordings of the hearings—which were later sold as *Voices of Resistance, Volume I and II*, to raise money to fight HUAC. Today, even after half a century, those voices are as excitingly rebellious as the valedictory of Nathan Hale.

After all that, there was a slight lull, but the calm was deceptive. Plenty of trouble awaited Frank's initiation as the CCPAF's chief propagandist. The trouble came from the government's renewed efforts to have the National Lawyers Guild put on the Attorney General's List of subversive organizations. At the 1953 national convention of the ABA, Eisenhower's attorney general, Herbert Brownell, announced the NLG's blacklisting, declaring that "at least since 1946 the leadership of the Guild has been in the hands of card-carrying Communists and prominent fellow-travelers" who constantly followed the wishes of Moscow.[1]

The press did not ask for substantiating details, and the only major newspaper to even greet Brownell's sweeping accusation with skepticism—and it was very mild—was the *St. Louis Post-Dispatch*, which on August 29, 1953, editorially suggested that if the guild had been subversive for that many years, "a lot of pretty intelligent people have attended its meetings and not caught on."[2]

When the NLG managed to block Brownell's move with a court order, he began proceedings to bar from federal courts or federal agencies any lawyer who was a Communist or who wouldn't swear he had no Communist connections.

Doing legal battle against that sort of thing would cost lots of money, of which the NLG had little. Raising some was Frank's first big effort. He recalls:

To fight back, we decided we would hold a fund-raising banquet. That's the standard technique, but we were new at it. We had to develop the skills. We took the old Royal Palms Hotel—a miserable fleabag on Bonnie Brae Street just north of Sixth Street. We took it because they gave us a dinner for two dollars and everything else was profit. I think we charged ten, and on top of that had a collection.

But how were we going to get people to come out? Who could we get to defend the guild in the rip-roaring way we wanted? At that time we'd heard of a man by the name of Harvey O'Connor, the historian for the Oil Workers International Union, who had written many books, including the very popular *Mellon's Millions.* He was a muckraker who also exposed other large financial leaders, like the Guggenheims and Astors. He also wrote *Revolution in Seattle: A Memoir,* because Harvey had been a Wobbly [a member of the International Workers of the World] and a Socialist up in Seattle. He had written something in both English and Spanish regarding his appearance before the Joseph McCarthy committee. Harvey was called before that committee because his books had appeared in the overseas libraries of the U.S. government. Our State Department was trying to "teach freedom" to people around the world.

McCarthy found out about it and concluded the government was sending out subversive ideas. So McCarthy calls Harvey at his beautiful home on a point jutting into the Atlantic Ocean at Little Compton, Rhode Island, and makes him come down to Washington to appear before McCarthy's committee. That makes Harvey mad and he refuses to answer any questions on the grounds of the First Amendment. That was a dangerous thing to do in those days. Later he was called before HUAC a couple of times and he gave them the same treatment—and got by with it. Very courageous. I think Harvey was one of the first really important national figures called before McCarthy who refused to answer on First Amendment grounds. Harvey always won the legal battles. Later, when he was the chairman of the Committee to Abolish HUAC and I was executive director and I was fortunate enough to go to jail, Harvey would jokingly say to me, "What will I ever say to my grandchildren when they ask me, 'Grandpa, why didn't *you* go to jail during the McCarthy years?'" Harvey's comment was, "God knows I tried, but I never made it."

In other words, he was a very radical guy—just the sort to bring in a crowd for our banquet. Here I am feeling like a pariah and I'm calling across the country to a well-known person to ask him to come out here to speak to defend the radical National Lawyers Guild under attack by the attorney general and by HUAC. I shall never forget the conversation— me, trying to explain the situation just right and his cutting me off with a robust, "Well, I should think so! I'll be glad to come." I don't know what I would have done if he had said no, because I was in no position to be put down.

Everyone was thrilled that he was coming. I think we got six hundred people, an amazingly large turnout, considering it was at the height of the McCarthy period. As I said, we charged ten dollars, a hefty price in those days, and the place was literally jammed. I'm not talking hotel tables, but long boards on sawhorses, like in a church basement–type dinner. It was packed. I'm sure if the fire marshals had come to the banquet, they would have closed it down.

Harvey made a magnificent fight-back speech, and then others followed in the spirit of a football rally.

Many jokes were made about that dinner. We raised an enormous amount of money, but Harvey O'Connor still says his life was shortened by the piece of chicken that he got from the Royal Palms Hotel that night."

Beginning with that banquet—and from then on—every time any un-American activities committees, state and federal, or Senator Eastland's committee, or any group of an inquisitorial nature came to Los Angeles—and they were coming into California at least three or four times a year—Frank and his supporters fought back, raising funds, issuing pamphlets, picketing the committees, and recruiting supporters to crowd into the inquisitorial chambers.

▪

ONE REASON FRANK'S CCPAF fight-back operation was so successful was that its leadership was made up largely of professional people, or at least people who were from an upscale background. Frank—with an upper-crust upbringing and years spent honing his social and political talents in college and on the lecture circuit and as a housing bureaucrat with a program to sell—was a natural to lead this operation. And the CCPAF was remarkably successful in going to the employers of persons subpoenaed to appear at a HUAC session and asking for a period of tolerance.

"Time after time," he recalls, "we saved jobs."

We set up special committees to visit employers, to sit down with them and earnestly give our reasons for why they should be patient. "Don't fire this social worker. Don't fire this musician. Don't fire this teacher. Watch what's going on and see if you don't agree that this whole HUAC thing is an unconstitutional attack." We'd send distinguished citizens to visit a school principal, or a trade union leader, or a corporate big shot, and reason with them on their level.

Because there were no headlines to be made by rounding up riff-raff, HUAC subpoenaed mostly people of special talents—writers, lawyers, teachers, artists, publicists, actors, musicians. This was a break for Frank, since such people could be put to creative use in the fight-backs: writing newspaper ads deriding HUAC, or sending out flyers of the same temper (when the FBI hadn't stolen CCPAF's mailing list, which on several occasions it did), or doing radio spots.

Perhaps the most creative fight-back was put on by a group of subpoenaed musicians. When they gathered for Frank's usual briefing, somebody looked around the room and said jokingly, "Hey, we've got a whole orchestra here. All we're missing is a piccolo player. Let's have a concert." The suggestion was immediately taken up. There weren't really enough musicians, but by recruiting some help from non-subpoenaed musicians—including a distinguished cellist—they had an acceptable ensemble for a concerto. The program was planned, to be followed by a jazz set.

Los Angeles being the swinging city it was, when word of what these suspected subversives were up to got out to the art colony, enough money poured in to enable Frank to rent the Embassy Auditorium and pay for a full-page ad in the *Los Angeles Times*—with a picture of an English horn in the center of the ad, and all around the horn many little Sherlock Holmeses. They were dressed in London Fog raincoats, each holding a spyglass and obviously looking for Communists. Under the title line of the ad were printed the words "Force and Violins," and below that was the invitation: "Come to the Concert, Embassy Auditorium."

Twelve hundred people showed up.

But perhaps the most impressive evidence of this fight-back's success was the influence it had on Mrs. Norman Chandler, the mainstay of the Los Angeles Philharmonic Orchestra. Among the musicians subpoenaed by HUAC on this occasion were four members of the Philharmonic. Chandler's husband was the publisher of the *Los Angeles Times*, and the *Times* hated Communists, but she wasn't going to let that interfere with the most prized part of her life. She personally announced that no member of the Los Angeles Philharmonic Orchestra would ever be removed simply because they were called for questioning by those busybodies from Washington.

CHAPTER 16

The Slow Evolution Toward the First Amendment Challenge

PANIC WAS USUALLY the first reaction of those subpoenaed to appear at a congressional inquisition. After 1953, when hearings were held in Los Angeles, it was Frank's job at CCPAF to round up the people subpoenaed and get them all together in one room. For every hearing, that meant at least half a dozen potential victims whom he needed to calm down before they did something stupid. The most effective calming drill was to explain how to get through the legal maze that lay ahead. For this, Frank would get one of his lawyer friends at the ACLU (the Los Angeles ACLU was far more eagerly combative toward HUAC than was the national ACLU) to drop around and inform the group of the available choices.

Actually, there was only one *safe* choice. If a witness refused to answer questions and gave no constitutional reason for his or her silence, that was an almost guaranteed way to be convicted of contempt of Congress. Also, the Supreme Court was still a long way from making it safe to cite the First Amendment as a reason for silence; the Hollywood Ten had all taken the First in 1947 and wound up in prison for contempt. So all that was left was the Fifth Amendment. Unfortunately, its wording—"nor shall any person . . . be compelled in any criminal case to be a witness against himself"—was easily interpreted to mean that whatever a person refused to say would have indeed been "against" that person. The Fifth had a spotty reputation; too many bootleggers and swindling bank presidents had stood mum behind it. In the public mind, taking the Fifth had come to be equated with silently admitting guilt. Given its reputation, the inquisitorial committees became rather fond of the Fifth and accepted a witness's taking it as a satisfactory victory.

In 1947, screen star Zero Mostel confronted HUAC in a small dining-room-turned-hearing-room at the Hollywood Roosevelt Hotel. HUAC craved big headlines, which is why they so often targeted film stars. Mostel got huge headlines this time, and his performance disappointed no one inside the closed hearing room. The scores of radio, TV, and newspaper reporters were left packed outside the door; but thanks to Mostel's lawyer, Frank got a seat at the counsel table.

Frank recalls:

> It began with the committee's counsel immediately launching his attack. "Mr. Mostel, are you or are you not a Communist?" I mean, bang, bang, like that. Zero leaped out of his chair behind the counsel's table, knocking the microphones to the floor, and reached for the throat of HUAC's attorney while shouting, "That man called me a Communist! Get him out of here! He asked me if I'm a Communist! Get him out of here!"
>
> The committee was roaring with laughter. They were delighted. Here they had Zero Mostel all to themselves, on stage, in a private dining room. Zero went on playing and parlaying with them for at least twenty minutes, responding to their questions by reciting each amendment in the Bill of Rights.
>
> Finally, HUAC's lawyer cautiously said, "Mr. Mostel, we know all about those amendments. We simply want to know are you, or are you not, claiming the Fifth Amendment."

He didn't ask Zero, "Are you or are you not a Communist." He asked him, "Are you or are you not claiming the Fifth Amendment." What they wanted him to say was "Yes." After another ten minutes of sparring, Zero said, "Yes, I'm claiming the Fifth Amendment."

The hearings were stopped right there. The committee's PR guy goes to the door and opens it. He doesn't say a word to the crowd of reporters. He just holds up five fingers, and the press dashes off to the telephones there in the hotel. The headlines the next morning: "Zero Mostel Pleads Fifth Amendment at HUAC Hearing."

Obviously, the government was beginning to successfully reduce the Fifth to little more than a theater prop. That made Frank very angry and very unhappy.

To bring the fight with HUAC back to its proper constitutional focus, somebody would have to risk his or her freedom by challenging the committee on First Amendment grounds rather than on the Fifth. This was Frank's challenge.

From then on, at his meetings with subpoenaed witnesses, after going through the usual drill, Frank would ask if among them there was anyone willing to risk taking the First Amendment. That daredevil volunteer, he promised, would be given support by the ACLU all the way to the Supreme Court. As an added enticement, he promised—quite accurately—that if they won at the Supreme Court level, their name would have a revered place in legal history.

Not surprisingly, no volunteer willing to swap the certainty of Fifth Amendment freedom for the vague chance of First Amendment honor appeared.

Then came HUAC's 1956 visit to Los Angeles. It would have been just one more visit like all of its other visits, except that Frank Wilkinson had just read Alexander Meiklejohn's testimony to the U.S. Senate, and it had changed the direction of Frank's life and the entire nature of the fight-back against HUAC.

◼ FIRST, AS BACKGROUND, "THE" TESTIMONY OF 1955

Alexander Meiklejohn was one of those people who have an enormous influence on life in the United States but never become well known to the general public. Meiklejohn was no lawyer—he was an educator, and a very distinguished one[1]—but for many years, among the practitioners of constitutional law, he was considered to be one of the nation's foremost authorities on the First Amendment.

His interpretation of that amendment was already well known to scholars, but it started getting more public notice when in 1947 HUAC successfully put the "Hollywood Ten" into prison for refusing to say whether or not they were or had ever been Communists. The First Amendment had traditionally been used to protect the right to *do* certain things (freedom of speech, press, assembly, etc.), but the Hollywood Ten took the position that if it protected the right to speak, it also protected the right *not* to speak. So they were silent—except for the abundant insults they flung at the committee—when asked about their politics.

When this case reached the Supreme Court, Meiklejohn and Carey McWilliams, editor of the *Nation*, submitted an amicus curiae brief (and recruited many distinguished Americans to cosponsor it) arguing that the First Amendment implied the right to silence because citizens might hesitate to participate actively in politics if they could be called before inquisitorial committees and questioned about their beliefs in circumstances where the answers might hurt them.

Today this point of view is taken for granted; then it was not. In fact, it was considered heretical. Meiklejohn wrote a shorter version of the brief for the December 12, 1953, issue of the *Nation*, a magazine whose stock in trade was heresy.[2] At that time, Frank Wilkinson was not yet paying attention to Supreme Court arguments about the First Amendment. Nor was he aware of Meiklejohn's testimony before the Hennings Senate subcommittee in 1955—which was hardly surprising, since the general press gave it no attention, either.

■

THOUGH A CLOSE reading of the history of the 1950s might lead one to conclude that Congress in those days was quite hopeless, in fact, some members were fighting the good fight. Senator Thomas Carey Hennings Jr., of Missouri, was among them. He was elected to the Senate on a platform opposing McCarthyism—and this was in 1950, when McCarthyism was at its most virulent and when opposition to it was most dangerous.

Senator Hennings decided to do what he could to purify the atmosphere. So when he was named chairman of the Senate Judiciary's Subcommittee on Civil Rights in early 1955, he changed its name to Subcommittee on Constitutional Rights and authorized it to investigate possible violations of the Bill of Rights. To open the investigation with just the right tone of gravity, he invited four of the nation's most distinguished Bill of Rights scholars to drop in and enlighten the senators.

Meiklejohn was one of them. Here is just a fraction of what he told the senators in the stern but long-suffering tones of an aged professor (Meiklejohn was eighty-three) addressing a group of cocky undergraduates who have failed to do their homework properly. It's quoted here at length because Frank Wilkinson says reading it "changed my life," and that was no exaggeration.

> The First Amendment seems to me to be a very uncompromising statement. It admits no exceptions. It tells us that the Congress and, by implication, all other agencies of the government are denied any authority whatever to limit the political freedom of the citizens of the United States. It declares that with respect to political belief, political discussion, political advocacy, political planning, our citizens are sovereigns, and the Congress is their subordinate agent. . . .
>
> We, the people, who have enacted the First Amendment, may by agreed-upon procedure modify or annul that amendment. . . . We Americans, as a body politic, may destroy or

limit our freedom whenever we choose. But what bearing has that statement upon the authority of Congress to interfere with the provisions of the First Amendment? Congress is not the government. It is only one of four branches to which the people have denied specific and limited powers as well as delegated such powers. And in the case before us, the words "Congress shall make no law . . . abridging the freedom of speech," give plain evidence that, so far as Congress is concerned, the power to limit our political freedom has been explicitly denied. . . .

Whatever may be the immediate gains and losses, the dangers to our safety arising from political suppression are always greater than the dangers to that safety arising from political freedom. Suppression is always foolish. Freedom is always wise. That is the faith, the experimental faith, by which we Americans have undertaken to live. . . .

If men are not free to ask and to answer the question, "Shall the present form of our government be maintained or changed?"; if, when that question is asked, the two sides of the issue are not equally open for consideration, for advocacy, and for adoption, then it is impossible to speak of our government as established by the free choice of a self-governed people. . . .

No belief or advocacy may be denied freedom if, in the same situation, opposing beliefs or advocacies are granted that freedom. If on any occasion in the United States it is allowable to say that the Constitution is a good document, it is equally allowable, in that situation, to say that the Constitution is a bad document. . . . If it may be said that American political institutions are superior to those of England or Russia or Germany, it may, with equal freedom, be said that those of England or Russia or Germany are superior to ours. These conflicting views may be expressed, must be expressed, not because they are valid, but because they are relevant. If they are responsibly entertained by anyone, we, the voters, need to hear them. When a question of policy is "before the house," free men choose to meet it, not with their eyes shut, but with their eyes open. To be afraid of any idea is to be unfit for self-government. Any such suppression of ideas about the common good, the First Amendment condemns with its absolute disapproval.

The freedom of ideas shall not be abridged.[3]

■

THE GOVERNMENT PRINTING Office's record of that sub-committee meeting does not tell us whether members were sleeping by the end of Meiklejohn's long lecture, or whether they were standing and cheering. Since much of what he said was aimed at diminishing the power that Congress had assumed and scolding it severely for its attempted limitations on political association and speech, the reaction was probably mixed.

But the effect on Frank, when he got around to reading it, was to inspire undiluted worship of Meiklejohn's philosophy and—to only a slightly lesser degree—of the man himself.

■ WILKINSON'S EPIPHANY

In early December 1956, a three-man subcommittee of HUAC (Clyde Doyle of California, chairman, plus Harold Velde of Illinois and Gordon H. Scherer of Ohio) announced that it was coming to Los Angeles to inquire into the suspiciously subversive activities of the Los Angeles Committee for the Protection of the Foreign Born, another of the harassed organizations that Frank had helped to organize.

The subpoenaed people met and decided to hold a large, public fight-back meeting the night before the HUAC inquisition was scheduled to open. Somebody in the group was inspired to suggest that Meiklejohn be recruited to make the rallying speech and to build it around the testimony he had given to the Hennings committee. Since Frank did the inviting for the group, he thought it only polite to read Meiklejohn's lecture before he met him.

He read it, and then he reread it that evening, and he was overwhelmed. On finishing the second reading just before midnight, his decision came with remarkable ease: the next time he was summoned to confront an inquisitorial committee, *he would stand on the First Amendment.*

He didn't have long to wait. A subpoena from HUAC arrived the next morning at seven o'clock. He phoned A. L. Wirin and Fred Okrand, lawyers at the ACLU office in Los Angeles, and said, "We've been looking for months to get a First Amendment volunteer. OK, we've got one. Me!"

Most of the men who operated at the heart of the Los Angeles ACLU were strongly behind Frank, which made it unique among its chapters in the nation. None was more supportive than Wirin, the Southern California ACLU's general counsel, who would be Frank's attorney when he appeared at the HUAC grilling. Wirin was such a devout believer in the First Amendment that he even had the grudging and bewildered admiration of California's "Little HUAC," which in its June 1961 report acknowledged that he was "somewhat of an enigma." It pointed out that, on the one hand, he was a member of the National Lawyers Guild, which had been cited as a Communist-dominated organization, and had participated in other organizations that were openly sympathetic to the Communist cause; but that on the other hand, "his defiance of the Communist Party line, his ouster as counsel of the Communist-dominated CIO unions and his representation of anti-Communist organizations and individuals speak for themselves."

The committee then offered what it said was a typically bewildering example of Wirin's First Amendment devotion: when the anti-Semitic prophet of doom Gerald L. K. Smith applied for permission to speak at a Los Angeles high school, the only organization that insisted on letting him speak was the ACLU, through Wirin.

Then, when permission was granted by the Board of Education and Smith started his program at the appointed time, Wirin, himself a Jew, joined the picket line outside the building carrying a sign urging people not to attend a meeting addressed by a notorious anti-Semite. But when he found people being physically restrained from entering the building, he began picketing to protest that restraint.

We presume that three signs would probably have been necessary for Mr. Wirin under these circumstances: one urging that Smith had a right to speak, the second urging people not to go hear him, and a third protesting against people being prevented from hearing him.

Sometimes these matters can become very complicated.

■

HOWEVER, SOME OF Frank's most faithful supporters up to this point, lawyers who had been part of the Hollywood Ten's defense team and knew the inevitability of prison and heartbreak that came with taking the First, begged him not to do it. They tried their best arguments: the besieged left-wingers of Southern California needed him to keep organizing anti-HUAC rallies, and he couldn't do it from prison.

The Communist Party also was averse to Frank's taking the First Amendment. Their imprecations didn't get him to budge when he was subpoenaed to appear at HUAC inquisitions and Communist leaders pleaded with him to take the Fifth, as the safest way to avoid testifying. That wasn't Wilkinson's way. Safe or not, he was going to take the First Amendment. When they argued, "If you go to prison, we'll wind up having to support your family" he replied, "I wouldn't take a penny from you. Not a penny." And he didn't.

And what about his family; how would Jean and the three kids get by with him in prison? Nothing stirred him. He was determined to be a martyr. How did his family interact with this decision? For his daughter Jo, one of her most vivid memories and, as she says:

> . . . pivotal moments came when there was a discussion in
> our apartment on Waverly Drive in Los Angeles, about

Dad taking the First Amendment and challenging HUAC, in order to make it a test case before the Supreme Court. . . . I listened to the adults debate the plusses and minuses of such a position, and heard that the minus would be a prison term, away from his family. He said he was ready to face that.

He came into the living room, sat in a big chair, and I crawled into his lap. I asked him, privately, away from everyone else, what they had all been talking about. . . . In my mind, as a ten-year-old, I understood that what he was doing was a powerful and principled thing to do. But, I also wanted to know, right then, right there, whether or not he actually was a communist. . . . So, I asked him, sitting on his lap, in a special daughter-to-father, whispering private conversation, whether he actually was a communist. His body language and voice changed, and he spoke the words I had heard him speak over and over again at public rallies and meetings. "Until such time as . . . there is a free marketplace of ideas . . . I will refuse to answer that question . . . under the grounds of the First Amendment.[4]

"From that point forward, my relationship with my father fundamentally changed. I felt, right then, that I was no more special than the people sitting in the audience that he spoke to." She says she has tried to regain that specialness for most of the rest of her life.

■

AT THE HEARING, the manner in which Frank was questioned by Richard Arens, HUAC staff director, proved Frank's theory had been correct: HUAC's primary objective was to force or frighten witnesses into taking the Fifth Amendment. It was the easiest route to victory. Arens's coaxing shows that he fully expected, and wanted, Frank to take a Fifth Amendment defense from the very start.

After asking Frank for his name and getting it, Arens asked

for his address. Frank responded: "As a matter of conscience and personal responsibility, I am refusing to answer that question."

Arens answered sarcastically: "Do you have any other little reasons you want to give us now besides your conscience?"

Frank said he challenged the constitutionality of the committee.

Arens asked: "Do you have still another reason?"

Frank answered: "It is my belief—"

Arens responded: "We don't want to probe your beliefs here now. What is the reason why you don't want to tell us what your address is? Let's get to the point."

Frank said: "I feel that the House Committee on Un-American Activities stands in direct violation of the First Amendment of the Constitution."

Arens replied: "You have still got another reason now, haven't you? Let's get to that one. Do you honestly apprehend that if you told this committee truthfully what your address is you would be giving information that might be used against you in a criminal proceeding?"

Frank said: "I have the utmost respect of Congress to have the broadest possible powers to investigate. But Congress cannot investigate into areas in which it cannot legislate. And this Un-American Activities Committee attempts, by its mandate and by its practice, to investigate—"

Arens said: "You still have another reason, haven't you, in the back of your mind? Let's get to your real reason and then get on with the next question."

The "other reason" for not talking that Arens kept pressing and probing for was, of course, the Fifth Amendment, which, by that time, it was clear Frank was not even going to mention, much less take.

The committee was rattled. The three members, noticing that Frank wore a hearing aid, kept asking him if he understood or could even hear their questions. One member came down from the dais and stood behind him and asked in a loud voice if he could hear. Frank, in a loud voice, assured them he could.

Congressman Scherer was the most stubborn in trying to get it out of him. After one question Frank said, "I am answering no questions, on the grounds of my initial answer."

Scherer asked: "Does that initial answer include an invocation of the Fifth Amendment?"

Frank answered: "My initial answer stands as I made it."

Three more times Scherer asked Frank questions about his "initial answer" or his "original answer," got the same rebuff, and each time again asked if the rebuff was "based on the Fifth Amendment." And finally Scherer said, "If he's not going to take the Fifth Amendment, let's move on."

Surely, never was an unused Fifth Amendment such a disappointment to the members of HUAC.

■

TO PUNISH HIM for his silence, the subcommittee voted to ask Congress to indict Frank for contempt. But for some reason, they didn't push to see that Congress followed through on that threat. Perhaps they thought it wasn't a good time to challenge a First Amendment defense. Or perhaps they weren't certain he had even used the First Amendment. After all, except by implication, he had mentioned it only once, and then not as a personal defense but only to say that HUAC was violating the amendment.

So Frank had failed in his initial effort to be convicted of contempt of Congress and thereby finagle a way for the First Amendment defense to be tested in the Supreme Court.

■

BUT SOMETHING ELSE had happened in that same HUAC hearing that would ultimately guarantee a visit to the Supreme Court. This was the appearance of a witness we'll call Mrs. X.[5]

Before Frank testified and after Mrs. X had given the subcommittee a couple of documents, she recounted, at its request, her background: she was the wife of a naval officer stationed in

San Diego and had been approached by FBI agents several years earlier. They persuaded her to become an informer on the Democratic Party of San Diego. With a lucky break for an informer, she became chairman of the party's special committee dedicated to the abolition of HUAC. The year before the hearing, she had tried to set a trap for Frank. After he'd finished talking to several hundred people at the Rosslyn Hotel in Los Angeles, she introduced herself, said she had been impressed by his denunciation of the witch-hunters, and asked if he would come down to San Diego to deliver a similar lecture. He'd begged off and arranged to have Rev. A. A. Heist, the retired director of the Los Angeles ACLU and chairman of CCPAF, take his place. That being the first and last time Frank had seen Mrs. X, he promptly forgot her.

Now, halfway through his monotonous questioning of Frank, Arens asked, "If Mrs. X is still in the room, would she stand?" Then, to Frank: "Mr. Wilkinson, would you kindly look around over your left shoulder there at the lady who is standing in the rear of the hearing room? That lady, Mr. Wilkinson, testified here a little while ago under oath that she knew you as a member of the Communist conspiracy. Was she lying or telling the truth?"

Frank did not turn to look at the rather nondescript woman standing at the rear, and he gave his usual response, with only a slight variation: "I am answering no questions. This committee should be abolished, and the answer to that question is none of your business."

True enough, but the specter of this mystery witness would not be that easy to dismiss. It would, in fact, haunt him for years. So would the answers she had given earlier to Arens's questions.

Referring to the CCPAF, Arens had asked, "Was it Communist-controlled?"

Mrs. X: "Yes."

Arens: "Who was the ringleader in that organization?"

Mrs. X: "I didn't work in that organization and I don't know who the ringleader was. My contact on that committee was with Frank Wilkinson, I believe."

Arens: "Did you know him as a Communist?"

Mrs. X: "Yes."

Arens: "Have you any further information with reference to these two documents to which you are now alluding?"

Mrs. X: "Yes. Mr. Wilkinson asked me to start a similar organization or branch of that organization in San Diego. He said that he would give me a list of professional people—teachers, doctors and lawyers—in the San Diego area and that I should contact them in an attempt to set up such a committee in San Diego. When I discussed this with Frank Wilkinson in Los Angeles, I said that since I wasn't a professional person—at that time I wasn't active publicly—perhaps it might be better to have somebody else head it."

The remarkable thing about Mrs. X's comments was that they were so unremarkable. The existence of the CCPAF and Frank's leadership in it had been the focus of many stories in the Los Angeles press. It was hardly a startling revelation that the CCPAF had recruited many professional people and intended to go on doing so as the best way to arouse public opinion against HUAC. Although she admitted she had never worked in the CCPAF and knew nothing about its leadership, Mrs. X was still absolutely certain it was "Communist-controlled." Any good defense attorney (if HUAC had allowed defense attorneys to speak, which it didn't) could have torn that claim to shreds, and the same fate would have befallen her wispy claim of a working relationship with Frank. He was her "contact"? "I believe" so, she said. And she offered the same amount of evidence—none—when asked about Frank's political persuasion.

Indeed, the dialogue between Mrs. X and Arens had been so brief, so undramatic, and essentially so trivial that the reader will wonder how in the world it could have had any impact on Frank's life. On the surface, the exchange seemed ridiculous, not damaging, and certainly not dangerous. But the FBI and HUAC would make it dangerous in many ways. Perhaps the most effective tactic was the FBI's circulation of literally thousands of copies of Mrs. X's testimony—edited and elaborated in such a way as to make it sound like an alarming exposé—to audiences wherever Frank gave his anti-HUAC lectures in the years ahead.

And it remains interesting that the person in Frank's Communist Party circle in Los Angeles, who didn't have to expand on the truth to say that he knew Frank as a Communist—even if a Rotarian kind of Communist, was not called to testify. This was a man—we could call him Mr. Y—who was in the small meeting and reading circle of social workers in the Communist Party in Los Angeles. He and Frank were the last members of that circle, and this man's quite reliable information to the FBI was cited by HUAC, and obviously known to the FBI. But they didn't use Mr. Y at the very public HUAC hearings—the California's Little HUAC, or the big national Atlanta meeting of HUAC. Why? What would he have said? That Frank just met with his local group, argued a lot about the CPUSA ordering him around to keep the Chavez Ravine project integrated when he wanted it more based on need? It's pretty likely the testimony wouldn't have been very exciting, but we'll never know. His words were not used to convict Frank. It was Frank's work to expand CCPAF and its work to abolish HUAC that made Frank truly dangerous, as Mrs. X alleged.

CHAPTER 17

The East Coast Was Watching with Admiration

ALTHOUGH FRANK HAD failed in his effort to become a First Amendment martyr in 1956, he and his Los Angeles compadres considered the hearings a success. He hadn't been the first in the nation to defy HUAC by taking the First. In fact, fifty-six others had beaten him to it—including his friends Pete Seeger, Corliss Lamont, and Harvey O'Connor. But he was the first to do it on the West Coast. Moreover, he had done it in such a sly fashion that members of the committee weren't even certain what his defense had been. The CCPAF and the local chapter of the ACLU were so pleased with the outcome that they printed up a thousand copies of the hearing's record and sent them to allies around the country.

In New York, their allies were particularly impressed. But they had already been impressed for some time with the CCPAF's Los Angeles fight-back campaigns and the local ACLU's enthusiastic part in them. In L.A. there was a spirit and a cooperative arrangement that had largely disappeared on the East Coast because of the strange Cold War attitude of the national ACLU's bureaucracy. The ACLU showed little enthusiasm for protecting the civil liberties of radicals and none at all for giving legal defense to persons suspected of being Communists. By the early 1950s, in the heart of the McCarthy era, things had gotten so bad that many "liberal" organizations like the ACLU seemed as fearful as politicians of being considered "soft on Communism."

Indeed, the ACLU even asked the FBI to screen its own boards and committees for their loyalty. This was part of a Faustian working arrangement that the ACLU and the FBI had started in the 1940s and that would continue into the 1960s. A number of ACLU insiders—including Irving Ferman, onetime director of the ACLU's Washington office, and particularly Morris L. Ernst, for many years the ACLU's general counsel (and ironically the lead attorney in a number of famous First Amendment cases) agreed to pass along to the FBI all sorts of intimate details of the ACLU's own functions. They also shared information on the politics and private lives of individuals who had confided in the ACLU.

In return, Hoover promised to help it keep Communist-free and prevent the HUAC from publishing any report critical of the ACLU. Hoover carried out his part of the bargain. But he got much more in return from Ernst and his crew. To help counteract the criticisms that liberals were constantly hurling at the FBI's conduct, Ernst made flattering speeches and wrote articles like the one that appeared in the December 1950 *Reader's Digest*, "Why I No Longer Fear the FBI." On occasion, Ernst actually served as Hoover's personal attorney, for which his reward would be a night out with Hoover at the Stork Club. He publicly called Hoover "a treasured friend."[1]

This left a dangerous void in the defense of civil liberties that needed to be filled. In 1951, Corliss Lamont, Carey McWilliams, I. F. Stone, Paul Lehmann, H. H. Wilson, Clark Foreman, and a few others took the initiative of setting up the Emergency Civil Liberties Committee (ECLC).

Even before the committee was formed, McWilliams of the *Nation*, Stringfellow Barr from Rutgers College, and Thomas I. Emerson of Yale had signed an open letter calling attention to "the critical need to provide adequate legal defense for the political pariahs of the Cold War"—the national ACLU certainly wasn't doing it. The response from "Cold War liberals" was typical. One of their leaders, historian Arthur Schlesinger Jr., was so outraged by the appeal that he took the pulpit of his *New York Post* column on September 2, 1951, to deliver a papal denunciation:

> None of these gentlemen is a Communist, but none objects very much to Communism. They are the Typhoid Marys of the Left, bearing the germs of infection even if not suffering obviously from the disease. . . . Those whose belief in the importance of civil freedom is so feeble that they could collaborate with Communists in the 1948 election at home [Schlesinger meant those who voted for Henry Wallace for president on the Progressive ticket—Wallace, the former Democratic vice president, former secretary of commerce, and lifelong corn farmer] . . . are clearly less interested in civil liberties than they are in something else. I doubt whether many liberals will fall for the [Thomas I.] Emerson bait. There can be no compromise between liberals and doughfaces.[2]

Schlesinger was further outraged when McWilliams observed in the *New Statesman* on December 8, 1951, that Schlesinger's "was the language of McCarthyism even if spoken with a Harvard accent."[3]

▪

THE PRO–COLD WAR forces, ranging from people like Schlesinger in the center to J. Edgar Hoover on the right, created such an intimidating climate of opinion in the early and mid-1950s that wealthy donors were reluctant to be identified with liberal publications like the *Nation*. Its readers were loyal, but sponsors were hard to find. Indeed, it wouldn't have survived if McWilliams hadn't got help from Aubrey Williams's *Southern Farmer* in Alabama. McWilliams installed a teletype system over which copy was transmitted from New York to Aubrey Williams's plant in Alabama. Williams also extended a generous amount of credit.

For a period of some years in the 1950s, only the *Nation*, along with the *National Guardian*, edited by James Aronson and Cedric Belfrage (until the FBI drove Belfrage out of the country), and I. F. Stone's newsletter, which made its debut in January 1953, survived as "intellectual" publications of general interest that were critical of the Cold War.

The *New Republic* was a different creature. First of all, in regard to budgetary comforts, it had the good luck to be edited by Michael Straight and Frank Wilkinson's friend Gilbert Harrison, both of whom had tons of money at their disposal—Straight by birth and Harrison by marriage. Furthermore, while both men were liberals, they were not critics of the Cold War. (Straight had even once been a spy for the Soviet Union, then was reconverted to capitalism and became an informer.)

But this split personality of the liberal Left was, by 1957, beginning to show a few, if only a few, signs of dissipating. Pressures were beginning to ease, if only slightly. McCarthy, like Dickens's Marley, was dead (he died in 1957) and the clanging chains of McCarthyism did not ring quite so loudly in the nation's ongoing nightmare. The most promising development of the year was two decisions handed down at the U.S. Supreme Court on June 17, 1957—which conservative commentators quickly dubbed "Red Monday." In *Yates v. United States*, the justices virtually killed the prosecution of Communists under the Smith Act by ruling that only overt acts, not just abstract advocacy, could be considered an effort to overthrow the government. And in *Watkins v. United States*, the Court struck down a congressional contempt citation by ruling that (1) a subpoenaed witness could not be forced to talk about the Communist activities of others, and (2) congressional hearings must have some legitimate purpose and Congress could not turn a hearing into a sporting event—that is, "expose for the sake of exposure." It was this case of which Chief Justice Earl Warren mused, "Who can define what is meant by the term *un-American*?" (a remark that made Frank and his attorneys think they might have some chance when their case reached the Supreme Court in 1961).

Encouraged by these developments, and impressed by the program Frank was running in Los Angeles, the founders of the ECLC invited Frank to join them in New York, to become the ECLC's field director of an effort not only to supply legal defense for victims of HUAC subpoenas, but to launch a national campaign to actually get rid of it altogether.

Frank couldn't resist the offer. He loved the idea of going national, and the thought of having New York as his base set him on fire with enthusiasm. It gave him, he says, "unbelievable dreams, energies, drives." Having already learned that an underdog could not win in ideological combat without a reasonable amount of money, he started planning a giant fundraiser in New York even before he left Los Angeles. What more appropriate place to pass the hat than Carnegie Hall?

Frank's family packed up and went with him, living first with Corliss Lamont and then in a small apartment in New York. This job was the beginning of Frank's national touring to abolish HUAC and defend the right of dissent. The field trips would continue a lifetime, and make him pretty much an absentee father and husband. Through the tribulations to come, Jean and the kids would have to weather their storms on their own terms. Frank would be the national hero and martyr.

Frank was full of confidence in going national. He had just arranged a dinner that had raised a hefty amount—at least, it was the most the CCPAF had ever raised in Los Angeles—to subsidize the lawsuit *Wilson v. Loew's* against the motion picture studios' blacklist. Eight hundred had paid to hear speeches by noted historian Henry Steele Commager and by Dalton Trumbo, who had become one of the superheroes of the "Hollywood Ten."

HUAC may have made Trumbo a jailbird, but his great talent had again quickly, if surreptitiously, rocketed him to the top of his profession. Navasky wryly recounts Trumbo's comeback victory: "In 1956, the Academy Award for the best motion picture story went to one 'Robert Rich' for *The Brave One*, and when he failed to show up to accept it (those in attendance were told he was at the bedside of his wife, who was about to give birth to their first baby), rumors spread that Rich also traveled under the name of Dalton Trumbo."[4]

Having survived the worst that HUAC could do, Trumbo now had the kind of sympathetic appeal that Muhammad Ali had when he regained his heavyweight title after being banned from boxing for opposing the Vietnam draft.

He would be delighted, he said, to star at Frank's first New York fundraiser. But Frank also wanted an academic. He went after Hugh H. Wilson, the left-wing Princeton professor who was spending the summer at a Connecticut inlet.

Aware of Wilson's reasonable affection for alcohol, Frank took along a half-gallon of gin to make his recruitment more appealing. By midnight, both men were diving off Wilson's dock nude, the professor repeatedly yelling, "Of course I'll be there." Frank's only worry was that "Hubie" might not be sober for the Carnegie Hall event.

But he was, and he made a brilliant and prescient speech that night, calling for a term limit for the FBI directorship, an idea that became law in 1968 when Congress enacted legislation limiting the tenure of the FBI director to ten years and requiring Senate confirmation. So sensitive was the FBI to criticism that from then on its file on Wilson would contain the inflated accusation that he had called for the utter demolition of the bureau.

■ A NIGHT TO REMEMBER

The night of the fund-raiser, September 15, 1957, was unpleasantly hot and humid, and a hundred Hungarian "freedom fighters," whose ire was up because of the Soviet crushing of Hungarian rebels in 1956, stood outside Carnegie Hall spitting at and cursing the people who streamed into the packed hall. The program was about half over when the "freedom fighters" ignited a stink bomb inside the hall. The audience, in amazing good humor and good order, retreated to the street while the auditorium was aired out, then returned for a comical riff—Wilkinson and Trumbo arguing over whether the bomb should properly be pronounced "stench" or "stink"—and settled down for more of the rhetoric they had come to hear.

Frank was convinced that the harassment had been orchestrated by the FBI, but data obtained years later indicated it could just as easily have been stage-managed by the CIA.[5]

The Carnegie Hall success was followed in December 1957 with a Civil Rights Banquet (Frank was the main speaker this time) that drew more than eight hundred people. There had been no advance commitments, but it raised twenty-five thousand dollars, a huge amount in those days. His pitch had been: "From now on, we will do nationally what our group did in Southern California. We'll organize. We'll save jobs. We'll build opposition to the un-American committee. Call ECLC! If HUAC comes to your town, call ECLC! We'll meet every HUAC hearing with an organized protest within twelve hours anywhere in the country. We'll provide competent legal counsel for free. We'll fill every hearing room with family and friends determined to honor each subpoenaed individual with an effective fight-back. We'll kill these witch hunts with the Bill of Rights!"

Frank remembers the two fundraisers as "putting the ECLC, nationally, way, way up high in terms of being the organization that was working for the abolition of HUAC. There was a real resurgence. There began to be a feeling, 'We're out of the Cold War. We're leaving McCarthyism behind'"—which, unfortunately, was far from accurate.

■ A BIG TEST, UNDER IMPOSSIBLE CONDITIONS

Frank didn't have to wait long in the winter of 1958 before he was called to organize fight-backs in several cities. The one that showed most dramatically that his strategy could work began with a panicky telephone call from Gary, Indiana. Five days had elapsed since the subpoenas had been handed out, which made a successful response unlikely.

The caller wouldn't give his name. "I can't tell you. But I know what you look like. Take such-and-such flight and I'll pick you up at the airport." There, the caller introduced himself as a music teacher and head of the Communist Party in Indiana. Thus began the kind of trip that East Germans must have taken to shake pursuers when fleeing to West Germany before the Berlin wall was built. Frank was driven to three locations, each time changing cars and drivers, before being deposited at the home where he was to stay.

He had entered a world of pure panic. During this circuitous trip, he learned the cause: There were ten United steelworkers in Gary who had been subpoenaed to appear at an upcoming HUAC hearing. Somebody had identified them as Communists. They were so fearful that for the five days since they'd gotten their subpoenas they had refused to meet anyone—including each other. They wouldn't even allow their attorneys to talk to the other attorneys. One family of five steelworker siblings was divided by the fear that one might be an informer.

Frank was holed up in the home of a sympathetic Gary businessman and somebody lent him a very old car that had no heater. The weather was ten degrees below zero and Frank, having just returned from Los Angeles, had rushed from New York in such a hurry that he was still wearing a gabardine suit and a light trench coat. The family he was staying with in Gary loaned him a scarf and gloves, but it was a rough three days spent driving around Gary trying to talk to the spooked accused, trying to get them together to plan a strategy. Some of them would only open the door a crack and size him up while he talked to them from the porch.

"Finally," Frank recalls, "my pleas were heard. A meeting was arranged at the home of the oldest among the group. We all gathered there with a great sense of relief, because they had found that the informer wasn't one of them."

But the men had stalled so long that Frank was desperate for help in building a fight-back. As part of it, his clients obviously needed legal advice in the worst way. U.S. Steel had announced that anybody who was called before HUAC and took the Fifth would be fired at once; the union, United Steelworkers of America, supported the company's position. If the steelworkers took the Fifth, they would be blackballed throughout the industry, and in the late 1950s being out of work in Gary was not a pleasant prospect. On the other hand, if they stood on the First Amendment, they would likely follow the "Hollywood Ten" into prison.

These liberal people I was staying with told me, "Well, there used to be an ACLU chapter here in Gary and Rabbi so-and-so used to be head of it. But it's dormant now." I called the rabbi and got some of the ACLU people together to plan a strategy. We raised $1,200 and took a full-page ACLU ad in the morning *Gary Post* on the day of the first hearing, urging everyone to show up for all the hearings. The *Gary Post* was a small paper, so a full-page ad stood out. And as a result of the work I had been doing for several years, I could fill the ad with all kinds of information about prominent people, like Eleanor Roosevelt, who were speaking out against HUAC.

The fight-back was wonderful. We were able to pack the hearings, not just with friends of the subpoenaed people but with remnants of the liberal community. The men had excellent legal representation. The ECLC had sent out Victor Rabinowitz, a Lawyers Guild member and one of the best civil liberties lawyers in New York, but the local Gary lawyers handled most of it and the ACLU chapter suddenly showed signs of life.

Pragmatically, my ten steelworkers decided to use the First. It was hardly philosophical idealism that moved them. It was the necessity of holding on to a job, at least until their case reached the Supreme Court in a few years.

After the hearings, everyone felt wonderful. The subpoenaed people got together with the liberal people who placed the ad—the ACLU people—and everyone was so happy they'd taken on HUAC. As it turned out, the government, apparently sensing it had a very weak case, agreed to select one of the men as a "test" and give him only a few months in prison—and let the others go free. I felt there was a touch of humor in the outcome; it could be said that HUAC—and U.S. Steel—saved nine "First Amendment Communists."

Almost as heartening to me, the old Calumet chapter of the ACLU voted to revive itself.

■ DESCENDING FROM CLOUD NINE

Frank came back to New York on a high, feeling he had achieved a breakthrough under almost impossible conditions. A special meeting of the ECLC was called that night to hear his report.

The people of Gary had fought back. The accused had obtained superb legal counsel for free. They had made a First Amendment challenge successfully. Above all, Frank had helped bring a dormant ACLU chapter to life, leaving the town with an organization to defend the future. Who could ask for more? It hadn't been easy. He spoke of the trouble he had had getting the defendants together. He described the fear and yet the coordination of the Communist Left in Chicago and Gary.

Most of the ECLC board was impressed. Izzy Stone and Carey McWilliams and Harvey O'Connor (who was at that time president of ECLC) certainly were. But to Frank's intense irritation, there were quibblers; somehow, the board had wound up with a couple of Cold War liberals as members. David Haber, a distinguished Rutgers professor and authority on civil liberties, told Frank he was wrong to work with Communists. The ECLC, he continued, should avoid them. Was Haber using this board meeting as an opportunity to criticize what everyone at ECLC must have been aware of: Frank's frequent and open visits to the New York City office of the Communist Party?

Frank became even angrier when Clark Foreman, who ran the ECLC office, said, "Well, why did you form an ACLU chapter? Why didn't you form an Emergency Civil Liberties Committee chapter?"

Trying to keep cool, Frank says, he answered, "Look, where there is an existing body, it is our job to work with them, not to set up something competitive. The fact that I left behind a viable ACLU chapter was one of the more important products of my trip. I feel that as an organizer, my job is to try to straighten out the ACLU wherever I can. Anyway, the ECLC is deliberately called the *Emergency* Civil Liberties Committee, and as soon as we can get the ACLU to clean up its act, then the emergency will be over and there will be no need for another group."

But he probably overreacted. He says he felt he had been called a traitor. In fact, most of the committee—and certainly the members he most respected—had judged him to have achieved an ingenious victory. But, he says, "from that moment on I was ready to go"—that is, return to Los Angeles. Probably his yearning to return to the old, familiar battleground was one reason he exaggerated the criticism.

But above all, he resented the quibbling from Clark Foreman. He considered Foreman a dilettante, a sluggard, lacking verve and the kind of aggressiveness the job called for. When Frank arrived in New York to take his new job, Foreman wasn't around. He was winding up a cushy three-month visit to France. Typical, thought Frank—just when the ideological wars needed him.

One incident, more than any other, persuaded Frank that, at bottom, Foreman was the kind of liberal he wanted little to do with—a "Cold War liberal" who joined conservatives in believing that those who maintained their political privacy by taking the Fifth Amendment were, in fact, probably disloyal to the country.

He had come to this conclusion when Congressman Francis E. Walter, a Pennsylvania Democrat and chairman of HUAC, wrote an article for the *Philadelphia Inquirer* describing the ECLC as a Communist-front organization. Foreman got permission from the *Inquirer* to write a response, in which he said that the ECLC could hardly be considered a Communist front since not a single member of the organization was a Communist. Before sending in his reply, he asked Frank to give it a critique. In Frank's memory of the resulting conversation, Foreman said, "What do you think of it, Frank?" "I think it's terrible," Frank replied. "Why?" asked Foreman. "Well, in effect," said Frank, "you sound just like the national ACLU, and you're heading an organization that was set up to shame the ACLU into defending the civil liberties of anyone, even Communists. By answering Walter's charges, you are acknowledging his power to do exactly what we're trying to take away from political inquisitors—the power to get answers to questions that aren't any of their business. Until such time as one can be a member of a proscribed political party without economic sanctions for refusing to answer, we won't have our civil liberties back. So those who are not Communists should not answer the questions, either."

Frank went on: "Beyond that, you say there are no Communists in ECLC. How do you know? Like any organization, we have fifty or sixty names running down the left margin of our letterhead. How do you know there are no Communists among them? How do you know there aren't any Communists on our board?"

Foreman replied, "I know, because I wouldn't allow them to be there."

"Clark, how do you know *I'm* not a Communist?"

Foreman laughed. "Well, Frank, you couldn't be. You used the First Amendment."

What a pity, thought Frank. Foreman had obviously bought into the very tactic that HUAC considered its greatest achievement: spreading the assumption that those who took the Fifth were probably Communists, could be dangerously disloyal, and should be shunned.

Although Foreman's adoption of this position did seem to undercut the very foundation of the ECLC, Frank should probably have been a bit more forgiving. In the first place, some of the left-wingers Frank admired most shared Foreman's judgment of the Fifth Amendment. Jumping into the future for a moment, we find I. F. Stone arguing in his March 6, 1961 *Weekly* that neither Frank nor his soon-to-be-jailmate Carl Braden was a Communist, and he was certain of that because "if they were, they would have taken the Fifth [instead of the First] as scores of hounded Communists and ex-Communists have done."

In the second place, as executive director of the ECLC, Foreman had over the years played a crucial role in raising money, for lawyers and bail, to keep integrationists out of jail. And Foreman had been fighting a good fight against the powers of darkness longer than Frank had, and could perhaps be forgiven for being gun-shy.

Foreman also played a bit part in another drama whose plot line would eventually converge with Frank's. To understand that drama, we next turn south.

CHAPTER 18

The South: Integration and Civil Liberties Entangle, and the SISS

■ FOREMAN, DOMBROWSKI, AND WILLIAMS

After serving as President Roosevelt's special adviser on race, Clark Foreman joined the Southern Conference for Human Welfare (SCHW), which had been founded with the support of Eleanor Roosevelt and a coalition hoping to inject more of the New Deal philosophy into Dixie. The administrator of the SCHW was James A. Dombrowski, a Christian socialist trained at Harvard and the Union Theological Seminary—which was enough to make him suspect in the Deep South.

Foreman and Dombrowski did not get along. Foreman felt that the influence of Communists was poison to left-wing politics, while Dombrowski had no trouble working with Reds. Their bickering reached such a peak that Foreman left to work in the Wallace campaign, and Aubrey Williams came in as codirector of the Southern Conference Educational Fund (which replaced the SCHW). To many southerners, the new partnership was surely subversive. For years, Dombrowski had guided the South's only integrated grassroots effort to end segregation. Williams had been one of the most talented—and most controversial—young men in Roosevelt's leadership as director of the National Youth Administration (NYA), which gave jobs to millions of young people, blacks as well as whites. Mississippi congressman John Rankin was among many southerners who saw such actions as "the beginning of a Communist dictatorship." That it might have helped enfranchise or empower blacks was certainly a threat.

When congressional right-wingers shut down the NYA in 1944, Roosevelt tried to appoint Williams to head the Rural Electrification Agency, a job Williams greatly desired because he knew electricity would transform rural life. He had many powerful supporters in and out of government, but their influence could not beat the racist conservatives who accused him of everything from "coddling" youth to creating equal employment opportunities where "whites are forced to use toilets with the blacks." (That accusation was the contribution of Senator Theodore Bilbo of Mississippi.) Several senators described him as a "Communist sympathizer," and the very accusation was enough to scare others away. Actually, he was one of the most anti-Communist officials to work in the New Deal.

His nomination was defeated in the Senate, fifty-two to thirty-six. Nineteen Democrats had voted against him; all but two were from the South.

■

OUT OF GOVERNMENT, Williams did not have to scramble for a livelihood. He was rescued by Marshall Field, the immensely wealthy Chicago department store heir who had been one of the investors in the short-lived but very liberal New York newspaper *PM* and continued to publish the *Sun* in Chicago. In 1945 Field bought the nearly defunct farm monthly *Southern Farmer*, published in Montgomery, Alabama, where the flag of the old Confederacy still flew over the state capital (and would continue to do so for half a century). Then he turned the magazine over to Williams, a longtime friend, with instructions to hire editors and writers of unbending liberalism who would start challenging the dominant political backwardness of the South. While publishing the magazine, Williams also served on the board of directors of the Southern Conference Education Fund (SCEF, a successor to civil rights group SCHW).

Proof that Williams and Dombrowski were making some headway was evident when they were subpoenaed to appear in New Orleans at a hearing of the Senate Internal Security Subcommittee on March 18, 1954.

■ A FEW WORDS ABOUT THE SISS

The Senate Internal Security Subcommittee (SISS) was not nearly so well-known as the HUAC, but it was much more powerful. Since 1951, it had been a permanent part of the Senate Judiciary Committee, through which passed 40 percent of all bills—bills touching on everything from immigration to civil rights, as well as judicial appointments and appointive jobs in the Justice Department. Usually the SISS's chairman was also chairman of the full committee, and in the congressional hierarchy, that made that person fearsomely powerful.

■

THE FOUNDING CHAIRMAN of SISS, and author of some of the most oppressive "national security" laws of the 1950s, was Patrick McCarran, a Nevada Democrat who became so successful in blocking the appointment of decent judges and federal attorneys that many would have agreed with Harold Ickes's appraisal of him as "the most socially retarded member of the Senate."[1] Such judgments didn't bother McCarran; he had no fear of losing his Senate seat, since he was in the pocket of the mining and gambling interests that ran his state. Nor did he care that President Truman hated him for turning his attorneys general into reactionary puppets. Because McCarran considered all immigrants, but especially Jews, to be potential Communist subversives, he used the McCarran-Walter Immigration Act of 1950 to keep their inflow down to a relative trickle. Laws he authored and pushed through Congress made it easy to fire federal employees without telling them why or giving them a way to appeal, and set up a mechanism for establishing concentration camps in this country for imprisoning left-wing dissidents during "emergencies."

The next chairman of SISS was the Republican senator from Indiana, William Jenner, about whom Dwight Eisenhower made one of his wisest judgments: "I felt dirty from the touch of the man."[2]

Jenner was followed by James Eastland, who was not nearly as important as McCarran as a witch-hunter but was one of the era's leading racists.

■ PERHAPS THE DEEP SOUTH'S GREATEST DEMAGOGUE

Senator Eastland was a rich planter who owned many thousands of acres around his home in Sunflower County, Mississippi—where 68 percent of the population was black, living and dying in uncomplicated peonage; where white-on-black violence flowed out as naturally as the passage of the seasons; and where one could easily stand in the middle of the Delta's steaming sameness and honestly believe that the world went straight out forever, flat all the way, made by a God who in his infinite wisdom gave Adam a cotton allotment.

Known in Mississippi as "Our Jim," a pillar of the Democratic Party and of every white-supremacy organization, Eastland was considered by most of his neighbors to be, as one admirer put it, "a kind planter who never whips his n*****s and would fire any white worker who did." But his black workers told another story. Most families who lived in his plantation shanties (some sleeping four to a bed) earned no more than a thousand dollars a year, and that much only by putting their children to work, sunup to sundown.

In *Time* magazine's judgment, Eastland was "the nation's most dangerous demagogue." Others had more colorful descriptions. Clarence Mitchell, spokesman for the NAACP, called him everything from "stinking albatross" to "accessory to murder and treason" to "mad dog loose in the streets of justice," designations that only made him more popular among white Mississippians.

His hold on the Judiciary Committee and its Civil Rights Subcommittee put him in a position to shape, retard, and pervert the civil rights movement more than any other man in America.

The *New York Times* credited Eastland's influence in the Judiciary Committee with bottling up 122 civil rights bills. He complained that the correct number was 127—"not one ever emerged."

His most famous speech in the Senate, delivered after the U.S. Supreme Court handed down its *Brown v. Board of Education* school-integration order in 1954, was a call to rebellion: "I know that Southern people, by and large, will neither recognize, abide by, nor comply with this decision. We are expected to remain docile while the pure blood of the South is mongrelized by the barter of our heritage by northern politicians in order to secure political favors from Red mongrels in the slums of the East and Middle West."[3]

▪ THE FARCICAL CONFRONTATIONS

So it was hardly surprising that Senator Eastland would summon two of the South's most aggressive integrationists—Dombrowski and Williams—to be publicly reviled at the SISS's 1954 hearing in New Orleans. It was the subcommittee's first hearing in the South and, not surprisingly, considering the outcome, its last. Doubtless Eastland assumed he could easily humble the men. He was in for a shock.

Also subpoenaed was Virginia Durr, an upper-middle-class native of Birmingham, Alabama, famous for her part in the SCEF's crusade to help blacks get the vote by ending the poll tax.

Her patriotism was obviously suspect, because not only was she aggressively pro-integration, she was (1) the sister-in-law of that well-known subversive Supreme Court justice Hugo Black, and (2) wife of Clifford Durr, the most liberal member of the FCC during the New Deal years. Durr had quit the FCC in protest against President Truman's antiliberal "security" program. Worse than that, Durr was a former president of the NLG. Indeed, it was during Durr's presidency that Hoover worked most furiously through his friends in the press to spread suspicions of the NLG's "subversive" character. Durr was on hand at the New Orleans hearing as Williams's attorney.

But it was Mrs. Durr who more or less saved the day. She had phoned her friend Lyndon Johnson one night shortly before the hearings were to be held and asked if he could persuade the two smartest senators on the SISS, John McClellan of Arkansas and Patrick McCarran of Nevada, to stay in Washington. He could, and did, leaving the inquisition to be presided over by a single senator, "Our Jim," who was simply not up to the occasion.

■ LET THE LYING BEGIN!

Like so many congressional inquisitions, this one became almost immediately incomprehensible, with overtones of farce. Unless Eastland was completely out of the loop, he must have known that none of the people he had subpoenaed were Communists and that, even if they were, they would never admit it. In three days of hearings, the only people who admitted they had ever been Reds were the two informers he was using, one by the name of Jack Butler—whose biography has been lost in the mists of history—and Paul Crouch, whose reputation was already so infamously tawdry that one has to believe Eastland was simply ignorant of it or he would never have asked for Crouch's help.

Each of the subpoenaed witnesses readily swore that they had never been a member of the Communist Party, so the only excitement Eastland's hearings could possibly provide would be believable testimony from others that they were lying and therefore subject to charges of perjury. For that, Eastland relied mainly on Crouch.

Twenty years before his starring role in the Eastland fiasco, Crouch had been court-martialed by the U.S. Army and sentenced to forty years in Alcatraz for trying to start a revolution in Hawaii. At his court-martial he admitted that he was, well, sort of a nut: "I am in the habit of writing letters to my friends and imaginary persons, sometimes to kings and other foreign persons, in which I place myself in an imaginary position."[4]

Somehow the government recognized that he had the makings of a swell patriotic liar, because he was freed after only three years and began working for congressional witch-hunters. But his "informing" about others was of questionable worth; in a case in which the Communist Party was a defendant, the U.S. Supreme Court ordered his testimony stricken from the record because he was known to have committed wholesale perjury in many other proceedings.[5] Informer Butler said he thought Mrs. Durr was a Communist, but he wasn't sure. Informer Crouch was sure. He said that back in the days when he was still active in the Communist Party, he'd known her as a very important undercover agent for the Soviet Union who used her kinship with Justice Black to introduce top Communists into White House circles and thereby make the Roosevelts unwitting accomplices to the "world Communist conspiracy in the interest of overthrowing our government."[6]

Later, when the committee room began to clear and her husband got close enough to make the threat meaningful, attorney Durr leaped to put his hands around Crouch's throat, yelling, "You dirty dog, I'll kill you for lying about my wife." Federal marshals separated them. Photographers loved the scuffle, but in fact Durr's chivalry wasn't nearly as eloquent an act as Mrs. Durr's insouciant powdering of her nose immediately after Crouch made his absurd accusation. Photographs of that gesture made front pages across the nation.

Back on the witness stand the following day, Crouch identified both Durr and Williams as Communists he had known in a prior part of his life, but his mind became a black hole when he was asked for details and dates. Rattled by the way his hearings were falling apart, Eastland then did something virtually never done in a HUAC or SISS hearing—he let Durr, attorney for the accused, cross-examine the accuser. Result: Crouch's answers became so obviously make-believe that spectators and reporters began to laugh, joined occasionally even by Eastland, who finally admitted he didn't think Williams was a Communist.

At first indifferent to the hearings, the press soon began to focus on them, to the embarrassment of some of the locals. The *Montgomery Advertiser* editorially orated in its best antebellum manner: "There is a matter of Southern honor involved here. A Southern gentleman and lady have been publicly branded with the most opprobrious term of the hour. They have denied it under oath. . . . This is the type of character lynching which Southern Senators should deeply resent."[7]

Some of the northern press poured scorn on the whole affair. The most effective was a widely syndicated series of columns by Joseph and Stewart Alsop, who studied countless court records and came up with such a detailed history of Crouch's false testimony over the years that Attorney General Herbert Brownell announced he would never again be used as a government witness. Crouch, acting with the kind of absurdity this era engendered, counter-attacked by accusing Brownell of being a Communist and asked the ACLU to help him in his fight. The next year, Crouch died; his widow, left penniless, appealed to Aubrey Williams for money, and got it. And from Durr, writing in *I. F. Stone's Weekly*, Crouch got a remarkably balanced obituary: " . . . not the source of evil, but its mere conduit. He did what he was hired to do. . . . He died a lonely and despised man by those who used him, but those who hired him remain in respectable and powerful positions."[8]

■ BUT IN THOSE DAYS, NICE GUYS SELDOM WON

By any civilized measure, Dombrowski and the Durrs and Williams had demolished Eastland. But this was an unsophisticated part of the United States, sodden with suspicions of anything "liberal" or "foreign," and they could not win. Because he had been identified as a Communist—never mind that the identification came from someone totally discredited—Durr's law practice in Montgomery, Alabama, never recovered, and his social circle shriveled.

Eastland worked an even greater vengeance on Williams. Before releasing the official version of the hearings, a copy was sent to the American Legion. Under the heading "Communism in Agriculture," the legion turned over two entire issues of its monthly publication *Firing Line* to long, cleverly edited excerpts from the New Orleans hearings, plus commentaries implying that Williams, his magazine, and the SCEF were instruments of the Communist conspiracy.

Firing Line had a huge circulation in the South, as indeed it had throughout the nation, and the legion's assault was devastating to Williams's printing business; the circulation of his magazine, *Southern Farm and Home*, plummeted, as did its advertising. In four years it was defunct.[9]

But Eastland wasn't through. For two decades, congressional "Un-American" investigators had been itching to get their hands on the files in Dombrowski's New Orleans headquarters. At the hearings, Eastland had twice threatened to charge Dombrowski with contempt if he did not produce all of the SCEF's records, including the names of the organization's three thousand patrons. Dombrowski refused, and in the hubbub of the hearings there was no follow-up.

But Eastland hadn't forgotten. Much later, he figured out how to get those records—with the cooperation of the New Orleans police and some members of the Louisiana Joint Legislative Un-American Activities Committee (an intriguing organization that had investigated and cleared the Ku Klux Klan, finding it to be only a "political action group" with "a certain Halloween spirit"). In a late-night raid, a dozen cops, guns drawn to make sure Dombrowski would not interfere (which was absurd, because Dombrowski was so arthritic he was on crutches), used a sledge-hammer to break down the door into his SCEF headquarters.

A charge of "criminal conspiracy" had been the pretext for the raid, and while Dombrowski and two SCEF attorneys were running around trying to find a judge who would throw out that charge, the invading force carted off the SCEF's twenty-year collection of extremely important data—and sent it to Senator Eastland.

Eventually he returned the records to SCEF, but only after every single piece had been photographed. For months thereafter, Eastland, with obvious glee, read into the *Congressional Record* the private correspondence to and from Dombrowski[10]—especially a number of poisonous letters that showed some sharp disharmony in the ranks of civil rights leaders.

It may not seem that the theft of Dombrowski's papers by Eastland is related in any way to Frank Wilkinson's crusade to destroy the HUAC, but in fact it has a vital relationship. A few years later, the two were brought together by outstanding teams of lawyers to ask the highest courts to outlaw the House Un-American Activities Committee because *its very existence*—which was to suppress opinion—was a violation of the First Amendment.

After the Louisiana raiders finished looting his office, Dombrowski and several people on his staff were charged with violating Louisiana's Communist Control Act, a crime that could land them in prison for ten years. In addition, Ben Smith, the SCEF's attorney, was charged with belonging to a "subversive organization," namely the NLG. If those charges were supported in court, the threat of their being used elsewhere would freeze the voter registration drive and other civil rights activities across the South. Their indictments had to be overturned.

For years nobody had been able to persuade a federal court to interfere with a state court's criminal proceedings and stop it in its tracks as unconstitutional. Nor had anyone been able to persuade any federal court to strike down states' antisubversive laws as violations of the First Amendment. But Arthur Kinoy, a combative Rutgers University law professor who seemed to pile into every civil rights fight, did both. He persuaded the U.S. Supreme Court in 1965 (*Dombrowski v. Pfister*) to declare the state antisubversive laws to be in violation of the First Amendment; the Court agreed with Kinoy's argument totally. Justice Brennan, speaking for the Court majority (only Justices Harlan and Clark dissenting), declared that the federal courts must prohibit any government action which has "a chilling effect upon the exercise of the First Amendment rights."

Any government action? Would the Court feel the same if asked to do away with Congress's "chilling effect"—namely the HUAC? Frank Wilkinson and Kinoy, asking that question in different but overlapping ways, would eventually find out.

CHAPTER 19

Tracking the Muddy Footprints
of the American Legion

THE TREATMENT AUBREY Williams got from the American Legionnaires was quite in keeping with their long record as patriotic vigilantes—tough guys who had been giving important support to strikebreakers, corporate propaganda campaigns, and government inquisitors since as far back as World War I.

With seventeen thousand posts and more than 3 million members down at the grassroots level—farmers, small-businessmen, skilled workers—it was one of the most powerful antiradical lobbies. It influenced the making of Hollywood's blacklist. Many in Congress paid close attention when the Legion's "Americanism Commission" gave a thumbs-down to labor and welfare programs, and a thumbs-up for bigger military budgets.

■ A GRAND PLOT TO GET RID OF "THAT RED IN THE WHITE HOUSE"

While its members were known for violently attacking striking workers, notably in 1919 against the Wobblies in Centralia, Washington, the American Legion was far better recognized for intellectual combat. There was, for example, the time when some officials of the legion played roles in, or at least approved, one of the most bizarre plots in American history. Hatched in the summer months of 1934 by some of the nation's top capitalists, its aim was literally to overthrow President Roosevelt's administration—and with it the government of the United States. In its place would be installed a group that would do the bidding of Wall Street. The plotters hoped to persuade members of the American Legion and the Veterans of Foreign Wars to become an army that would march on Washington in a coup d'état.

Knowing they needed a leader who could rally the troops, the plotters in the summer of 1934 sent Gerald MacGuire, a lawyer in the brokerage office of Grayson M. P. Murphy and an official of the American Legion, to recruit General Smedley Butler, former commandant of the Marine Corps and holder of two Congressional Medals of Honor. He was probably the most popular military man in America.

It's odd that the plotters thought Butler would be interested in joining their fascist plot; his hatred of fascism was headline material. A couple of years earlier, he had publicly described Italian dictator Benito Mussolini as "a mad dog about to break loose in Europe." The Republican State Department was upset by this honesty, and President Hoover told Butler either to retract the statement or resign. He resigned.

MacGuire's pitch to General Butler was that, under President Roosevelt, the nation was in great danger of a "Communist menace and could only be saved by the veterans." He said that, considering Butler's popularity, at least half of the American Legion and Veterans of Foreign Wars—easily five hundred thousand men—would follow him in a march on Washington.

MacGuire had a letter of support from Louis Johnson, the former national commander of the American Legion (and later President Truman's assistant secretary of defense). And MacGuire assured Butler that money would be no problem. That was certainly true; his employer, Grayson M. P. Murphy, was treasurer of the recently founded American Liberty League, whose 156 sponsors either headed or were on the boards of directors of the nation's biggest corporations: General Motors, U.S. Steel, E. I. Du Pont, etc. They were already sponsoring, in the name of the American Liberty League, many nationwide radio addresses demanding that "all government regulation of business should be abolished."[1] The planned overthrow of the Roosevelt regime would bring that about.

Butler strung the plotters along until he had the full picture of what they wanted to do, then went to J. Edgar Hoover. But Hoover, as Curt Gentry puts it, "knew a loaded gun when he saw one."[2] The plot sounded real to him, but he wasn't about to make enemies of all those corporate moguls; he said that because no federal laws had been broken, he couldn't investigate.

Butler next took his story to a private session of the Special House Committee on Un-American Activities, which called James Van Zandt, national commander of the Veterans of Foreign Wars, and Paul Comly French, a crusading reporter for the *Philadelphia Record*, both of whom had been taken into the confidence of MacGuire and learned of the plot. Both French and Van Zandt, under oath, corroborated what Butler had testified.

Apparently afraid that digging further might precipitate a national crisis, the committee stopped its investigation at that point. None of the corporate leaders implicated in the conspiracy were even called for questioning. The committee suppressed some of the evidence, but its official report on February 15, 1939 (note the five-year delay) confirmed the plot to overthrow Roosevelt.[3]

Gerard Colby Zilg notes in his history of the event that the committee's report brought a thundering silence from the press: "Of all the country's large newspapers, most of which were (and are) controlled by well-financed syndicates, only the liberal *New York Post*, French's Philadelphia *Record*, and two New Jersey papers printed the details of the conspiracy and the corroborating testimonies."[4]

Roger Baldwin, head of the ACLU, issued a properly prickly last word, noting that although the congressional committee acknowledged "the Fascist plot to seize the government was proved, yet not a single participant will be prosecuted under the plain language of the federal conspiracy act making this a high crime [a law J. Edgar Hoover apparently overlooked on purpose]. Imagine the action if such a plot were discovered among Communists! Which is, of course, only to emphasize the nature of our government as representatives of the interests of the controllers of property. Violence, even to the seizure of the government, is excusable on the part of those whose lofty motive is to preserve the profit system."[5]

Compared to planning the overthrow of the government or the cleaning up of Hollywood, the American Legion must have considered the destruction of Aubrey Williams's business small pumpkins indeed. When you consider that the American Legion believed it had the authority to overthrow the government, then it's obvious and even frightening that it was prepared to rid the country of every last Communist, Communist sympathizer, or like-minded individual—with the HUAC or without it.

CHAPTER 20

On Various Levels, a Momentous Year

IN ADDITION TO *Brown v. Board of Education*, in 1954 two other events of national implication were important in shaping Frank Wilkinson's life. One was Senator Eastland's revenge—via the American Legion—in driving Aubrey Williams out of business and, ultimately, into Wilkinson's anti-HUAC crusade. The other was a dynamite explosion in Louisville, Kentucky, that blew up a black family's home and, coincidentally, sent Carl Braden to prison—for the first time. Later, he would go back to prison with Frank.

Carl Braden (named after Karl Marx) was a gruff, no-nonsense copy editor on the *Louisville Courier-Times*. He was the son of a radical, often unemployed, railroad-worker father and a Catholic mother. She got Carl into a Catholic preparatory seminary, where he stayed for three years, or long enough to learn that religion wasn't the answer. Neither, he decided, was fighting or boozing, though in his tough neighborhood he had learned to do both. Having helped put out the school newspaper for a couple of years, Carl quit school at sixteen and got a job as a police reporter. True, he had little schooling, but he was a voracious reader—happily spending hours poring over dictionaries and encyclopedias (a habit that was great for killing time when he was in prison)—and, anyway, backwater newspapers didn't expect stylish writing. Later, he began reporting on labor affairs for various regional newspapers, and by 1954 he had graduated to the *Louisville Courier-Journal*, which had some class.

He and his wife, Anne, were liberal activists, a reputation easily earned in Louisville in those days by not doing much more than talking liberal and perhaps voting for Henry Wallace. But Carl was a pushy kind of fellow, just waiting to put a real dent in society's conservatism, and in 1954 he got his chance.

Andrew Wade IV was an African American World War II veteran who had come back to Louisville from the war with the notion that his service at least entitled him to buy a decent house in a decent neighborhood. The U.S. Supreme Court had outlawed restrictive covenants in 1948, but real estate agents and lending institutions helped whites keep their neighborhoods white by raising all sorts of hurdles. Consequently, most Louisville blacks continued to live in seedy, segregated housing projects. In the five years before 1954, about twenty thousand new homes were built in Louisville, but only about 1 percent of those were built for blacks.

Although Wade was a light-skinned black, he wasn't light enough to get past wary real estate agents. But he had his eye on a two-bedroom house that he really liked, in an area called Shively, just outside the Louisville city limits, and he was determined to get it, even though he could have bought a house in a black neighborhood not more than a quarter of a mile away. So in March 1954 he developed a scheme, and went to Carl and Anne Braden for help. Why them? Well, Wade had asked around and learned that they were sympathetic to black hopes.

The scheme was simple: Carl Braden would buy the house Wade had selected and then sell it to him. Neither the homeowner nor the real estate agent nor the bank would know what was going on until the deed was already done.

Everything came off just swell for about the first twenty-four hours after the transfer, and then all hell broke loose.

Were Wade and Braden so naive they thought it wouldn't? Or were they just indifferently confrontational?

Public transportation in Louisville was already integrated, but in all other things, segregation was fixed both in fact and state of mind, to be defended with the fervor found farther south—or, to be geographically fair, also found in some neighborhoods of Chicago and New York and Boston. Buying in the Shively area was particularly tricky because it was a lower-middle-class neighborhood of folks who were not known for their sophistication. Violent reactions were not unknown.

And making it even trickier, Wade's new home was right next door to the home of "Buster," son of the contractor who was building the subdivision. Well, it wasn't much of a subdivision yet—just three dinky houses on an unpaved street. But the contractor had dreams, and he understandably saw a black resident as the end of those dreams.

The first day of the Wades' residency, a Saturday, a rock was tossed through their front window. That evening a cross was burned next door. Very early Sunday morning, half a dozen shots were fired at their home. And the next day, May 17, 1954—"Black Monday" to segregationists, for on that day the U.S. Supreme Court handed down *Brown*, its school desegregation ruling—racists everywhere swore perpetual war. There would be no armistice.[1]

The Wade-Braden integration plan was doomed.

So was the Wade home. A midnight dynamite bomb demolished one whole side of it.

Doomed also was Carl Braden's career as a journalist. It happened rather fast. Since being an integrationist was not a crime, Jefferson County's politically ambitious commonwealth attorney, A. Scott Hamilton, decided to attack Braden in the most effective way possible for the mid-1950s—as a subversive who'd concocted the Wade home purchase as part of a Communist plot to create racial strife. It was a theory widely supported in the community; the grand jury completely agreed with Hamilton.

Braden was accused of (1) violating Kentucky's sedition law, which hadn't been used in more than three decades, and

(2) "conspiracy to damage property to achieve a political end—communism." Sedition is a vague, old-fashioned term that is defined as actions or language inciting rebellion against a government entity. Actually, the Kentucky Constitution was unusually fair about that sort of thing, for it granted citizens the right to "alter, reform, or abolish their government in such a manner as they deem proper," although it, too, was a bit vague about how much "deeming" would be allowed.

As it turned out, definitions and law were beside the point. The thirteen-day trial made clear almost from its beginning that prosecutor Hamilton had no evidence whatever that Braden had conspired to do anything but help—not encourage, just help—a black man to buy a house where he was excessively unwelcome. As for proving a "Communist plot," Hamilton pulled the same trick that prosecutors all over the country were using against left-wing suspects—he used a search warrant to hunt for "Communist literature" in the Bradens' large home library. It was a fruitful hunt. Since Braden was a longtime student of Soviet affairs, many boxes of "suspicious" books were lugged into court, and Hamilton spent hours exciting the jury with juicy readings from them.

For his finale, Hamilton produced the standard HUAC and FBI performers, professional circuit-riders—ex-Communists turned informers-for-profit—who were appearing in similar trials all over the country to identify the subversiveness of the books some suspects had in their homes.

The only fresh prosecution witness was a local woman whom the Bradens had considered a friend, but who, alas, turned out to be another paid FBI informer. She, of course, said they were Communists.

The Bradens' defense attorney tried to bury her testimony under a mound of dirt by telling the jury that, after she was hired as an informer by the FBI, she had been discovered in the backseat of a car with a black man and arrested on a morals charge. The gambit was quite in keeping with the character of the whole trial. But in the mid-1950s, not even illicit interracial sex could trump sedition.

Braden's sentence was fifteen years in prison and a fine of five thousand dollars. Of course his attorneys appealed—he was getting lots of help from the ECLC—but the court kept him in prison for six months (the first forty-two days in solitary confinement) while his friends laboriously collected forty thousand dollars to post the highest bond ever set in Kentucky.[2]

On April 2, 1956, Braden gained freedom from further harassment via the U.S. Supreme Court, which on that day ruled that sedition laws that had for years been cluttering up the statutes in forty-one states were invalid because they were superseded by the infamous federal Smith Act. It was probably the only decent result the Smith Act ever brought about.

■

BRADEN'S IMMEDIATE PROSPECTS for employment were bleak. The editor of the *Louisville Courier-Times* flatly refused to rehire him because, he said, Carl lacked the "objectivity" needed for newspaper work. (By this time, it may have been true.) For a year the family lived off Anne's fifty-four dollars a week as a do-it-all clerk. They were outcasts in surprising places. The Kentucky Civil Liberties Union, which Carl had helped found, shunned their efforts to participate in its work. And the chairman of the Louisville NAACP told Carl "your presence on the membership committee threatens to disrupt the entire campaign."[3]

The Bradens were rescued from the ash heap by Aubrey Williams, James Dombrowski, Harvey O'Connor, and, of course, Frank Wilkinson, who got the Bradens involved in a variety of ways but most usefully as "field representatives"—meaning organizers—for Dombrowski's SCEF. Their assignment was to convince newly awakened civil rights activists that to succeed they would have to join forces with the civil liberties anti–witch hunt movement. There was no other way to drown out the Right's clamorous effort to pin the "Communist" label on all integrationists.

The South's embattled moderates had tried to avoid that label ever since the Progressive Party's candidate, Henry Wallace, campaigned through the South (amid a hail of rotten eggs and ripe tomatoes) in 1948. With self-defeating timidity, most had shunned relationships with the very people who were trying hardest, and risking their own reputations, to silence the Right. That's why the Kentucky branch of the ACLU and the Louisville branch of the NAACP had shut the door on Braden.

That kind of Red-baiting in "liberal" organizations—trying to remain socially respectable by passing one anti-Communist resolution after another—was happening all over the country, but with special intensity in the South. Even Dombrowski's baby, the SCEF, succumbed to a long, hard debate at one board meeting as to whether they should adopt a ban on Communists. Anne Braden recalls, "We debated it for hours, until Jim Dombrowski pointed out very quietly—as was his way—that we had wasted all afternoon on this question while the violence of the segregationists was rising all around us. He said one thing that stayed with me: 'I'm not sure it's important whether SCEF survives, but I think it's important that American democracy survive. If we adopt this policy, we will be supporting the witch hunts that threaten any hope of democracy.'"[4]

■

SADLY, FIFTEEN YEARS after the Wades' house was destroyed, the Wilkinson house was firebombed. Only Tony and Jo were home. Jo was downstairs with the neighbors, and on her way back up the hallway stairs, she noticed a dark bottle full of liquid on the stairs. After going to bed, Jo and Tony woke to a loud bang. When they opened the front door, they saw the staircase in flames, and went out the back way.

When the police came, they took Jo and started questioning her, which scared her even more. Little damage was done to the house, but there was lifelong damage to her. Soon after, someone painted a black swastika on the duplex. At that finally the landlord told them to move. Years later, Jo was diagnosed with post-traumatic stress disorder, as she puts it, "not from just the bombing, but the constant surveillance and pressure our whole family was under."[5]

CHAPTER 21

The Black Rebellion Begins to Rumble across Dixie

THE U.S. SUPREME Court's declaration on May 17, 1954, that "separate educational facilities are inherently unequal" was a call to arms for both sides. For the old stand-pat Dixiecrats, the first truly ominous sign of things to come was Rosa Parks's simple act of taking a seat at the front of the Cleveland Avenue bus in Montgomery on December 5, 1955, and refusing to give up the seat to a white man. The bus stopped, she was arrested, and the next day Montgomery blacks (who normally made up 75 percent of the city's bus passengers) declared a boycott. It was the first action in which the Reverend Martin Luther King Jr. had a leadership role. One year later, Montgomery's white establishment surrendered, but only after its income from bus fares had reached a perilous low and after the Supreme Court declared segregation on buses unconstitutional.

But that victory was deceptive. Wherever they could fight without damage to themselves, the segregationists were passionately ready to do so. One of the most ominous actions had been taken shortly after the *Brown* decision, when thirteen citizens of Indianola, Mississippi, met on July 11, 1954, in the home of the manager of the cotton compress. These ordinary citizens—the town banker, the dentist, the pharmacist, the city attorney—had a plan to defend segregation across Dixie by almost any method. It would be called the Citizens Council of America (CCA) (or, sometimes, superfluously, the White Citizens Council). By 1956, the CCA had an estimated quarter of a million members across the South, and many were politicians in high places. Walter Sillers, speaker of the Mississippi House of Representatives, called it "the greatest force we have in this battle to save the white race from amalgamation, mongrelization, and destruction."[1] Although some of the CCA's charter members had murder in mind (most notably, fertilizer salesman Byron De La Beckwith, who shot Medgar Evers, Mississippi's most aggressive civil rights worker, in the back), their real motive was to freeze public opinion around time-honored cultural ways and frustrate all integration laws. Compared to typical members of the Ku Klux Klan, its members seemed almost mild, Rotarian-like. They weren't. If they did not personally take part in violence, they wholeheartedly approved of it. The day after Medgar Evers was shot, Louis Hollis, the executive director of the Citizens Council in Mississippi, said, "We hoped that this would be a cold war. But if it isn't, it is still a war, and we don't intend to surrender."[2] That became plain enough when, at De La Beckwith's second murder trial, Mississippi governor Ross Barnett came down to the front of the courtroom, shook hands with the defendant, and engaged him in five minutes of jovial conversation—right in front of the jury. The jury took its cue from Barnett and did not convict De La Beckwith.[3]

■

WHILE MISSISSIPPI WAS a bit of a backwater, it was in Georgia, the most promising state in the Deep South, that Frank Wilkinson would meet his downfall. The state was indeed promising, but it had a bipolar character. It was also the state where the political power of the CCA was most dramatically illustrated in the life of one man, Roy V. Harris, who was for a time the council's president.

Harris, a Svengali-like magical maker-and-breaker of Georgia politics, had a decisive role in the election of every governor over a period of two decades, and was particularly influential in the totally corrupt, segregationist administrations of Herman Talmadge (who, fittingly, had the "grand dragon" of the Georgia Ku Klux Klan on his staff) and Marvin Griffin, the two governors just preceding Frank's arrival in Georgia in 1958.

In gratitude for his help in getting them elected, two governors appointed Harris to the University of Georgia's board of regents, where he is best remembered for (1) trying to close down the university's newspaper because it was full of "Communist influences and the crazy idea of mixing and mingling of the races," and (2) praising rioters who, on the university's first effort to integrate, "had the nerve to stand up in the face of federal court decrees and to defy the police and the army of deans and get nigras out of the university."

In the fall of 1957, when it looked like the Little Rock, Arkansas, high school might be able to integrate without violence, Harris and Governor Griffin went over to Arkansas and harangued the Little Rock Citizens Council with claims of how "blood would flow in the sewers of Atlanta" before *they* "would let one nigra enter a public white school." Arkansas governor Orval Faubus says that after their visit, the attitude around town "hardened" to the point that any chance of quieting Little Rock was ruined; the school was integrated only after President Eisenhower sent in a thousand paratroopers and ten thousand Arkansas National Guardsmen to get it done, despite a mob that threatened to drag the black students out and lynch them.

■

THE *ATLANTA CONSTITUTION* was considered the most progressive newspaper in the South—was it in favor of segregation? No. What it supported—as the voice of the city's power structure—was *not rocking the boat*. Atlanta, "the gateway to the South," boasted of its cosmopolitan attitude, but in fact it was ingrown and defensive;

its upper crust was as embarrassed by the city's small cluster of liberal activists as it was by the loud rednecks who roosted under the capitol dome.

The moneyed establishment was quite willing to go along with the rednecks so long as that resulted in a social calm that was good for business. When Governor Talmadge, scion of a redneck dynasty, forced Adlai Stevenson to come to Georgia to make peace with southern Democratic segregationists (who had not supported him in 1952 because of his racial liberalism), Ralph McGill, editor of the *Atlanta Constitution*, wrote that he feared Atlanta's "grim liberals, with their stiff-necked demands for conformity, will not wish Stevenson's southern visit to be a happy one. They will try to enmesh him in the dialectics of civil rights and associated issues."

And when Governor Talmadge, responding to the Supreme Court's desegregation edict, threatened to close the public schools and subsidize private ones, the *Constitution* called that move "sensible, calming" and gave an editorial "salute to the Governor who, for all his extreme feelings on the subject, has risen to the challenge of it and come forward *with the only two proposals possible for a civilized people dedicated to Christian ethics.*" (Emphasis added.)[4]

James Dombrowski and his allies would encounter the same lack of press support in their effort to combat HUAC when it invaded Atlanta, which it was about to do.

■ HUAC GOES PROSPECTING FOR MORE HEADLINES

With the nation's eyes now glued on the explosive South, the House Un-American Activities Committee (a majority of whose members were from the South) decided it was time to go down and get its share of the publicity. It scheduled a well-rehearsed subcommittee hearing for Atlanta, Georgia, to be held over the last days of July 1958. Congressman Edwin Willis, Democrat of Louisiana, would be nominally in charge, but the ax hanging over each subpoenaed witness would be in the hands of the most experienced executioner in the business, staff director Richard Arens.

Congressman Willis said the purpose of the hearings would be to investigate "Communist Party propaganda activities in the South and to trace the web of Communist penetration into the industrialized areas of the South."

But James Dombrowski and others in the SCEF suspected the hearings would be an extension of Senator Eastland's 1954 hearings in New Orleans, with the general aim of harassing civil rights workers. It determined to organize a public campaign to oppose the hearings, including having a significant presence at them. Frank would join the effort. To begin the campaign, the SCEF wrote an open letter to the U.S. House of Representatives; it was circulated and signed by two hundred black ministers, college presidents, and other leaders. Obviously enjoying an opportunity to use the words "subversive" and "un-American" correctly, the cosigners urged Congress "to see that HUAC stay out of the South unless it can be persuaded to help defend against these subversives who oppose our Supreme Court, our federal policy of civil rights for all, and our American ideals of equality and brotherhood."

It continued:

We are acutely aware of the shocking amount of un-American activity in our Southern states. To cite only a few examples, there are the bombings of homes, schools, and houses of worship of not only Negroes, but also of Jewish citizens; the terror against Negroes in Dawson, Georgia; the continued refusal of boards of registrars in many southern communities to allow Negroes to vote; and the activities of White Citizens Councils encouraging open defiance of the United States Supreme Court. There is nothing in the record of the House Committee to indicate that it will investigate these things. On the contrary, all of its activities suggest that it is much more interested in harassing and labeling as "subversive" any citizen who is inclined to be liberal.

For this reason, we are alarmed at the prospect of this committee coming South to follow the lead of Senator Eastland, as well as several state investigating committees, in trying to attach the "subversive" label to any liberal white Southerner who dares to raise his voice in support of our democratic ideals.

Turning the letter into a full-page ad, Dombrowski tried to get it published in the *Atlanta Constitution*, but editor Ralph McGill refused to accept it, claiming it might offend some pro-segregation politicians who would sue the paper for libel. (It was published seven hundred miles to the north, in the *Washington Post*.)

More likely, the ad was rejected because it might conflict too glaringly with the campaign then under way by Lieutenant Governor Ernest Vandiver, running for governor with the support of the *Constitution*. Coming from different political climes, Frank was rather startled, his first day in Atlanta, to open the *Constitution* and find a full-page ad promoting Vandiver as a last-ditch segregationist. In the middle of the page was the candidate's heart-felt promise:

TO THE MOTHERS AND FATHERS OF GEORGIA . . .
Neither my three children nor any child of yours will ever attend a racially mixed school in this state while I am governor.

Frank says he closed that newspaper with the feeling that this time he was in truly hostile territory.

■ INTO THE MESS BY REQUEST

Even if he had been a bit jittery about those Georgians the *Constitution* had called "a civilized people dedicated to Christian ideals," Frank would undoubtedly have gone down anyway after Carl and Anne Braden called from Louisville to ask for help in opposing the upcoming HUAC hearing. They had never faced the committee before and they knew he was a veteran. Over the phone he began telling them how to adopt Meiklejohn's petition to abolish the committee. But the Bradens, says Frank, cut him off, saying,

"The South is not ready to consider abolition of the committee. Southerners don't know anything about the committee. But they would understand a petition that said, in effect, 'Keep HUAC out of the South, because we don't need it down here supporting race terrorists by pinning a Red label on our effort to get white folks to obey the Supreme Court's school decision.'" So that was the petition the Bradens wrote, with Frank's long-distance help. And he agreed to meet them in Atlanta to work out other details.

Actually, he had doubts about his usefulness in the region. "I had never been in the South. I was a Californian and a briefly transplanted Northerner," he says.

> I thought it would be silly for me to go down there. I brought the problem to Clark Foreman's attention and suggested that he go instead. After all, as director of the ECLC, he would have more clout. Besides, he was directly related to the family that founded the *Atlanta Constitution*. But he said, "I'm not going to go down there. They haven't got a chance. They're all Communists and Jews." He was talking about the people who had been subpoenaed.
>
> So I asked him if ECLC would pay my way. I reminded him we had raised $25,000 to go anywhere that HUAC goes. But he refused. He said, "If you want to go, go, but I'm not going to pay for it."

Dombrowski put up the money.

Frank had to hurry. He was due in Atlanta the next day. He packed, called Alan Reitman, associate national director in the New York ACLU office, to find out which ACLU lawyers he could contact in the South, and was off to the airport. Arriving in Atlanta the next morning, he checked into the Atlanta Biltmore Hotel, and then . . .

> I go into my room, close the door, and I hadn't even opened my suitcase when there's a knock on the door, and here's this fifteen-foot-tall marshal with a subpoena for me.

I brought him into my room and asked, "How did you know I was here?" He said, "I know nothing about it except that they called me from Washington yesterday saying you were on the way and they were sending a courier down with a subpoena for you and I'd find you at the Atlanta Biltmore Hotel this afternoon."

FBI records later obtained by Frank's attorneys show that the bureau almost always knew where he was.

▪

NATURALLY, TOP OFFICIALS of city and state offered southern hospitality to HUAC's illustrious inquisitors. Governor Griffin, the soiled son of Bainbridge, Georgia, even dropped by on the opening day of the hearings to give the panel his blessing. But some officials coupled their hospitality with questions as to the need for the Communist hunt. Mayor William B. Hartsfield, a moderate who had dominated city politics for more than two decades, said, "I'm always happy to have our congressmen come here. But I think there's very little Communist activity in this area." And Attorney General Eugene Cook echoed those sentiments, saying, "I'm delighted they're going to hold hearings here. But I believe Georgia probably has fewer Communists than any other state. In fact, I don't think there are any here. But if there are, the committee's presence will have a beneficial effect to let them know they are being watched. It might keep them out."

Margaret Shannon, one of the best reporters on the *Constitution*, cut through the fluff with her opening story about the upcoming hearing: "Since the departure of Homer S. Chase in 1950, the Communist front has been without a publicly identified leader in these parts. . . . If the House Un-American Activities Committee brings out anything at all about Communist activities in Georgia other than generalities, it will be more than has been told publicly in five years. [More accurately, eight years.] Any evidence of major Red doings in the state would be a surprise, indeed."[5] And the

Journal, although it supported HUAC's intentions, questioned the existence of its target: "The last flurry of Communist activity around here was during the Henry Wallace Progressive Party campaign," ten years earlier.

Most remarkably, Armand Pena, an undercover FBI man for seven years in the South and HUAC's chief informer for this event, admitted that the party had had little, if any, success in its efforts to organize in the region. So why the hearings?

The list of subpoenaed witnesses further underscored the strange vacuity of this invasion, HUAC's first into the Deep South. What did it hope to achieve? Congressman Willis, the chairman of the subcommittee, had informed the press before the hearing opened, "We are here to trace the web of Communist penetration into industrialized areas of the South." Then why so few subpoenaed witnesses from the South who worked in industry? And why subpoena a twenty-two-year-old employee from a Brooklyn, New York camera manufacturing plant (whose only contribution was to shout angrily, "I told you I'm not a Commie! I have never been a Commie! I never intend to be a Commie! So far as I know, I've never even *seen* a Commie!")? Why subpoena a junior college student from Chicago whose only connection with the South was that he had once sold vegetables on the streets of Atlanta?

The one industrial employee the subcommittee hauled up was a woman from Greensboro, North Carolina, whom FBI informer Pena had identified as a "colonizer" for the Communist Party. But the only thing they seemed to have against her was that when she applied for work at a textile mill, she failed to mention that she had a master's degree from Syracuse University. After she explained, "They didn't ask," the panel seemed to run out of questions.

When Hunter Pitts O'Dell, a black insurance man from Montgomery, Alabama, took the stand, Arens began to lecture him about how "a hundred years ago Karl Marx launched a Communist movement that is trying to destroy this government, the last bastion of freedom." O'Dell interrupted to say he wanted "to call attention to three hundred years of slavery in this country," and asked to read a two-page statement. His request was denied.

The closest the subcommittee came to getting a confession from anyone was when a witness (an air-conditioner salesman) admitted he "may have" let his name be used eight years earlier in a movement to get support for removing our troops from Korea, and he "may have" written an article for the *Daily Worker* urging that the eleven persons convicted in the first big Smith Act trial be freed.

The congressmen were so grateful for getting even that much from anyone that they thanked him for being a "courteous witness."

Among the thirteen witnesses who took the Fifth Amendment was a poet-philosopher-farmer—one of those offbeat characters almost fondly tolerated in the South—whom the *Journal* wryly described as "an enthusiastic Communist in the '30s who has since refused to say what he is. He has taken the Fifth Amendment so many times count has been lost." Among the other Georgians, the *Journal* added, "are some considered to be at least fellow travelers but who are equally shopworn and so well known as to be caricatures."

■

THAT LEFT THE two subpoenaed witnesses who did not take the Fifth Amendment but instead took the First: Carl Braden and Frank Wilkinson. And the spectators who crowded into the hearing room of the federal courthouse for three days, beginning on July 29, 1958, were there mostly to see how the committee handled these two, the ex-con integrationist and his associate, the already accused Communist from L.A. Indeed, it became obvious that the entire hearing, otherwise so flimsy and foolish, had been set up solely to trap Frank and Braden into once again responding as the congressmen knew they would. There was good reason for HUAC (and J. Edgar Hoover) to look upon them as quarry who had escaped deserved punishment. Frank had successfully defied HUAC in Los Angeles in 1956. Carl had been rescued by the U.S. Supreme Court from a fifteen-year sedition sentence. But they wouldn't escape this time, not if they responded as expected to the committee's questions.

Of the two, Frank got star billing, which was appropriate. After all, avowed integrationists were not that scarce even in Georgia, but a real live accused Communist (usually designated as "Stalinist stooge") was never seen in the flesh. Alas, the crowd would not get the verbal duel they expected, but their disappointment was not the fault of HUAC staff director Arens. With Frank in the witness chair, he started with a dramatic series of accusations that were somewhat muddled by his torrent of bureaucratese:

> It is the information of this committee that you are now a hard-core member of the Communist Party;[5] that you were designated by the Communist Party for the purpose of creating and manipulating certain organizations, including the Emergency Civil Liberties Committee, and including a certain committee in California the name of which is along the line of the committee for cultural freedom, or something like that. I don't have the name before me at this instant.
>
> It is our information that in anticipation of the hearings here in Atlanta, Georgia, you were sent into this area by the Communist Party for the purpose of developing a hostile sentiment to this committee and its work. We intend to pursue that area of inquiry and undertake to solicit from you information respecting your activities as a Communist on behalf of the Communist Party, which is tied up directly with the Kremlin; your activities from the standpoint of undertaking to destroy the Federal Bureau of Investigation and discredit its director and undertake to hamstring the work of the House Un-American Activities Committee, and your work along these lines with the Emergency Civil Liberties Committee, of which you are the guiding light.
>
> Now, sir, I put it to you and ask you to affirm or deny the fact that you are part of an enterprise to destroy the very Constitution of the United States under which we all have protection, and that you are an agent of the Communist

Party as an arm of the international Communist conspiracy
sent into Atlanta for the purpose already mentioned. If that
is not so, deny it under oath.

And this is only about half of his opening statement. Like the calm
after the last house has collapsed in a tornado, Frank offered, no
doubt to the keen disappointment of the crowd, a one-sentence
reply:

"I refuse to answer any questions of this committee."

■

THE DIFFERENCES BETWEEN Carl Braden and Frank Wilkinson
are worth pointing out. They were different in personality and
to some degree in purpose, and yet they became exceedingly
close, both in and out of prison, where they usually had adjoining cells.

Braden's consuming purpose was not free speech, free press,
free assembly for blacks; it was *total* freedom for them—by doing
away with all laws and customs that prevented them from having
the same opportunities as whites. He hated HUAC because it was
on the side of the racists.

Frank's goal was in one way possibly in conflict with Braden's.
He wanted full protection and enjoyment of the First Amendment
for people of all colors and creeds and customs—yes, including
racists, so long as their enjoyment of the First did not restrict in
any way the liberties of others.

Frank was outgoing and congenial. He took powerful, unbending positions without insulting—or at least without going out of
his way to insult—his opponents. He was by now quite a professional organizer, having traveled the country to oppose HUAC,
and this hearing was important, regardless of family concerns or
possible jail sentence. His conduct on the witness stand at HUAC
hearings had been honed down to the essentials: at some point
in the interrogation, he would say that he was there under duress,
that HUAC was operating in direct violation of its congressional

mandate, and that by delving into areas relating to free speech, religion, and peaceful association, it was in violation not only of the First Amendment but of recent Supreme Court edicts.

He would give that explanation for his refusal to cooperate only after he had answered one question, "What is your name?" Beyond that, he answered nothing. He would not even give his home or business address, and he most emphatically refused to answer when asked if he was or had ever been a Communist. Having once cited the First Amendment, he thereafter usually said no more than, "My answer is my answer."

Arens's thunder got only more quiet refusals. Frank wasn't there to debate HUAC's members. That wasn't part of his strategy. He was there simply to resist their questioning in such a way that he could reach his ultimate goal, a test case for the U.S. Supreme Court. That was his gamble, his toss of the dice. "Either the U.S. Supreme Court, when we get there, will turn down my appeal and I'll go to prison," he would say, "or it will side with my argument that the First Amendment permits all witnesses *not* to answer HUAC's questions. If it does that, HUAC will be totally disarmed and will die."

Braden, on the other hand, loved to insult the questioners on HUAC's panel. He snarled and snapped at them. Although he took the First when asked if he was a Communist and when asked other questions about his politics, unlike Frank he would engage the congressmen and Arens in a dialogue—but only in the most insulting way. "Carl was a tough guy," Frank recalls admiringly. "He was uncompromising. If you disagreed with him, he would say right to your face what he thought about you. He was that way with everybody. It was a very admirable quality because he was like John Brown, an absolutist on civil rights in the South. With his white hair, he even looked a little bit like John Brown."

Unlike Frank, Braden didn't take the First because it was a guaranteed prison sentence. That was the last thing he wanted. He had had enough of prison, and he had a family to help support. He took the First, well, simply for a John Brown reason: defiance.

Braden was wise to answer some of the questions and engage

the panel in at least a limited dialogue because—as Frank knew
only too well—to remain completely silent led many folks to think
that for sure you must be a Communist. The suspicion flourished
all over the South, Braden's home base. As field secretary of the
SCEF, he relied heavily on support from black preachers, and they
had enough baggage to carry without allying themselves with
somebody considered a Communist.

Witnesses were expected to appear with at least one attorney.
Braden had four: three black lawyers (another plug for his SCEF
job) including C. Ewbank Tucker, presiding bishop of the Tenth
Episcopal District of the AME Zion Church in Louisville, and
Leonard Boudin, considered by many to be the best constitutional
lawyer in the country. Boudin, an NLG attorney, had come down
from New York at the behest of the ECLC and would have been
happy to represent Frank, too. But Frank, encouraged by memories
of his very active pals on the West Coast, wanted to encourage
ACLU chapters everywhere to become more militant in defending
persecuted left-wingers.

Not only could Frank have had Boudin, he could have had any
number of other ECLC lawyers, or New York ACLU lawyers.

But he wanted to feed some red meat to Atlanta's affiliate. So
he called twelve lawyers the New York office had told him were in
Atlanta's ACLU. As it turned out, each one was very sorry, but his
tight schedule just wouldn't enable him to attend the hearing that
day. So Frank came by himself. But as he took his seat at the witness table, he happened to glance over at the jury box. The twelve
lawyers he had asked for help were sitting there as spectators.
A suspected Communist was apparently meat too red for their
legal practice. Frank finally got the ACLU to provide him Rowland Waits, general counsel of the ACLU from Baltimore, to take
his Atlanta case in July 1958.

■

HUAC COULD CITE a witness for contempt of Congress, but the
House of Representatives had to confirm the citation in order to

get the defendants into court. The House confirmed the charge against Braden by a vote of 434 to 1, the nay vote coming from Rep. Robert N. C. Nix, a black representative from Philadelphia, probably because Nix had heard about Carl and Anne's selling the house to a black GI in Louisville.

The House vote to charge Frank was 435 to 0. Nobody voted for him, which was a rather accurate measure of congressional courage in the Cold War 1950s. He didn't even get the vote of Jimmy Roosevelt, the congressman for the California district in which he lived. But that didn't surprise Frank. He had always found the Roosevelt offspring a slippery ally. On January 9, 1959, for instance—after much prodding and after hundreds of dignitaries (including his mother) had signed a full-page ad in the *Washington Post* denouncing HUAC as "an agency of repression"—Jimmy had introduced a bill to kill the committee. Then he chickened out. In a January 12 speech he said he didn't mean to stop HUAC-type investigations, but only to turn them over to a committee with a better reputation.

On January 22, 1959, Frank had his trial in the Federal District Court in Atlanta. It was rather perfunctory. U.S. attorney Robert Sparks, echoing Arens, told the jury, "This is a man assigned by the Communist conspiracy to destroy the Federal Bureau of Investigation and the House Committee on Un-American Activities and wreck the reputations of such men as J. Edgar Hoover and Rep. Francis Walter," chairman of HUAC.

If Sparks had left out the stuff about the Communist conspiracy assignment, that would in fact have been an accurate description of Frank's efforts. And the twelve-man jury (one black) came in with a guilty verdict in forty-five minutes.

In Braden's trial the next day, his attorney, John M. Coe, president of the reliably feisty NLG, gave a blistering attack on HUAC, calling its investigators "twenty times as dangerous as any Communist who ever crossed the sea." That apparently was impressive enough to delay Coe's jury an extra five minutes (total: fifty minutes) before coming in with a guilty verdict.

It was curious that these jurymen, all native sons of a state where the Confederate battle flag still flew over the capitol, were so quick to condemn two rebels.

▪

OUR REBELS, OF course, filed an appeal to the U.S. Supreme Court. For Frank, everything was developing just as he had hoped it would. Perhaps.

But it was scary. What if he wound up in Lewisburg, which was not at all like those latter-day prisons the press derides as "country clubs"?

Frank and Rowland Waits, his ACLU attorney from Baltimore, had adjoining rooms in their Atlanta hotel. The night before Frank was to be sentenced, Waits came into Frank's room with a bottle of bourbon and two glasses. Frank recalls:

> He poured one for himself and one for me. A tumbler—three, four, five jiggers—of straight bourbon.
>
> He says, "As your lawyer, I have to say something to you now. I have reason to believe"—he didn't say how he learned it—"that if tomorrow you'll tell the judge you are not a Communist, or that you have never been a Communist, you'll never serve a day in jail."
>
> I had been so very strong about taking my position that I could see Rowland was sort of, well, almost embarrassed to have to tell me that.
>
> I said, "Thank you, Rowland. You've discharged your legal responsibilities, and my position is still my position. I will answer no questions of that kind ever again."
>
> He leaned forward with his tumbler full of bourbon, we clicked glasses, and that night I drank more bourbon at one time than I've ever done in my life.

CHAPTER 22

Youth Joins In, Lending Enormous Vigor to Frank's Crusade

LET'S STEP BACK a moment from Frank's trial in Atlanta to look at how the movement around his effort to topple HUAC was forming nationally. A good amount of time had passed between his HUAC hearing, the trial, the appeal, and the Supreme Court hearing, and it was prime organizing time. In 1953 most of his help—and most of the interest shown in his effort—had come from adults. Even in 1958, when he and Carl offered folks in Atlanta the rare opportunity (for that city) to watch two rebels defy Congress, only a few dozen spectators showed up, and none of them were of college age or younger.

Then came the explosion of 1960—after Frank's conviction in Atlanta, but before the Supreme Court heard his appeal.

Black adults had been galvanized by the victorious desegregation of bus lines in Montgomery, Alabama, in 1955, and by the desegregation of Little Rock's high school—with the help of a thousand paratroopers—in 1957.[1]

But nothing stirred black youths to do combat with white authorities like the simple act of four black college students who took seats at a Woolworth lunch counter in Greensboro, North

Carolina, on February 1, 1960, and ordered Cokes. The lunch counter was whites-only territory, and they were arrested for their impudence.

That did it. The technique for protesting segregation immediately spread throughout the South—there were sit-ins at lunch counters in fifty southern towns, and wade-ins at all-white beaches, and read-ins at libraries. There were many arrests and many violent clashes, but the revolt kept spreading.

To nobody's surprise—considering the decades-old radicalism embedded at the University of California, Berkeley—white UC Berkeley students jumped into the civil rights fray. The South's segregated bus lines and schools had been causes too difficult for white students outside the South to conveniently show support for, but denying four young college students the simple pleasure of having a Coke in a Woolworth store was something they could respond to more easily.

And they did. Two weeks after the eruption in Greensboro, some of the more radically inclined Berkeley students shut down Woolworth in Berkeley with massive picket lines, telling management, in effect, "You're not going to sell anything to a Berkeley student until a black student can get a Coke in your southern stores. So make up your mind."

That was so much fun that the young UC firebrands looked around for another cause to protest. They found it, conveniently enough, at the San Quentin penitentiary, where Caryl Chessman was scheduled to be sent to the gas chamber on May 2, 1960.[2] On the night of May 1, just hours before his ninth date with the gas chamber, people like Marlon Brando and Shirley MacLaine, pilgrims begging mercy for Chessman, camped out on the lawn of the governor's mansion in Sacramento.[3]

Also on hand, both at the governor's mansion and at the penitentiary, was a sizable army of University of California, Berkeley students. But for them it wasn't a one-night stand. Some of them had been picketing both places for days. And the fact that they lost this battle with the Establishment did not lessen their zeal; they remained in the demonstrating mood. Thus, they were only too eager to respond as an unwelcoming committee for the House Un-American Activities Committee when it arrived in San Francisco in mid-May to hold hearings at city hall.

■ ON TO SAN FRANCISCO!

The circus that rose up around these HUAC hearings was like nothing the city had ever seen. Perhaps the closest—in drama, but at an entirely different level of violence—was the general strike of 1934, which paralyzed San Francisco for days and resulted in cripplings and deaths. In 1934 the issue was working conditions and wages. In 1960 the issue was civil liberties, and—though the headlined participants included several well-known, seasoned radicals who had been subpoenaed to testify—the demonstrators were mostly college students. And this time the violence came from cops using plenty of muscle and fire hoses. Frank was in the middle of all of it—watching, and, finally, being targeted—again.

HUAC immortalized the San Francisco hearings on film "borrowed by the government" from various San Francisco television stations whose cameramen had covered the engagement inside city hall, on the sidewalks outside, and in Union Square across the way. HUAC titled the patched-together film *Operation Abolition*, and it was emceed by four members of the committee who must have reminded at least a few viewers of Walt Disney's famous dwarfs Dopey, Sleepy, Grumpy, and Doc.[4] In making the film, HUAC's purpose was to show the rebellious ways of young people who were supposedly under the sway of subversives. "But what had the greatest impact on public opinion," writes Richard Gid Powers, historian and biographer of Hoover, "was the film's unflattering contrast between the youthful, idealistic demonstrators and the anticommunists on the Committee: beefy, balding, bullying, lashing out against their enemies with wild, red-smearing invective, a crude and embarrassing relic of unreconstructed McCarthyism."[5]

Congressman Francis E. Walter, HUAC's chairman at the time, opens the film by explaining that its title "is what the Communists call their current effort to destroy the House Un-American Activities Committee and to render sterile the security laws of our government. Scenes you will be seeing were taken by newsreel photographers at our hearings in San Francisco on May 12, 13, and 14 in 1960. You will see the longtime tactics that a few hard-core Communists use to incite non-Communist sympathizers to do the dirty work of the Communist Party."

This was, of course, false on several levels.

First, the tactics used to stir up the demonstrators on this occasion were certainly not "longtime tactics," because never before, anywhere in the United States, had HUAC been thrown off balance so effectively as by the virulence of opposition it encountered in San Francisco.

Second, much of the "incitement" engaged in on those three days was clearly HUAC's fault. The committee overreacted to the basic liberalism of San Francisco and its legendary refusal to be pushed around by outsiders—especially by fourth-rate, back-East congressmen.[6]

Congressman Walter was right about one thing: the monumentally effective opposition he ran into came not from the few real Communists among the subpoenaed witnesses, but from a multitude of "non-Communist sympathizers" who didn't like to see anyone—Communist or not—subjected to the kind of inquisitions that HUAC had for years been infamous for.

Another HUAC commentator in the film, August E. Johanson of Michigan, said *Operation Abolition* showed that Communists "have chosen the minds of students for their insidious attacks" and that "these students are toying with treason." He added, "The carefully organized protest was climaxed with a student directive on the front page of the official University of California student newspaper, the *Daily Californian*, just prior to the hearings. The directive reads as follows: 'The Student Committee for Civil Liberties plans to picket the hearings today. It has issued a call for students to attend the rally and hearings and suggests that people laugh out loud in the hearings when things get ridiculous.'"

If it was "toying with treason" to "laugh out loud . . . when things get ridiculous," the UC Berkeley students who turned up at the hearings were obviously traitors, for they did a great deal of laughing—and hooting and jeering and singing, inside the hearing room, in the corridors of that wing of city hall, and on the sidewalks facing city hall. They were there by the hundreds. Long before the doors opened, huge lines were waiting to get in. But they certainly didn't look like scruffy traitors; most of the young women were dressed for a social occasion, and many of the young men were wearing ties and sport coats or suits.

■ HUAC'S UNINTENDED HEROES

It surely wasn't what the filmmakers set out to achieve, but *Operation Abolition* had two clear heroes. The first hero was Archie Brown, a middle-aged longshoreman whom Chairman Walter, perhaps correctly, identified as the "second in command of the Communist Party in California." He was obviously a great favorite of the young demonstrators, and he also had a loyal following among San Franciscans generally; he'd received thirty-five thousand of their votes a few months earlier when he ran for a seat on the board of supervisors. When he shouted insults at the committee, his admirers turned them into thunderous chants: "*Open the door! Let the people in! What are you afraid of? Let the people in!*" Actually the chamber was already crowded by two antagonistic groups: a large number of people from religious groups and the John Birch Society and DAR—who'd received special passes from HUAC—and a much smaller but more vocal group of high-spirited hecklers.

The chants went on so long that the committee summoned a police squad to physically drag Archie out of the chamber. But he got back in, and the next time he grabbed a microphone and began shouting at the committee, "*Get out, you un-Americans! Pack up and get out! That's what you should do—just pack up and get out!*" Once again his followers picked up the chant with all the gusto of the Mormon Tabernacle Choir. This time, as the cops again descended on Archie to carry him out, his admirers shamed them by singing the national anthem. On this patriotic note, his part in the melodrama for the first day was brought to a close. (But he would be back the next day—under subpoena this time—only to be thrown out again when he refused to stop making a statement about how his family was being threatened.)

During the noon recess, more than a thousand students and spectators gathered in Union Square across from city hall to hear two San Francisco assemblymen and a prominent clergyman bitterly denounce HUAC. If, as *Operation Abolition*'s moderator claimed, "It was a call for further action and more volunteers," it certainly succeeded. That afternoon, hundreds more students crowded into city hall attempting to get into the hearing room, but it was already overflowing. Students forced to stay outside expressed their disappointment by increasing the volume of their chanting and singing and clapping and laughing. They turned it into a chaotic, festive occasion.

The HUAC inquisitors were totally distracted. Unfortunately, bureaucrats and judges elsewhere in the building also found it impossible to carry on their work. So the city's storm troopers were summoned. The young protesters did not go quietly; some of them threw their shoes at the cops. Many others sat down, linked arms, and began singing, "We Shall Not Be Moved." The police were unsuccessful in trying to shove hundreds of young protestors out of the building, so they uncoiled fire hoses and began blasting the students out of the corridors and down three levels of marble steps.

When the water's force was not enough to send them all the way to the bottom, the police wrestled and dragged them the rest of the way. Television cameras caught it all, and it was pretty ugly to see those thoroughly drenched co-eds sliding down dozens of slippery, rump-bruising steps as they tried to save themselves by hanging onto the cops' legs. The storm troopers seemed to favor dragging the young men by their legs, or by the neck of their shirts, like sacks of potatoes.

The day after the students were washed down the marble steps of city hall, about five thousand protestors confronted the congressmen going into the building with cries of "Sieg Heil!" and the straight-arm Nazi salute.

■

IF ARCHIE BROWN was the James Cagney of HUAC's flick, William Mandel, wearing dark glasses, fittingly, was its Clark Gable. They were even in their defiance of the committee, but Mandel was handsomer and more eloquent. Congressman Walter introduced him as a "top propaganda instructor in Communist Party training schools while in public circles he pretends to be a respected newsman in the San Francisco area."

Mandel had been subpoenaed—as an unfriendly witness, of course—and it immediately became quite clear that he was not a beginner at testifying. Why HUAC thought he would be a good witness to feature in the film is a mystery, for no one could have been more attractively insulting.

From the first question asked, he was on top of them, full-throated, tossing his head for emphasis:

"If you think [pause and head toss] I am going to cooperate with this collection of [pause] *Judases*—of men who sit there in violation of the U.S. Constitution—if you think I am going to cooperate with you in *any* way, you are *INSANE!*"

Loud applause.

Later, asked about his role as a lecturer at the labor school in San Francisco, he replied:

This question has *no* purpose or veracity. I was asked this question last in '53 by the late Joseph McCarthy. And let me say that I am honored—though I may not deserve the honor—when people come up to me on the street and say, "You're the fellow who killed Joe McCarthy" because I appeared on the first day of the book-burning hearings and I did my best to conduct myself then in the way I am conducting myself today.

If there were *any* evidence against me under *any* law,

the *proper* authority would move against me. This body is improperly constituted! [His voice rises.] It is a kangaroo court! It does not have my respect! It has my *utmost contempt*! And I am not going to answer that question![7]

Thunderous applause.

Mandel was a very hard act to follow, but HUAC's script-writers saved what they considered the best, and most dangerous, for last—although his appearance was a mere cameo.

Congressman Gordon H. Scherer, Ohio Republican, introduced him:

One of the top Communist agents in Operation Abolition is Frank Wilkinson, recently convicted of contempt of Congress for refusing to answer questions regarding his Communist Party membership and activities. Frank Wilkinson's job for the Communist Party consists of one prime duty: to incite opposition and trouble for the House Un-American Activities Committee in any given location where the committee is to conduct hearings.

Frank Wilkinson was in San Francisco during the May hearings. He arrived in the city prior to the committee to organize the so-called spontaneous public demonstrations against the committee and the hearings. Moreover, he was actually in the corridor during the hearings inciting hostile actions and issuing instructions.

Frank Wilkinson was interviewed by a newsman shortly after he had been educating among the student demonstrators. Listen to this interview closely because in it you will hear Frank Wilkinson, a Communist agent, using his Communist jargon to explain his role in the Communist Party.

That dour introduction hardly prepared the viewer for the smiling face and friendly voice of the "Communist agent" as he chatted with a TV microphone in his face:

Question: Did you have anything to do with the demonstrations in front of city hall today?

Frank: No. I have only been an observer of those.

Question: I understood you said you were organizing protests against the House Un-American Committee.

Frank: Yes. One of the things our committee [the CCPAF] does which I do for our committee is to come to each community to assist subpoenaed persons and others in the community who are not familiar with the kind of unconstitutional behavior that HUAC carries on, and to assist those subpoenaed persons in their own self-defense.

Question: In the hearings today you were called an international Communist agent. Are you?

Frank: [Laughs] That's a very flattering remark. I've been frequently called a hard-core Communist, a local Communist, by Mr. Arens [HUAC's lead counsel], but never an international Communist. As for your question, until the Supreme Court has answered the fundamental issue that is now pending in my case, until they have resolved this matter and declared these kinds of questions under compulsion to be illegal and unconstitutional, I have refused to answer the question when I am away from the committee just as I have refused to answer the question to the committee when I have been called.

∎

IT WAS A rather undramatic interview, but Congressman Scherer tried to pump it up a bit:

> You have been listening to a top Communist coordinator of Operation Abolition. And during the last forty-five minutes you have been witnessing only the surface manifestation of an extensive operation by the Communists that in many phases is subtle, takes the form of articles, in letter-writing campaigns, and a wide range of other such activities. Not for the purpose of

improving the investigative techniques of congressional committees, and not for the purpose of protecting civil liberties as they would have you believe, but for the avowed objective of destroying the Committee on Un-American Activities and our nation's entire security program.

You have seen Communism in action, that same Communism that is at this instant trying to devour the world through subversion, revolution, deceit, sabotage, and vicious propaganda. You have, through this film, seen Communism with its mask ripped off, with its sweet facade uncovered, and with its hard and bitter core revealed.

■ A MOMENTARY ASIDE

Whether it was Communistic or not, the city hall riot—thanks to the spirit of the collegians—did indeed have a partially sweet facade. The students went home with bruises, but they could joke about them later. And they could sing about them, too, if they wanted to join in a song written (probably by Pete Seeger) to the tune of the folk classic "Billy Boy":

> Did they wash you down the stair, Billy Boy, Billy Boy,
> Did they wash you down the stair, charming Billy?
> Yes, they washed me down the stair,
> And they rearranged my hair
> With a club, in the city hall rotunda.
> Were there pigeons in the square, Billy Boy, Billy Boy?
> Were there pigeons in the square, charming Billy?
> There were pigeons in the square,
> And stool pigeons on the air,
> And they fouled up the city hall rotunda.
> Did they set for you a chair, Billy Boy, Billy Boy,
> Did they set for you a chair, charming Billy?
> No, the DAR was there,
> And there wasn't room to spare,
> So we stood in the city hall rotunda.

Was the House committee there, Billy Boy, Billy Boy,
Was the House committee there, charming Billy?
The committee, it was there,
Throwing slander everywhere,
While we sang in the city hall rotunda.
Did the people think it fair, Billy Boy, Billy Boy,
Did the people think it fair, charming Billy?
No, they didn't think it fair,
And they notified the mayor,
And he wept, and he wept,
And he wept, and he wept,
While they mopped up the city hall rotunda.[8]

■

THE WHOLE EPISODE was such a public-relations disaster for
HUAC that it never again tried to hold a hearing in San Francisco.
And the committee became incredibly thin-skinned in response
to songs and jokes about its San Francisco performance. In a
special October 10, 1962, report, it reprinted the above ditty to
show how demonic Communists could be in their efforts to kill
the committee, and it noted that the song was featured in *Sing
Out!*, "an alleged folk song magazine," whose editors were Irwin
Silber and Pete Seeger, "who have been identified as Communist
Party members." The committee also condemned the publication of *A Quarter Century of Un-Americana*, a book of cartoons
about HUAC, published jointly by Angus Cameron and by Carl
Marzani. HUAC said Cameron was "identified" as a Communist
by the SISS, and noted that Marzani had served time in prison for
denying he had been a Communist.[9]

■ FRANK WAS NOT SAN FRANCISCO MASTERMIND, BUT HE GREATLY BENEFITED FROM THE BLAME

Was Frank guilty of masterminding the riot in San Francisco?
According to the FBI, on April 4, 1960, Frank organized in San

Francisco a chapter of his CCPAF "for the specific and immediate purpose of opposing hearings by the committee which were to be held in that city the following month."[10] That much was true. Unfortunately, though he would have loved to have taken credit for putting together the splendid, three-day show of defiance, he was, to his great disappointment, innocent. He had indeed, as usual, gone to San Francisco to organize opposition. But he had started so late that his plans were limited to handing out copies of Jimmy Roosevelt's pioneering anti-HUAC speech, "The Dragon Slayers," given in Congress on April 25. Far from organizing the disturbance, Frank could not have guessed the size and scope of what was about to happen.

He had gone by city hall to attend the hearing and found, to his surprise, "a block-long line of students down the street and up the city hall's front steps to the hearing room."

> There were certainly more than six hundred waiting to get in, and 95 percent of them were students. They had been waiting since seven o'clock, so they got pretty mad when down the hall comes a couple hundred women with white cards that let them in first. Turned out they were members of the John Birch Society and various religious organizations. After the last woman got in and the students tried to follow, very few made it. The others were told the room was full. The students began yelling, "First come, first served!"
>
> I could see I couldn't get in, so I went back to the St. Francis Hotel where I had an appointment to talk to a *New York Times* reporter about our program to abolish HUAC. Then I heard on the radio about the riot at city hall and I grabbed a cab to go back there. When I arrived, firemen and police were dragging students out of city hall—soaking wet—and putting them in paddy wagons. They were all being arrested out there in the street.
>
> I went up those wet steps and into the hearing room. There was one seat vacant, by the door. At this point HUAC's counsel, Arens, the guy I'd clashed with both in San Diego and Atlanta,

was in a swivel chair browbeating one of the witnesses. He had his back to me, but he must have seen me come in. He said to the guy on the stand, "In organizing these diabolical, godless riots, were you influenced by, or did you consult with, that international Communist agent who is sitting over there?" And he spun around and pointed right at me.

Then there was a brief adjournment, and the newspaper and television reporters were all over me, asking questions.

So in fact, Frank's only role in the demonstrations and resulting riot came later, when he rushed around recruiting lawyers to get the wet college kids out of jail.

■

THE UNEARNED CREDIT Frank got for the San Francisco agitation greatly invigorated his crusade, which certainly needed it. In fact, this credit, and Frank's brilliance in seizing it, deserved or not, was probably a life-saving development for the movement to stop HUAC. The battle with the congressional inquisitors had been going on since 1952—confrontations at hearings everywhere; anti-HUAC speaking tours and rallies in dozens of cities; constant recruitment of supporters—and he and his followers had developed considerable fatigue. They were uncertain what to try next. In 1958, a small group within the hierarchy of the CCPAF had proposed that the organization disband. Frank smoothed that over, but it was clear the gas tank was running low. The young people's response to the San Francisco hearings refilled the tank—to overflowing.

And Frank's fame, thanks to his enemies, grew. First, HUAC distributed hundreds of copies of *Operation Abolition* to colleges and civic and veterans' organizations all over the country. Then the Department of Defense used *Operation Abolition* as part of a training program. And then the FBI came out with a pamphlet—it printed a half-million copies—titled "Communists Target Youth." In it, J. Edgar Hoover called Frank "the brains and energy of the San Francisco riots."

In fact, Frank first saw *Operation Abolition* by invitation from students at UC Berkeley. This occasion was also the first time he had seen any of the students involved in the city hall affair. Although he'd had no part in it, and didn't know any of the people who'd organized the demonstration, he was suddenly a famous agitator. He began to get invitations from student organizations all over the country.

■ THE REAL CONSPIRATORS OF THE GLORIOUS CITY HALL CHAOS

We can't leave San Francisco without touching upon who the main source of the agitation really was. If it wasn't Frank, who was it? No one knows for sure, but it was probably SLATE, a student political organization founded in 1957. By 1960, its accomplishments included opposing compulsory ROTC, supporting a fair-housing proposition, rallying against capital punishment, and fighting with the university over its shifting rules against political expression. So for once, the California Senate Fact-Finding Subcommittee on Un-American Activities was probably correct when, in June 1961, after a yearlong investigation of the riot in San Francisco and other student opposition to the thought police, it fingered SLATE as the chief villain. Warning that "a wave of Communism is set to break across the campuses of every major university in the state," it looked back to the ruckus at city hall in San Francisco as a portent of things to come and confirmed that J. Edgar Hoover had been right: young Communists were behind it.

The *Los Angeles Times* was delighted with that verdict, probably because it spread the guilt sufficiently to warrant a front-page banner headline:

**ALARMING RED DRIVE
IN COLLEGES DESCRIBED**
Student Recruitment
at Berkeley Charged;
Public Apathy Scored

Digesting the Senate report for its readers, the *Los Angeles Times* had to admit that, while the senators didn't exactly accuse the UC student group of being Reds, it did claim that "some of the most active leaders are oriented toward Marxism and communism."

And the orientation, it implied, was inherited. Early leaders of SLATE, the article noted, had been Carey McWilliams Jr. and Pat Hallinan. "McWilliams was identified as the son of the noted writer and editor of *The Nation*. . . ." (Enough said!)

"Hallinan, whose two brothers were also said to be associated with SLATE, was identified as the son of attorney Vincent Hallinan, candidate for president in 1952 on the Independent Progressive Party ticket. The Independent Progressive Party, the report noted, has been 'thoroughly exposed as a creature of the Communist apparatus and completely dominated by the Communist Party from start to finish.'

"David T. Rynin Jr., a SLATE activist, was identified as the son of a professor in the speech department who in the 1930s signed a petition to let the Communist Party get on the ballot and in the 1950s urged the faculty senate to adopt a rule that all faculty members would refuse to cooperate with the FBI or any other government organization asking about the loyalty of students applying for jobs."

The state senators traced radical left-wing rot not only into the UC faculty, but all the way to the top, criticizing President Clark Kerr for permitting speeches on campus by "the Communist activist" Merle Brodsky, another of those who was physically ejected from HUAC's hearings in San Francisco, and Frank Wilkinson, "the Communist propagandist and strategist."[11]

CHAPTER 23

Eloquent Words, but Was Anyone Paying Attention?

FRANK AND CARL Braden, meanwhile, had appealed their case to the Supreme Court in a constitutional challenge to Congress's right to demand information about a person's associations without evidence that they were involved in a crime. Even though they were fully aware of the odds against them when they reached the Supreme Court in February, Frank and Carl and their supporters opened 1961 with a quixotic attack, filling two pages of the first section of the *Washington Post*'s January 2 edition with an appeal to be rescued from the House Un-American Activities Committee.

Such petitions for help usually have a questionable impact on Washington, D.C., which is often petitioned into a coma; even less impact would be felt by one of the city's most rigidly inflexible organisms: Congress.

In 1961, reactionary southerners still chaired most of the important committees of Congress; as the chairmen went, so went, usually, the whole. No pressure to kill HUAC would come from the White House; one of John F. Kennedy's first actions after taking office that year was to signal his support of witch-hunters by reappointing FBI boss J. Edgar Hoover. And the background of the new attorney general, Robert Kennedy—who had once been a conspiracy blood-hound for Joseph McCarthy himself—promised little relief.

Still, the Left and civil libertarians had to keep up their morale, and a two-page spread in Washington's most influential news-paper was a good place to start. The inch-high typeface boldly proclaimed:

> Petition to the House of Representatives
> Of the 87th Congress of the United States
> We, the undersigned, petition the 87th Congress to elimi-nate the House Committee on Un-American Activities as a Standing Committee.
>
> We believe that the U.S. Supreme Court has, in *United States v. Watkins*, made it clear that the Committee has habitually misused its mandate in unconstitutional ways for political purposes; that it has an agency for repression; that it has usurped the functions of the executive and judicial branches of government.

The catalog of HUAC's evils continued, with five examples of how HUAC had perverted the whole concept of congressional inves-tigations, had discouraged free study and inquiry, had critically retarded efforts to establish peaceful relations with other countries, and had increased bitterness between racial and religious groups. And it wound up: "Let us rid ourselves of this agent of weakness and folly"—a quote selected from one of Eleanor Roosevelt's speeches.

What good would it do? Well, there was always the chance that the relatively few readers who would pause to scan the list of 346 signers would at least be somewhat impressed by the number of leaders, past and present, in their various fields.

As always in such civil-libertarian appeals, the arts and lit-erature galaxy was generously represented; Ben Shahn, William Carlos Williams, Lewis Mumford, Carl Sandburg, Catherine Drinker Bowen, Matthew Josephson, Louis Untermeyer, Thornton Wilder, J. Frank Dobie, and a score of other stars all signed.

Among the handful of scientists were such standouts as

Harlow Shapley and two Nobel laureates, Harold Urey and Linus Pauling. Theologians of various stripes were the most abundant (they numbered seventy-six), and included marquee types like Reinhold Niebuhr, Paul Tillich, and Harry Emerson Fosdick; of course, the Rev. Martin Luther King's name was there, as one of only two signers from the state of Georgia (the other, gaining brief fame for the company he kept, was attorney Austin T. Walden). All sorts of professors were sprinkled over the petition. Strangely, considering the subject, only about one-tenth of the signers were lawyers—or maybe that wasn't so strange. Some were probably spooked away from the petition because the president of the NLG, Pearl M. Hart, was a petitioner.

Of course, most of Frank's close circle had signed: Alexander Meiklejohn; Clifford Durr and Aubrey Williams, who made up two-fifths of the names from Alabama (a state that also supplied the only petitioner listed as "farmer"); and others such as Thomas I. Emerson, Carey McWilliams, Robert Kenny, Daniel and Dorothy Marshall, Vern Countryman, H. H. Wilson, and that unique Wall Street banker, James Imbrie, who was on the board of the ECLC when Frank was there and later helped organize the NCAHUAC.

Vast areas of the U.S. map were blank in this roll call—as blank, it's fair to say, as most Americans' awareness of, or interest in, the witch hunt. It could be argued as well that some—even those already affected—didn't sign out of continuing fear of HUAC.

■ WINNING ONE OUT OF TWO WAS DECEPTIVELY PROMISING

As Frank Wilkinson and Carl Braden approached their Supreme Court showdown, they had two (and possibly three) fairly recent rulings to guide them in betting on the outcome.

The first was *United States v Watkins*,[1] which the Court handed down in 1957. It was the case of a trade union official accused of being a Communist. When subpoenaed by HUAC, he had talked freely about himself (denying the accusation) and about people he knew currently to be Communists. He refused, however, to talk about the *past* affiliations of others. For that refusal, Congress had convicted him of contempt.

But the Supreme Court, speaking through Chief Justice Warren, said in a six to one decision that Watkins was innocent, because HUAC had handled him in a lawless, incoherent manner. With this decision, the Court pushed into radically new and promising territory, ruling that Congress was subject to all First Amendment restrictions, and that while Congress had the power to obtain information, "there is no congressional power to expose for the sake of exposure" or "to expose where the predominant result can only be an invasion of the private rights of individuals."

Then—after noting that Congress had given HUAC authority to investigate "the diffusion within the United States of subversive and un-American propaganda"—the Court declared that "when First Amendment rights are threatened, the delegation of power to the committee must be clearly revealed in its charter, and 'un-American' is so vague that it is difficult to imagine a less explicit authorizing resolution." With a final blast, Chief Justice Warren's opinion required that, when HUAC asked a witness a question, the witness be told why the question was pertinent to the investigation; HUAC's chairman had been "woefully inadequate" in meeting that requirement.

In short, in 1957 the Supreme Court had mopped the floor with the witch-hunters.

If that had been the Court's most recent decision regarding HUAC's conduct, Frank and Carl's chances would have looked very good indeed. The *Watkins* decision seemed to condemn most of HUAC's conduct over the previous two decades as violations of everything the First Amendment stood for.

But *Watkins* was a fluke. In the 1950s, when the investigating committees were most vigorous in harassing Americans, only once—in *Watkins*—did the Supreme Court rule against any congressional action for violating an individual's constitutional rights to free expression, due process, or privacy. In fact, rarely in its history has the Supreme Court invalidated either congressional legislation or congressional investigation as an abridgement of free speech. In periods of agitation, when the tide of national emotions is running high against dissenters and those on the fringes of orthodoxy, the practical effect of the Bill of Rights is put to the gravest test, and it is at such moments that the Supreme Court and the lower courts usually fail to stand firm behind the Constitution.

Watkins was a mini-earthquake with several aftershocks. It made arch-conservatives furious. Dismay and anger were voiced from other courts, and from many conservatives in Congress and the press, who probably spoke for much of the public. A typical editorial overreaction came from the Cleveland *Plain Dealer*: "Well, Comrades, you've got what you wanted. The Supreme Court has handed it to you on a platter."[2]

In another positive—and even more controversial—decision, *Jencks v. United States*, a Supreme Court case also tried in 1957, the Court upheld the right of a man to see the documentary evidence against him as well as hear the testimony of FBI informants.[3] Clinton Jencks was a union official accused of lying on an affidavit that he was not a member of the Communist Party. While Harvey Matusow and J. W. Ford testified that Jencks was a Communist, the FBI refused to give the defense their notes, and no other proof of his membership was offered. After this decision, Congress passed the so-called Jencks Law to try to minimize the impact of this decision.

In the year following the *Watkins* and *Jencks* decisions, the parliamentarian skills of Democratic Majority Leader Lyndon Johnson managed to block half a dozen bills that would have restricted the Supreme Court's appellate powers.

■

THE SUPREME COURT would probably have continued on this course had not its membership changed, and with it the majority's viewpoint. Eisenhower appointed two new members, Charles Evans Whittaker and Potter Stuart, and the tilt toward conservatism was dramatically illustrated two years after *Watkins*. The Court, by a five to four vote, ruled that Lloyd Barenblatt, a young

Vassar College instructor, should be imprisoned for six months because he had refused, on First Amendment grounds, to answer HUAC's questions about an alleged fling with Communism as a student at the University of Michigan.

Why was refusing to answer questions about one's own ideology (*Barenblatt v. United States*)[4] considered more punishable than refusing to answer questions about the ideology of others (*Watkins*)? There was no answer, except that the Court's ideological tilt had shifted.

According to Robert Wagman, if libertarians found anything promising in *Barenblatt*, it could only have been that with the appointment of Brennan the year before, the case "represents the first time the four-member minority of Justices Black, Brennan, Douglas, and Chief Justice Warren came together and formed what eventually became the core of a strong pro–First Amendment majority."[5]

Justice Black's fiery 1959 dissent in *Barenblatt*, joined by the other three justices, opened with the libertarians' customary damnation: HUAC had been created with such "sweeping, unlimited, all-inclusive and undiscriminating compulsory examination powers" as to violate the Fifth Amendment, and compelling Barenblatt to answer was a violation of the First Amendment.

But Black was just getting started. Next—focusing on the really dirty tactics—he accused HUAC of pursuing a course of "pitiless publicity and exposure" (to which HUAC admitted) in order to drive suspected Communists and "subversives" out of virtually all employment, public and private. And by doing that, wrote Black, HUAC was "improperly seeking to try, convict and punish suspects, a task which the Constitution expressly denies to Congress and grants exclusively to the courts, to be exercised by them only after indictment and in full compliance with all the safeguards of the Bill of Rights."[6]

Black's eloquent fury was the only thing about *Barenblatt* that Wilkinson and Braden could enjoy. In other respects, the outcome of that case clearly and accurately pointed to the probability that they would be knocked down when they approached the bar in 1961.

CHAPTER 24

Showdown at the Supreme Court's Not-So-OK Corral

THE FOLLOWING ARE thumbnail sketches of some of the Supreme Court justices who weighed the constitutionality of the charges against Frank and Carl:

Potter Stewart, who wrote the majority opinion, was one of four Eisenhower appointees. The FBI had investigated his past, something it did for all Court appointments. But Stewart got special attention from J. Edgar Hoover, perhaps in part because of his (and others') isolationist views in the 1930s. Otherwise, Stewart had been an ordinary Republican ward heeler in Cincinnati and was an average judge on the U.S. Court of Appeals when, in 1958, a vacancy opened on the Supreme Court. Hoover personally picked Stewart to fill it, and Eisenhower promptly obeyed. Why was he Hoover's choice? Maybe because, as a young Yale graduate, Stewart had tried to become an FBI agent. Maybe because the FBI's investigation of Stewart had found he had "not rendered any opinions which can be construed as anti–law enforcement or anti-Bureau."[1]

In Gifford Phillips's *Frontier Magazine* in April 1961, Daniel Berman, then of American University, wrote:

A year and a half ago I published a preliminary appraisal of Justice Stewart for the *Cincinnati Law Review*. The article led to an invitation from the Justice to visit him. Our 40-minute conversation took place in his chambers in the Court on Jan. 27, 1960—thirteen months to the day before he announced the Court's disposition of the Wilkinson and Braden cases. One of the principal subjects covered in our conversation was the deciding vote Stewart had cast in the *Barenblatt* contempt case in the preceding year.

The discussion left me with a feeling of utter incredulity. [Among other key facts about HUAC] . . . it was news to him that J. Parnell Thomas, a former chairman of the Committee, has gone to jail for padding his payroll. In fact, he seemed totally ignorant of all aspects of the Committee which had not been covered in the briefs submitted to the Supreme Court—and some which had.

One knows there are lawyers whose only source of information is court cases, but it is staggering to find an example in the robes of a Supreme Court justice. The man who was to send Carl Braden and Frank Wilkinson to jail seemed the archetype of the lawyer who has sharpened his mind merely by narrowing it.

Stewart must have been putty in the hands of Justice Felix Frankfurter, who assigned the writing of the *Braden* and *Wilkinson* opinions to him. Frankfurter, in fact, had been the real villain in almost every one of the tragic decisions institutionalizing a genteel variety of McCarthyism. It was he who persuaded the Court's majority that abridgments of personal beliefs . . . are acceptable as long as the governmental purpose . . . outweighs the constitutional rights of the individual and the public.[2]

Felix Frankfurter was an FDR appointee to the Court in 1939. Because as a young man Frankfurter had helped establish the ACLU and the NAACP and had been something of a liberal activist in the early New Deal, he carried, through the rest of his life, a leftist reputation he did not deserve.

During the 1940s and 1950s, all liberals and most centrists of the judicial world came to believe that the First Amendment (freedom of speech, press, religion) and the Fourteenth Amendment (in which all constitutional safeguards of freedom are made applicable to state courts) deserved special status. Some called it "the preferred freedoms doctrine." To his dying day, Frankfurter disagreed.[3]

It was fitting that Frankfurter was chosen in 1940 to write one of the Court's historic blunders, in which the appeal of two Pennsylvania children, Jehovah's Witnesses who had been expelled from school for refusing to salute the flag for religious reasons, had been rejected. "We live by symbols," he wrote with puzzling logic. "The flag is a symbol of our national unity, transcending all internal differences, however large, within the framework of the Constitution. It is not for the courts to interfere with a school board's right to awaken in the child's mind considerations as to the significance of the flag contrary to those implanted by the parent." With war breaking out in Europe and threatening to suck in the United States, hyperpatriotism was in the air, and even the liberals on the Court complied in the eight-to-one ruling. But three years later, an ashamed Court reversed itself, ruling six to three that a couple of West Virginia kids, also Jehovah's Witnesses, could keep their hands down when the flag went up. Frankfurter didn't switch. When the choice was between state's rights and the Bill of Rights, he usually sided with the former.

Tom Clark had been on the Court since 1949. He had been one of Truman's bad attorneys general—and the most damaging to the Bill of Rights. A lawyer from eastern Texas, Clark had no tolerance for dissenters—or for people who tolerated them. He had fiercely opposed the NLG and had tried to persuade national and state bar associations to disbar attorneys they believed to be Communists. He publicly advocated harsh punishments—even jail time and suspension of licenses—for attorneys who defended Communist clients so enthusiastically as to offend "the dignity and order of our courts."[4] His suggestion caught on—with chilling effect.

MONSIGNOR PAUL O'DWYER, Los Angeles Archdiocesan director of charities. Frank's mentor for twelve years in the Citizens Housing Council. Unknown photographer, circa 1940s. Wilkinson family collection.

FRANK and others in a housing protest in Los Angeles, circa 1939.
Unknown photographer

TONY, JO, FRANK, and **JEAN WILKINSON** playing in the snow.
Photo by Leonard Nadel, noted L.A. housing photographer. January 1949.

"You Read Books, Eh?"

YOU READ BOOKS, EH? Originally appeared in the *Washington Post*, April 1949. *The Herblock Book*, Herbert Block, Beacon Press. Boston, 1952. p. 141. Used with permission from Beacon Press.

JAMES DOMBROWSKI, CARL and **ANNE BRADEN, FRANK WILKINSON,** and **REVEREND MARTIN LUTHER KING JR.** at dinner before Frank and Carl head to jail, April 1961. Unknown photographer. Wilkinson family collection.

FRANK and **CARL BRADEN** in Atlanta, in a police car heading to jail, May 1, 1961. Probably by Tracy O'Neal. Permission from Special Collections, Georgia State University.

JEFFRY, JO, and **TONY WILKINSON**, with dog. 1961. Family photo by Adya Bryant. This is the photo Frank had with him while he was in jail.

FRANK and **CARL BRADEN** in jail, 1961–2. Unknown photographer. Wilkinson family collection.

Would you believe Concentration Camps for Americans?

WOULD YOU BELIEVE CONCENTRATION CAMPS FOR AMERICANS?, 1968 NCARL flier cover. Key flier for campaign with the Japanese American Citizens League to eliminate part of the McCarran Act.

AUBREY WILLIAMS, probably from Chicago NCAHUAC meeting 1963. Unknown photographer. Rachel Rosen DeGolia collection.

FBI MEMOS regarding assassination attempt against Frank. March 1964. Obtained in FOIA lawsuit against the FBI.

A March 2, 1966, *News & Observer* photo shows UNC student president Paul Dickson (left) greeting students who had gathered at what became known — and labeled — as "Gov. Dan K. Moore's Wall" prior to Frank Wilkinson's address.

It's time to bury the Speaker Ban Law

University of North Carolina
Chapel Hill, NC

SPECTATOR

MARCH 30-APRIL 6, 1995

March 1966: Frank Wilkinson speaks to UNC students across a wall dividing the campus from the rest of the town

FRANK WILKINSON, banned from speaking at UNC, addresses crowd from across a wall, March 2, 1966, then March 1995, invited back to campus. March 2, 1966 *News & Observer*, reprinted by permission. *UNC Spectator* April 1995.

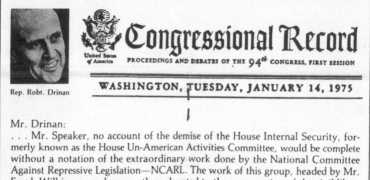

Rep. Robt. Drinan

Congressional Record

United States of America — PROCEEDINGS AND DEBATES OF THE 94ᵗʰ CONGRESS, FIRST SESSION

WASHINGTON, TUESDAY, JANUARY 14, 1975

Mr. Drinan:

. . . Mr. Speaker, no account of the demise of the House Internal Security, formerly known as the House Un-American Activities Committee, would be complete without a notation of the extraordinary work done by the National Committee Against Repressive Legislation—NCARL. The work of this group, headed by Mr. Frank Wilkinson, and many others devoted to the preservation of the civil liberties of Americans, has been uniquely valuable to Members of this Congress who have sought to excise from the dignity and majesty of the House that self-inflicted wound called HUAC-HISC which now after 30 or more years will no longer be an embarrassment and indeed a disgrace to the Congress of the United States . . .

REP. ROBERT DRINAN comments in January 14, 1975, *Congressional Record* acknowledging the critical role of NCARL in the abolition of HUAC.

NCARL FAMILY PORTRAIT at 1975 meeting following abolition of HUAC. Unknown photographer.

FRANK WILKINSON, General Counsel **PAUL HOFFMAN**, ACLU of Southern California, and Attorney **DOUGLAS MIRELL**, Loeb and Loeb, with some of the files on Frank and NCAHUAC from the successful FOIA suit against the FBI. *Los Angeles Times* October 18, 1987. Copyright, 1987, *Los Angeles Times*. Reprinted with permission.

REP. JOHN LEWIS, FRANK WILKINSON, and civil rights leader and First Amendment Foundation board member, **REV. C. T. VIVIAN,** Washington, D.C. 1989 celebration of Frank's seventy-fifth birthday and thirtieth anniversary of NCARL. Photo by Rachel Rosen DeGolia.

First Amendment Foundation and NCARL meeting 1989. Frank's sister **HILDEGARDE**, **FRANK** and **DONNA WILKINSON**. Kit Gage, photographer.

FRANK and **DICK CRILEY** at ACLU 1999 biennial, where Frank received ACLU Earl Warren Civil Liberties Award. ACLU photo. Wilkinson family collection.

Apparently approving of Clark's Americanism at the time (though years later Truman would describe his former attorney general as a "dumb son of a bitch"), in 1949 Truman next appointed him to the U.S. Supreme Court, where he joined three other Truman appointees—Fred Vinson, Sherman Minton, and Harold Burton—to support federal and state suppression of individual freedom.[5]

Clark's anti-Communist crusade drew him into a close alliance with J. Edgar Hoover. Although as head of the Justice Department he was officially Hoover's boss, Clark was subservient to the FBI director and rubber-stamped most of his requests. One of these requests expanded the FBI's wiretapping power to include subversive activities (beyond actual deterrence) and certain types of criminal cases, such as kidnapping.

When Clark moved to the Court, their friendship grew closer. The hallowed table at Harvey's eatery reserved for Hoover and his constant companion, Clyde Tolson, was now frequently occupied by Clark as well. Some in Washington believed Clark was an informer for Hoover, and would pass along gossip about the justices' musings in cases that might relate to security matters.[6]

■ ON THE OTHER SIDE . . .

There were also, of course, four justices who voted to set Wilkinson and Braden free.

It was Earl Warren, former attorney general and governor of California, who provided the decisive support that got Eisenhower the GOP nomination in 1952. He was rewarded by being appointed chief justice. Eisenhower was perhaps misled in his expectations by the fact that Warren, as attorney general, had treated some labor unions severely and, as governor, had supported putting Japanese people living in California in detention camps during World War II (an act that, later in life, Warren wept to remember). On reaching the Court, and following the *Brown* decision, he showed a radically different side—so different that the southern segregationists began putting up highway billboards calling for his impeachment.

Eisenhower called Warren's appointment "the biggest damn fool mistake I ever made." Understandably: in important cases, Warren almost always voted contrary to Eisenhower's position. The president sympathized with the South—he told Warren shortly after he arrived in Washington, "These are not bad people. All they are concerned about is to see that their sweet little girls are not required to sit in schools alongside some big black bucks."[7] Warren's very first act as chief justice was to somehow magically persuade the entire Court to support *Brown*, the landmark school integration ruling.

He brought a new atmosphere to the Court. According to Alexander Bickel, "When a lawyer stood before him arguing his side of the case on the basis of some legal doctrine or other, or making a procedural point, or contending that the Constitution allocated competence over a given issue to another branch of government than the Supreme Court or to the states rather than to the federal government, the Chief Justice would shake him off by saying, 'Yes, yes, yes, but is it *right*? Is it *good*?'"[8]

William Joseph Brennan Jr. was a seven-year veteran of the New Jersey judiciary and another Eisenhower appointee who no doubt disappointed his patron by virtually always voting to support individual rights.

Though he had a long and distinguished career, he is perhaps best remembered for crafting the majority opinion in *New York Times v. Sullivan*. A number of Alabama politicians, including the governor, had sued the *New York Times* for a total of $3 million (big bucks in those days) for carrying an antisegregation ad on March 29, 1960, that they claimed constituted libel. The Brennan opinion declared that libel actions brought by public officials could prevail only if they could prove the defendant had *knowingly* published false information or had done so *in reckless disregard of the truth*. That lofty standard made it virtually impossible for public officials to punish their critics by libel lawsuits. It has been called "the epitaph for sedition in America."[9] Meiklejohn, the philosopher of free speech, said the Court's opinion was an occasion for "dancing in the streets."[10]

And the revolution had only just begun. Three years after the Wilkinson case, in *Curtis Publishing Co. v. Butts*, Brennan cowrote the Court's majority opinion that public figures must meet the same "reckless disregard" test as public officials in libel cases. (Stewart was among the dissenters.)[11]

The one and only—abysmally dark—stain on Brennan's First Amendment record was his writing the majority opinion condemning Ralph Ginzburg to prison in 1966 for violating the outdated (to say the least) ninety-three-year-old Comstock anti-obscenity law.[12] Brennan later admitted it was the worst decision of his career, and many legal scholars consider it one of the worst ever written by anybody.

Stewart, writing for the minority in that case, came up with the smartest thing he ever said: "Most of the material strikes me as both vulgar and unedifying. But if the First Amendment means anything, it means that a man cannot be sent to prison merely for distributing publications which offend a judge's aesthetic sensibilities, mine or any other's."[13]

But the "absolutist" defenders of First Amendment rights and, therefore, the most controversial justices, were William Orville Douglas and Hugo Lafayette Black.

Their backgrounds were very different. Douglas was a Minnesotan with an Ivy League law degree who was teaching securities law at Yale when Roosevelt picked him to oversee the Securities and Exchange Commission. Black's background was less lofty. He was an Alabaman with a law degree from his state's mediocre university. His law practice in Birmingham tended to support working stiffs: labor and personal-injury lawsuits were a natural springboard into Democratic politics, and the Democratic Party was then dominant in the South. He also joined the Ku Klux Klan—which in those days was looked upon by many white men as no more extreme than the American Legion. But he strategically quit the Klan to run successfully for the U.S. Senate in 1927. There he became known as a firebrand reformer. In 1935, he spoke on the radio to warn the public that lobbying in Washington "has reached such a position of power that it threatens the government itself. Its size, its power, its capacity for evil; its greed, trickery, deception, and fraud condemn it to the death it deserves."[14] FDR, who was having some trouble with the Supreme Court and needed a fighter there, named Black to the Court in 1937.

So uncompromisingly did Douglas and Black support First Amendment rights that they infuriated some of the other justices— particularly the snobbish Frankfurter, who sarcastically referred to them as "those great libertarians." One of Black's legal opinions, Frankfurter said, "makes me want to puke." Another time, he likened Black to "the cheapest soapbox orator." After one of their arguments, Black told another colleague, "I thought Felix was going to hit me today, he got so mad."[15]

Nor was there any love lost between Frankfurter and Douglas, whom Frankfurter called "the most cynical, immoral person I've ever known" and "the most systematic exploiter of flattery I have ever encountered in my life." Douglas's opinion of Frankfurter was much briefer: "A prevaricator."[16]

It was hardly surprising, then, that Frankfurter did not join Black and Douglas in defense of Wilkinson and Braden. It was certainly no surprise to Frank. He and Meiklejohn were sitting together in the audience listening to the lawyers debate his fate before the Supreme Court when a page came down and handed a note to Meiklejohn. It was from Frankfurter. It said, "Alex, how could you!" Meiklejohn looked up and saw Frankfurter shaking his head sadly.

■ THE SUPREME COURT OUTCOME IN A NUTSHELL

The three pages the *New York Times* gave to the Supreme Court debate over this case might have been a bit hefty for the typical subway rider to digest, but for five cents he or she could buy the liberal *New York Post* and get a very good brief summation of its outcome:[17]

> By a vote of 5 to 4, the Supreme Court has given the House Un-American Activities Committee another reprieve. In affirming the contempt convictions of Frank Wilkinson and Carl Braden,

the Court majority—Stewart, Frankfurter, Clark, Harlan and Whittaker—has affirmed the committee's power to question any American who criticizes its operation and has the misfortune to be labeled a Communist—justly or falsely—by almost any professional informer or amateur snooper.

The decision will keep the committee in business for a while. Growing numbers of Americans have begun to ask out loud what function the committee really serves, and by what standard it presumes to be the arbiter of "Americanism" and thereby dishonor us in the world. All of them are now subject to inquisition if the committee merely asserts that somewhere some alleged authority accused the skeptical one of being identified with "subversion," the area which is the committee's private playground.

We do not naively suggest that Wilkinson and Braden are conservative Republicans who are hapless victims of mistaken identity. What is clear is that both men were hauled before the committee as a direct result of their efforts to organize public opposition to the committee's works. In upholding the committee's right to subject them to its inquisition, the majority relied solely on the unproved allegations that they were Communists. As Justice Black pointed out in his eloquent dissent, every member of the Court has been the target of the same charge from some know-nothing source.

■

STEWART, AS SPOKESMAN for the majority, shrugged off the petitioners' complaint that HUAC's only motive in subpoenaing them was to punish them for their criticisms. He said, "It isn't for us to speculate as to the committee's motivations," and, "We can find nothing to indicate that it was the intent of Congress to immunize from interrogation all those (and there are many) who are opposed" to HUAC.

Furthermore, said Stewart, HUAC had a good reason to

subpoena them, because they had previously been identified as Communists—Frank by a paid FBI informer at the HUAC hearing in San Diego, Carl by a paid informer at Senator Eastland's SISS hearing in New Orleans.

That was about all Stewart had to say, but after he finished reading his written opinion he took the very unusual step of adding something, off the cuff, that made it sound like he didn't want anyone to think he was happy to be taking the side of the HUAC riffraff; Anthony Lewis, the *New York Times'* court reporter, quoted him: "Of course it is unnecessary for me to say that these opinions do not imply any *personal views* as to the wisdom or unwisdom of the *creation or continuance* of this committee." (Emphasis added.)

At the very least, wrote Lewis, Stewart by that comment was "going out of his way to disassociate himself and the Court from the House committee."

■

ALL OF THE justices in the minority—Black, Douglas, Warren, Brennan—expressed the same contempt for HUAC, but they also expressed contempt for their conservative brethren's tolerance for its inquisition.

Black, joined by Douglas and Warren said, " . . . it is clear that this case involves nothing more nor less than an attempt by the House Un-American Activities Committee to use the contempt power of the House of Representatives as a weapon against those who dare to criticize it. The dominant purpose in subpoenaing Wilkinson was to harass him and expose him for the sake of exposure.

"The majority does not and, in reason, could not deny this, for the conclusion is all but inescapable for any who will take the time to read the record. They [the Court majority] say instead that it makes no difference whether the Committee was harassing Frank Wilkinson solely for reason of his opposition."

Brennan and Douglas argued that HUAC had known in

advance that Frank wouldn't testify, and so had looked upon him as a sitting duck. "A scant 19 months before the hearing in question, Wilkinson was summoned before this very committee and refused to answer questions on substantially the same grounds as those he claimed in this instance. Nor did his conduct in the interim afford any basis for the hope that he may have repented, for he continued to proclaim his hostility to the committee and his belief that it had no power to probe areas of free expression.

"Furthermore, HUAC's staff director came perilously close to admitting—on cross-examination by Wilkinson's counsel—that Wilkinson was called to the stand only because of his opposition to the committee's activities."

As for Stewart's argument that HUAC had probable cause to subpoena Frank and Carl because (paid) informers had identified them as Communists, Black pointed out that the defendants had not been allowed to cross-examine the informers. And anyway, "information from paid informers is totally worthless" because "perjury among them is commonplace."

Then Black began to raise his voice to a tone of militant outrage, a performance for which he was famous: "In the atmosphere existing in this country today, the charge that someone is a Communist is so common that hardly anyone active in public life has escaped it. Every member of this Court has, on one occasion or another, been so designated. And a vast majority of the members of the other two branches of government have fared no better.

"Thus, in my view . . . the only real limitation upon the Committee's power to harass its opponents is the Committee's own self-restraint, a characteristic which probably has not been predominant in the Committee's work over the past few years.

"The result of all this is that from now on anyone who takes a public position contrary to that being urged by the House Un-American Activities Committee should realize that he runs the risk of being subpoenaed to appear at a hearing in some far-off place, or being questioned with regard to every minute detail of his past life, or being asked to repeat all the gossip he may have heard about any of his friends and acquaintances, of being accused by the Committee of membership in the Communist Party, of being held up to the public as a subversive and a traitor, of being jailed for contempt if he refused to cooperate with the Committee in its probe of his mind and associations, and of being branded by his neighbors, employer, and erstwhile friends as a menace to society regardless of the outcome of the hearing.

"With such a powerful weapon in its hands, it seems quite likely that the Committee will weather all criticism, even though justifiable, that may be directed toward it. For there are not many people in our society who will have the courage to speak out against such a formidable opponent.

"If the present trend continues, this already small number will necessarily dwindle as their ranks are thinned by the jails.

"Government by consent will disappear, to be replaced by government by intimidation, because some people are afraid that this country cannot survive unless Congress has the power to set aside the freedoms of the First Amendment at will.

"I can only reiterate my firm conviction that these people are tragically wrong. This country was not built by men who were afraid and it cannot be preserved by such men."

■ FROM THE MAINSTREAM PRESS, LITTLE SYMPATHY

Considering the spirited attention given to this case as it wound its way to the Supreme Court—there were numerous anti-HUAC rallies on college campuses and in Washington, D.C., plus anti-HUAC petitions signed by hundreds of notable people—and then the front-page attention given to the Supreme Court's judgment by the *New York Times* and the *Washington Post*, there was little editorial comment.

An exception was the *New York Post*'s columnist Murray Kempton, famed for defending underdogs and deflating stuffed shirts. On February 28, 1961, he wrote a slashing attack on Justice Frankfurter in which he portrayed him as the elitist manipulator behind the Supreme Court's decision. Kempton wrote, in part:

The majority opinion was delivered by Justice Stewart, but make no mistake, it was Frankfurter's opinion. He is the most voluble man alive, but in this case he preferred to sign in silence.

Justices Black, Douglas, Brennan and Chief Justice Warren dissented. They are men who in the main lacked Justice Frankfurter's great advantages of early acquaintance with the great. Chief Justice Warren is the product of one of the most unproductive educational institutions in the land, the California Republican Party. Justice Brennan is the son of a building trades labor skate, and went to a parochial school. And Justice Black was once a Birmingham, Alabama, night court judge. I am proud to be an American and a citizen of a country which is fed from unfashionable sources. Harvard gave us Frankfurter; and the Alabama police court gave us Black, and we're almost even. . . .

I am sure that my liberties and Justice Frankfurter's are safe from the Un-American Activities Committee. The issue is the liberty of Frank Wilkinson.

Mr. Justice Frankfurter, in his habitual glorification of the collective over the individual—which in essence means the friend in high station over the unknown humble—can be as zealous as he wishes in defending the right of Congressmen to make fools of themselves. But he cannot argue—and retain our respect—that Congressmen can defend that right by sending a man to jail for questioning it. . . .

In moments like this, I always seem to remember a discharged subway switchman who came to see me once. He was a security risk: the authorities believed that, in the emergency after the Soviets drop the hydrogen bomb on us, our safety might be imperiled if, under [Communist] Party orders, he threw the wrong switch on the Queensboro line.

"What I want to know," the poor man said, "is who goes to glory by taking away my job?" All right, Mr. Justice Frankfurter, who goes to glory when Frank Wilkinson goes to jail?[18]

CHAPTER 25

An Organizing Interlude before Jail

AFTER HIS CONVICTION for contempt of Congress was upheld by the Supreme Court, Frank became an even more romantic outlaw to many collegians. As a speaker, he was very much in demand.

Shortly after the Court's decision came down in February 1961, to great national publicity, the Berkeley student organization SLATE (which had helped organize the wonderful and raucous protest of the HUAC hearings in San Francisco) invited Frank to come up and speak to "thirty-five" of its members. He must have misunderstood. He spoke not to thirty-five students, but to five thousand: one thousand were crammed into Wheeler Auditorium, more than three hundred into Wheeler room number eleven, and about three thousand outside listening via loudspeakers—a total of almost a quarter of the student body. He outdrew Governor Nelson Rockefeller, who had spoken there in the fall.

The crowd was made even bigger by the organized opposition. Led by Assemblyman Don Mulford of Berkeley and three well-known Baptist ministers of that area, an eighty-car caravan carried two hundred Bay Area residents to Sacramento to storm the capitol and demand that Governor Brown refuse to let Frank speak at UC Berkeley. Brown, who was also chairman of the Board of Regents, did not oblige. Neither did Berkeley president Clark Kerr, who said, "The University is not engaged in making ideas safe for students. It is engaged in making students safe for ideas." As FBI records later revealed, this was just one of a number of things Kerr said and did that convinced J. Edgar Hoover that he was a Communist.[1]

Naturally, it was curiosity stirred by the headlined opposition to Frank's appearance rather than a real awareness of the constitutional issues at stake that prompted much of the attendance. Many of the students must have been as uninformed as Dick Dean, a political science major from Castro Valley, who told a *San Francisco Chronicle* reporter, "Life's never dull around here. I've heard speakers from Adlai Stevenson to . . . to Wilkinson. Who the hell is this guy, anyway?"[2]

But without question, the response that developed at Berkeley, with Frank's encouragement, in the early sixties was part of the first stirring of what in 1964 would become the revolutionary Berkeley Free Speech Movement, which sent waves of revolt across campuses around the nation.

■

BY THE TIME Frank was invited to speak at Berkeley by SLATE leaders Michael E. Tigar, who later became a celebrated attorney, and Michael Myerson, who later headed the World Peace Council, he was already something of a celebrity. The *New York Times* had considered his appeal to the Supreme Court enough of a landmark case to give the Court's opinions three full pages.

But when Frank and Meiklejohn passed through Sather Gate and were met by television crews and a crowd of about three thousand, Frank was struck dumb. He had no prepared speech, and he tried to get Meiklejohn to take his place.

"Let me introduce you, and then you talk to these students," he said.

"Oh, no, Frank," responded Meiklejohn. "This is your day. Just get up there and tell them about Emerson and Thoreau."

"I looked at him blankly," Frank recalls.

> He says to me, "You know, Thoreau went to jail just like you're going to do. You know, he failed to pay taxes for the Mexican Civil War and spent the night in jail and Emerson came to see him."
>
> I'm about to be introduced and I'm very impatient with Meiklejohn, who keeps encouraging me. "You know, Emerson said, 'What are you doing in there, Henry?' and Thoreau said, 'What are you doing out *there*, Ralph?'
>
> Meiklejohn looked at me like he'd made a great point and I'm still blank. He said, "You've read Emerson and Thoreau, haven't you?" I said, "No!" He said, "Oh, Frank. Oh, Frank. Oh, Frank."
>
> Then *he* became alarmed and said, "You get up there and you make the best speech you can. And once you're in prison, I'll send you books so you'll know why you're in there."

Some talented and aggressive students were so angered by the riots and inspired by Frank's speech that they dropped out of college to volunteer for his new organization, the National Committee to Abolish HUAC (with the impossibly long acronym NCAHUAC), which had been set up in August 1960. Though the speech had been his first to students, and he admits it wasn't very good, it at least included his memorable remark: "We will never save the First Amendment unless we are willing to go to prison to save it. I am willing."

One convert to the cause was Arnold Lockshin who had done Phi Beta Kappa undergraduate work at Berkeley and doctoral work in biochemistry at the University of Wisconsin. He was also a pianist talented enough to have played, at the age of twelve, with the San Francisco Symphony Orchestra. Lockshin was living in Berkeley in 1960 and had gone across the bridge to attend the hearings. He got caught up in the movement, gave up his brilliant career writing scientific papers, and volunteered to run the abolition office in Boston—at forty-five dollars a week. It was he who persuaded the National Council of Catholic Bishops to take a stand against HUAC.

Classy recruits were always the hallmark of Frank's organizations.

When Lockshin gave up his NCAHUAC job to join a peace movement, his replacement in Boston was Peter H. Irons, a PhD in history and a graduate of Harvard Law School who was later a leading counsel on the Japanese American restitution case and a nationally known historian.

Another outstanding recruit was Burton White. One scene in *Operation Abolition* shows him standing in a city hall corridor cheerily leading a group sing-along during the demonstration. In the film, the HUAC commentator says he is using a Communist songbook. This enraged White, a graduate student at UC in medieval history, who knew nothing about Communism and had never had a radical thought in his head until the cops washed him down the city hall steps. After that, he dropped out of school, signed on with Frank, and went around the country speaking on behalf of the NCAHUAC.

■

FROM THE TIME of his Berkeley speech until he went to prison on May Day, 1961, Frank, usually accompanied by Carl Braden, had a packed coast-to-coast schedule, giving speeches mostly on university campuses in Los Angeles, Boston, New York, Chicago (several times), Madison, Milwaukee, Baltimore, Salt Lake City, and Denver. A Pete Seeger concert drew a turnout of five thousand to hear them in New York. At Yale University, the law school chose Frank and Carl's First Amendment case as the "moot court argument" (traditionally, a school-wide event where students learn to argue important issues) that spring and gave a dinner in their honor.

On their last night of freedom, Frank and Carl were guests

of honor at a reception at Morehouse College. They were the only white people there. Their hosts were black clergymen, led by Dr. Martin Luther King. King told them, "These men are going to jail for us. We'll never achieve peaceable integration in the South until the Un-American Committee is abolished." Later they had a private dinner with just Dr. and Mrs. King.

In some respects, it was a triumphant tour—Frank's work, at least, was being noticed as never before. But he remembers it with painful modesty. Before this speaking tour, his work had been mostly that of an organizer, and while he was masterful at the conversational level, dealing with small groups or one on one, he wasn't yet the powerfully persuasive platform speaker he would become through endless experience. "I just remember reaching the point where I didn't really know what to say. I was not prepared to speak. Carl was making these rambunctious statements, very well informed, very radical, very [he laughs] Carl Braden-ish, and I was just getting up there and sayings things like, 'For every person silenced in jail by the committee, a thousand new voices will be raised and many of these will be students.' Frankly, I was just relieved to go to jail—because I didn't know what to say and I was speaking all over the country."

CHAPTER 26

Guests of Honor, then Off to a Hairy Atlanta Jail

FRANK AND CARL were ordered to show up in Atlanta to start their imprisonment on May 1, 1961. May 1, of course, is the original Labor Day, the day Communists everywhere celebrate as their equivalent of July 4. Was the government playing a little joke on them?

At 10 A.M., Frank and Carl showed up at the federal courthouse. Frank, ever the optimist, carried a briefcase and some books to read. These were immediately confiscated. Next they were taken to the stainless steel Fulton County Jail, where they were grabbed and half-pushed through rooms to be fingerprinted and have their mug shots taken before being separated into different holding cells, each of which was about twelve by eighteen feet and contained sixteen bunks, a table, and a very small amount of space in which to walk. The rooms had two toilets, neither of which had a seat. Frank recalls, "You squatted on the toilet with fifteen guys watching you, telling you not to fart, not to stink—'Flush it, goddamn you!'—while you're trying to do your business."

Toughness—physical and/or mental—determined the hierarchy among the sixteen inmates. The top dogs decided who got which bunk, who got the most food, who got to use the table. Frank was low man on the totem pole He sometimes had to sit on the concrete floor. The height of generosity was when one of the tough guys watching him eat asked, "You want this?"—and tossed half of a piece of bread from his own plate to Frank. It was the first and only bread he got that day. But Frank knew better than to complain. Some of his cell mates were in for violent crimes, and, having been stuck in that fetid room for months, were about to explode again. It was better if they didn't even notice him.

Segregation was total: whites on Frank's floor, blacks on the floor below.

The atmosphere was dicey from the moment he was shoved into the room.

I came in there still wearing my suit. They hadn't taken my clothes yet. I saw on the table a newspaper—I'm sure it was the warden's doing, because I never saw newspapers generally getting into the prison while I was there. It was the *Atlanta Constitution* with pictures of Carl Braden and me being embraced by Dr. King. The headlines in those days were that Freedom Riders had been arrested in Alabama after the police stood by and watched them being beaten. It was a very, very angry situation.

The concept of two guys being jailed for a First Amendment challenge of the Un-American Activities Committee was beyond my cell mates' comprehension. They were all classic rednecks. Crackers. They assumed we were Freedom Riders and we were being jailed because of it. We were friends of Dr. King, and that was an even worse identification.

I hadn't been in the room a minute before I sensed the hostility. I had to do something for self-protection. I noticed there was a Bible on the table—the only book in the room—and I went directly over, sat down, and starting read it. I just sensed that any eye contact would be dangerous.

I don't know how many minutes it was, but very shortly after that the door clanged and a guard came in with a paper sack, and calls out my name as though he didn't know who I was. He'd just brought me in there. He hands the sack to me, and as soon as he leaves, one of the bigger guys in the room takes it from me.

He reaches inside and pulls out a book. Stuck in the book is a rosebud on a short stem. (I didn't know how this happened until much later, when I was out of prison. The book and rose had been sent by Isabel Carney, a very devout Quaker lady from northern California. Actually, she had come to the prison with a bouquet of a dozen roses, but they let her send in only that one rosebud, stuck in this book of writings by George Fox, the seventeenth, eighteenth-century Quaker who had been jailed for his religious beliefs. She thought I would like to read it because I was being jailed for my views, the same as George Fox was.)

The moment that rose came out of the sack, there was a powerful psychological effect on the whole cell. It took their eyes off me and their minds off the Freedom Riders. These guys had not seen sunlight for maybe five or six months. They had seen nothing of nature in that time. One guy took this rose and held it in his hand for a moment, then passed it to another, real carefully. Another guy picked up a tobacco can off the table, went over to the toilet and scooped it full of water, brought it back to the table, and then two of them worked, very carefully, at propping up the rosebud in the can. During the eleven days I spent in that room, they kept that rose alive.

And maybe the rose kept me alive. If the other inmates had decided to beat me up or gang-rape me—and gang rape was a real possibility in those places—I would have had no chance at all. By the time the guards would have come, whatever they were going to do to me would have been done, and I would have been severely hurt or killed. But after the rose, it seemed the possibility of attacks on me went away.

While he was in the holding cell, Frank got a good look at racism in action. When black inmates were brought up from the floor below to mop the corridor outside his cell block, white inmates would take human feces out of the toilet, throw it in the corridor, and taunt the blacks. "You know the language. I don't think I'd ever heard the term *motherfucker* before. Now everything was motherfucker, motherfucker, motherfucker. 'You black mother-fucker, clean up that shit.' I watched that and it just paralyzed me because all I would have had to do was to protest—'That's no way to talk to someone' or, 'You shouldn't do that'—and believe me, I would have been in deep trouble."

Fortunately, he could be deaf to much of this simply by turning off his hearing aid.

One of the miracles of his stay in the Fulton County Jail was that, for some reason, the authorities allowed a package to get through to him containing Ray Ginger's *The Bending Cross: A Biography of Eugene Victor Debs.* "I would sit there, often on the floor, amazed that they were letting me read these wild speeches that Debs made about the ruling class and the working class. Some of Debs's writing had been done in the Atlanta penitentiary, a short distance from where Carl and I were jailed forty years later. His rhetoric was like Carl's, not like mine. I never talked about the class conflict, but Carl did. Here I'm reading this radical material and looking around at my 'working-class' cell mates and wondering if they had ever had a Debsian impulse in all their life."

Their lawyers made a real effort to get Carl transferred to a prison in or near Kentucky so that his family could visit him more easily, and to get Frank transferred to a California prison.

So they were transferred to a prison in Greenville, South Carolina.

∎ THE LAND OF MOONSHINERS AND ILLITERACY

For the first time, a note of loathing creeps into Frank's retelling of his odyssey through the federal prisons. It wasn't directed at his fellow inmates, but was reserved almost entirely for the police, guards, and prison officials at whose mercy the prisoners suffered.

Frank and Carl had not been convicted of an antisocial

crime. They had been convicted of a mere misdemeanor. And when they failed in their efforts to have their convictions overturned, they voluntarily surrendered to begin their punishment. And yet, every step of the way, they were treated as though they were the most dangerous criminal felons plotting to flee at the first opportunity.

Frank's loathing really began to develop on the trip from Atlanta to Greenville. The doors to the back seat, where he and Carl rode, had no handles and could not be opened from the inside. There was a heavy screen separating the back seat from the front, where the two officers were sitting. Obviously, there was no way Frank and Carl could escape, and yet they rode in chains: very short chains around and linking their ankles, so that even if they somehow miraculously got out of the car, they could not run or even walk normally, but only hobble along. And there was a chain around their waist, to which their manacled hands were chained.

En route, Frank told the officers he had to urinate. At first they told him to just hold it for another hour, but finally they stopped at a dirty little gas station. They went through the police farce: checking their guns to see that they were loaded, then checking Frank's chains to see that they were still tight, then finally allowing him to hobble to the restroom. But Frank was so tightly chained that he couldn't reach his fly.

At that point, he says, he was suddenly swept with "a sort of cynical vicious feeling toward these guys. I said, 'Will you pull down my fly so I can urinate?' I felt like saying, 'Will you *hold it* for me so I can urinate?' It was security madness. They wouldn't even release one of my hands so I could urinate."

■ GREENVILLE

Once he and Carl were handed over to the guards at the Greenville prison, their chains were removed and they could walk around rather freely. They were sent to the warden's office for an "orientation" session—i.e., to get a work assignment.

When Frank entered the office, the warden was busy over some papers. In front of his desk was a chair that was obviously intended for new prisoners to sit in for the interview. So Frank sat down.

Immediately, the warden looked up at Frank and shouted, "Get out of that chair! Get out of it! Don't sit down! I know all about you. I don't want any of your teaching here. Get out!"

That was Frank's "orientation." He never learned what the warden meant by "teaching," although he supposed the FBI had warned the warden to watch out for his spreading left-wing doctrines.

The inmates could certainly have used some "teaching." Forty of the four hundred prisoners signed their names with an X. Most inmates had gone through only the third grade in schools buried out on dirt roads in northern Georgia, South Carolina, and North Carolina. The prison had equipment in its library that could have changed their lives: up-to-date projectors and all the films for teaching reading and writing to adults. Although Frank was assigned to the library, he wasn't allowed to touch that equipment. It was always kept under plastic wrap.

His job was to test incoming prisoners for their IQ and skills, to note down their background and recommend where they should work in the prison. But measuring their intelligence was mostly a matter of guesswork, because he didn't have the equipment to do it properly. It couldn't easily be done verbally, and a written test was out of the question. "These men were capable of doing anything they were asked to do in the way of hard work," says Frank, "but when I would tell them that at two o'clock that afternoon they'd have to go to the education building and take an examination, they came apart. When they sat at a desk, they would begin to sweat. I'd hand them a piece of paper and a pencil, and the sweat would literally break out. Their most common excuse for not taking the test was their glasses 'was busted' and they couldn't see. Could they wait? These guys never *had* glasses."

For months, every new inmate had to pass through Frank's examination. Over time, he got to know many of these hard-luck folks rather well, and he admired them as survivors. Many became his good friends.

But upon their arrival in Greenville, he'd gotten off to a bad start. Carl had no trouble being accepted, because his accent, his dialect, was southern; further, he was considerably overweight, and even in a suit he looked rumpled. By comparison, Frank was pure, neat bourgeois and very non-southern. Frank's first cell mates were so sure he must be a government revenue agent trying to spy on them they wouldn't even tell him their last names or where they were from. A prisoner in the cell across the corridor asked Frank, "Hey, are you a stool pigeon?" Frank said, "No, no, no, no. You don't understand. I made a First Amendment challenge of the House Un-American Activities Committee and . . ."

The prisoners' faces clearly showed that his explanation was only making them more suspicious. Carl, overhearing this exchange from two cells down the hallway, cut in with a shout: "Shut up, Frank!" Then he said with a growl, "Hell no, man, we're not stools."

Something about the way Carl said it—a gruff, unchallenge-able declaration reverberating down the corridor—changed everything. Suddenly Frank's cell mates were friendly and gave him their names and hometowns. Carl was always useful as an ambassador in that foreign land.

■

AT THE INMATE level, the prison was integrated and even fairly democratic. After his experience at the Fulton County Jail, Frank was astounded to find "an inmate population which was so won-derful in terms of their respect for their fellow inmates." About one-third of the prisoners were black. They joined with the whites in a mutual hatred for the guards. Many prisoners of both races also shared a professional background: bootlegging, moonshining, illegal whiskey running.

Frank judged the integration to be "completely natural. Blacks and whites sat with each other because of friendships. There would be a bootlegger and moonshiner combination. They'd worked together on the outside and they got together on the inside. The moonshiner would often be a white dealing with a black bootlegger who would sell his 'white lightning' in the ghetto areas."

> In the mess hall, there were tables for four or six. You could sit with any group and you could visit without rushing. The only thing they guarded in the mess hall was the sugar box. There'd be a guard standing at the sugar box to prevent an inmate from taking more than one spoon of sugar in his coffee. The inmates made whiskey from the sugar they could steal, and they managed to steal quite a lot. We were forever being offered whiskey made in the kitchen.

> The only place in South Carolina that was integrated was the prison. The *only* place. We often said that if we could just get Strom Thurmond in there for one weekend, we could clean up his act. We joked about it with other inmates. There was never any fighting between blacks and whites. It was a very good relationship and it came out of the shared poverty system in the Piedmont area that drove them to making and selling whiskey because they couldn't scratch any tobacco out of soil that was so poor it had no nurturing chemicals for raising tobacco.

▪

THE FBI ORDERED the Greenville prison to photocopy all the mail sent to Carl and Frank, and since the prison had no Xeroxing or other copying apparatus on hand, all of their mail was rushed back to the Atlanta penitentiary for photocopying before being returned to Greenville. Still, Greenville constantly double-checked to make sure nothing uncopied got through. That's why Frank often returned to his cell to find several guards going through his letters.

Most of the inmates got maybe one letter a week; many got none. Frank and Carl got as many as regulations allowed, but that wasn't many. Frank did receive wonderful letters from his daughter,

Jo. She remembers, "I wrote him long and detailed letters while he was in prison. I loved writing every detail of my teenage life at the time, and he told me how much he loved receiving those letters, and how important they were to him."[1] Jo was in the ninth grade when Frank went to jail. Frank's brother, Alan, stood in for Frank at Jo's graduation. But Frank sent her a present to mark the occasion: a purse and belt made out of cigarette wrappers. He didn't smoke, but that was all the material available to him to mark this important milestone.[2]

For birthdays, the limits on correspondence were lifted. So in August—their birthdays were just a week apart—Frank and Carl got a flood. Somebody among the many anti-HUAC chapters had started a letter-writing campaign to cheer them up, and over a two-week period, literally thousands of birthday cards and birthday letters poured in—wheelbarrows were used to deliver them to their cells. Prison management was furious, for there were far too many to send back to Atlanta for copying.

But the other inmates were bowled over. How could anyone have so many friends? "They didn't quite understand what was going on, and didn't quite understand us," says Frank. "In a way it was a healthy thing and it helped us, because it clearly gave our fellow prisoners the feeling that we were something unique and different."

Prison management and the FBI must have noticed, too. Were the two subversives getting too popular? And were they becoming dangerously influential with other prisoners? They were making real friendships, of the sort that inspired invitations to visit homes and families if they ever dared return to the region.

■

ALONG WITH FRIENDSHIP came trust. Many of the inmates who were illiterate or only semiliterate used Frank and Carl to dictate letters home.

"We wrote their letters constantly," says Frank.

It was fascinating because of the way they would filter personal things through us, transformed for the moment into grown children as they talked to the folks back home—"Dear Mommy," or "Dear Mommy and Daddy, I miss you so much. I been a good boy," and go on with such simple sweetness about their plans and their promises to do better next time.

Carl was better at that than I was because he understood the language. They would say they were from such-and-such a town. "Greenville" would come out "Gre'vul," and "Spartanburg" would come out "Spatna." There I was sitting right next to them, and I'd have to ask them to repeat words. I struggled. I really wanted to help these guys.

In writing their letters, they mentioned details back home that I would later ask them to elaborate on. They would tell me how they had one pig a year that they always slaughtered for Thanksgiving or Christmas, and they'd describe how they fattened that pig for months. Then they would cook it and the whole family would just eat, and eat, and eat like it was the only meat they would have for another year. And it usually was. Other than that pig, they usually ate only beans and grits. Their land was so worn out they couldn't raise much in the way of vegetables.

The overwhelming problem for many inmates was that not only did they make and sell liquor, they also drank the stuff—too much of it. Alcoholics Anonymous meetings, open only to men who had a record in their folder indicating they could attend, were held in the evening. The nice thing about those meetings was that guards, who were omnipresent everywhere else, weren't allowed into AA meetings. Frank and Carl, not being alcoholics, wouldn't have been allowed in, either, except that somebody had to read the twelve-point pledge aloud and keep a written record of every meeting (evidence of inmates' attendance helped when they sought parole). Reading aloud without stumbling and writing coherently were challenges most of the members trembled to contemplate, so they asked prison officials to let Frank and Carl come in and do it for them. Actually, the alcoholics probably just wanted their company; all that letter-writing had made a lot of friends.

The stories the members told, night after night after night—how they'd gotten drunk and beat up their wives, or their kids, or the neighbor, or committed some other crime, and how sorry they were, and how much they meant to reform, and how they feared their willpower wouldn't protect them from the lure of whiskey when they got out—were deadeningly repetitious.

Abbreviated accounts of those dreary recitations were what Frank and Carl wrote up in the minutes. Not included were the interlarded bull sessions, which included many other topics. "We talked about everything," Frank recalls. "There were no holds barred. It was the one free-speech place in the whole damn prison. I think the prison authorities had no idea how dangerous it was to have us in there with twenty-five to forty men, no guards around, to rap about anything. You could tell the guys who ran the place were worried. The guards kept asking us, 'Why are you in there? What's going on? What do you talk about?' I've always wondered why they didn't wiretap us. Maybe they did, and we didn't know it."

■

IF NOT WIRETAPS, Greenville, like all prisons, had snitches. So the warden learned what was said and done behind those closed doors. And through him, so did J. Edgar Hoover.

■

MUSIC PIPED INTO the whole cell block was chosen by one inmate. He liked the loud popular music of the day, so that's what everyone had to listen to. It didn't bother Frank; he could just turn off his hearing aid. But it bothered the hell out of many others, who wanted old-time country music and religious hymns once in a while. They complained to Frank, and changes were made. The cell block elected a committee that listed the music the majority of inmates wanted to hear, and that's what they got.

A nice piece of democracy, true, but to the warden, and to the FBI, it was another warning sign of Frank's growing popularity and influence with the inmates.

●

FRANK ALSO GAINED popularity by occasionally cheating for his friends at church services. He didn't attend the services, but the warden's office had assigned him the task of sitting outside the room where they were held and taking down the number worn by each inmate who entered. Being good sinful southerners, virtually all of the inmates were also devoutly religious. And those few who weren't devout wanted to look like they were. Frank's roll-taking went into the files, and if it showed they went to church three times a week—Sunday morning, Sunday evening, and Wednesday prayer meeting—the parole board would probably be impressed.

Some prisoners who didn't attend would occasionally come to Frank privately and ask him to check off their names. Naturally, he obliged.

Presumably God was aware of what he did, but more importantly, so was the warden. Another black mark.

●

AS PRISON LIBRARIAN, Frank had come to the conclusion that the library was virtually worthless. No prisoners ever used it. No books were ever checked out. And no wonder. The shelves were full of books that kind-hearted citizens had contributed—books they wanted to get rid of because they were boring or difficult.

What the prisoners did like were comic books, and the library had a great collection of them. So Frank and Carl went to the warden and said, "Although most of the prisoners here aren't very good at reading, they do love comic books. But the only time they're free to read them is Sunday afternoon, and you have the library closed all Sunday. If you'll have it opened at two in the afternoon after church for a couple of hours, we'll be glad to handle the checking out and checking in of the comic books." Without hesitation, the warden said, "Well, that seems like a nice idea. Sure."

The next Sunday, everything went great. The inmates lined up to check out the adventures of Batman and Robin, et al. That night in the mess hall, Frank and Carl got a lot of thanks.

Monday went normally.

The following day, Frank and Carl were summoned to "control"—the security part of the prison. A summons to "control" was never a good thing. The moment they passed through the door, four guards jumped them, throwing cuffs and chains on their hands, chains around their waist, and chains around their ankles—all the while moving them across the room and out a door, into a waiting security bus.

No explanation.

"Wait, wait," Frank pleaded. "I've got to have my hearing aid batteries! Wherever you're taking me, I've got to go back to my bunk and get my batteries."

Shut up! Just shut up!

"My books! I've got to get my books!" Frank pleaded. He meant not only his personal books, but all his correspondence from Meiklejohn and others.

Gear, clothing, everything was left behind.

The bus stayed on rural roads. They had no idea where they were going, other than that they were going north. About ten o'clock that night—they were given no food, no nothing along the way—they arrived at a prison in Petersburg, Virginia. Food was shoved under their cell door. Bed was a concrete slab. One blanket. Then up at six o'clock and back on the bus, still heading north.

■

WHAT HAD TRIGGERED this bureaucratic kidnapping?

Could the success of the comic books have been the last straw? Had the FBI in Washington, tired of hearing about the popularity of Frank and Carl, decided to punish the irritating subversives by moving them to a much tougher prison? That was one theory

Frank sometimes considered. Another theory was that it was the FBI's response to an effort going on at that moment by friends of Frank's to convince President Kennedy to grant the two men a pardon.

In any event, the FBI apparently felt the kidnapping should be explained, so they accused the two men of something heinous, and ridiculous: they were charged with spying for Russia. Yes, spying, right there in prison. Several guards had gone to the security forces at nearby Donaldson Air Force Base and reported that they had caught Frank and Carl observing the landing and takeoff of planes, and that they were—somehow—reporting this activity to the Soviet Union. No theory was offered as to how the information was passed on. And since the plane traffic from Donaldson could be observed much more easily from almost any other place in the surrounding countryside, why would the Soviets use people in the prison as spotters? And why would the Soviets want such absurdly mundane information, anyway?

Of course the government never made a formal case against the "spies." The charge had the hallmarks of J. Edgar Hoover's absurdity. In any event, it allowed the government to say that for the security of the United States they must be moved from easy-going South Carolina to the penitentiary in Lewisburg, Pennsylvania, which over the years would house not only Mafia bosses like Joe Adonis, but a horde of interstate auto thieves and head-liners of the anti-Communist era—such as David Greenglass, Alger Hiss, William Remington, and Harvey Matusow.

Their transfer was carried out so secretly that when Aubrey Williams wrote them at the Greenville prison, his letter came back "Address Unknown." He tracked them down only after soliciting the help of an old friend, the director of the Bureau of Prisons, who called back to say: "Aubrey, you may find it hard to believe, but your boys got caught spying for Russia and they are in solitary at Lewisburg at this time."

CHAPTER 27

A Bitter Introduction to Penitentiary Life

THE LEWISBURG PRISON, built on a federal reserve about the size of New York's Central Park and with great views of the Allegheny Mountains, opened in 1932. It was part of a reform movement that had been trying to get away from the violent penal fortresses in Atlanta, Leavenworth, and Alcatraz. If that ambition had not been fulfilled by the time Frank got there—the races were still segregated, and riots still occurred—a melancholy reminder of the early hopes was still visible over the entrance to the administration building, where it was written: "Let those who control the lives of the men who enter here ever bear in mind that the path to better things lies upward always and is steep, and that God's choicest blessings come to him who helps the weary climber."[1]

From outside, the Lewisburg penitentiary architecture, with its heavy masonry and Gothic arches and windows, reminded Frank of Duke University or the University of Chicago.

Inside, the atmosphere was anything but collegial.

New prisoners were almost immediately put in solitary confinement. Not for punishment, supposedly, but for "orientation"—

i.e., they were given a taste of the discipline they would receive, in spades, if they ever got out of line.

This is Frank's description:

It was a terrifying experience. There was a long row of cells, perhaps twenty. A guy at the end of the block would pull a lever and that opened every door simultaneously. The walls were concrete. You entered your cell through a heavy steel door with a tiny peephole in it, about three inches at the top. At the other end of your cell was a tiny little window, but you couldn't see anything out of it. The only light came from a twenty-watt bulb in the ceiling, about eight feet up, which burns night and day. There's a metal bed and a toilet without a seat on it. There's a wash device above it for cleaning your hands.

Because the battery in my hearing aid was dead, I was wrapped in silence. Not total, but almost. That, plus the lack of illumination, gave me a horrible dose of claustrophobia.

You had to respond with military precision. When they gave a call for meals, all doors were automatically flung open, you quickly stepped out into the corridor and lined up. Then they pulled the lever and all doors slammed shut. Then you marched off in lockstep.

My deafness caused me to miss the meal calls most of the time. And I missed a couple of calls to be let out for a bath. You had to be ready. Sometimes they would feed you at six o'clock in the morning, sometimes at ten o'clock at night. There was no schedule. You didn't know when the call would come. I would sleep on my bunk with my head jammed against the wall, and Carl, in the next cell, would bang on the wall when there was a call. Sometimes I felt the vibrations, sometimes I didn't.

When you marched off in lockstep, not a word was allowed. You didn't speak to anyone. The men in solitary ate separately, not with the rest of the prison population. You go through the line almost as fast as you marched in. Inmates behind the counter throw your food on the tray—boom, boom, boom.

At the end of the counter, the guard points, "Sit there." You've got ten minutes to eat—no conversation.

On Frank's first march through the meal line, he looked up in surprise at the man dishing out mashed potatoes. It was his friend Junius Scales, whom he had known in New York when Scales was being tried—he was the last to be tried—under the Smith Act.

They didn't speak, but their eyes met. They would have their conversation, thanks to the subversive talents that prisoners develop for getting around rigid regulations, but it would come later, after Frank was transferred to the Allenwood sub-camp of the Lewisburg penitentiary.

The only bright spot in the week he spent in solitary at Lewisburg came on the day he heard the call and was outside his cell when the guy giving orders yelled "Library!" The line marched about a hundred yards down a long corridor to double doors, wide open, and lockstepped right into a room full of books.

"As soon as we got in," says Frank, "they told us, 'All right, five minutes. Take any books you want. Five minutes.' What do I find? I find Matthew Josephson's *The Robber Barons*, I find Harvey O'Connor's *Mellon's Millions*. I find another one on Benedict Arnold's treason in the Revolutionary War. I asked, 'How many can you take?' They said, 'As many as you can hold.' I had eight books in my arms. Lockstepped back to my cell, I stumbled in with these eight books and said to myself, 'Boy, only in America could you have prisons like this.'"

At the end of a week of solitary, he and Carl were transferred to the Allentown prison, eighteen miles away. Before leaving, they were ordered to shed their Lewisburg garb and were given shoes and denim shirts and pants that had been washed so many times they were threadbare. This was in mid-November. For the eighteen miles to the Allentown prison, they rode on the back of a flatbed truck. The Susquehanna River they rode beside was frozen. So were they.

When they were unloaded into a wooden prison building, Frank rushed over to a steam radiator and put his hands on it. It was too hot, so he just held his hands close to it. "After I'd done that for a few minutes," says Frank, "some guy came up to me, laughs, and says, 'There's no heat coming out of that thing.' I touched it again, and sure enough it was cold. The heat was coming from my imagination. That's how cold I was."

■ SUBVERSION TRIUMPHANT!

The very next day, Frank was told to get back on the truck for another frigid ride, back to Lewisburg. He was being ordered to take an X-ray.

These transfers from prison to prison were not a simple matter. Lewisburg was surrounded by a series of gates and walls and thirty-foot-high metal fences. There were ten checkpoints, at each of which a guard had to come out and see if Frank looked like his mug shot, and to have another mug shot taken.

Finally, they got to the X-ray offices. A guard told Frank, "Sit down; we'll get to you when we can." When the guard left, an inmate orderly said quickly, "Come with me." They went through two X-ray rooms, and in the third, Frank was instructed, "Just wait here. Somebody wants to talk to you."

Suddenly Junius Scales was brought in. The orderly said, "Okay, guys, you've got five minutes," and left them alone.

It had all been done with military precision: Frank was brought eighteen miles, Junius was brought half a mile, each had to pass through a passel of checkpoints, and they wound up together at exactly the right time.

They embraced and spoke quickly. Frank, astounded because he had been under constant surveillance, asked how the meeting had been achieved. Scales said, "You have no idea how wonderful these guys are. They'll do anything for you. They're totally apolitical, but if you want to meet somebody, it's, 'Sure, I'll get him in. Where is he located? Allenwood? Sure. When do you want to see him? I'll arrange it.'"

The inmate orderly was back in five minutes, on the dot, and the illicit adventurers reversed their trails. Frank never got an X-ray.

This episode, along with some of the experiences he'd had

previously in Greenville and would have later in Allenwood, left Frank with something of a circa-1935 MGM view of the people he met behind bars: "I came out of these prison populations," he says, "with more respect for their solidarity, their brotherhood, their friendship. They'll do anything for another inmate. Their hatred is for every hack, every guard, in prison."

Of course, this was a grossly idealized description of fraternalism that overlooked the segregation, the riots, the rapes, and the stool pigeons who made prison life anything but a bastion of brotherhood. But that was Wilkinson: always—well, almost always—upbeat.

■ MOMENTS OF PEACE AND CONTEMPLATION, MOMENTS OF TERROR

Allenwood could be called a sub-camp of the Lewisburg penitentiary. It was for minimum-security inmates who, even if they faced long sentences, were not considered potential troublemakers. Frank was once again assigned to work in the library, but the education level of the inmates this time was considerably higher. After all, many were white-collar criminals. One whom Frank enjoyed chatting with was an American Nazi serving a life sentence for having gone to Germany in World War II and broadcast propaganda to U.S. troops.

The penal atmosphere at Allenwood was pretty relaxed. On some occasions, the relations between guards and inmates were downright amiable, as when they gathered around a checkers game to give advice and cheer good moves. Frank wrote to his wife about one such checkers game, but censors sent it back marked "Unsuitable." Apparently, the prison administrators didn't want to get a reputation for softness.

But as prisons go, Allenwood *was* soft. During certain hours, before twilight, inmates could walk around freely. The prison was surrounded by eighty-five hundred acres of federal land in an attractive valley. It had been built on the site of some long-forgotten village, the only vestiges of which were a graveyard and a very old stone church about a mile down the road. It was, Frank recalls, "an unbelievably solitary place. No other prison in America could have produced such an experience, where you walk a mile away from the place of your imprisonment, with nobody near you, only deer now and then, and you watch the sunset over the snow—indeed, you watched it carefully because you wanted to get back before the deadline. But you had freedom, and time to think."

The atheist couldn't shake the old days. The old church provided wistful memories of the Methodist churches Frank had grown up in, in Arizona and Hollywood. And as he walked, he says, his feet would set the meter for some of the old hymns going through his head—maybe "Doxology" or "Onward Christian Soldiers."

Chapel services were held in the church on Sundays, and he was always there. As in Greenville, he was assigned to take down the prison numbers of the inmates who attended.

■

THE ALLENWOOD PRISON was also where he buried himself in a systematic course of study, knowing that, once free again, he would be too busy for books. He studied under the guidance, and the goading, of his close friend and mentor, Alexander Meiklejohn.

In 1961, when Frank first went to jail, books started arriving regularly from Meiklejohn, as promised, to educate Frank about why he was in prison. Meiklejohn had told Frank that he needed to learn, in depth, the history of the First Amendment and the importance of dissent. And Meiklejohn was as good as his word.

Frank recalls: "They [the prison authorities] wouldn't let some of them in. He was sending me things like Zechariah Chafee's book on civil liberties, *Free Speech in the United States*; the prison guards in South Carolina wouldn't let it in. They wanted to know who this Zechariah is: 'Is he a Communist?' He was the dean of the Harvard Law School."

At Allenwood, his traffic in books went more smoothly.

The ones Meiklejohn insisted on Frank reading during the first few weeks—Plato and Milton's *Areopagitica* and *Paradise*

Lost—might have been considered, for a beginner, more of a hazing than an introduction to classics dealing with freedom. But when he moved on to reading the lives of Nehru and Gandhi, written when they were in prison for their beliefs, Frank was moved. "It had the same impact," he says, "as reading the book by Debs when I was in the Atlanta jail. There I was, behind bars for my radicalism, and I had never read about one of America's greatest radicals who was in prison for years because of his beliefs. That's how ignorant I was."

Finally, Meiklejohn let him read the Constitution, along with some books about it. Not until then did Frank learn that when the Constitution was written, a black person was considered to be only three-fifths of a person. "I never knew that till I was in prison. I had all the good gut reactions for freedom and against loyalty oaths and against witch hunts, but I hadn't read things I needed to know about. I was ignorant, ignorant, ignorant!"

The winter curriculum in Allenwood made him less so.

▪

CARL, TOO, WAS studying. In his dictionary. Not just any dictionary, but a very large one, a magnificent India-paper compilation of the sort usually found only on a pedestal in a good public library. Day after day, line by line, page by page by page, he went through it, holding it in his lap. It was the only book he had, or wanted.

Frank was also busily trying to cram more words into his own brain. He had taken a cluster of index cards from the library at the Greenville prison and, for the past several months as he ran into words in his reading that were new to him, he'd been copying them down on the cards. About a week before he was due to be released from prison, he learned that no one was allowed to take out any written material whatsoever. They even inspected the bottoms of the feet of people being discharged, lest they be carrying phone numbers or any other information that would link the inside with the outside. Memory, as far as possible, was to be banished.

Frank pleaded with prison officials to exempt his cards, covered with about two hundred words, but they told him his handwriting was so tiny it might hide code messages. He would have to leave them behind.

There was still time to memorize a few more from the list, and he went to Carl to help him drill. And that's when he learned something new about his friend. Carl, who had never even graduated from high school, knew all the words; for many, he knew their Greek and Latin derivation; and for a few, he even knew the Sanskrit. He had learned the Greek and Latin while studying for the priesthood, and he'd gotten interested in Sanskrit when he started reading the works of Gandhi and Nehru. They used words like *satyagraha*, meaning civil disobedience, that are Anglicized Indian words.

For the most part, Frank's effort at last-minute cramming was a failure.

■ A VERY NARROW ESCAPE

The comparative freedoms of Allenwood made Frank careless, and he fell into a trap that a more experienced prisoner would have avoided.

Unlike Lewisburg, Allenwood was integrated. At meals, you could sit anywhere you liked. Not many white prisoners sat with blacks (at least in the prisons he sampled, Frank found much more racism in Pennsylvania than in South Carolina) but you could if you wanted to. Frank and Carl often did.

One day Frank was eating at a mixed table when a white inmate came over and squatted down by his chair and said, "We used to have a forum here and we'd like to get it going again. Do you know anybody who would come to speak if we can get the forum started?"

A forum? Frank says he couldn't believe the guy was serious. (This was before "country club" prisons came into existence.) "It just made no sense at all, having a forum in prison. I had not encountered anything like that. The only outsiders who ever got into any of the prisons I was in were the Bob Jones University evangelists down in South Carolina who had the right to walk into your cell and preach Christianity to you. They had the right to sit right there and go on and on, while you did your best to tune them out.

"Anyway, though I thought he was crazy, I said to the guy, 'Well, okay. I've never heard of it, but if there is going to be a forum, sure, I know some people who would come talk.' He asked me to give him some names, so I started out with Dean John Bennett of the Union Theological Seminary, Reinhold Niebuhr, Martin Luther King Jr., and I named the man who was secretary to the World Council of Churches. That was it. That was all. The guy scribbled down something and left. All of that couldn't have taken more than three minutes."

To Frank it was a meaningless encounter, and he promptly forgot it. Two days later, he was summoned to the warden's office.

One of the requirements to reach the rank of warden is apparently to develop a face as hard and rigidly uncompromising as an iron skillet. This warden was a classic example. With no emotion, the warden told a terrified Frank:

"Get your things together. Pack your gear. You're going to the wall."

"Going to the wall" meant he was being sent back to Lewisburg. It was the most dreaded punishment. Being in Allenwood meant that, though you might be a lifer, you have established enough good points that the prison management no longer fears you. To be sent back "to the wall" means that they look upon you as incorrigible. More than that, for Frank it meant he would be put in solitary, and this time without Carl Braden next door to communicate by banging his shoe on the wall.

Worst of all, it meant that instead of getting out of prison in eight days—as he was scheduled to do, thanks to "good behavior"—he would have to serve out the three months to complete his year's sentence.

After a moment of stunned silence, Frank began to complain forcefully. "What's going on? What's happened? What have I done? Someone's misinformed you. I have no idea what you're talking about." The warden cut him off. "You know damned well what I mean. You've been teaching Communism. You go get your gear. You're going to the wall."

A warden's power is absolute. What could Frank say to break through? He pleaded so hard he began to cry.

Finally, the warden relented. He told Frank, "Go back to your bunk and think about what you've been doing, and come back and make a clean breast of it."

A clean breast of what? For twenty-four hours Frank got no answer to that—and no sleep.

Then he got a break. Word of his terrible luck had passed along the prison grapevine, and when he went into the bathroom and stood at one of the dozen urinals, he heard behind him the low voice of a convict who hardly paused as he walked past: "Your problem is helping to arrange the forum. And if you know what's good for you, you'll stop sitting with black inmates at mess."

So that was it! Frank rushed to the warden's office "bubbling," he says, "with relief."

> I met his stern glare with, "Oh, thank God, I've got some friends here. I've found out what your problem is. You said you were told I was teaching Communism. No, no, I was just answering an inmate who said you used to have a forum here and wanted some names of possible speakers." The warden looked like he didn't want to hear what I was saying. When I said, "Thank god for the friends I've got here," he cut in with, "For every friend you think you've got here, I have ten. You mind your business." Then, still staring at me like he wanted to send me to the gallows, he said, "Watch out, or you're going to the wall." I had come into his office on a high. When he made the threat again, I crashed. I was petrified, but at least he hadn't done what he threatened to do.
>
> For the last days of my sentence, I was afraid to say anything to anyone. I felt they were eager to frame me; if not for one thing, it would be for another.

■

POSTSCRIPT: YEARS LATER, when Frank's attorneys forced the FBI to release its huge file on him, he learned the reason behind this harrowing episode. Sitting at the next table in the prison mess hall and listening in on the conversation about the bogus "forum" was Frank's cell mate. In return for spying on other inmates, the warden occasionally allowed him to take a prison car and run errands for him in town—which meant, of course, access to sex. So passing along a false story about Frank's "teaching Communism" was simply a way of making himself seem useful to the warden.

But his cell mate had another reason; he considered Frank a Communist, and he hated Communists. He had once been the cell mate of William Remington, one of the tragic victims of the Cold War. Remington had been a high official in several New Deal departments when one of the FBI's most infamous informers, Elizabeth Bentley, named him among some 150 others as being peripherally involved in a Communist spy ring. An activist grand jury foreman, John Brunini, working with the Justice Department, created a politicized and harassing environment. Nevertheless, two grand juries failed to indict Remington, and after he lost his government security clearance because of Bentley's television appearance on *Meet the Press*, a government loyalty review board cleared him. And then Remington won a settlement in a libel case against Bentley and NBC.

But hoping desperately to revive Bentley's sagging reputation as an informer, the government finally got a grand jury to indict Remington on charges that he had lied when he said he had never been a Communist. A jury convicted him, but this conviction was overturned by the court of appeals. Then a new grand jury indicted him on five counts of lying, and he was convicted of two of those counts, and finally this conviction withstood an appeal.

The initial grand jury foreman, John Brunini, was a piece of work. Judge Learned Hand thought the foreman and the prosecutor guilty of "misconduct, coercion, and deceit." Within the grand jury, they forced Remington's estranged wife to testify against him. Further, while the grand jury was in recess, Brunini collaborated with informant Bentley to write a book about her experiences, helped get her a book contract, and was, until the deal was exposed, to have shared the royalties for it.[2] It was just another bit of sleazy Cold War justice, and ended with Remington sharing a cell in Lewisburg with the chap who, a decade later, ratted on Frank.

One night somebody got into Remington's cell (or was already there when he came in) and crushed his skull with a brick. The culprit was never identified. For refusing to give information, his cell mate was given extra years in prison, which is why he was still there when Frank arrived. He had already hated Communists; those extra years made him hate them even more. And those guys Frank recommended for the forum sure sounded like Reds to him.

■THE FAMILY HAD ITS TROUBLES, TOO

While Frank was still in Allenwood, the *Los Angeles Herald Examiner* reportedly didn't help matters for his family at home in L.A. when it published an editorial calling for locals to, as daughter Jo puts it, "do their patriot duty and take care of this 'Commie traitor' when he returned home." The family had to put up with strange men wandering around the house or sitting in unmarked cars parked in front, day and night. Jo remembers one fire inspector who told them that at least some of these folks were trying to prevent another firebombing. He told the family to give him the license plate numbers and he'd be able to tell them if they were his guys. Some were, and some weren't.[3]

■GIVING A FINAL FINGER TO PRISON AUTHORITIES

During the process he underwent leaving the prison, Frank saw just how hopeless it would have been to try to sneak out his vocabulary cards. The exit, as he described it, went like this:

> You go into a long room. You take your clothes off, strip down nude. Everything off. You go a few yards forward. They come up to examine you. They look in your mouth, look through

your teeth, put a light up your anus, pull back your foreskin, look in your armpits, look at the bottom of your feet. You're just so much flesh.

Then you're allowed to walk five feet forward to get your clothes. They were picked out for you a week before, so they had been searched. You put on your clothes and you're free to go. You walk out of there feeling that you've been stripped of everything human, everything of value. You feel you are just as naked intellectually as you were when you stood there and they pulled your foreskin back to see if you had slipped somebody's address under your penis.

But Frank came out of jail with a pretty interesting education—both in humanity and in books. And he was the same pesky ideological rebel on February 1, 1962, that he had been on May 1, 1961, when he began his sentence at the Fulton County Jail. He proved that immediately.

Courtesy of U.S. taxpayers, he and Carl had been given bus tickets—to Louisville, Kentucky, for Carl, and to Los Angeles for Frank. Neither man intended to go directly to his city. They intended to go to New York first, where anti-HUAC fans of Frank's were going to throw a big welcoming rally. He had mentioned in a letter to his family that he was going to be released at 10:30 in the morning, and some of those fans arranged to pick him up for the trip to the rally. Of course, all of his mail passed through the hands of the FBI—and so his release time was suddenly switched to 3:40 in the afternoon, supposedly too late to make the rally. A drive from Allenwood to New York City would take at least five hours.

Frank learned of the planned delay via the prison grapevine. How could he get word to his friends in New York? The only inmate getting out the day before him was a black Jew who wore a yarmulke and Jewish prayer shawl and had kept himself totally isolated from the rest of the prison population. He didn't seem a likely courier. Frank went to him and begged for his help. "Will you *please* learn this phone number and, when you get out, will you immediately call them and tell them the problem, that we won't get out until late afternoon and we're being put on a bus heading west. Tell them to have a car there. We'll get off the bus immediately."

The black Jew was hard to deal with. He was not only apolitical, but he seemed to have no interest in anything other than reading the Torah. Reluctantly, he finally agreed to do it.

But would he remember the number? And if he did, would he remember the message?

Prison guards took Frank and Carl to town and delivered them to the Greyhound bus at around 4:30 P.M. The prison rule is: a prisoner is free as soon as he gets on the bus. They climbed aboard. The door closed. *They were free!*

"So, right in the faces of the guys who had put us on the bus," says Frank, they immediately got right off the bus, laughed at the guards, and then ran behind the bus and "here is not one car but several carloads of people from New York. We hop in and with horns honking we turn around and head back to New York. We got there around 10:30 [that night]."

▪

ON JANUARY 26, 1962—five days before Frank was released from prison—the Hearst newspapers, a favorite outlet for Hoover's leaks, had run a column that laid out Frank's immediate schedule with amazing accuracy. After saying of his organization, the NCAHUAC, that "a bigger batch of pro-Communists would be hard to find," it went on to say,

> A hero's welcome is being prepared for the "big brains" behind the abolition drive—whose jail term ends on February 1. The "coming out" parties are planned for Wilkinson, an identified Communist Party member, and another imprisoned partner, Carl Braden. . . .
>
> Wilkinson will be hailed at a New York reception the night he gets out of jail. A pro-Communist Chicago group does the honors the next night, and then there's a welcome home party scheduled for Los Angeles February 14, among others.[4]

J. Edgar Hoover had been right on schedule.

■

THE RALLY IN New York was still on tap. The crowd had been entertained while they waited by Pete Seeger, whose music seemed to be omnipresent at all protest rallies, and by speeches from people like Willard Uphaus, a white-haired seventy-year-old pacifist who had once taught Christian ethics at Yale. He'd recently finished a stint in prison as the result of the same Supreme Court decision that put Frank and Carl behind bars. Uphaus and pacifists like Ammon Hennacy (who served time in federal pens for protesting both World War I and the Cold War) and A. J. Muste were "Communists" only in the sense that they tramped around the country advocating a friendly solution to the United States' differences with the Soviets. Uphaus had established a World Fellowship camp in the mountains of New Hampshire. His neighbors didn't like it because his black guests swam in the lake. The state's attorney general, who called Uphaus "one of the worst fellow travelers in the state," demanded he release the names of the camp guests. His refusal sent him to prison.

So the atmosphere inside the auditorium, where more than a thousand fans waited, was suitably revolutionary when Frank walked out on stage. The stomping and cheering, which lasted at least ten minutes, made it impossible to speak. Finally he began to talk—about life in prison. He spoke of how, the day before he was to get out, five lifers with little schooling had come to him and asked if he knew Alger Hiss. Assured that he did, the spokesman for the group said, "Mr. Hiss used to read to us, and write letters home for us. If you ever see him again, tell him we miss him. Tell him we love him."

Hiss happened to be in the audience that night. As Frank finished this anecdote, Hiss walked down to the stage, and the crowd exploded again with cheers as the two alumni of Lewisburg's educational program embraced.

Carl Braden did not participate in the rally. He had gone instead to a Fair Play for Cuba Committee dinner in New York. Frank could never figure out why his friend had disappeared. One probable reason was that Carl was sick of being inaccurately linked to the Communist movement. Of course, the Fair Play for Cuba crowd wasn't exactly conservative. But it wasn't hated by Hoover and HUAC nearly as much as Gus Hall, a top official in the Communist Party USA, was, and Gus was going to be at Frank's rally.

What's more—and this must have really ticked Carl off—Gus was going to be there at Frank's invitation. When the rally's organizers wrote to Frank about their plans, they asked him if there was anyone he especially wanted them to invite. He responded with a short list, among whom were Matthew Josephson (he wanted to tell him how much he had enjoyed reading *Robber Barons* in prison), the editors of the *Guardian*, who were militant civil libertarians but not necessarily Communists, and Gus Hall.

Why the invitation to Hall? It was a bit odd, for Frank had never met him and, from what he had heard, didn't expect to like him. So was he just showing respect for Hall as a fellow ex-con who had done time for his beliefs? A Smith Act conviction plus another three years for jumping bail had put Hall in prison for most of the 1950s. But free again, he had got control of the CPUSA and ran it like a feudal kingdom, surrounding himself with sycophants whom he rewarded with vacations and special trips abroad. He—and they—always flew first class. The CPUSA, already fractured by quarrels, split further. So did this guy deserve an invitation?

Yes, said Frank, for solidarity: he wanted to bring together the Socialist Workers Party, the Trotskyites, the Stalinists, the fussing and feuding Communists, and left-wingers of all sorts, and remind them that they had a common enemy. The enemies of his enemy were to be considered his friends, no matter their flagrant defects. To him it was simple: "We've got to have everybody with us on the campaign to abolish HUAC."

He would need more than solidarity. He would need stamina. It would be another fourteen years before the House Un-American Activities Committee (by then operating under a new name) went out of business.

CHAPTER 28

Picking Up the Pieces, Twice

WHEN FRANK AND his allies set up the NCAHUAC in August 1960, the future looked reasonably bright. The notoriety he'd received as the alleged organizer of the San Francisco disturbance—plus the many speeches he and Carl Braden made on college campuses before going to prison and the multipage anti-HUAC petitions placed in major newspapers—had shown the public an organization with a vibrant character.

But when Frank went to prison in 1961, he stepped down as national director and turned the job over to Aubrey Williams. For a while Williams handled it skillfully. Having held important political jobs in the Roosevelt administration, he knew what to do to influence Congress. When the first letterhead for NCAHUAC was being drafted, he told Frank, "You can't just have me, Meiklejohn, and Bob Kenny listed in these top offices. You've got to have other people on the letterhead." Aubrey thought thirty or forty prominent people would do the trick.

So Aubrey, with the help of Sylvia Crane, drafted a letter urging a select group to become members of the board. The letter assured them that, unlike several other national liberal organizations—

such as the NAACP, the ACLU, and the Americans for Democratic Action—the NCAHUAC would not require its directors to take a loyalty oath. This was also, of course, a polite way of saying that the new organization wasn't interested in directors who would be afraid that at board meetings they might be sitting next to a Communist.

They mailed the invitation to 600 people, hoping to get 30 or 40 acceptances. They got 150. Success did create a new problem: they wound up with a four-page letterhead.

During his years in Washington, Aubrey had grown to despise lobbies that claimed to be "national" but in fact had no widespread support outside the capital. So he decreed there would be no office in Washington for the NCAHUAC until it had established grass-roots organizations in at least fifty congressional districts in at least fifteen states. Since the objective was to persuade House members to cast abolition votes, they would have to be shown that many of their constituents wanted them to. Ergo: organize locally.

Frank had learned this as early as 1957, when he was trying to get Jimmy Roosevelt, the congressman in his district, to go after HUAC. Jimmy was reluctant. So the gung ho Southern California ACLU—the one organization in Frank's odyssey that performed heroically over and over—rounded up twenty-two thousand signatures from Jimmy's district; suddenly he was a believer. Aubrey Williams didn't demand that much, but he set a firm quota: get at least one hundred community leaders, real leaders, in each congressional district to sign a public petition to abolish HUAC. Do that in enough districts, and you might move Congress.

It was a great idea, but then, with Frank taking a nine-month sabbatical—in prison—things started falling apart. Just when firm leadership was needed, Aubrey was diagnosed with cancer. He began running out of energy, and was unable to prevent considerable disharmony—even serious quarrels—from breaking out among leaders of the organization. FBI records later released by court order show that Hoover had planted informants in the NCAHUAC. They were tasked with disrupting the committee's work, spreading doubts, and stirring up fusses, as well as with reporting on its every move. But that wasn't the only cause of the quarrels; some members were just naturally hard to get along with.

Sylvia Crane for instance. She was one of the most creative of the people who set up NCAHUAC. Married to an heir to the Crane Plumbing Company of Chicago, she had sufficient social status—and dough—to make good things happen, such as entertaining Nobel laureate scientists (potential anti-HUAC petition signers) at her big house in Woods Hole. She probably did more than anyone else to lure the prestigious people who agreed to sponsor the committee. In fact, she worked so hard at it that she never finished her PhD in history under Henry Steele Commager, then at Columbia University.

At the same time, she had an amazing talent for irritating others in the crusade. Frank recalls that Professor Otto Nathan, cochairman of the New York branch of NCAHUAC (he was also executor of the Einstein estate), wouldn't even sit down next to her.

Aubrey Williams himself was responsible for one of the most serious splits. Although he was a stout-hearted populist and an ardent First Amendment supporter who did not believe in persecuting Communists, he did not trust them, either. He was convinced that Russ Nixon, cochairman of the New York branch, was a Communist—or something close to it. A few others in the organization shared that suspicion.

But Nixon also had strong supporters who weren't finicky about his ideology. They valued his loyalty to the cause, which did not waver despite the fact that he was constantly sniped at as an executive of the United Electrical, Radio, and Machine Workers of America (better known simply as "UE"), a union with a radical leftist tradition and consistently identified as Communist by J. Edgar Hoover and HUAC. Frank was among Nixon's friends, and recalled gratefully that whenever he had work to do in New York City, especially in the year he was there with the ECLC, Nixon let him make his headquarters in one of UE's well-equipped offices, right next to St. Patrick's Cathedral.

But Frank couldn't smooth things over from Lewisburg prison.

Finally Aubrey drew the line: "Either Nixon goes or I go." Nixon went, but he left much anger and dissension in his wake. NCAHUAC virtually ceased to function. And Aubrey, devastated to see what he had caused but too ill to do anything about it, withdrew except as a figurehead (he was chairman emeritus until he resigned in 1963). Harvey O'Connor temporarily stepped in to take Aubrey's place. And then Richard Criley took over.

■ SAVED BY AN EXPERIENCED EX-COMMUNIST

The change was instantaneous and electric. Aubrey Williams had steered clear of anyone suspected of being a Communist. Dick Criley was one. Or at least, he had been one for most of his adult life. As a Bill of Rights absolutist, he had quit the party in 1960 when party officials took the position that the First Amendment should protect them but not the Ku Klux Klan.

Long, long ago, during the UCLA student rebellion on free speech in Frank's undergraduate days in the 1930s, when many students at UC Berkeley rebelled in sympathy, Criley had led the Berkeley rebellion. Frank, of course, had at that point been something of a stool pigeon for the UCLA administration. Now, more than a quarter of a century later, they were very much on the same side.

Criley came from an old Californian family; they had been at the founding of one of the state's most beautiful villages, Carmel. Standing before the towering window in the front room of their home, looking out at the Pacific, one could feel as much in possession of the world as from Hearst's 150-room castle down the coast at San Simeon. Criley would spend his last years in Carmel. But most of his life he was tied to Chicago. He moved there in 1946 from California, where he had headed the Young Communist League. In 1947 the United Packing House Workers expelled him as a suspected Communist.

When he and his wife, Florence, moved to Chicago, they settled in the community known as Lawndale. It was mostly white. Twenty years later the neighborhood was almost 100 percent black. He liked the change, and worked hard to help his neighborhood as a member of the advisory council for Lawndale's Urban Progress Center (LUPC), which administered part of the city's antipoverty program. In 1966, Mayor Richard Daley forced him out of the post, implying that Criley was subversive, even though LUPC's seventy-seven-member advisory board voted overwhelmingly not to remove him. Father Mallette of the Presentation Catholic Church said Criley had "an extremely good reputation as a neighborhood worker. He's a fine man. All the little people know him."[1]

Throughout the ideological wars of the 1950s and 1960s, Criley and Florence (a remarkable organizer for the progressive and activist UE) were able to reach across racial lines to build political coalitions—including black working-class people at the precinct level—to fight the oppressive Daley machine. But they also had good credit with large segments of the establishment class, including important parts of the University of Chicago and the Chicago Theological Seminary. Several renowned theologians from that institution were on the Chicago Committee to Defend the Bill of Rights (CCDBR), of which Criley was director, even though they had received letters from J. Edgar Hoover warning them of its subversive character. It was with their help that Criley had rounded up the names of hundreds of noted theologians to petition President Kennedy to pardon Wilkinson and Braden. During the years that the ACLU was weak and timid in Chicago, the major part of the work it should have been doing was being carried out by Criley's CCDBR.

Criley was the target of numerous FBI "black bag" jobs, as they were known (because of the color of the satchel in which FBI agents carried photographic equipment and their tools). But the agents worked only at night, making copies of his mail and of everything relating to his organization. Years later, by suing the FBI under the Freedom of Information Act, Criley learned that the break-ins had begun in 1962, when he took over NCAHUAC from Aubrey. After a trial run to get an idea of what sorts of things Criley's office contained, the agent in charge sent a memo to the FBI: "The Chicago office has recently developed an anonymous source close to

CCDBR headquarters. This source presents a great potential for obtaining the personal correspondence and financial records of Richard Criley." (The "anonymous source close to" euphemism was simply the standard way of identifying the target and saying it had been penetrated—often by an illegal break-in.)

The memo continued, "The office building is locked from the inside at 10 P.M. each night, after all the tenants have departed. The building is not reopened each morning until 7 A.M., upon the arrival of the building engineer. In view of the maximum security which can be secured, it is recommended that authority be granted to make contact with these sources on or about Feb. 10, 1962, sometime during the period of 1 A.M. to 6 A.M."

Although the FBI claims it quit black-bagging Criley when he left the Communist Party in 1960, records show they continued to burgle his office for another five years. "They paid more attention to me when I was out of the CP than when I was a member," says Criley. In or out, he had plenty of company. In 1985, FBI Special Agent M. Wesley Swearingen told the *Chicago Tribune* that, as the head of the Chicago office's break-in squad, he had committed possibly five hundred illegal black bag jobs in that city during the 1950s, with special attention paid to "various Communists, religious officials, black leaders, union officials, liberal attorneys, and others." He received regular commendations—and sometimes cash bonuses—from Hoover for his efficiency.[2]

Frank credits Criley with holding together the NCAHUAC during its most rickety, self-destructive period.[3]

■ FRANK'S BACK

Frank's second stop after leaving prison was Chicago, where another Roman-style blowout was held for the returning warrior; then, finally, he was off to California. First stop was UC Berkeley to speak to SLATE. By this time SLATE was forced to hold its talks off campus, because it continued to invite radical speakers, even known Communists; however, it got special permission to use Wheeler Hall for Frank's speech.

Next stop, hometown Los Angeles. Here he was to be greeted by more hosannas and, finally, to see his family—briefly. Coming out of jail, Frank was ready for a full schedule of events; his children, who had looked forward to a little time alone with him, would be disappointed. His daughter, Jo, remembers how she felt at the time: "When he got out of prison, I was in the tenth grade, at Los Angeles High School. He didn't come immediately home, but took time to stop and speak on his way back. He did the same thing on his way to prison, leaving early so that he could make public appearances and meet with as many people that he could, than to hurry home, or remain home as long as possible. That was the reality of him being my father." But they were not lonely at home. Night and day there were armed friends guarding the house. This was a new house, bought and given to them by friends after it became clear after the firebombing and swastika in the yard that they would find it tough to find a place to rent.[4] Frank arrived back in L.A. in time to participate at a town meeting of Democrats in the Shrine Auditorium, where five thousand people paid one dollar each to hear heated denunciations of the Right. It was becoming downright popular to be anti-extremist; for the committee organizing the rally included the president of the California Bar Association, the chairman of the Los Angeles Board of Supervisors, two school board members, and actor Robert Ryan, writer Rod Serling, comedian Steve Allen, and singer Helen O'Connell. The main speakers were Senator Clifford Case (R-NJ), Senator Eugene McCarthy (D-MN), and two ministers whose homes had been bombed two months earlier while they were speaking at a rally in Los Angeles against extremism.

Frank's first order of business back in L.A. was to taunt—with the help of about eight hundred mostly college-age picketers—the House Un-American Activities Committee subcommittee, which opened hearings on April 23, 1962. It had subpoenaed sixty witnesses, some of whom were from Frank's crowd.

But the HUAC inquisitors, mindful of what had happened to them in San Francisco, were obviously afraid of getting another shellacking. This time they ducked possible public rowdiness by holding closed hearings. And they traveled to the hearing room not by going through the federal building's open lobby and taking a regular elevator, but via the basement and a freight elevator.

Though many were called—union members, lawyers, students, doctors, housewives, members of civic organizations—few were chosen to testify, and it turned into one of most barren inquisitions in HUAC's history. Why the subcommittee even bothered to come west was a mystery, unless it was to gain a little hometown publicity for its chairman, Los Angeles congressman Clyde Doyle, who predictably warned the *Los Angeles Times* that "this county is the No. 1 hot spot for Communist infiltration."

It certainly didn't seem very hot. The only witness called to testify the first morning was Ben Dobbs. That was hardly newsworthy. Dobbs and Dorothy Healey had been the two best-known Communist leaders in Southern California for a quarter of a century, and both had been among the famous "second tier" (as the press called them) Communists convicted under the Smith Act. But they were also among the "straightest" Communists, having turned totally against the Stalinists in the party. They were also working closely with the New Left, and were accepted as interesting characters by parts of the Southern California establishment.[5] But Congressman Doyle would not have wanted to hear that—even if Dobbs had been willing to talk, and he wasn't. He was quizzed for three hours but, predictably, said virtually nothing.

The star of the second day was Dorothy Marshall, at that time executive director of Frank's CCPAF. She was also an executive of NCAHUAC, and she had been chairman of the oldest anti-HUAC group in the nation, the Committee for the Protection of the Foreign Born, established in 1952 in Los Angeles by the Reverend A. A. Heist, a Methodist minister, to fight then Attorney General Herbert Brownell's effort to denaturalize and deport ten thousand citizens.[6] Marshall had many contacts within the liberal element (which was in the minority, but still influential) of the Catholic Church leadership across America. She sometimes accompanied Frank as his ambassador to this group on his national tours.

Around town, the indomitable Marshall was better known for

her civic activities: she was past president of the Catholic Women's Club of Los Angeles, a former director of the Los Angeles office of the National Conference of Christians and Jews, and a member of the Los Angeles Realty Board. Only HUAC could have seen something subversive in these organizations. HUAC was equally suspicious of her husband, a former trustee and general counsel of Loyola University of Los Angeles.

HUAC had ordered Marshall to bring all documents relating to the CCPAF to the hearing, but she couldn't comply. The FBI's minions had been busy again; those documents, including mailing lists, had been stolen in a burglary the previous June—just one of a recent wave of burglaries of civil rights and civil liberties organizations.

After she took the First Amendment in response to the committee's first substantial question, they knew she would answer no further questions. But perhaps because this wasn't the first time they had met, they let her make a statement. They were probably sorry they did, for she told them in curt, matronly tones: "This hearing is ridiculous. A man like Dobbs has been identified as a Communist for years. You know that. And you already knew that I consider you carpetbaggers of the Far Right. This is not the first time your committee has brought its road show to a community on the eve of an election. There are Birch nuts running for office in California and your appearance will be utilized by them to smear responsible candidates as 'soft on Communism,' which you gentlemen know full well is a completely phony issue."

■

THIS WOULD BE HUAC's last invasion of the West Coast. Once upon a time, Californians had found the committee somewhat fascinating—because it could inspire fear; but the fear was fast disappearing, and thus the committee became simply boring. As a road show it was beginning to suck air, and committee members were apparently smart enough to realize it.

If they needed proof that they were becoming passé, they got it in their complete failure to stir up headline material from the testimony of Robert C. Ronstadt, a candidate for Congress from the Twenty-seventh District. He had been an FBI informer who'd posed as a Communist from 1947 to 1954. During that time, he told HUAC, he'd known four men who were guaranteed Communists. One of them, he said, was the fellow whose endless campus crusade had already made him nationally known as the number one anti-HUAC pied piper, the fellow J. Edgar Hoover had publicly denounced as "Mr. Abolition"—Frank Wilkinson. Ronstadt claimed their relationship had been very close from 1949 to the end of 1953. True, Ronstadt's testimony was given behind closed doors, but that had never stopped HUAC from leaking before. So why didn't they leak it now? Or, if they did, why did the press ignore it? A close reading of the committee's report suggests that the answer was that not a single thing in Ronstadt's testimony even vaguely implicated Frank. Indeed, for someone who claimed he'd known Frank very well for five years, Ronstadt was impressively ignorant about his "comrade." For example, the committee's attorney asked him, "What is the interest of the Communist Party in Frank Wilkinson?" He got only the vaguest of answers. "Well," said Ronstadt, "the party's interest, as I stated before, is, he is a very intelligent person. He makes a very good appearance. He's a good speaker. I think he was a loyal party member, and he could carry on the work of the Communist Party." Uh-huh, but what did he *do*? Was Wilkinson a good recruiter? As a top official at the LAHA, did he pilfer inside information that the Communist Party could use for propaganda? Just what *did* Wilkinson do for the party all those years? Ronstadt, allegedly Wilkinson's buddy, had no answers.

Either HUAC realized their hoped-for bomb was a dud and avoided embarrassment by not releasing Ronstadt's testimony, or they did release it and the press judged it too weak to print.

Fighting His Way through Tangled Grass Roots

BACK WHEN THE U.S. Supreme Court ruled against him, Frank had said, "I am serenely confident that for every voice which asks for abolition of the Un-American Activities Committee and is silenced in jail, a thousand new voices will be raised; and, most significantly, many of these will be the new generation of American students." More than ever convinced of this by the San Francisco hearing, Frank had thereafter guided his steps with the faith that the youth of America would be the first line of offense against HUAC.

It was a sensible faith, because the young in particular are equipped with the kind of robust irreverence that can easily handle right-wing fundamentalism. This was shown particularly well in the DuBois–Boys Club conflict.

The campus-oriented clubs known as W. E. B. DuBois Clubs, organized in 1964 to promote "Marxism, peace, civil rights and civil liberties," were named after the black historian who helped found the NAACP and who, in 1961 at the age of ninety-three, joined the Communist Party. One should not take "Marxism" in the DuBois Clubs' stated goal too seriously. The clubs were not designed, nor did they function, to bring about the "revolution."

At its height, the DuBois Clubs' membership was about the size of the turnout at a high school basketball game. But J. Edgar Hoover, as usual, sounded the alarm: in his Law Enforcement Bulletin for October 1964, he warned that the DuBois Clubs were spreading across the country. The "spread" was pretty thin; there were chapters at Harvard and a few other colleges, but it was mainly active on the West Coast. Its national headquarters in San Francisco was under the guidance of three of the battling Hallinan brothers: Terrence, national secretary; Patrick, counsel; and Matthew, educational director. Frank had worked with their father earlier in his organizing days.

Hoover noted that at the founding convention of the DuBois Clubs, the majority faction "had voted overwhelmingly to work in unity with mass organizations such as the trade unions and with the liberal wing of the Democratic Party." That might not sound very dangerous, but Hoover went on, "This is the present tactic of the Communist Party and the Socialist Party." The *Los Angeles Times*, always sensitive to Hoover's warnings, reported in depth on the new threat and was doubtless overjoyed to find that the organization's president, "Phil Davis, 25, looks the part. A 200-pound 6-footer, he wears leather boots and a sport shirt open at the neck. He admittedly needs a haircut." Better yet, when the *Times* asked him if he was a Communist, hairy Phil invoked the name of one of Los Angeles's best-known ex-convicts: "'I learned from Frank Wilkinson not to answer that question,' he smiled."[1]

Hoover wasn't the only one who wanted to get rid of the DuBois Clubs. So did his friend Richard Nixon. By March 1966, former vice president Nixon was national chairman of the Boys Club of America. Nixon had noticed, in his paranoid fashion, that "DuBois Club"—when "DuBois" was pronounced as the author pronounced it—sounded just like "the Boys Club," and he charged that the Communists "are not unaware of the confusion they are causing among our supporters and among other good citizens. It is an almost classic example of Communist deception and duplicity."

So Nixon and Hoover asked Attorney General Nicholas Katzenbach to use the Subversive Activities Control Board (SACB) to get rid of the DuBois pests. The SACB had been established by the McCarran Act of 1950. It required that every Communist-front organization register its officers and list the source of its funds. Over time, it became an almost totally meaningless agency; in sixteen years, not a single organization had registered, because of the Court's Fifth Amendment ruling. But the Justice Department had found that when it did order a group to register, its membership fell off and the organization eventually collapsed. That was the desired result when the SACB ordered the W. E. B. DuBois Clubs to register.

The order got a typical Hallinan response. The club's attorney, Patrick, snorted: "The administration knows we aren't a Commie front. They're just mad at us because we're against the Vietnam War. Well, let them jump on [Wayne] Morse and [William] Fulbright [two antiwar senators]. Attorney General Katzenbach can stick his registration in his ear."[2]

■

STICK HIS REGISTRATION in his ear. That was the rebellious spirit of youth Frank Wilkinson exploited everywhere he could as he traveled around the country organizing chapters for his NCA-HUAC. And he always squeezed in speaking engagements with campus audiences. Most faculties and student groups received him with at least hospitable curiosity, and occasionally with militant support. But college administrators—sensitive to the wishes of trustees, legislators, alumni, and patriotic groups—sometimes found it easier to pretend the First Amendment didn't exist. A few large universities in the early 1960s were so timid as to submit to subpoenas from HUAC for the membership lists of student organizations.

This was a period in which controversies over invited speakers raged on many large campuses. Because the Right-Left conflict was so intense, some college administrators preferred to simply remove the welcome mat for speakers on both sides. For example, Frank was barred at Marquette University—but so was Revilo P. Oliver, a national leader of the conservative John Birch Society.

Some "liberal" schools were squeamish about hosting an anti-HUAC speaker; some "conservative" schools took it in stride. Perhaps because once upon a time its Mormon founders had been badly treated for their unorthodox religious beliefs, the University of Utah was among the latter. Not that Frank's scheduled appearance didn't cause some tense disagreement between the school's administration and several notable members of the church (including Reed Benson, Utah coordinator for the John Birch Society, and Utah secretary of state Lamont Toronto). But the school held firm. Academic Vice President Jack H. Adamson announced: "These people object on the grounds of Mr. Wilkinson's alleged affiliation with the Communist Party. . . . It is not only impossible to insulate students from controversial ideas, but it is also unwise. It is good to have a free exchange of ideas."[3] Frank was received by an overflow audience there in November 1963.

Later, the administration did sponsor a rebuttal lecture by two political science professors, Dr. S. Grover Rich and Dr. Reed Frischknecht. They were supposedly going to argue against Frank's position, but in fact they supported much of what he had said. Dr. Rich thought Frank had made a "valid argument." Furthermore, he said, "Extremism plays a vital role in American society and through men advocating abolishment [of HUAC], we will eventually achieve healthy change." Dr. Frischknecht didn't favor doing away with HUAC, but he did consider it to be a bungling, undemocratic, superfluous mutation. As for whether they thought Frank was a Communist, both profs treated that as a frivolous question.[4]

Since Frank was almost invariably asked at these lectures if he was a Communist, the answer he gave at the University of Utah—which was his standard answer everywhere—might as well be put into the record here. This is how Sandy Gilmour, managing editor of the *Utah Chronicle*, took it down: "For 14 years of my life I answered every loyalty oath that could possibly be given. I swore I was not a Communist. I swore I was not a member of any organization advocating force and violence. I came to the conviction that this sort of forced thinking was part of the sickness of our society. The only oath I'm willing to take now is to uphold the Constitution of the United States. My position is that until HUAC and its source of law, the McCarran Act, shall have been repealed, I will not answer any questions of this kind and I discourage people from asking them." He said that his accusers were usually careful to call him "an identified Communist," but that the identification had only been made in hearings before the House committee, where such accusations were protected from the libel laws.

Reportedly, the applause that followed this statement was impressively loud.

■

SCORES OF COLLEGES and off-campus organizations offered to host Frank for a lecture—the reception could range from polite to enthusiastic. But some were quite hostile in their refusal, and on some occasions his lectures were broken up by violence or jeering. Given the temper of the times, some of that was to be expected. But Frank didn't learn the source of most of his troubles until 1983, when his lawsuit forced the FBI to surrender the 132,000 pages covering its surveillance of him. He had been watched by the FBI and various police agencies since the 1940s, but after he was released from prison in 1962 and it became evident that he was going to fight HUAC to the bitter end, he became a prime target of J. Edgar Hoover's so-called Counter Intelligence Program, or COINTELPRO. It was designed to disrupt, discredit, and neutralize Communist, leftist, and dissent organizations. Upon learning of COINTELPRO's existence in 1973, one headline writer aptly called the FBI "the Department of Dirty Tricks."

In Richard Criley's book *The FBI v. The First Amendment*, a nutshell summation of the 132,000-page record of the guerrilla war against Frank, we learn that on April 30, 1962, J. Edgar Hoover sent a directive to the FBI's field offices with instructions to start thinking up ways to disrupt Frank's speaking engagements. The agents who thought up the best tactics would receive an "Incentive Award." The first award was given for an action that would be repeated numerous times; it went to an agent who persuaded Minneapolis labor leaders to withdraw their agreement to let Frank use their hall.

Frank describes the FBI process:

> I was averaging at least 150 field trips a year. Every one of them was covered by the FBI. They had my plane schedule, my flight numbers, at whose house I would be staying, where I'd be speaking, who my contacts were. They kept detailed records of all my movements, as if I were doing something illegal. Here's a classic example: They have me coming into Ypsilanti Airport on an American Airlines flight fifteen minutes late. I was picked up by a woman wearing a brown plaid suit. I got into a 1949 Buick. I was seen driving east. This is the report.[5]

When the FBI failed to get his lectures cancelled, it relied increasingly on some of the more rabid anti-Communist groups to either picket the place where he was going to speak or interrupt his lecture with heckling questions. Many times he found that somebody had preceded his arrival by distributing to the audience reprints from the 1956 HUAC hearing in San Diego where a female informant ("Mrs. X") had accused him of being a Communist.

The American Legion, by far the FBI's most loyal auxiliary, could always be counted on to do these sorts of things. When Frank was scheduled to speak at the University of Toledo, the American Legion tried to persuade the university to ban him. Failing at that, the group took out newspaper ads asking people not to attend his lecture. And then it packed the hall with its members to disrupt the lecture.

"When I entered the hall," Frank recalls, "I could sense trouble ahead."

> The room was so full that people were standing along the wall. Many of them were wearing their Legion caps. As I walked down the aisle, there was complete silence. I stepped up on the stage, and here was a man in Legion uniform at the podium waiting for me. I paused, looked around the stage, then walked up to him and quietly, without comment to the audience, said, "You have no American flag flying here, and I don't speak without an American flag."
>
> And this guy who had been painting me as a Communist, as an awful, unpatriotic person, completely accepted the fact that I would not speak without an American flag. So he held up the meeting, called a janitor—the FBI records of this episode are so complete they list the name of the janitor who searched that building and at least one other building looking for an American flag—and he finally came down the aisle holding this little flag. It was just a pitiful little thing. The audience applauded him. He put it down, and the Legion leader on the stage with me explained to the crowd, "Mr. Wilkinson does not speak without the American flag." Thereafter I had an audience that didn't heckle me once, listened to me, and asked very good questions.

He had out-patrioted the Legion's superpatriots. It was probably the most successful ploy of his entire speaking career.

Hoover's agents were ordered to work especially hard at sabotaging Frank's lectures on college campuses. But if its disruptive tactics were to be uncovered, the FBI could face a potential public relations disaster. The director warned: "Since Wilkinson's speaking engagements are scheduled to be held on college campuses, the utmost discretion will be necessary to avoid any possible basis for allegations that the Bureau is interfering with academic freedom."[6]

The American Legion and some very conservative legislators exerted enough pressure to keep Frank off the Ohio State University campus in 1962. A group called Students for Liberal Action (SLA) had invited him to speak, but OSU President Novice G. Fawcett, using his powers under something called the Speakers Rule, cancelled the invitation. As he always did when he ran into this kind of opposition, Frank gave the students a lesson in fighting back. He recruited two from the SLA to join him in a federal lawsuit to overturn the ban. They got support from an unexpected source, U.S. Rep. Robert Taft, Jr.—Ohio Republican. Enough other influential Republicans followed his lead that the ban was set aside (by the university, before the court acted). So Frank was invited to speak at OSU in 1965.[7]

In 1963, students at the University of North Carolina invited Frank and Herbert Aptheker, a leading theorist of the Communist Party, to give some lectures. The state legislature responded by passing a resolution banning Communists or persons pleading the Fifth Amendment from speaking at state-supported schools. Aptheker, a devoted Communist, was easily covered under the ban. But Wilkinson wasn't. He had never been proven a Communist and had never taken the Fifth. But he was banned anyway.

Quite a few UNC students were embarrassed, for just up the road at Duke University, Wilkinson and Aptheker were welcome lecturers. How come those rich Duke brats got the fun of hearing radicals, but the children of mill workers and tobacco farmers didn't? Complaints were actually put in such terms. Student threats of a lawsuit prompted UNC trustees in 1966 to lift the restrictions and replace them only with the requirement that speaking invitations be made by "recognized" student groups and that the invitation be approved by the school's chancellor.

As soon as the ban was lifted, Paul Dickson III, student body president and chairman of the Students for Free Inquiry group, invited Frank and Aptheker to come back. Frank did, and on March 3, 1966, he and more than 350 students and faculty members gathered outside the locked doors at Carroll Hall at 7:30 P.M. A university cop blocked the way; Chancellor J. Carlyle Sitterson still hadn't made up his mind whether or not to approve the lecture. Well, said young Dickson, how about letting the crowd in to hear one of Frank's speeches delivered by tape recording? No, not even that. So the group marched three blocks to Hillel House, an off-campus Jewish student center, to hear him speak.

The next day, Chancellor Sitterson had made up his mind: the answer was no. Thereupon, Frank participated in his most pictur-esque demonstration of First Amendment devotion. Since he was *verboten* on UNC territory, he stood on a city sidewalk bordering the university, giving his spiel to about a thousand students and faculty members who were standing or sitting on the university's lawn, just a few feet away. Between him and his audience was a waist-high stone wall.

His short speech (the outdoor acoustics weren't very good) was interrupted by applause five times. The event—his 132nd on a campus—ended right: he and young Paul Dickson filed a lawsuit to get Chancellor Sitterson straightened out.

■

ON A FEW occasions, Frank's audience gave off an aura of poten-tial violence, but on one occasion, October 10, 1963, it developed into more than an aura. All day, a rumor had swept the cam-pus at American University in Washington, D.C., that George Lincoln Rockwell's Nazis would appear at the school's Leonard Gymnasium that evening. The reason? They planned to attack that night's speakers—Frank Wilkinson; James Forman, execu-tive secretary of the Student Nonviolent Coordinating Commit-tee (SNCC); and Frank's close friend Aubrey Williams, president emeritus of the SCEF and by that time pretty ill. Their topic was the struggle for racial integration. What else was there to talk about, since in recent weeks the University of Mississippi and the University of Alabama had been forced to enroll their first black students, and Dr. Luther King had given his "I Have a Dream"

speech at the Lincoln Memorial to the largest civil rights demonstration ever?

In response to the rumored invasion of the Nazi toughs, a
big group of muscular students waited outside the gym. But
since it was impossible to identify the Nazis, several slipped in
unnoticed.

Williams had hardly started to speak when two young men
in the front row began coughing, loudly and without letup. Two
cops grabbed one of them, but he dragged them onto the stage
and shouted, "This is a Communist meeting!" One of the cops hit
him on the head with a nightstick. The crack was heard all over
the gym. The other cougher was dragged out yelling "Sieg Heil!"
When Williams started to speak again, another young Nazi jumped
up and started shouting. He was brought down with a thump by
two students. Half-conscious, he still managed a Nazi salute as
he was carried out.

Williams, who was seriously ill, didn't try to resume his talk.
Wilkinson took over. But he had said only a few words when a
blond girl rushed on stage, clawed his face, yelled "You race-mixing
swine!" and kneed him in the crotch. A cop grabbed her in a
hammer lock and took her away. Meanwhile, a fight had started
between Nazis and AU students, but by that time there were so
many cops in the room that order was quickly restored. Frank,
obviously in some pain, finished his lecture sitting down.

After all the excitement, when Forman rose to give his talk
he was understandably subdued, and the press quoted only one
of his remarks: "It's really sad—these are the people HUAC gave
birth to."

CHAPTER 30

Too Much Travel, No Home Life Equals— Well, Of Course!

AFTER HIS INITIAL targeting at the eminent-domain hearing, Wilkinson had gradually become, in effect, a vagabond missionary, so intensely—perhaps a better word is fanatically—committed to his mission that he simply didn't have the time or the interest to succeed as a husband and father. He was off speaking an average of 150 days a year—for decades. Frank's youngest child, Jo, born right after World War II, talks about her father's zeal:

> "The Cause" took our father away. It swallowed him up, completely. I don't blame The Cause. It was great—worthy—noble. And though I will never be certain of it, I believe that if Frank Wilkinson had become a Methodist minister, his ministry would have swallowed him up as well. Given those two choices, I think being the daughter of "Mr. Civil Liberties" was by far the better choice.[1]

When he got out of the penitentiary, Frank exuded the glamour of an ex-con who had suffered for a good cause. There were piles of editorials and columns and news stories written about him and Carl Braden. They were invited to come and speak all over the country. More than Braden, Frank ate it up. After the huge welcome-out meeting in New York, and after going to Chicago and then back to Los Angeles for large protest demonstrations against the HUAC hearings taking place in those cities, he returned to the Atlantic coast for a series of lectures, and then reversed his field again to lecture in "every little town you ever heard of" (his appraisal) in Michigan, Illinois, Ohio, Wisconsin, and Minnesota. "We had big, big, big meetings in Madison, some fair-sized ones at Marquette and Milwaukee, Cleveland, Toledo, Oberlin, Cincinnati, Antioch College."

In other words, after nine months in prison, he had hardly taken any time to get reacquainted with his family in Los Angeles. Psychologists can argue over the causes of the neediness of an individual who is driven to travel and speak and advocate, who needs to be consistently at the center of attention. But the results on their family life are often the same.

■

GROWING UP IN the Wilkinson family was often painful for the children. Their parents were pariahs, were fired and blacklisted; the house was firebombed and a swastika was burned in their yard; unknown men shadowed the family constantly; and their schoolmates sometimes harassed them. Jo recounts a period in the ninth grade during the Cuban Missile Crisis of 1962, when classmates would "literally throw themselves up against the hallways when I would walk by" to avoid her. When her class watched President Kennedy speak about the Russians having nuclear weapons in Cuba, Jo recalls, "one of the boys stood up and yelled 'Communist! Traitor!' at me. There I was, just as afraid as everyone else that our world was about to be blown apart, and this kid yells at me that it's all my fault!"[2]

Another time, Frank was on a local television show hosted by a right-wing talk-show host, Tom Duggan. At home the phone rang. Jo picked it up and the man on the line asked her if her dad was on television. When she said yes, the man said, "We're gonna take care of him," and hung up. Perhaps more frightening to her, when the police came to their house to investigate the threat, they asked if Wilkinson was "a member of the ACLU or something?" When the answer was affirmative, the police then left without saying another word or investigating further. Jo says, "Those were strange times . . . I also remember the feeling that, if we can't trust the police to protect us, how would my father get home safely?"[3]

Growing up Wilkinson was often traumatic—and sometimes hardscrabble. Children often get pigeonholed within their families as one "type" or another. It can be tougher when they all have to stand in the shadow of a nationally known figure, especially one who spends little time with them. Jeffry, the oldest child, had to contend with never meeting Frank's expectations—and hearing about it repeatedly. Tony, the middle child, was the "perfect" one, and no one who is given such a label is ever able to live up to it. Jo, the youngest and the only daughter, felt like no one ever listened to her. Certainly none of the children got the emotional support they needed; their mother was busy trying to keep them in clothes and food, and their father was off saving the country.[4]

Jo does note that, despite these travails, "I learned many wonderful things from the times we lived in and the people we were privileged to know."[5] Among these remarkable and famous people were some very sympathetic folks, many of whom were similarly targeted. At a time when Jeffry (being a typical teenager) was feeling rebellious, he went to stay with Alger and Isabel Hiss in New York. When Hiss came to California, this most controversial and mild-mannered "Communist" stayed with the Wilkinsons. When Frank started working at ECLC in New York, his kids got to spend three months at Corliss Lamont's posh upriver estate, canoeing and fishing and playing. They developed so much affection for the mogul that when he came to visit Frank in Los Angeles, they put up a sign in their front yard that read, "Welcome Dangerous Corliss Lamont."

At one of the large fundraisers held at the Lamonts' while the kids were staying there, Alger Hiss came up to Jo and asked her how she felt and what she liked to do. After listening to her answers, he said that her grandfathers must be proud of her. Jo responded that her grandfathers were both dead. At that, Hiss asked her if she had a godfather. Jo remembers "thinking that it was a strange word, especially in our family, because we were brought up as atheists. I told him that we didn't believe in God and that I didn't know what a 'godfather' was. He smiled and said that it was somebody who looked after a special child . . . and that if it was all right with me, he would like to be my godfather." And so he became, just between the two of them, her godfather. Years later she found out about the famous Alger Hiss, who to her was just a gentle and compassionate man.[6]

And the kids got to know eccentric radical geniuses like Linus Pauling, who invited the whole Wilkinson family over for dinner just before Frank went to prison. And they got to know Paul Robeson, and Pete Seeger—who had Jo and Tony stay with him for a weekend when Frank first went to prison; Jo fondly recalls Seeger teaching her to play the banjo. And when Frank got out of prison, Joan Baez had the Wilkinson family up to her place at Carmel for a couple of days. And of course there were all those times when the youngsters got to eavesdrop on exciting battle plans being worked out by people like Harvey O'Connor and Alexander Meiklejohn. They got to meet, and to see their dad work closely with, some of the most remarkable people in the civil rights movement, including the Reverend Fred Shuttlesworth, James Forman, Robert Moses, and Fannie Lou Hamer.[7]

So there was an upside to being Frank Wilkinson's offspring.

■

AND SO IT came to pass that when Frank's lecture tour took him to Columbus, Ohio, his already fragile family life began to shatter.

The plan was to have dinner before the lecture at the Unitarian Church in the home of John and Donna Childers, and then return for a reception at the Childers' large, snazzy home situated on about three tree-filled acres that sloped down to the river. John was a successful lawyer and president of the local ACLU. The mood was amicable, to say the least. The guests were upscale. Frank was the center of attention, of course. It could have been a movie set for a romantic flick. And Frank fell in love.

With John Childers's wife, Donna.

It was, he says, borrowing an age-old rationale for a change of heart, "love at first sight." Donna was a small, good-looking, smart, vivacious, independent-minded woman. Columbus was a conservative city, but her talent for organizing was largely responsible for bringing together five hundred mainline Columbus citizens into one of the NCAHUAC's most effective anti-HUAC lobbying groups. Donna was partly drawn to Frank because he was a radical, and she adored radicalism. Frank had gone to prison for the cause of First Amendment freedoms, so he was obviously a left-wing extremist. "I wanted to fall in love with a Communist," she said.

She began driving him around to speaking engagements in nearby cities. Being a kind of traveling salesman of ideas, Frank was content with the age-old traveling-salesman arrangement. In other words, it was a perfect affair: there was wife Jean and three children, all of whom he still loved very much, back home in Los Angeles. And there was adoring Donna (also with three children, but they didn't figure significantly in his ideal equation) on the other end in Columbus. He managed to sustain the affair for three years before Donna, to his distress, compelled him to tell Jean what was going on.

There were divorces on both ends. Mr. Childers took it sportingly and was soon married again. Donna brought her children to their new home: John, William, and Robert Childers, twelve, ten, and eight years old when Frank and Donna married in 1966. They were a decade and more younger than Frank and Jean's kids. Donna had custody, child support, and was on good terms with the children's father, Jack. The kids pretty quickly acclimated to having Frank as their "True-True"—or true friend—but also didn't see him very much as they grew up. Jean felt totally betrayed and did not remarry. While Jean and the kids had been forced to function independently of Frank, it wasn't their choice or their preference. It's no surprise that Jean was shocked. They had been married for twenty-seven years. Her close friendship with Frank had started when they were at UCLA. When he came back from his post-college tour through the Middle East and Europe spouting his God-is-dead dogma to the irritation of many of his old friends, she stuck by him. They were married in 1939 and had three children in quick succession in the 1940s: Jeffry in 1942, Tony in 1945, and Jo in 1947.

In the first few years of their marriage, Frank had worked here and there—sometimes at manual labor—but it was Jean's job as a teacher that kept them in groceries. Then, when he was fired from his high-paying LAHA job, her closed-mouth loyalty got her fired, too, although the school board had nothing against her except that she was Frank's wife and had rebuffed the questioning of California's "Little HUAC."

For the next decade, she was forced to rely on pickup jobs as a teacher at private schools, at much lower pay, and sometimes doing home tutoring for no more than five dollars per day.

It seemed that for most of their married life, except when Frank was a top executive at LAHA, the lack of money and options had clouded Jean's life. During the years of his anti-HUAC crusade, Frank never earned more than ninety dollars a week, and when he went out of his way to get thrown into prison for the cause of the First Amendment, Jean became the sole supporter of herself and three children. She was so strapped for money during that period that friends got together and chipped in the equivalent of Frank's former salary to tide her through his absence. Because the Communist Party had disagreed with Frank's taking the First Amendment partly because it didn't want to support his family, Frank refused to take any money from the party while in prison.

Also, just before Frank went to prison, some anti-Communist devotee set off a bomb outside Frank and Jean's apartment, rocking the whole neighborhood. Neighbors had insisted that they move.

But where to? Again, their friends came to the rescue, raising enough money to buy them a small house.

It was swell to have such friends, but it was still charity. And Jean wasn't the charity type.

In short, she had shown dogged loyalty through some very financially lean, ideologically mean times. So it wasn't surprising that getting the heave-ho from Frank came with a rather large load of bitterness. Jean had stuck by him through all the ordeals.

Then Jean moved to Berkeley and started over.

■

AS IT WAS, when Jean did finally break out of the blacklist in 1965 and get a job teaching in Berkeley's public schools, the school district took into consideration only the five years she had previously taught in public schools—not the ten years she had taught in private schools—which put her way down on the salary schedule.

The witch-hunting era made Frank a celebrity. But what did Jean get out of it? "I was thinking just this last day or two," she told an oral historian, "what has been the effect of McCarthyism on my life? Financial, for God's sake . . . If I had continued in public schools and accrued automatic raises, I would have gotten a much better salary [in Berkeley]. My retirement is based on what I made in public schools, so I have a very low pension, and that means that I'm broke."[8]

CHAPTER 31

Suddenly, or So It Seemed, Protestors Were Everywhere

UP TO 1961, it must have felt pretty lonely protesting the existence of HUAC. But after Frank got out of prison, he and his small band of longtime activists suddenly had plenty of company. For thousands of Americans, protesting became the thing to do—to counteract all sorts of political grievances and push for all sorts of reforms. As never before, blacks, college students, and women were the prime energizers; civil rights, civil liberties, and peace were the prime issues.

In a long essay in the *New York Times* of May 14, 1962, reporter Nan Robinson, who had just returned from a visit to ten major campuses in all parts of the country, wrote:

The "silent generation" has found a voice.

Before today ends, American college students will have picketed something or someone, started a sit-in somewhere or marched someplace.

Two years ago, they might have been demanding later dating hours or making a panty raid on a girls' dormitory.

Today the students may be picketing a Communist or

John Birch Society speaker, sitting in a segregated lunch counter in Alabama, calling for the abolition of the House Un-American Activities Committee, marching in a "Ban the Bomb" demonstration or rallying for Senator Barry Goldwater, the national political hero of the student right.

Just a tiny fraction, but that fraction of the student body on the right and on the left is vocal, militant, organized, growing and full of determination.

Then she took note of a phenomenon that must have lifted Frank's spirits:

But few human molders of opinion have appeared before as many students as has *Operation Abolition*, the film picturing students at Berkeley and, by projection, American youths, as dupes of the Communist conspiracy for demonstrating against the Committee on Un-American Activities. On every campus reached in this survey, it has been shown at least once and often several times amid boos, catcalls, and cheers from students that packed auditoriums.

■

FRANK'S FIRST AMENDMENT crusade itself would be dwarfed by—but maintain a guiding role in—the coming era of great political protest movements, the most massive and sometimes the most violent of which centered on civil rights. In August 1963, two hundred thousand demonstrators in Washington, D.C., heard Rev. Martin Luther King deliver his "I Have a Dream" speech. In March 1965, King led a march from Selma to Montgomery, the participants swelling from thirty-five hundred to twenty-five thousand along the way. Alabama police and state troopers beat and jailed many of them. King had already been marked by Hoover as one of the nation's most dangerous Communists and as "the nation's most notorious liar." In such an environment, King and Frank Wilkinson were close allies and were often in touch. In many of his speeches across the country, Frank built his argument around civil rights, arguing that Congress wouldn't have enough politicians willing to kill HUAC until blacks got the vote in the South—a rather naive assumption that the black vote would change the reactionary character of Dixie's politicians.

•

THE VIETNAM WAR was also beginning to heat up. Young American males subject to the draft were becoming quite aware of who would fight future wars. In 1961, the Student Peace Union in Chicago had 150 members. In 1962 it had 12,000 members on seventy-five campuses. By then, with bad news from Vietnam filling the headlines, the antiwar movement was expanding on hundreds of campuses. Thousands began demonstrating. At the University of Chicago, student protestors seized the administration building and held it for three days. When the Students for a Democratic Society (SDS) announced plans to stage antiwar demonstrations in eighty-five cities across the nation in 1965, President Johnson said he had "no doubt" that Communists were behind the plan. In hearty agreement, J. Edgar Hoover told Johnson the SDS was "largely infiltrated by Communists" and that the plot was "woven into the civil rights situation which we know has large Communist influence."[1] In October 1967, 35,000 peace marchers descended on Washington; hundreds were arrested, and many were knocked around, when they tried to enter the Pentagon.

■ THOSE PEACE-LOVING WOMEN REALLY KNEW HOW TO FIGHT

One could reasonably argue that the most effective opponents of militarism in this period were women. And just as Frank's anti-HUAC crusade received an invigorating injection from the youthful rebels of San Francisco in 1961, he got an equally powerful lift from Women Strike for Peace (WSP), founded in 1961 by the irrepressible Dagmar Wilson, a commercial artist and illustrator living in the suburbs of Washington, D.C.

Before WSP came along, the most prominent peace organization in the country had been the Committee for a Sane Nuclear Policy, better known simply as SANE and, much more recently, Peace Action. When the SISS demanded that it prove that its members, one and all, were patriots without even the hint of a pink tinge, SANE panicked and adopted an exclusionary rule: swear one's anti-Communism, or get out. The result was disastrous. Membership collapsed. Many chapters withdrew to protest the violation of civil liberties, and SANE's entire youth section was suspended for challenging the policy.[2]

In contrast, Women Strike for Peace was much too smart to go down that path. Women of all political beliefs were welcome to membership, no questions asked; as a result, the WSP grew quickly and harmoniously across the nation. This was shown when it held simultaneous demonstrations in sixty cities to protest the arms race.

And like Frank's organizations (over the years he had at least four), and to some extent thanks to their example, WSP refused to be intimidated by congressional inquisitors.

These were mostly middle- to upper-class women who had previously led lives free of much public political passion, but they became such outspoken, unbending peaceniks that some parts of the government considered them to be subversive and capable of violence. The women were put under steady surveillance by the FBI and the CIA, and by "anti-Communist" divisions common in most big city police departments of the era.

Some of the larger WSP chapters suffered the same indignities as Frank's organizations: they were burglarized and had their membership lists stolen by Hoover's intrepid gumshoes.

In 1962, HUAC committed one of the great mistakes of its existence by subpoenaing leaders of WSP to appear for three days of hearings in Washington.

As soon as they were subpoenaed, WSP leaders wired members all over the country to come to the hearings in Washington and insist on testifying. They were told to "bring your babies, if necessary. Hospitality provided."

So the hearing room was jammed with women and babies and diapers and babies' bottles—and determination. In Bud and Ruth Schultz's book *The Price of Dissent*, Dagmar Wilson recalls: "It was much more like an enlarged PTA than a congressional hearing. But the tall guys with the helmets were there, too, standing around the wall. . . .

"I was the last to be called. As I listened, I could see very clearly what a simple-minded plot or scenario the committee had thought out, about who we were and how to 'trap' us. They tried to set us up as being run by a group of clever Communist women in New York. They had me down as an innocent victim, a 'duped' leader, who was being manipulated by these wicked Communist ladies. If we had fallen for the committee's line, our organization, like some before us, would have been split by dissension.

"But the strength of Women Strike for Peace was that we did not allow ourselves to be intimidated by the fear of Communists in our midst. We were not about to examine each other and say, 'Are you or aren't you or were you ever . . . ?' The committee's ghost was not our ghost, so we were not haunted by it. We felt, really, that we were a sisterhood of fellow spirits, and we would march with Communist women and every other woman in the world to abolish war and to work on nuclear disarmament."

The women had worked out their responses. When one was called to take the witness stand at the HUAC hearing, all would stand. But the very first time they did this, the committee declared it to be a demonstration, and demonstrations were forbidden. So the next day they had a new strategy: they would all applaud when the first woman was called to testify. No! That was also forbidden. "Then," says Wilson, "with the typical ingenuity of our sex, we decided that every woman who went up for interrogation would be presented with a bunch of flowers by her sisters, which we did. And everyone who came off the stand was hugged and kissed and congratulated."[3]

Not even the hairiest member of HUAC dared suggest forbidding such sweetness.

But as always, the committee's members, having built their careers on compulsive rudeness, tried to browbeat the witnesses. It didn't work. In fact, it failed almost comically. When Alfred Nittle, the committee's attorney, took off his glasses and jabbed them in the direction of a witness as he demanded answers in his best courtroom style, the answers always came back with candor wrapped in ornate politeness. The committee members were too dense to see that they were being smothered in irony and parody.

Thus, when Nittle asked Wilson, "Would you permit Communist Party members to occupy leading posts in Women Strike for Peace?" she answered, "My dear sir, I have no way or desire to control those who wish to join our efforts for peace. Unless the whole world joins in this fight, then, God help us."

To his next question, "Would you permit Nazis or fascists to join?" she answered, *If only we could get them!*"

■

ONE NEWSPAPER SUMMED up the hearings with the headline: "Peace Gals Make Red Hunters Look Silly." Most major newspapers, except those under the thumb of Hearst and Colonel McCormick, joined the razzing. The *Washington Post*'s Herblock drew an editorial cartoon depicting HUAC in session, with one member saying sotto voce to another, "I came in late. Which was it that was un-American—women or peace?"[4]

Years later Dagmar Wilson could still relive that confrontation with great satisfaction: "There was no question that I made them look awfully silly. I remained polite throughout, though, and I never lost my cool. Once in a while, I did turn around and grin at the house behind me. It was a great day. I probably will regard it as the one great moment in my life."

In her triumph, though, she did not forget that she was benefiting from battles that had been fought for years by Frank and others who knocked massive holes in HUAC's battlements often at great cost to themselves.

"But, look," she went on, "were we ever lucky! We came along at an opportune moment. We had much more public support than victims of this committee had had before.... Actually, they treated me with kid gloves. I don't know what would have happened if it had been earlier, when there was still so much fear, when this country was so hysterical about Communism."[5]

∎

MEMBERS OF HUAC, stung by defeat, took their revenge by subpoenaing the women for a return engagement on December 7, 1964. Would they never learn?

As soon as the engagement was announced, the press across the country began to hoot and jeer, recalling HUAC's previous rout. The *Charleston Gazette* editorialized:

> If we're not mistaken, Mrs. Wilson and Mrs. [Donna] Allen are the same two ladies who turned a HUAC hearing last year into a total shambles.
>
> A nation roared with laughter, as the press reported daily how they and other housewives frustrated repeated HUAC attempts to link them to an international conspiracy.
>
> So devastating was HUAC's defeat, so one-sided the performance, that the show closed long before it was scheduled to, and HUAC members slunk back into the woodwork to await a more propitious time to carry out their ridiculous investigations.
>
> It's small wonder the committee wants no more open hearings with the likes of these women. Asking for secret testimony is about the smartest move this committee has made since Congress unwisely established it.[6]

The *Washington Post* echoed those thoughts: "Some of the Women Strike for Peace, including Mrs. Wilson, were hailed before the

Committee once before; their manifest candor, good faith and good humor made the Committee look very foolish indeed. No doubt, this is why the Committee prefers to talk to them in executive session where its embarrassment can be concealed."[7]

Allegedly the new hearings were called to learn if the government was properly carrying out the McCarran Act of 1950, which had been passed by Congress when Europe still was overflowing with displaced persons pleading to come to the United States. The law was as mean and conservative as the senator who rammed it through Congress: Pat McCarran of Nevada, chairman of the Senate Judiciary Committee and thereby dictator of immigration legislation. Since he hated all Jews, domestic or foreign, and suspected all immigrants of being potential spies, his goal had been to restrict immigration as much as possible.[8]

These HUAC hearings were being held a decade after McCarran's death; the use of the immigration law had become saner by then. That change didn't please everyone. Certainly not HUAC. It feared that too many Communists were slipping into the country, and the hearing on December 7, 1964, would be the ninth of ten scheduled to find out if enforcement of the McCarran Act had become too loose.

Which is why Dagmar Wilson of WSP, Donna Allen of WSP (and NCAHUAC's first Washington coordinator), and Russ Nixon, formerly with Frank's NCAHUAC and now general manager of the *National Guardian*, were being subpoenaed. In 1963 they had gone to the State Department and persuaded it to grant a visitor's permit to the Japanese peace leader Professor Kaoiu Yasui, dean of the Hosei University Law School and head of a group opposing nuclear weapons. Once in the United States, Professor Yasui had spoken to law schools and peace groups in ten cities, and at the *National Guardian's* fifteenth anniversary dinner in New York City. Like Dagmar Wilson and Donna Allen, the *National Guardian* constantly criticized the government's overindulgence of the defense industry.

As the *Washington Post* observed, "Certainly there is nothing 'un-American' in going to a department of the United

States government—openly and candidly—to submit a completely lawful request. The right to do this is specified in the U.S. Constitution."[9]

But it still smelled subversive to HUAC, which wanted tougher restrictions on visas for foreign visitors whose views opposed U.S. policy.

Once again, HUAC got trounced.

When HUAC said the hearing would be closed, the targeted trio, with polite cheerfulness, replied, "Not if you want us to testify." They attended the closed session, as they had been ordered to do, but answered nary a question. They would not budge; it would be open hearings or none. Outside in the corridor, about fifty WSP members and several children waited to see if they could get in. Also in the corridor were dozens of huge floral baskets, sent by their "sisters" across the nation, with messages saying such things as "Wish we were with you again" and "Sic 'em." One newspaper judged the corridor "so full of flowers it looked like a princess's wedding or a mobster's funeral."

Faced with another defeat and a public relations disaster, the committee threatened the resisting witnesses with a contempt citation and probable jail. Allen played along by telling a CBS reporter, "I can't imagine a better issue to go to jail for than this one."

A federal grand jury did indict them on December 30, but surely Allen knew she was in little danger of going to prison. In the previous fifteen years, HUAC had asked for the House to cite 129 individuals for contempt, and the House had routinely, mechanically acceded to every request. But the federal courts had almost always thrown them out; only nine of the citations had resulted in a final conviction. On August 2, 1966, it happened again; the District of Columbia Court of Appeals threw out the contempt case against the two women and Nixon. It was the fifth loss for HUAC since 1961.

In fact, the last HUAC contempt conviction to survive court review was the one the Supreme Court upheld against Frank and Carl in early 1961.

Speaking of contempt for HUAC, perhaps the most effective

response to being "identified" as a Communist came from Harvey O'Connor, Frank's close associate and compatriot in the fight against HUAC, at the conclusion of an anti-HUAC speech at the University of Utah on May 17, 1964. After O'Connor had finished speaking, a student in the audience produced a list of 30 "Communist-front organizations" to which O'Connor was said to belong. O'Connor politely replied that the list was not up-to-date. At latest count, he said, HUAC had linked him to at least 150 such organizations. In an annual report on his committee, Senator Joe McCarthy had written that Harvey was "the most contumacious witness ever to appear before the Committee." It was a sentiment Harvey asked to have put on his gravestone.[10]

■ SHUFFLING OFF TO BUFFALO— AND ANOTHER DEFEAT

After being thrashed by WSP in their first encounter, the members of HUAC apparently thought they could recoup some of their reputation as tough guys by picking on citizens in some out-of-the-way city. They scheduled Buffalo, New York, for the last week of April 1964. It was a poor choice. Any city not in the South probably would have been a poor choice, because in many parts of the country, and especially in cities on the West Coast and in the Northeast, people were beginning to think that a visit from the congressional thought police needed to be followed by strong fumigation.

Frank Wilkinson and his generals arrived in Buffalo early to start gathering the troops. The battlefield was hospitable to them; the last HUAC hearing in Buffalo had been in 1957, and the city was clearly disgusted at their return. The Buffalo Common Council, by a vote of eleven to four, refused to extend an official city welcome. The motion to table the welcome was made by Councilman Delmar Mitchell, who pointed out that "most of the committee members are from the dead South. I'm against their coming here and trying to brainwash us." At the State University at Buffalo, 180 professors signed a protest against HUAC's invasion, and students from three universities turned out for a big protest march. Folk singer Joan Baez raised the anti-HUAC temperature at a special meeting with two thousand students and at a concert attended by three thousand. Frank Wilkinson and actor Sterling Hayden—out on bail after being arrested in a massive civil rights demonstration in California—were among ten anti-HUAC speakers at a big community gathering. NCAHUAC sent attorneys to prep the subpoenaed witnesses for their ordeal, and the Buffalo Bar Association urged members to supply them with defense attorneys.

During the hearings, fifteen hundred picketers from New York City and upstate colleges walked six picket lines. That sort of opposition didn't faze HUAC, of course; they were accustomed to it, and probably appreciated the publicity that tended to come with it. But the kind of boisterous, snarling, insulting reception they got in Buffalo and were beginning to get wherever they went—and especially the total lack of deference, to put it mildly, that they were beginning to get from witnesses—must have taken some of the wind out of these notorious windbags.

The first witness set the tone for the three days of hearings. Paul Sporn, a tall, muscular University at Buffalo English instructor, could not have been more contemptuous. He was on the stand for three hours because the committee practically had to pull his answers out of him with pliers. He gave circuitous replies, elliptical replies, conflicting replies, and always insulting replies when he wasn't simply citing the First, Fifth, Sixth, Ninth, and Fourteenth Amendments, to frequent applause from the audience. Now and then he would lace his answers with claims that some members of the committee—including Acting Chairman Joe Pool—were there illegally because blacks in their districts had no voting rights.

The *Buffalo Courier Journal*, obviously proud of its obstreperous citizens, rewarded Sporn with an eight-column front-page banner headline:

UB INSTRUCTOR RIDICULES HUAC

There were other stars in the melodrama. When Edward A. Wolkenstein was called to testify, he gave only his name, cited the First, Third, Fifth, Sixth, Ninth, and Fourteenth Amendments to justify his lack of cooperation, and then refused to say anything else except, "Is this Buffalo, New York, or Nazi Germany?" Mrs. Wolkenstein and her daughter Rachel, fifteen, applauded that remark. Chairman Pool told them to stop, but they kept clapping. Pool told her to leave. She said, "No, I won't leave. He's my husband." A U.S. marshal reached for her. Several spectators leaped on him and started kicking and punching; women clouted him with their purses. Wolkenstein jumped out of the witness chair and shouted for the marshals to leave his wife alone, then charged through the audience and grappled with one marshal while several other marshals bodily carried him back to the witness chair. The spectators started shouting "Storm troopers!" and singing "We Shall Not Be Moved."

Of the seven witnesses called to testify, not one cooperated even slightly, except for an undercover agent the FBI had paid to be in the local Communist Party for six years as a spy. Some in the audience shouted "Fink!" when he stepped down. Pool ordered marshals to carry a few more rowdy spectators from the room, squirming and shouting all the way. This manhandling of witnesses, attorneys, and spectators by U.S. marshals was something new to HUAC hearings, but it would become more commonplace, especially with Congressman Pool in the chair. Headlines of any sort were manna to him. But because Buffalo was too remote to get much coverage from the national press, it was unlikely Pool's constituents back in Texas would hear much about his antics. Still, he tried to make his visit to Buffalo sound productive:

"The facts developed in this hearing and the conduct of the witnesses, all of them identified as members of the Communist Party, are enough to refute the claim that communism presents no problem.

"Basically, there are only two ways of life in the governmental or political sphere—the way of the law and the way of the jungle. Communism, through the conduct of its adherents in these hearings, has been shown to be a throwback to the jungle movement."

▪ ONE OF HUAC'S WORST

Ever since its founding in 1939 under chairman Martin Dies, another Texan, the House Un-American Activities Committee had been infamous as a haven for the House's most primitive members. Some were perhaps more vicious than Congressman Joe Pool, but none was a more crude exhibitionist. He never rose to the chairmanship, but on several notorious occasions he sat as acting chairman. And since he would ultimately preside over a Washington, D.C., hearing in such a flamboyant, incompetent, disgraceful manner as to help speed HUAC on its long descent into oblivion, he deserves more attention.

While serving Dallas in the Texas legislature, Pool distinguished himself by introducing bills to outlaw horror comic books and to make membership in the NAACP a felony. In 1958 and 1960, he ran losing campaigns for a U.S. House seat. In 1962 he was one of two dozen candidates for a new congressman-at-large seat. The candidates, as Larry L. King accurately wrote in *Harper's* magazine, were "all so obscure they might have profitably robbed liquor stores without wearing masks."[11] Pool made the runoff with Woodrow Bean, a county judge from El Paso who would certainly have won if, halfway through the campaign, he hadn't been indicted for swindling the IRS.

Texas's new congressman immediately asked for a seat on the most unpopular committee in Congress: HUAC. Pool also began to rack up a perfect record, of sorts, by voting against unemployment compensation, against Medicare, against aid for education, against the war on poverty. But those votes would not have distinguished him from many in the House, so he began to go further. Asked why he was the only member of the House to vote against the Wilderness Bill when it passed 388 to 1, Pool explained, "Well,

I figured I could throw my conservative friends an anti-Lyndon vote and at the same time not do much damage."

HUAC—indeed, the House as a whole—was the perfect place for his cynicism to flourish. But he carried it to such an extreme when he presided over HUAC's stormy hearings in 1966 that it drew outraged responses from the press all over the country. Editorial writers even began snickering at his physical appearance, calling him "tubby" and "O-shaped" and the like. But this would come after some exciting developments in Chicago.

■ UNPLEASANT PREDECESSORS AT HUAC

HUAC tended toward mindlessness from its inception. Rep. Martin Dies, who helped found HUAC in 1938 on promises it would "not permit any character assassinations or any smearing of innocent people" quickly helped it violate the promise.[12] He typically used the committee as a platform to try to destroy the Roosevelt "gigantic bureaucracy" of subversives.[13] It was through Attorney General Robert Jackson that Dies struck a deal in which he would not publicize HUAC findings until they were cleared by the Justice Department—effectively by Hoover, and the FBI would send HUAC information on unprosecutable cases. It was a marriage made in hell, virtually guaranteeing HUAC would be a slander pit.[14]

Rep. J. Parnell Thomas, a New Jersey political hack was on HUAC from its inception in 1938, and reached his notoriety with the Hollywood Ten hearings of 1947.[15] Hoover's quick and quiet assistance with background on the Ten saved the day for HUAC. Thomas ended up pleading guilty to swindling and joined two of the Hollywood Ten in jail at Danbury prison.

It was Rep. John Rankin of Mississippi, who in 1944 slipped in a vote to make HUAC a permanent committee, a feat he managed without even being chair of HUAC. For Rankin, HUAC was a forum for race and ethnic baiting—especially of blacks and Jews.[16]

So-called friendly witnesses to the Committee would have

all the time in the world to read their novel-length statements. Unfriendly witnesses would almost never be allowed to read any statements, and only rarely, introduce them into the printed record.

■ INFORMERS

The friendliest of the friendlies were the big three informers—Harvey Matusow, Elizabeth Bentley and Whittaker Chambers. Matusow, after a brief stint as "a Communist flunky" switched to FBI stool pigeon and HUAC shill, and then back again to admitting he was a "perpetual and habitual liar."[17] Elizabeth Bentley was mistress to Jacob Golos, a spy for the Soviets. When he died, she sold a tell-all and became the "Red Spy Queen" and one of the most prolific and imaginative and unreliable stool pigeons.[18] It was Bentley who testified against William Remington, who had preceded Frank in his penitentiary cell.

Whittaker Chambers's great feat was sending Frank's friend Alger Hiss to prison. It was a takedown of a highly respected State Department official that simultaneously made Richard Nixon's career with HUAC. The story has been told elsewhere in great gory detail, but is most briefly summarized by Roger Morris as "not only a political spectacle but one of the judicial travesties of the century."[19] It was built on bizarre, headline-grabbing, partly inflated and mostly fraudulent evidence.

Of this material were HUAC and the informants made. And by those measures alone, HUAC was a nightmare and a fraud. Poking fun at the lunacy was the best medicine.

CHAPTER 32

Chicago: One More Nail in HUAC's Coffin

HUAC'S VISITS TO the Northeast had confirmed that region as an inhospitable place for the congressmen. But there was still the Midwest left to offend. The drama to come in Washington would wait in the wings.

And so, because the gentlemen of HUAC never learned, they scheduled a hearing for 1965 in Chicago. Of course, there were reasons to think that city would be hospitable to an anti-Communist posse. Many Chicagoans were immigrants from Eastern Europe and hated anything that smacked of Communism. As for Mayor Richard J. Daley, he was a strange mixture. A proud Democrat, he may have stolen enough votes in Chicago to give John Kennedy his state and thereby the presidency in 1960, but this didn't mean he liked left-wingers. Far from it. Another of his complexities was that, despite a reputed hatred of the Vietnam War, he had no sympathy for peacenik demonstrators.[1] Indeed, according to the *Washington Post*, Daley sent agents from Chicago's police department to infiltrate and disrupt antiwar groups in Los Angeles, San Francisco, and New York.[2] He was a brutal law-and-order guy. After the murder of Martin Luther King Jr., there were riots all over the country, and Chicago was among the hardest hit. Daley hit back equally hard, ordering his police to shoot to kill arsonists and "shoot to maim or cripple looters."[3]

HUAC also had good reason to expect a friendly reception from Chicago's conservative newspaper, the *American*, and from the Midwest's most influential right-wing rag, the *Tribune*.

However, other influences that should have put HUAC on its guard. First, it should have known that while industrial Chicago was proud of its stockyards and its fabled reputation as the hog butcher for the world, it also considered itself, and rightly so, as the culture capital of the Midwest. It was just as touchy and defensive as San Francisco, and wasn't likely to be happy about any portion of its upper-crust residents being judged by a fourth-rate congressional committee, a majority of whose members were from what they undoubtedly considered to be the most backward part of the country. It didn't help that it was chaired by a mean Louisianan, Rep. Edwin Willis.

HUAC had scheduled the Chicago hearings fully expecting opposition ads, mass protest demonstrations, speeches by people who hated it, and some chaos during its hearings. But there was a new undercurrent this time. With the peace, civil rights, and civil liberties movements growing in numbers and strength, many people—including many important people of both parties—had turned to concentrating on these issues; they were getting fed up with HUAC's endless search for "Communists" whose sins seemed to present no threat to the life of the community whatsoever. A kind of anger built up, which needed only the right personality to spark a revolt.

In Washington, the irrepressible Dagmar Wilson of WSP had supplied the spark. In Chicago, it would be Dr. Jeremiah Stamler.

Despite HUAC's built-in repulsiveness, its members might have come out ahead of the game if they hadn't gone one step—or one victim—too far in 1965. Napoleon once said, "Never interfere with the enemy when he is in the process of destroying himself." Picking on Dr. Stamler was part of HUAC's self-destructive process.

The committee issued subpoenas for Stamler, for his assistant Yolanda Hall, and for Milton Cohen, a young social worker. Ten other "suspects" were also subpoenaed, but for publicity purposes those were the important ones. Doubtless HUAC chairman Willis thought they made good targets. Stamler was an outspoken opponent of the Vietnam War, as he had been of the Korean War, and it was widely rumored that in the early 1950s a radical group had met regularly in his home. Hall was a defense witness at the 1949 Smith Act trials of Communist Party leaders. Willis, in a not unusual violation of HUAC's own rules, leaked their names to the *American*. He of course denied having made the leak, but since the list was delivered to the newspaper by police from Daley's "spy squad," the denial was obviously spurious.

Stamler, one of the world's leading cardiologists, was director of the heart disease control program of the Chicago Board of Health, a post he had held since 1958. He had also recently been awarded the Lasker Award for medical journalism, and was widely admired for his many public service activities. Naturally, he had many close friends and admirers among Chicago's establishment. And he was not about to take Willis's smear without launching an all-out counterattack. On receiving the subpoena, he cleared the deck by immediately signing a loyalty oath and giving Dr. Eric Oldberg, president of the Board of Health, his word that he had never engaged in subversive activities or associated with groups that did. The directors of the Board of Health said that was good enough for them, and so the Establishment was obviously going to stick with Stamler.

That included the local congressmen. Rep. Sidney Yates, the Democrat in whose district the hearings were held, introduced legislation calling for the abolition of HUAC. But more significant was the reaction from U.S. Rep. Donald Rumsfeld (Republican of Illinois, and yes, *that* Donald Rumsfeld), who represented the extremely conservative district—thick with John Birchers—just north of Yates's district. Rumsfeld stood up to HUAC, demanding that the investigators be investigated themselves, since "recurrent charges can no longer be ignored that the committee is unconstitutional (by investigating ideas and beliefs, not acts), denies witnesses due process, and has not served a legislative purpose commensurate with its costs."

Perhaps the best appraisal of the organized dissent that preceded the Chicago hearings was made by James West in *Political Affairs* magazine:[4]

> There was a time when the coming to town of the House Un-American Activities Committee would send people scurrying for the storm cellars. That was in the Frightful Fifties. But when HUAC announced it would be in Chicago starting May 25th, 1965, for three days of hearings, it gave rise instead to widespread indignation and determination to fight back. In less than two weeks a mighty array of forces gathered to give HUAC the kind of reception it deserved.
>
> Much of the organizing work was done by the [Richard Criley–led] Committee to Defend Democratic Rights and [its sister organization, Frank Wilkinson's] National Committee to Abolish HUAC, whose national leaders were, by chance, in town for a national conference on the eve of the hearings. ["By chance" must have been written in jest.]
>
> Not long after the hearings were announced, the Chicago *American* "leaked out" the information that 10 people had been subpoenaed (it turned out to be 12, of whom 4 were Negroes, 4 were women, 5 were shop workers and nearly all were active in civil rights, labor and peace movements). It was also learned that 100 people had received letters from Chairman Edwin Willis (D-La.), telling them they had been named as Communists and offering them a chance to "clear themselves" in executive session.
>
> At the opening session, when Chairman Willis announced that he had received not a single reply to his stool pigeon bait, a mighty cheer and burst of applause went up. This set the tenor of the hearings. The committee soon got the message: It wasn't welcome in Chicago. . . .
>
> Its appearance was therefore that of an old, toothless wolf

which could only make noises reminiscent of the ferocious beast of old. As Donna Allen, former legislative director of the Women's International League for Peace and Freedom [and D.C. coordinator of NCAHUAC] . . . said at the mass protest meeting of over 1,000 which took place two days before the inquisition opened: "HUAC fears people who are not afraid of it."

That protest meeting was sponsored by thirty peace, civil rights, and civil liberties organizations. On the platform with Donna Allen were Rev. Fred Shuttlesworth of the Southern Christian Leadership Conference (SCLC), James Forman of the Student Nonviolent Coordinating Committee (SNCC), Victoria Gray of the Mississippi Freedom Democratic Party, Professor Robert Havighurst of the University of Chicago, and Frank Wilkinson.

Opposition to HUAC's appearance came from the usual sources. A half-page ad urging abolition of the committee appeared in the *Daily News*, signed by more than 230 academic and professional leaders solicited by Criley. Picketing and anti-HUAC demonstrations went on throughout the hearings, with large turnouts from the University of Chicago, Northwestern, Loyola, several theological seminaries, Lake Forest College, and from the University of Wisconsin and even some Michigan schools. Picketing went on from 9 A.M. to 7 P.M.; sometimes as many as a thousand people were involved.

As it had at its San Francisco hearings, HUAC tried to stack the crowd by issuing passes to the John Birch Society and the right-wing American Security Council on a priority basis, letting its members get in before the general public. But enough college students shouting anti-HUAC slogans and singing "America" managed to attend that the occasion was given a rowdy flair; over the three days, only seventy young people were arrested.

Also before the hearing, Dr. Stamler asked some of Chicago's top business executives to suggest the best attorney for his fight. The consensus: Albert E. Jenner Jr., senior partner in an illustrious Chicago law firm and a highly respected figure in Illinois and national law. He had been attorney for the Warren Commission on the Kennedy assassination and was a former member of the U.S. Loyalty Review Board.

Neither Stamler nor Jenner wanted to take the First or Fifth Amendment route to avoid testifying. They wanted to really fight back. But how? When Jenner seemed stumped, Stamler called an old friend from his student activist days, Arthur Kinoy, and asked for help. He asked the right person.

Physically Kinoy was a shrimp, but in court he was a fighting cock. To the general public he was not famous, but among lawyers and civil libertarians he was held in awe as one of the scrappiest practitioners of the trade. He said, "I am proud that everything I do in court is vigorously pursued." Indeed it was. True, he often lost, but that was because he always took on the toughest cases: desperately trying to keep A-bomb spies Julius and Ethel Rosenberg out of Sing Sing's electric chair, for example, and organizing the legal assault team that tried to unseat Mississippi's congressional whites and replace them with blacks.

Kinoy had fought in the stifling courtrooms of the rural South and in the cool marble chambers of the U.S. Supreme Court, and it was in the latter that in 1965 he led an ACLU team to a stunning, landmark victory known as *Dombrowski v. Pfister.*[5]

▪ DOMBROWSKI EXPANDED

Dr. James Dombrowski, a good buddy of Frank's, was founder and director of the SCEF, the only organization made up primarily of white southerners committed to the black civil rights struggle. They had worked closely with Aubrey Williams in the South and had clashed with Clark Forman of ECLC. In 1964 the SCEF's office had been raided by New Orleans police and toughs from the Louisiana Un-American Activities Committee who stole the SCEF's files and membership lists and, in violation of a court order, shipped them off to Senator James Eastland, chairman of the SISS.

Eastland and Louisiana officials then trumped up indictments against Dombrowski and two of his top executives for violating state laws prohibiting membership in "subversive organizations," namely the SCEF and the NLG. If they were convicted, the conviction would eventually be overturned, for those laws were clearly unconstitutional. But it could take years to move their appeal up through the federal courts. In the meantime, it was feared that while Dombrowski and the others stood convicted and waiting to be cleared, the threat of the charges being used on others would bring the southern integration movement to a halt. So even if they eventually did win, they would have lost precious time. But why wait? Why not try to get the federal courts to rule the Louisiana antisubversive law unconstitutional *before* the prosecution got started? True, no one had ever yet persuaded the federal courts to overturn a state law as unconstitutional in advance, before it was used for prosecution. But it was worth a try. So Dombrowski approached Kinoy and his legal team. They agreed to go on the offensive by seeking preemptive justice: first getting a federal injunction to put the indictment on hold, and then persuading a federal court to kill the state antisubversive laws that Stamler and his associates would soon be accused of violating.

And somehow they did it. Early in 1965, Kinoy and his law partners, in *Dombrowski v. Pfister*, convinced the U.S. Supreme Court in a vote of five to two to preemptively block the states' use of those laws—to knock them out before anyone was even convicted of breaking them. As Justice Brennan put it (only Justices Harlan and Clark dissenting), the mere *existence* of the state antisubversive laws has "a chilling effect upon the exercise of First Amendment rights" and must be condemned and prohibited by the federal courts.

■

SO NOW KINOY urged Stamler and Jenner to try to use the brand-new *Dombrowski v. Pfister* ruling to stop HUAC in its tracks.

After all, if the Supreme Court approved of preemptively blocking unconstitutional state actions, why not ask the Court to preemptively block unconstitutional congressional actions? Specifically, why not try to persuade the Court that HUAC's whole purpose and modus operandi was an unconstitutional suppression of First Amendment freedoms, and that the committee should therefore be put out of business? Of course, there was the little matter of separation of powers. The Court had frequently blocked illegal actions by the executive branch and had often nullified laws passed by Congress, but never before had it tried to actually interfere in Congress's way of operating. Kinoy wanted to ask the Court to make that huge leap.

It was hard to convince Jenner that it was a good idea, but finally he said, "I'm with you. It's sound. Let's draw up a federal complaint based on *Dombrowski* and we'll ask for an injunction against the committee itself."[6]

Which they did. And to make their intentions clear, Jenner took his clients into HUAC's hearing room and told Chairman Willis they would not testify because the committee itself was an unconstitutional creature. Then the witnesses, including Stamler, marched right out of the hearing room. As expected, the Department of Justice immediately indicted them for contempt of Congress. Their fight-back was under way. It would not be easy—or quick.

■

BY WALKING OUT of the HUAC hearings, Stamler made them look futile and pointless. Without him as a witness, the hearings collapsed. For three days the committee went through the motions of a public investigation, but only two witnesses testified—both shopworn FBI informers.

Desperate to make something out of nothing, committee counsel Alfred Nittle pulled one of his old tricks. He asked a woman witness who refused to answer any questions, "Are you aware that Dr. Stamler was one of those in charge of setting up the Communist Party underground in the 1950s?" Stamler's name up to this point had not been so much as mentioned by any witness under oath—nor would he be mentioned by any witness still to be questioned. And yet he was now actually accused—not by a statement of fact, but in a question.

The *Daily News* bade the committee farewell with a thumbs-down: "The three-day visit to Chicago of HUAC was a disgrace from start to finish, from the hearing room to the picket line. Nothing positive was accomplished and a great deal of harm was done."[7] Even the reactionary *American* admitted "the committee has succeeded only in publicizing information long known to the FBI and hardly a surprise to anyone."[8]

The best responses came from newspapers outside Illinois. The *Blade* of Toledo, Ohio, wrote with malicious accuracy, "For three days last week, HUAC staged performances which had the pungent aroma of a circus. They were billed loudly in advance as an investigation into communism. But so far as what was publicly revealed, not a shred of evidence was uncovered that Illinois, let alone the nation, is about to succumb to communism." It was all quite in keeping, said the *Blade*, with HUAC's "long black record of character assassination, sensationalism, unsupported charges, abuses of authority, and a total disregard for the rights of individuals."[9]

Quite accurate, yes, but unfortunately a long way from reflecting the national judgment, or even Ohio's. The *Blade* was addressing a heavily unionized, industrial, Democratic island in the midst of northwest Ohio's Republican ocean. Toledo's congressman was Thomas Ashley, who was among the few on record as wanting to gut HUAC, but elsewhere in the state, voters had elected such representatives as Republican John Ashbrook, one of the most hardened members of HUAC.

Ashbrook's crowd, not Ashley's, was on top—for the moment. To be sure, their days were numbered—but in the thousands. Those fighting HUAC needed unbelievable stamina.

■ CONGRESS RATIFIES HUAC CONTEMPT CHARGE

An even more impressive display of resistance to change was shown on October 18 and 19, 1966, when the House debated whether to obey HUAC's recommendation to punish Stamler, Hall, and Cohen (also known as the Chicago Three) for walking out on the Chicago HUAC hearing.

Never before had a contempt citation met with such an avalanche of impressively motivated opposition. On October 18, Rep. Silvio O. Conte, a Massachusetts Republican, handed the House a petition opposing any punitive action against the Chicago Three. It was signed by 415 constitutional law authorities, 1,000 political scientists, 700 biomedical scientists, 300 historians, and 500 religious leaders. It was the most far-reaching petition Congress had ever received from the "brains" of America. In the *Congressional Record*, it took up twenty-one pages of small type.

To a large degree, the signers of the petition had been recruited by branches of Frank Wilkinson's NCAHUAC. He had started creating this network before going to prison; since getting out he had stepped up his pace, traveling constantly. After the San Francisco riots, he sent one of his young recruits, Arnold Lockshin, to run the NCAHUAC's Boston office. Lockshin made friends everywhere. He persuaded the National Council of Catholic Bishops to sign the petition, and he also persuaded Dr. Paul Dudley White of that city to be the front man in getting medical signatures. White, nationally known as the doctor who pulled President Eisenhower through his heart attack, was a great catch. But it didn't take much persuasion; Dr. White and Dr. Stamler were old acquaintances.

For once, many members of the House seemed impressed by the public's opposition to HUAC. At least they were impressed enough to keep debating the contempt issue far into the night and into the next day.

At one point in the debate, the issue shifted abruptly from the conduct of the accused trio to the conduct of some members of HUAC. Briefly, the House was split into shouting factions. It happened when, probably by accident, a congressman said he'd heard that a witness who testified against Stamler had been paid by the committee. What! Paying a witness for friendly testimony? By House rules, that was strictly a no-no.

Rep. Barratt O'Hara, an Illinois Democrat who was pro-Stamler, stormed, "If the reputation of this great Chicagoan is being sold for a price, I want to know the name of the man who received it." That, in turn, prompted several members of the committee to angrily proclaim that they would never approve such an underhanded trick. HUAC member Richard H. Ichord huffed, "I would fire anyone, or ask the chairman to fire him, if I knew that money had exchanged hands." Chairman Willis gave solemn assurance that the committee was totally innocent. Alas, he was lying; they were all lying. Wayne Hays, Democratic maverick from Ohio and chairman of the House Contracts Administration Committee, had left the floor briefly and now came back with records proving that HUAC had not only paid one thousand dollars to a witness to testify against the antiwar group but that it had been buying witnesses for years, calling them "consultants."

Perhaps proof of lying and skulduggery caused HUAC to lose face for a moment, but the House, forgiving as always of wayward members, ultimately handed it a victory. The contempt citation passed, 228 to 78. Rep. Don Rumsfeld, representing Chicago's fat-cat district, had once said HUAC needed to be investigated, but apparently he either didn't really mean it or he had heard from his constituents, for he voted aye.

So, with HUAC ratified by Congress, Stamler, Hall, and Cohen were facing criminal contempt of Congress charges in court. John de J. Pemberton Jr. was selected for the honor of taking their petition to U.S. District Court Judge Howard Corcoran. Pemberton was the first lawyer to serve as executive director of the ACLU. Among his accomplishments, he made the organization more democratic, cut off relations with Cold Warriors such as Joseph Rauh (who wanted Pemberton to stop cooperating with the NLG), and moved it into a new age of militancy, most notably by organizing a powerful coalition of all the major civil rights groups. This was the Lawyers Constitutional Defense Committee (LCDC), which became famous as the first line of defense for civil rights workers in the Deep South during its most violent postwar era.[10] The twofold request of Pemberton and his team of lawyers was simple enough. Judge Corcoran was asked (1) to issue a temporary restraining order to prevent HUAC from holding its next scheduled hearing and (2) to convene a three-judge appellate panel to decide—based on the *Dombrowski* ruling—whether HUAC's mandate to investigate "un-American propaganda" was constitutional. The petition was made on behalf of the next batch of subpoenaed witnesses but also on behalf of Dr. Stamler and his two codefendants, who still faced a possible jail term for walking out on HUAC in Chicago.

To the attorneys' amazement—indeed, Pemberton had told reporters they didn't expect success at that level—Judge Corcoran granted both requests, saying, "The committee's basic function, to investigate activity deemed un-American, has resulted . . . in exposing persons to public scorn because of their involvement in unpopular causes," and the constitutionality of that practice was sufficiently questionable that it deserved further study by a higher court before HUAC did any more mischief.

Washington was stunned and horrified. "A court telling a congressional committee it can't hold a hearing?" House Speaker John McCormack asked in incredulous tones. "Why, we might as well not have a Congress at all." No one suggested lynching Corcoran, but many members of Congress thought it would be a good idea to impeach him. Pool told the House he would ignore the restraining order and said, "I'll go to jail and stay there till hell freezes over to prove my point." It was a transparently flatulent boast, but many members on both sides of the aisle, closing ranks against the court's intrusion, gave him a standing ovation. The furor didn't last long. The three-judge panel Corcoran had assigned to handle the case quickly overturned the restraining order, and HUAC was free to proceed.[11]

However—and this was to have momentous consequences—the three-judge appellate panel said it still wanted to think about the constitutional question of HUAC's legitimacy. It was obviously taking the *Dombrowski* challenge seriously. So Kinoy and his "coconspirators"—as the right wing considered them—were still in business.

Kinoy and others slogged seemingly endlessly through the courts on behalf of Stamler, Hall, and Cohen. Not until four years after their indictment for contempt of Congress did they win their first, more permanent, victory. At that time, the Seventh Circuit Court of Appeals ruled that their lawsuit demanding a trial of the HUAC's constitutionality was entirely proper because "the Congress has no more right, whether through legislation or investigation conducted under an overbroad enabling Act, to abridge the First Amendment freedoms of the people than do the other branches of government." Furthermore, the court of appeals issued an injunction to stop the contempt of Congress indictments while Stamler's team gathered evidence of HUAC's long history of constitutional abuses to present in their suit.

But the roller coaster through the federal courts kept going, up and down, twice to the Supreme Court. After a total of eight years, Stamler, Hall, and Cohen were finally victorious—but it was only a kind of default victory. As Kinoy recalled, "It was not much of a surprise when, rather than proceed with such an explosive trial, the government in 1973 chose to dismiss the contempt indictments."[12]

CHAPTER 33

The Show Sinks to New Levels of Absurdity

A **SHORT WHILE AFTER** the HUAC disaster in Chicago, the committee decided to turn its attention once again to activists on the West Coast. This time, however, it would bring them east to see if that improved the performance. In the spring of 1966, students at Stanford, UC Berkeley, and other Bay Area campuses had collected blood (not much) for shipment to North Vietnam. Attorney General Robert Kennedy, who was gradually becoming a convert to liberalism, said he personally saw nothing wrong with sending blood to North Vietnam, as long as there was a surplus after helping our own troops. The American Friends Service Committee (AFSC, an organization of the Friends, or Quakers) gave money to the International Red Cross to help North Vietnam's war victims. Supplying humanitarian aid of that sort was not then illegal, though it is today. Of course, stiff penalties for giving aid to the enemy in a war formally declared by Congress had long been on the books. But the Vietnam War had not been formally declared.

Congressman Joe Pool was going to try to remedy that oversight. His legislation would have slapped a twenty-year prison sentence or a twenty-thousand-dollar fine on anybody who gave aid and comfort to the Communist government of North Vietnam. By interpreting that prohibition, the penalty might even apply to people who did no more than demonstrate or speak out against U.S. participation in the war. Or, as Monsignor Charles Owen Rice noted with alarm in the *Pittsburgh Catholic*, "You could break the law by simply giving a glass of water to an antiwar rioter or sending a food package to a starving family in Vietnam." Attorney General Ramsey Clark testified that the Pool bill was probably unconstitutional, and top officials at the Defense and State departments testified that ample laws to handle any eventuality were already in existence and that the Pool bill was completely unnecessary.

Nonetheless, Pool pressed ahead. To exhibit the kind of subversives he claimed were part of the anti–Vietnam War movement, he set HUAC hearings for four days in mid-August 1966 in Washington. Things got off to a typically underhanded start. As mentioned earlier, HUAC's rules specifically prohibited making public the names of subpoenaed witnesses before the date of their appearance. Of course, HUAC being HUAC, it had routinely violated that regulation, and Pool now violated it again. The chance to stir up publicity was too good to be missed. So, ten days before the hearings were to start he released seven names to Hearst's *San Francisco Examiner*. The most newsworthy name was that of Dr. Stephen Smale, star of the Berkeley math department.

The *Examiner*'s headline:

UC PROF DODGES SUBPOENA, SKIPS U.S. FOR MOSCOW

The story opened:

Dr. Stephen Smale, University of California professor and backer of the Vietnam Day Committee and the old Free Speech Movement, is either on his way to or is in Moscow, the *Examiner* learned today.

In leaving the country, he has dodged a subpoena directing

him to appear before the House Un-American Activities
Committee in Washington.

One of a number of subpoenaed Berkeley anti-war activists, Dr. Smale took a leave of absence from UC and leased
his home there before his trip abroad.

The next day, in the twelfth paragraph of a thirteen-paragraph
story, the *Examiner* avoided a libel suit by admitting, "A headline in yesterday's *Examiner* about Dr. Smale and the House Un-
American Activities Committee was open to an incorrect inference
that he had gone to Moscow to avoid the subpoena issued by the
committee."[1]

What the *Examiner* never told its readers was that in fact, Dr.
Smale had taken an authorized leave from Berkeley the previous
May in order to lecture for two months at the University of Geneva
in Switzerland before going on to attend the International Congress
of Mathematicians in Moscow as one of two thousand eminent
scholars. In Moscow he would be one of twelve to give lectures and
would receive the Fields Medal, considered the equivalent of the
Nobel Prize in math. (While there he also gave a speech, standing on the steps of Moscow University, in which he criticized U.S.
intervention in Vietnam—but made sure to remind his audience
that "it was only ten years ago that Russian troops were brutally
intervening in Hungary.")

■

THE OTHER SUBPOENAED witnesses included some young members of the Progressive Labor Party (PLP) and the Vietnam Day
Committee. Pool believed that "the key leadership of campus protest groups is made up of hard-core revolutionary Communists."[2]
He was at least 99.9 percent wrong about that, but a handful of
Marxists were proud members of the PLP. From experience, Congressman Pool knew they could be counted on to be combative or
even obnoxious, which would provide the headlines he desired.

But the headlines that really mattered—indeed, that would

help change history—were ones he blundered into by his own bullying. For Pool made the fatal mistake of mistreating some rowdy witnesses and then some tough lawyers who weren't about to take it lying down.

■ AN UNUSUALLY WILD SCENE OF CHAOS, EVEN FOR HUAC

The hearings in D.C. in the summer of 1966 heralded the end of the House Un-American Activities Committee's power to intimidate and abuse witnesses. One thing is for sure: the witnesses who showed up this time were not in the least intimidated, and nor were their antiwar friends who were on hand to lend support. Each day, the hearing room was packed with about three hundred enthusiastic spectators, with another several dozen supporters in an adjoining corridor. They were so unruly that a hundred U.S. marshals and police officers lined the walls; they strong-armed and ejected fifty of the rowdier participants during the three days of the hearings. One demonstrator was blocked from the hearing because he was wearing a Socialist button; he was then arrested for biting the policeman who restrained him. Several were so discourteous as to address Pool as "Tex." Some were—almost joyfully, it seemed— carried out bodily, struggling and shouting defiance all the way; they were arrested for disorderly conduct, but they quickly paid their ten-dollar fines and returned to the Capitol for more fun.

Attorney Frank J. Donner, author of *The Un-Americans* and a longtime student of this strange committee, wrote in the *Nation*:

> Until Tuesday morning, August 16 . . . the unfriendly witness tended to be a silent witness. But something went wrong. Of the 12 unfriendly witnesses who were subpoenaed, six took the stand and not one followed the script. All freely admitted their political views [for the most part, they were proud Marxist/Leninist Communists] and refused to take the Fifth Amendment except for the narrow purpose of blocking inquiry into the identity of others.

> Overnight, a new kind of witness was born: the witness
> who boils over with talk, who pleads no privilege and fills
> the record with his views and objections. He is free to talk
> bitingly, humorously, solemnly, and fearlessly. . . . Two wit-
> nesses were so eager to testify that they had to be forcibly
> removed from the witness stand.[3]

Jerry Rubin, for one, was excused from testifying, and that was
exactly what he did not want. Famed for baiting the establishment
(he would help organize the memorable 1967 march on the Pentagon), he understandably felt cheated. Some of the witnesses had
had a wonderfully good time insulting members of the committee,
and he wanted to share in the fun. Having waited almost three
days in his costume as a Revolutionary War soldier, complete with
brass buttons and tails, he became so belligerently insistent on
being allowed his hour on the witness stand that he was arrested
for disorderly conduct and carried out.

With good reason, Donner wondered, "Will the committee
persist in conducting its hearings after this most recent circus?
Some have claimed that the House will rally around HUAC to give
it a new lease on life. But its future looks most unhappy, haunted as
it will be . . . [to have created] a new breed of fire-breathing witness,
clamoring to testify, deaf to the committee's coaxing to plead one
of the good old amendments, clinging tenaciously to the witness
chair after the chairman had cried—'Hold, enough!'"

Pool was chairing the committee only because the regular
chairman, Rep. Willis, had been ill for days; Willis did put in a
cameo appearance, long enough to denounce the antiwar protestors as "dirty, yellow-bellied cowards." Immediately the crowd,
having worn out their other insults, began jeering at the committee: "Dirty, yellow-bellied, racist cowards."

No wonder Rep. Ashbrook, Pool's most loyal supporter, loudly
complained, "We can't have this mob rule!"

▪

IF MEMBERS OF HUAC loathed the young witnesses, their feelings about the witnesses' lawyers were even less affectionate. The loathing would have been there under any circumstances, but it was intensified because the lawyers were essentially trying to kill HUAC in court. Furious about that—and furious also because the impudent witnesses were causing him to lose control of the hearings—Chairman Pool was in an explosively vengeful mood. Attorney Kinoy, always combative, lit his fuse.

On the stand was Philip A. McCombs, twenty-two, a recent Yale graduate who had somehow infiltrated the PLP and had written an exposé of it for William Buckley's conservative *National Review*. Under questioning by HUAC's counsel, McCombs mentioned the name of one of Kinoy's clients, an antiwar protestor named Walter Teague III. Kinoy and his law partner, William Kunstler, were immediately on their feet, heatedly arguing that they were entitled to cross-examine McCombs on any testimony relating to Teague. Other lawyers joined in.

Pool shouted, "You are overruled!"

Kinoy responded, "We take strenuous objection to your ruling."

Pool (banging his gavel) shouted, "Sit down! Go over there and sit down! You are not going to disturb this hearing any further!"

Kunstler replied, "Mr. Chairman, you don't have to deal discourteously with an attorney in front of you."

Pool shouted, "I'll deal with him any way I want! I just told him to be quiet! I ask you both to sit down!"

At this point, all the other lawyers joined Kinoy in arguing with Pool, who, still banging his gavel, stood up, shook his finger at them and shouted, "Now you sit down!" He motioned for the U.S. marshals to move in on Kinoy.

Kinoy shouted, "I will not be removed from this hearing!" When the first marshal grabbed his arm, he shouted again, "Don't touch a lawyer!" A second burly fellow twisted Kinoy's other arm behind his back; a third smothered him in a choke hold. As they carried Kinoy out, he had barely enough wind to wheeze and sputter.

Kunstler shouted, "Throw us all out! Mr. Kinoy is my colleague, a professor of law at Rutgers, and a member of the bar of New York!"

The other attorneys had rushed forward and were now also loudly objecting. Jeremiah Gutman, with gestures of measurement, said, "Let the record show that Mr. Kinoy is five feet two inches and that he was carried out of here choked and trussed." Donner said, "In more than twenty years of appearances before this committee, I have never seen brutal treatment of this sort. I don't regard this as a hearing. I regard this as an armed camp." Pemberton said, "In all my years as an attorney, I have never experienced the shock I did this morning at the forcible removal of Mr. Kinoy." Beverly Axelrod, an ACLU lawyer from San Francisco, said, "As long as I am under fear of personal violence on myself, I cannot adequately represent my clients. I am not prepared to take physical violence."

All the lawyers walked out. The hearings fell apart.

Later that day, the lawyers came back to give a prepared statement to an army of reporters, who were delighted to be covering this donnybrook. It read:

> Although we have finally been able to bail Mr. Kinoy out of jail, the treatment offered him has all but destroyed any chance we may ever have had to represent our clients adequately.
>
> Attorneys cannot function in an atmosphere of terror and intimidation. The fundamental constitutional rights to be represented by counsel means by counsel free from brutalization and terrorization.

Kinoy was convicted of disturbing the peace by using "loud and boisterous language" at the committee hearing. Two days later, in court to be sentenced, Kinoy was totally *not* terrorized, and, still feeling scrappy, he told Judge Harold Greene: "Your honor may impose whatever your honor thinks is proper. I make no plea for mercy. I have no regrets or remorse for what I did. I will do it again and again and again and again." He vowed to take his appeal to the Supreme Court, "if necessary," and "take it there fast."

Kinoy wouldn't have to go that high. Justice wasn't served as quickly as he would have liked, but photos and stories about his ejection from the committee room had triggered a militant response from his peers all over the country, and two years later—after an amicus curiae brief was filed on his behalf by over a thousand lawyers and professors of law—his conviction was reversed by a unanimous court of appeals.[4]

■THE SHOW GETS VERY BAD REVIEWS ALMOST EVERYWHERE

As a cynical but wise commentator once said, "The Supreme Court reads the newspapers." If that were true, the Court would have noticed that some of the most powerful publications in the United States, and many of the moderately powerful, were portraying HUAC as an intolerable stain on the government, a stain to be eradicated. It may have been only coincidental, but every HUAC hearing since 1960 had received increasingly critical coverage from the press and, during the same period, the Supreme Court had overturned every contempt conviction stemming from a HUAC hearing.

The press response to Pool's folly in 1966 was the most damning yet.

The *New York Times*, which esteemed itself journalism's Vatican, offered a papal denunciation that also took a swipe at one of Congress's oiliest characters. "It is a measure of how low the House Un-American Committee has sunk in public esteem that Senator Everett Dirksen has joined those who condemn its unseemly spectacles and its legislative futility." The *Times* added, "The members of the House can expect an interminable round of futile and embarrassing controversies so long as they permit this committee to roam about with an inherently vague and unworkable mandate."[5] The *San Francisco Chronicle* wrote: "The Smear Boys have cranked up again. . . . The UnCommittee should have been abolished long ago."[6] The *Milwaukee Journal* wrote: "The Un-American Activities Committee is proving nothing but its unerring ability to make a great deal of to-do about nothing and give publicity to people who otherwise wouldn't be heard five feet from their own soapbox."[7] From the *St. Louis Post-Dispatch*: "An obscure Texas congressman named Joe R. Pool has done a wonderfully effective job in making the House Un-American Activities Committee look absurd using Hitler's bully boys tactics."[8] From the *Boston Globe*: "A leading candidate for the role of the late Senator Joe McCarthy in any resurgence of the hysteria of the decade is Rep. Joe Pool."[9] And the *Providence Journal* wrote: "The committee has displayed a remarkable facility for making headlines, for distorting situations, for trampling on the rights of witnesses in its widespread snooping forays, but its tangible accomplishments in more than thirty years of activity could be written, almost literally, on the head of a pin. . . . The question is: How much longer before the members of the House will stiffen their spines, take a hard look at the sorry record of this irresponsible committee, and do something about it."[10]

The *Washington Post*, which for years had been the most consistent and most insulting critic of HUAC, wrote: "HUAC has become a joke—but a bad joke. . . . Because HUAC has become ludicrous, serious legislators no longer care to be identified with it—and so its buffoonery is left largely to buffoons. The House would do well to join the general laughter and laugh this misbegotten body out of existence."[11]

Likening the committee to a circus and its members to clowns suddenly became commonplace, as in the *Detroit News* sneer at "the clownish HUAC."[12] Magazines also liked metaphors of that sort. Even the conservative *Saturday Evening Post* did, writing of the Pool hearings: "All members of the vaudeville cast certainly put on a good show—Congressmen snorting, students shouting, lawyers gesticulating, policemen strong-arming, with the audience booing and cheering each new comic turn. We wonder, though, whether it may not finally be time to drop the curtain on this long-running repertory show."[13]

The most extensive use of this theme appeared in *Commonweal* magazine. Its derision opened:

Back in the days of vaudeville, even a bad act could keep going if it could manage at least one good show a year. The House Un-American Committee, that last outpost of American vaudeville, has just registered its annual comic success, thus guaranteeing its existence for another season. . . .

If there was one flaw in the show, it was probably its ear-splitting noise. The line between broad comedy and outright silliness is at best a fine one. Too much wrestling and shouting are telltale clues that the line has been crossed. In this case, the arrest of some fifty people, including a lawyer, suggests that the stage directions are not being followed, and the actors were writing their own jokes as they went along. It is not customary, for instance, for witnesses to openly admit Communist affiliation. Nor is it customary (most of the time) for members of the audience to heckle and out-shout the Committee members. Hushed solemnity, an air of high seriousness and suppressed indignation is the expected etiquette. . . .

Even lovers of patriotic vaudeville balk when things get silly.

There is, however, a possible moral here. For years, many high-minded, utterly serious groups have tried to have the House Committee abolished. Every year a bill is introduced toward this end, a bill that gets nowhere at all. And every year, too, magazines like this one write editorials condemning the Committee and all it stands for. They don't get anywhere either. Far from going under, the Committee flourishes.

What the recent hearings show, however, is that the Committee can't cope with total and utter contempt on the part of the witnesses it calls and their supporters in the audience. Without the prop of nervous solemnity, a hearing just cannot be conducted. The witnesses pulled out this prop as violently as they could. They succeeded brilliantly in reducing the hearings to a silly shambles. Ordinarily, such antics would be reprehensible.

But the Un-American Activities Committee is not an "ordinary" committee, nor are its purposes "ordinary" legislative purposes. It is nothing but organized witch-hunting. If it can't be abolished by rational argument, then let it be abolished by laughter and shouting. Vaudeville is dead.[14]

▪ ANOTHER PYRRHIC VICTORY FOR HUAC

Whatever effect that kind of ridicule from the press may have had in shaping opinions on the U.S. Supreme Court, it clearly had little impact on members of the House. If anything, it made a majority of them—especially those from the South—resist reform even more stubbornly. On October 13, 1966, the House passed Pool's absurd bill to punish peace demonstrators by a vote of 275 to 64.

Congressmen from Dixie must have hoped that the folks at home wouldn't discover the details of the bill they had voted to approve. In the post-vote autopsy of the bill, it was discovered that during the turmoil of the debate, Pool had clumsily allowed the bill to be amended (quite against his intentions) in such a way that nobody would be punished for *advocating* resistance to the war effort, but only for taking *action* against it. Contrary to everything Pool and his southern supporters had in mind, Martin Luther King would not have been punished if he successfully persuaded a thousand people to lie down in front of a troop train, but an angry southerner who threw a pop bottle at a National Guardsman could have been subjected to a ten-thousand-dollar fine and five years in jail.

But who really cared anyway? House passage was just the first act in another kind of vaudeville show, one that was scripted to have the Senate kill the bill in the last act. Everyone knew that's how the show would end.

▪

SO DR. SMALE, Arthur Kinoy, and all those witnesses and all those rowdy folks in the HUAC audience came out of the hearings pretty unscathed.

CHAPTER 34

A Foul Atmosphere from the Top Down

TO FULLY APPRECIATE the occasional victories of Frank Wilkinson and his allies, it must be remembered that the anti-Communist hysteria was still constantly being stirred up—by both political parties.

Consider the presidential election of 1964. It offered nominees who were captives (as well as creators) of the muddy mess of reactionary politics. The Republican loser, Barry Goldwater, was generally thought of as the greater nut because he was supported by such outfits as the John Birch Society. The John Birch Society warned that Communists were fomenting racial hatred in the South as the first step to turning those states into a Soviet colony. It also "revealed" that Dwight Eisenhower, former president and famed army general of World War II, had been "consciously serving the Communist conspiracy for all of his adult life as a secret agent of the international Communist conspiracy." The Birchers also sprinkled the nation's landscape far and wide with billboards demanding that the "subversive" Chief Justice Earl Warren be impeached. The society had three goals: protect HUAC; get rid of the income tax; and ban all manufactured goods from Communist countries. It was so successful at burrowing into the national hysteria that by 1964 it was raising more than a million dollars a year (an impressive amount in those days) and had recruited a membership of tens of thousands.[1]

Actually, although Goldwater, in a casual moment during the campaign, gave an offhand endorsement of the kooks ("A lot of people in my home town have been attracted to the [Birch] society, and I am impressed by the type of people in it. They are the kind we need in politics [based on their real record of actions]"), Goldwater was not as frightening as the Democratic winner, Lyndon Johnson. Anyone scanning LBJ's record would have found enough rotten spots to be nervous about the future indeed.

During Johnson's eleven years in the House of Representatives, he had always voted yes, 100 percent of the time, against civil rights legislation—including an anti-lynching bill. He also voted to extend the life of Congressman Martin Dies's fledgling House Un-American Activities Committee. His maiden speech in the Senate, which lasted an hour and twenty-five minutes, was a contribution to a successful filibuster to kill civil rights legislation.

Shortly thereafter, in one of his dirtiest uses of a Communist smear, he rewarded the rich oilmen who'd put him in the Senate.

Leland Olds, a decent and public-spirited bureaucrat, was up for reappointment as chairman of the Federal Power Commission (FPC), which, among other things, regulated the price of natural gas sold to and by pipeline companies. During Olds's tenure, he had saved consumers a quarter of a billion dollars (very big bucks in those days) in rate reductions.

Two of Johnson's most important backers had just purchased a gigantic pipeline. If they could get rid of Olds and put in a more "cooperative" chairman of the FPC, their fortunes would be made. Johnson went to work. As a young man in the 1920s, Olds had written many fiery articles for left-wing publications denouncing the hideous working conditions found in many factories and mines. Using those articles, which showed that Olds had once been guilty of radical compassion, Johnson successfully portrayed him as a dangerous Communist. (In a gesture typical of Johnson, after killing Olds's confirmation, he met his victim in the hallway, put his hand on his shoulder, and said, "Lee, I hope you understand there's nothing personal in this. We're still friends aren't we? It's only politics, you know."[2])

The black marks continued. In 1954 Johnson opposed statehood for Hawaii, going along with Senator Eastland's argument that Hawaii was run by Communist labor unions. Johnson supported the appointment of Joe McCarthy's protégé Robert E. Lee to the FCC, although Lee's only experience in the field of radio was as master of ceremonies for H. L. Hunt's right-wing *Facts Forum*. Johnson voted against efforts to kill a $100 million loan to Franco, Spain's fascist dictator. He voted for the 1950 McCarran Anti-Subversive bill, a staggering frontal assault on civil liberties. And in 1957 Johnson supported retention of loyalty oaths for students getting loans from the federal government. But perhaps his dirtiest trick as Democratic majority leader in the Senate was to totally gut the 1957 civil rights bill while acting as its "savior"; he managed to win the support of some gullible northern liberals, such as Hubert Humphrey, while retaining the support of Dixie's segregationists in his quest for the presidency. Liberal columnist Thomas Stokes wrote, correctly, "Looking back on it all, we might say that never was a strategy so brilliant to bring about so evil a result."[3]

President Kennedy's fumbling anti-Communism was upgraded by his accidental successor. But the Texan's immediate need in his 1964 presidential campaign was to appear more moderate than his Republican opponent. To that end, Johnson assured the nation he had absolutely no war plans for Vietnam: "We are not about to send American boys 9,000 or 10,000 miles away from home to do what Asian boys ought to be doing for themselves." He made this promise thirteen days before the presidential votes were cast. Three months later, he was bombing North Vietnam; by June 1965, there were seventy-one thousand U.S. troops in the war—three times the number of the preceding December.[4] He obtained Congress's approval for going to war by inflating a probably contrived "battle" that occurred one night when U.S. destroyers were touring the Gulf of Tonkin. Allegedly, they were fired on by North Vietnamese PT boats—but no one actually identified enemy vessels on that pitch-black night. A great deal of shooting took place, but so far as could be proved, *all* of it came from U.S. guns. Nevertheless, that trivial and probably bogus encounter was inflated by Johnson into a critical international threat; it was all he needed to get a carte blanche resolution from the Senate to take any military action he desired. And so the war was launched.

Indeed, it's safe to say that whatever Johnson believed, or said he believed, could probably be explained by Johnson's remark to Olds: "It's just politics, you know."

After Kennedy's assassination put him in the White House, Johnson shed his racism as a snake sheds its skin. But his militaristic impulses increased—as did his willingness to cut corners on civil liberties. Just as Frank Wilkinson and his allies received no help from President Kennedy in their fight with the FBI's witchhunters, neither did they get any help from President Johnson. On the contrary. Johnson turned the FBI loose, as Johnson's idol, Franklin Roosevelt, had done, to crush any left-wing activists he thought might hurt him politically.

That tactic was put on full display at the 1964 Democratic convention in Atlantic City.

■

SOMETIME DURING THE night of June 21, 1964, civil rights workers Michael Schwerner, James Chaney, and Andrew Goodman were murdered in Neshoba County, Mississippi, by members of the Ku Klux Klan and its uniformed branch, the sheriff's department. On August 4, their bodies were found buried in a mud dam. Two days after that, Mississippi blacks mounted a kind of rebellion that had not been attempted in a hundred years: they set out to replace the only breathing political party in the state, the whites-only Democrats. Actually, the decision had been made on April 26 at a statewide convention of the brand-new Mississippi Freedom Democratic Party (MFDP) in Jackson. But the triple murder added fuel to the fire, and two days after the bodies were found the MFDP sent a letter to John Bailey, chairman of the Democratic National Committee, demanding that the sixty-eight Freedom delegates and their alternates be seated at the Democratic convention in Atlantic City in place of the all-white delegation, which, in violation of the U.S. Constitution, had been selected by a process that excluded blacks.

The MFDP hired Joseph Rauh as their lawyer and went to Atlantic City to continue lobbying for their rightful place. Obviously they believed that a leader of Washington's liberal legal establishment would crusade militantly to unseat the hopelessly reactionary delegates. They were wrong. When Arthur Kinoy and William Kunstler, two of the most radical and best-known "people's lawyers," dropped by to ask Rauh if he needed any help, they got an icy reception. "The coldness that emanated from Rauh," recalls Kinoy, "was as marked as any I could remember over the years."[5] There were several reasons for his coldness. First, Rauh knew that Kinoy and Kunstler were members of the NLG, which to him meant they were Communists.[6] Second and more important, Rauh was cozy with the Democratic establishment and, on its behalf, was at that very moment actually engaged in the process of betraying the rebel blacks who had hired him. Although Johnson's nomination was an overwhelming certainty, Rauh wanted to eliminate even the slightest bump in the path of Johnson's coronation parade, which meant frustrating everything the MFDP was attempting. The celebrated liberal Hubert Humphrey was Rauh's partner in this betrayal. Such was the split nature of "liberalism" in that era.

But their deviousness was nothing compared to Johnson's. On his personal orders, J. Edgar Hoover set up a political hit squad of twenty-seven FBI agents. Using bogus press passes and wiretaps and other spying apparatus, they learned exactly what the MFDP delegates and other civil rights and peace demonstrators were planning to do during the convention. And usually the combination of Rauh, Humphrey, and FBI subversion succeeded in thwarting the MFDP.[7]

·

IN OTHER WORDS, it's fair to say that everything civil rights and civil liberties activists achieved in the middle and late 1960s as they went about trying to win enough public support to lift repressive laws was achieved in spite of overt and covert disruption from the government and the powers that be. They took their knocks on picket lines, ceaselessly raised money (much of it their own) to buy newspaper space for their petitions, and refused to take any crap from HUAC, no matter how much legal drudgery and jail time resulted from their resistance. Their only real outside help came, in the 1960s as in the 1950s, from that truly gutsy, ever-shrinking group of radical left-wing lawyers who never let them down and worked on complex, drawn-out court cases for very little pay—when they got paid at all. And Frank always included civil rights and civil liberties as a matched set of essential rights in his and NCAHUAC's work in the South.

Support from members of Congress and from sympathetic media outlets did build up—slowly—in the last years of the 1960s, but it was never more than a pitiful fraction of the whole. Help from the White House, which means from the Justice Department, was incredibly slow in coming, if it came at all—and was always diluted by the spirit of "it's just politics, you know," when it wasn't being blocked or mis-channelled by superpatriotic "liberals" and by Hoover.

Over the years, Frank and his allies got thousands of the most respected and most illustrious professionals in higher education, religion, the arts, and the sciences to sign petitions begging for help in protecting civil liberties against HUAC. When these petitions landed on the doorsteps of the White House and of Congress, they simply lay there as the occupants calmly stepped around them—or on them.

■

OCCASIONALLY, SOMETHING WOULD happen to suggest that maybe the tide was turning—when it really wasn't. In the closing days of Congress in 1962, Rep. Jeffery Cohelan of California successfully led a fight to kill a HUAC-sponsored bill that would have revoked the security clearance of 3 million defense workers—thereby making them vulnerable to being fired if they were accused of being Communists—without letting them face their accusers in court. The vote to kill the legislation was by a promising two-thirds majority; it was the first major legislative defeat for HUAC since it was founded in 1938. But it was easy to read too much into that victory. It probably had little to do with congressional regard for civil liberties and much to do with its fear of labor unrest. With defense work spread all over the country, members could doubtless foresee a tidal wave of protest from nervous blue-collar constituents if the bill passed.

A more accurate measure of the soul of the House could be found in the efforts of some members to legislate HUAC out of existence. Their efforts came to nothing. Any bill aimed at killing it outright never got more than six votes. That's how many voted for its abolition in 1962: William Fitts Ryan of New York, James Roosevelt of California, Barratt O'Hara of Illinois, Thomas Ashley of Ohio, Robert W. Kastenmeier of Wisconson, and Edith Green of Oregon. Several dozen members could usually be counted on to speak out against HUAC, but when it came to voting to kill it, they backed off. The Washington bureau chief for the *Capital Times* of Madison, Wisconsin, wrote in disgust, "Almost everybody pooh-poohs the House Un-American Activities Committee these days. But nobody in the Administration or among the House leadership has screwed up courage for the messy job of knocking the committee in the head. So HUAC, though bruised and outcast, still lurks in the bush, still able to claw and spoil."[8]

Actually, some House members did have the courage; there

just weren't enough of them, not by a long shot. Realizing they would have to wait years before a majority of the House would vote for outright abolition, they changed strategy. They would try to starve it to death. To wit, they would keep reminding members of other House committees, most of which did a great deal of work, that HUAC did absolutely nothing of substance and yet got much more money than they did. In other words, their pitch would be: hey, suckers, don't you have enough pride to pull the budget plug on your do-nothing, lay-about colleagues?

Obviously, the answer was no.

In February 1963, Rep. Ryan of New York and Rep. Roosevelt of California read into the *Congressional Record* this appraisal of HUAC's costly uselessness:[9]

> The Supreme Court has held that congressional investigations must serve some legitimate purpose, yet in 24 years the House Un-American Activities Committee has been responsible for just three public laws. Of 13,420 bills introduced in the 87th Congress, 59 were referred to HUAC; the only one that became law was to correct one of the committee's own mistakes.
>
> In the 87th Congress, of the 19 standing committees that received appropriations, only two were given more money than HUAC. Its budget was more than three times as much as given the Foreign Affairs Committee, or the Armed Services Committee, and more than nine times as much as Agriculture. Its staff of 50 is exceeded only by that of the Appropriations Committee.
>
> And what does HUAC do for the budget it receives? Its members and staff have made a mockery of the First Amendment rights to free thought, speech, and assembly. For the most part they have spent their time investigating the expression of lawful ideas and constitutionally protected activities such as petition campaigns, rallies, picket protests, and so forth.
>
> The committee is notorious for ignoring the legal rights

of witnesses. It is largely to blame for the unfortunate and dangerous public contempt for the Fifth Amendment's vital protection of the accused against self-incrimination.

There is no justification for HUAC's existence. It does not catch spies or saboteurs; rather it produces embarrassing confrontations with women seeking a peaceful world; and phony movies about student opposition to its hearings; and the usual lists of alleged Communists already well known to the FBI.

The personal damage to witnesses is less important than the fact that its silencing of criticism enables our government to undertake stupid or perilous policies with only a few voices to oppose it.[10]

■

WELL SAID, BUT it had been said before—many times. Frank's group had made virtually the same argument in numerous ads in the big-city press beginning in 1962, and in dozens of speeches at major universities. It was the same argument, reduced to their individual experiences, that twenty or so House members made in letters to their constituents in 1963. The letter from Rep. Henry B. Gonzalez of San Antonio noted that his Banking and Currency Committee "handled 500 pieces of legislation the previous year while HUAC handled only 32. That committee has put through only three bills in its entire history."[11]

Considering that the House numbered 435 members, it was difficult to get very excited about the increase in support, but the 6 willing to vote against HUAC's budget in 1962 had grown to 20 in 1963. There was new blood: of the 20, 7 were freshmen elected in 1962—3 from California, 1 from Oregon, 1 from Michigan, 1 from Hawaii, and 1 from Minnesota. Almost as fresh was Gonzalez, elected in 1960. Only one of the naysayers was a Republican: Seymour Halpern of Queens, elected in 1959.

Ridicule was still perhaps the best way to undercut HUAC. As the *Washington Post* editorialized in March 1963: "Francis J.

McNamara, staff director of that remarkable research organization, the House Un-American Activities Committee, let it be known recently that there are 700,000 to 800,000 Communists in the United States. This is a rather striking contrast to assertions by J. Edgar Hoover, director of the FBI, that the Communist Party reached top strength of 80,000 in 1944, and has declined every year since then and nose-dived in 1961 to between 8,000 and 10,000." That was followed by a Herblock cartoon of a congressman pushing a wheelbarrow loaded with an enormous sack labeled "$360,000 Record Appropriations for HUAC." The grinning politician explains to a bug-eyed spectator: "We need the extra money to fight more and more Americans who are getting fed up with us."[12]

One of the myths the House preserved for years to justify its cowardice was that anyone who voted to kill or even restrict HUAC's work would be in danger of defeat in their next election. The election of 1964 proved otherwise. Of the twenty who voted in 1963 to starve HUAC, eighteen ran for reelection in 1964 and were successful, winning by resounding pluralities. And quite a few of the new members were known to favor not only cutting HUAC's budget, but killing the abomination outright. Nonetheless, their victories barely budged the mercury measuring courage in the House.

CHAPTER 35

HUAC's Grotesque Solution to a Problem It Helped Create

RACIAL TENSIONS THAT had been building steadily toward an explosion finally did explode, repeatedly, across America. The Watts neighborhood in Los Angeles—a mostly black slum neighborhood that might have been rebuilt by then if Frank had been allowed to continue running the city's low-income-housing program—was virtually destroyed over the course of five days of rioting, arson, and looting in August 1965. There were thirty-four deaths, a thousand injuries, two hundred businesses destroyed and seven hundred severely damaged. It started after the arrest and alleged mistreatment of a black drunk driver; it ended only after twenty thousand National Guardsmen were called in to quell it.

At around the same time, in Chicago, the death of a black woman hit by a fire truck driven by whites triggered a riot that left eighty injured. A year later, there was another race-related riot in Chicago, and then one in Atlanta.

Over four days in the summer of 1967, Detroit was the site of the most terrifying race riot in U.S. history; at the end, thirty-eight were dead and there was $500 million in property damage. "We have endured," said President Johnson, "such a week as no nation should have to live through." In the same month, there had been riots in Atlanta, Boston, Philadelphia, Birmingham, New York, and Cincinnati. The racial ingredient was not diffused by H. Rap Brown's haranguing a crowd of blacks in Newark to "wage guerrilla war on the honky white man. I love violence." Oddly enough, he had just been elected president of the Student Nonviolent Coordinating Committee.[1]

It wasn't very smart to use such words, because there were a number of crazy politicians, especially in the South, ready to take them seriously. Predictably, the nation's racial illness prompted the quacks of HUAC to come up with a cure-all: throw the urban ghetto "guerrillas" into concentration camps, without bothering to give them a trial. The argument went: it had been done to perfectly peaceful Japanese residents when World War II broke out, so why not do it to those tough-talking blacks who encouraged themselves with such foolish slogans as "Burn Baby Burn"?

Obviously eager for headlines, even headlines that would make the committee appear to have lost its marbles, HUAC in May 1968—speaking through Louisiana's Edwin Willis—actually suggested the concentration camp solution in the committee's report "Guerrilla Warfare Advocates in the United States." "Guerrilla warfare advocates" meant militant blacks particularly, but also peaceniks and other "commies."[2] The machinery for doing such a thing had been in place since 1950, when Congress passed the McCarran Act (and arguably since the presidential order of 1942 authorizing Japanese American internment). At the time of the McCarran Act, Congress's response to the imagined threat that domestic Communists were plotting to take over the government was Title II, Section 104(c), which resulted in the construction of six "detention centers" where persons considered "subversive" by the attorney general could be arbitrarily socked away. No trial. No appeal.

That era of hysteria passed without any Reds being rounded up and imprisoned to save the nation, but in the 1960s the camps were still available for use in a "national emergency." Allenwood, where Frank had spent most of his sentence for offending HUAC, was one of them—although that was a coincidence. At Frank's trial, the authorities—grudgingly, no doubt—had stopped short of calling his refusal to answer the committee's questions a threat to the government's very existence. And as we know, he was charged, had a trial, and even made an appeal to the Supreme Court—so Frank at least had been given due process in that respect.

HUAC chairman Willis said that if his recommendations were heeded, the urban "guerrillas" of 1968 wouldn't get that kind of "soft" treatment. His colleague, Pool of Texas, agreed that "they would be left in concentration camps for the duration of the war." What war? Was the undeclared white war of suppression against uppity blacks now to become a declared war?

■

U.S. ATTORNEY GENERAL Ramsey Clark, representing another segment of officialdom, disagreed with Willis and Pool: "These rumors [that McCarran would really be used against blacks] become rampant in times of tension like this. I don't feel [Title II] poses any kind of threat for us. It's all so academic because it's so remote." A lot of blacks, including their leaders, didn't feel it was academic. Fear of concentration camps was already abroad. Six days before he was killed on April 4, 1968, Dr. Martin Luther King Jr. told William Hedgepeth, a senior editor at *Look* magazine, "I see a ghetto perhaps cordoned off into a concentration camp. I haven't said there was a move afoot, just that it is a possibility. The more there are riots, the more repression will take place, and the more we face the danger of a right-wing takeover, and eventually a Fascist society."

And a week after Chairman Willis and his HUAC colleagues at least metaphorically declared war on uppity blacks, the influential *Washington Afro-American* newspaper hit the streets with a banner headline:

CONCENTRATION CAMPS FOR GHETTO?

Its story opened:

> The report by the House Un-American Activities Committee
> urging the use of detention centers in the event of guerrilla
> warfare confirmed rumors that this proposal is under seri-
> ous consideration by some official sources. . . .

An accompanying editorial was written several decibels
higher:

> Now it is admitted that if some colored Americans are suf-
> ficiently determined to assume by force their rightful place of
> manhood in this society, some of the white power structure
> is prepared to set aside [the] Magna Carta, the Constitution,
> preachments on due process and all the rest.
>
>   Now an instrumentality of the legislative branch of fed-
> eral government has admitted that in its sinister mind it is
> prepared to follow the morally verminous route of Hitler's
> Germany by using concentration camps in which to detain
> colored political militants.

Civic leaders and downtown business leaders in major cities with
large black populations were furious at the proposal. Wasn't there
any way to shut up that damned committee, which, contrary to the
Afro-American editorial, wasn't best known for having a "sinister
mind" but for having no mind at all?

The flabbergasted, disgusted voice of the Establishment was
promptly heard editorially in many cities. Typical was the *Pittsburgh Post-Gazette*:

> The bumbling House Un-American Activities Committee
> must be credited with consistency. In critical periods it can be
> depended on to compound confusion and heighten tensions.
> At a time when federal and local governments are trying to
> dampen smoldering racial hostilities, the HUAC had predict-
> ably burst into the scene with a can of kerosene.[3]

The *Courier-Journal* of Louisville wrote:

> In past weeks Rap Brown and Stokely Carmichael have been chilling audiences with claims that Whitey—the law, the government, the white community—was planning concentration camps for troublesome Negroes in case of riots or demonstrations. The charge seemed so obviously ridiculous that it was generally dismissed as an example of extremist irresponsibility.
>
> Now—incredibly—an official agency of Congress, the House Un-American Activities Committee, has actually come up with a scheme as hare-brained as Brown and Carmichael described.[4]

(If Frank's old prison mate, Carl Braden, happened to read that editorial, he would have been justified in feeling some grim delight in the *Courier-Journal*'s unease. The newspaper's record in promoting integration was spotty in Braden's day. The reader will remember that, in 1954, when Braden was a copy editor at that newspaper, his employers didn't seem much perturbed when Kentucky's racist judicial system sentenced him to fifteen years in prison for helping a black man buy a house in a white neighborhood.)

■ FRANK ENTERS THE FRAY

What a monumental and awful year 1968 was. Martin Luther King was assassinated on April 4, sparking riots in Chicago, Baltimore, Pittsburgh, and Washington, D.C., where fifteen thousand troops were needed to stem the rampage—some of them manning machine guns from the top of the Capitol building. Lyndon Johnson announced he was going to step down. Robert Kennedy entered the race to succeed Johnson, and was then assassinated.

Then the Democrats moved into Chicago for what turned out to be one of the most chaotic, ill-willed political conventions in the country's history, with Hubert Humphrey nominated to lead a party hotly divided over Vietnam and (because Dixie's influence in the party was still strong) over civil rights. Ten thousand young people arrived in Chicago during the convention to physically protest the Vietnam War, and six thousand National Guardsmen, six thousand soldiers, and Mayor Daley's twelve thousand cops responded to their taunts and spit with clubs, mace, and tear gas. Inside the convention hall, guards—properly called "thugs" by CBS anchorman Walter Cronkite—roughed up delegates and journalists; sixty-five of the latter were beaten or jailed, or both, during the week.

But for Frank Wilkinson and his eager army of anti-HUAC missionaries, there was an upside to all of this. How convenient to have all those politicians herded into one place! What better opportunity to remind them that one of the primary founts of violence and hatred in the country was the House Un-American Activities Committee?

And what better way to remind them than by printing and circulating a dramatically designed brochure including HUAC's concentration camp proposal, a selection of the most fiery editorials opposing it, and the best of the *Look* magazine piece by William Hedgepeth?

It was all printed on one side of a large sheet of paper, seventeen by thirty inches, which folded down to the size of a number ten envelope. On the other side of the broadside was a streamer: "Would You Believe Concentration Camps in America?" plus a drawing of barbed wire across the page, in two colors. "The artwork was done by a friend, a high-priced PR man in California, who volunteered his services," says Frank. "It was the most attractive thing we ever did."

Frank, Dick Criley, and their most persuasive cohorts, loaded with thousands of copies of this propaganda, made the rounds of each state's delegation at the convention. It wasn't easy. They had to go to fifty different delegations, find the leadership, and ask for a few minutes to talk about the legislation needed to repeal the McCarran Act. When they didn't feel they had scored in those visits, they would get the hotel room number of each delegate and go down the hall slipping copies under doors.

It was rather naive of them to think the delegates would pay much attention. There were far too many distractions. Why would the delegates get worked up over the hypothetical establishment of Nazi-style concentration camps in the future when, outside on the streets, they could at that very moment watch the reality of Mayor Daley's cops performing like Gestapo guards? As for the eventual winner, Hubert Humphrey, he—on orders from President Johnson—refused to endorse a peace plank for the Democratic Party's platform. Instead, in his acceptance speech he promised: "Where there is hatred, let me sow love."[5]

Remembering the rioting that followed Dr. King's assassination in April and listening to the rioting outside their hotels in August, many delegates were probably less interested in opposing laws to control rioters than they were in supporting Strom Thurmond's proposed legislation to make anyone who crossed a state line to incite a riot subject to five years in prison or a ten-thousand-dollar fine. Except, that is, those who managed to get beaten and teargassed themselves.

Indeed, the temper of the times was such that progress came mainly by trade-offs: although Dr. King's assassination created an emotional atmosphere in which Congress would pass the Fair Housing Act, that got accomplished only because Democrats submitted to the passage of Thurmond's anti-riot act.[6]

■ REMEMBRANCE OF THINGS PAST

The knowledge that the presidential contest of 1968 would be won by either Richard Nixon or Hubert Humphrey would have been enough to dampen the spirits of any reformer less stubborn than Frank Wilkinson. Those two politicians had been instrumental in creating Title I and Title II of the McCarran Act of 1950, perhaps the most repressive piece of legislation passed in the last half of the twentieth century, and yet here they were, eighteen years later, on top of the political heap. Frank hated Nixon for all the reasons the man had given to inspire hatred during the course of his career; he despised Humphrey as a craven "liberal" who capitulated to the right wing.

CHAPTER 36

The Slow Death of the McCarran Act

"ONCE HYSTERIA-SPONSORED MEASURES do become law, it becomes an all but impossible task for the people to repeal them." This was Frank's admonition to activists, and it was certainly borne out by the effort to repeal the McCarran Act.

Title I of the McCarran Internal Security Act sought to compel the registration of people who were members of the CPUSA or similar organizations, and then prohibit them from traveling and engaging in certain other activities. It would have sought to force people to testify against themselves—a clear constitutional issue.

The law was a creation of Senators Humphrey and Nixon as well as McCarran. Obliged by the McCarran Act to do so, Truman had named the five-man Subversive Activities Control Board (SACB) to administer the law. The effort was as costly as it was futile. For the next decade and a half, organizations and individuals spent a staggering amount of money in legal fights with the SACB over the "registration" provisions.

Although the McCarran Act was constantly challenged, it wasn't until 1961—after eleven years of nearly continuous hearings and litigation—that the Supreme Court finally got into the act. And then it screwed up. By a five-to-four majority (with Warren, Black, Brennan, and Douglas dissenting) it ruled that the Communist Party was a potentially subversive "action" organization, not just an organization for fellowship and political debate, and therefore would have to register.[1]

The majority opinion upholding the Subversive Activities Control Act, written by the increasingly reactionary Justice Frankfurter, was a sad declaration of (temporary) judicial surrender: "It is not for the courts to reexamine the validity of these legislative findings and reject them. They are the product of extensive investigation by Committees of Congress over fifteen years. We certainly cannot dismiss them as unfounded or irrational imaginings."

Incredibly, Frankfurter was speaking of committee investigations carried out by HUAC and the SISS—committees chaired by politicians like Rankin, Dies, Walter, Pool, Eastland, and McCarran, who were guided both by the wildest racism and by the "irrational imaginings" of Communists behind every curtain.

Justice Black was alone among the minority to read the act as a clear violation of the First Amendment. His dissent was as uncompromising as it was melancholy: "I do not believe that it can be too often repeated that the freedoms of speech, press, petition and assembly guaranteed by the First Amendment must be accorded to the ideas we hate or sooner or later they will be denied to the ideas we cherish. The first banning of an association because it advocates hated ideas—whether the association be called a political party or not—marks a fateful moment in the history of a free country. That moment seems to have arrived in this country."

Fortunately, "that moment" passed within five years. On November 15, 1965, the Supreme Court in a unanimous decision (Frankfurter had retired) came to its senses and declared the act unenforceable in regard to requiring the registration of alleged members of the Communist Party. And most promising of all, it made that decision in a case involving two men who were openly leaders of the party.

Oddly enough (or perhaps it wasn't so odd, for some Republicans were really libertarians in disguise) a couple of hidebound Republican leaders were quick to support the decision. Two weeks later, Senator Barry Goldwater tipped his hat to the justices: "Without softening for a moment any of my past and current criticisms of the Court, I applaud it wholeheartedly in this instance. It would be worse than irritating if a basic protection of our freedom were thrown out the window simply to inconvenience the Communist Party."[2]

William F. Knowland editorialized in his *Oakland Tribune*: "Before anyone should start hurling charges at the Court, he should first remember he too has the same constitutional guarantee and that if an exception was made once—it could be made again and again and, one day, he might not have the protection of the Constitution."[3]

Many millions of dollars had been wasted by the government trying to keep the useless SACB alive; many more millions had been spent to keep hordes of attorneys in the Internal Security Division of the Justice Department litigating on and on, wasting their lives and the lives of the accused while wrestling over an unenforceable law. But it was the waste of tax dollars, more than the waste of harassed citizens' lives, that finally turned the citadel of conformity, the U.S. Chamber of Commerce, against the SACB. In 1967, it admitted, rather wistfully: "After all, in its 17-year life it never controlled a subversive. It never has accomplished anything at all. This witch hunt had a fast start and a short life. The Act of Congress establishing it was so full of fault, principally in its violations of the Constitution, that the Board became inoperable."[4]

Seventeen years was "a short life"? Only the seemingly eternal U.S. Chamber of Commerce could think so.

■ IN CONGRESS, THERE'S LIFE AFTER DEATH

Any sane appraisal of the SACB would have shown that it was not only dead and embalmed but overdue for burial. The Supreme Court by unanimous verdict had indirectly declared it so by wiping out its sole reason for being. And yet, despite pleas from even economy-minded Republicans to make the dead past bury its dead, Congress passed a HUAC-sponsored bill that gave the board $295,000 to continue doing nothing for fiscal year 1967–68.

The absurdity of the situation did not go unnoticed. The *Wall Street Journal* noted that for the final approval of the bill "there were only five Senators in the chamber. . . . Thus by a margin of one vote out of a grand total of five the ayes had it, giving the do-nothing SACB in effect nothing to do, with pay. . . . Which is, in the words of an old expression, nice work if you can get it."[5]

The "nice work" continued with subsequent appropriations—despite protests such as Senator Sam Ervin's "Let us not go through the mockery of doing nothing but drawing salaries and breath"—until the end of 1973, when Congress finally stopped funding the SACB.

With the elimination of the SACB, Title I of the Internal Security Act was finally totally dead. It had been fertilized by Hoover in 1948 and hatched by McCarran in 1950. In a quarter of a century, its "registration" requirements had resulted in an ocean of mischief but not one ounce of national security.

■ DEATH OF THE EVEN MORE REPRESSIVE PART OF THE McCARRAN ACT

Title II of the McCarran Act was the "Emergency Detention" portion of the law (or, more accurately, the "concentration camp" provision). A mere twenty-one years after the bill was passed, the Senate took up its repeal. The repeal vote, on September 25, 1971, was unanimous in the Senate, and an overwhelming 356 to 49 in the House.

Senator Hubert Humphrey and his six misguided Senate colleagues had attempted to outwit McCarran, the malevolent old fox from Nevada, by being meaner than he was and thus keep the law from passing. Instead they'd made the bill worse and probably slowed its destruction. But by 1973 both Title I and II had been buried.

What precipitated the repeal of the McCarran Act? The short answer is: HUAC opened its big mouth once too often. It stirred up the wrong group when it began yammering about the need to put "threatening" people in "concentration camps." That threat brought back bitter memories among Japanese Americans. They would never forget that on March 2, 1942, a little more than two months after Japanese planes bombed Pearl Harbor, Lt. Gen. John DeWitt, acting on presidential orders to evacuate anyone who might be a threat during an invasion, began rounding up more than 112,000 Japanese people living on the West Coast. Not one verified act of espionage or sabotage had been committed by these people before they were summarily sent to detention camps.

Although, oddly enough, J. Edgar Hoover had not approved of the mass evacuation of Japanese Americans, General DeWitt's actions prevailed. "The Japanese race is an enemy race," he said. "It therefore follows that along the vital Pacific Coast over 112,000 potential enemies, of Japanese extraction, are at large today. They are . . . organized and ready for concerted action at a favorable opportunity.

"*The very fact that no sabotage has taken place to date is a disturbing and confirming indication that such action will be taken.*" (Emphasis added.)

Translation: innocence proves guilt! In those fear-laden times, even some liberals—including Frank's First Amendment mentor, Alexander Meiklejohn, and California's liberal idol, Congressman Jerry Voorhis—supported sending the Japanese to detention centers. To be sure, there were also officials, including Frank's friends Rep. Helen Gahagan Douglas and Carey McWilliams, then handling housing and immigration for the state government, who lobbied militantly for fair play for the Japanese Americans. The ACLU was with them as well. However, they were largely drowned out by voices like the *Los Angeles Times*, which warned its readers not to be fooled by the Nisei: "A viper is nonetheless a viper wherever the egg is hatched. A leopard's spots are the same and its disposition is the same wherever it is whelped."[6]

By 1968, popular sentiment about Japanese Americans in

general, and about the value of the World War II internment camps in particular, was virtually reversed. So when HUAC began talking about concentration camps for riotous blacks in the late 1960s, both Americans in general and many of the Japanese American survivors were outraged.

Japanese Americans had been interned by a 1942 presidential order and not by the 1950 McCarran Act. But the aroused leaders of the Japanese American community decided in 1968 to get rid of all traces of any law that would intern people. As the McCarran Act was still on the books and was being used by HUAC to threaten another group, the community decided it must be repealed.

With a vow of "Never again, for anyone," the Japanese American Citizens League (JACL), one of the older Nisei organizations, set up the Committee to Repeal the Emergency Detention Act and went to work. In 1942, many Japanese Americans had been successful farmers and small-businessmen, but they'd had virtually no political power. In 1968, they did have power, especially those from Hawaii, where Japanese Americans made up almost a third of the population and Caucasians were a distinct minority. Patsy Mink and Spark Matsunaga in the U.S. House and Daniel Inouye in the U.S. Senate were rising stars (Inouye, with an empty sleeve where his arm had been, and Matsunaga were both heroes of the fierce Italian battles of World War II).

But organizing that political power for specific goals other than elections was another matter. Some JACL activists asked Frank to lend them a hand. It wasn't that the JACL was interested in Frank's First Amendment crusade; they were interested in killing laws that denied due process. But his record as a political organizer in targeting a specific goal, of using his NCAHUAC branches around the nation to put pressure on individual congressmen for their support, was well known, particularly when the goal was to defeat HUAC and the Deep South cabal.

Frank's actual role was to help the more radical members of the JACL convince the rest of the organization that this repeal program was something they must take on. They used his wonderful flier—"Concentration Camps in America" with the barbed wire printed across it—and they got JACL moving.

"Unique and primary credit for killing Title II of the McCarran Act belongs to the Japanese American Citizens League," says Frank. "After three years and a wealth of practical experience in coping with HUAC, their political maneuvering led to the repeal of the Emergency Detention Act, one of the few great victories for civil liberties in those bleak years."

But the simple repeal left a threat still hanging over the nation. What if in the future some president decided on his or her own to be as high-handed as Roosevelt had been and intern people by presidential edict alone? Republican Rep. Thomas F. Railsback (R-IL) took care of that. He successfully offered an amendment to the repeal legislation that blocked any future president from imprisoning any citizen "except pursuant to an Act of Congress."

The triumph over this horrible act, orchestrated by some of his least favorite people, gave Frank enough personal satisfaction that he could crow: "Those who doubt the power of redemption for original sin should note that Hubert Humphrey was among those who cosponsored the repeal legislation. And President Nixon, apparently at long last feeling contrite, twice sent Justice Department Internal Security Division chiefs to testify that he was 'unequivocally in favor of repealing the act.'"

•

THE DEATH OF the McCarran Act marked another crucial development. Because the House Un-American Activities Committee had, of course, strongly opposed the repeal, this constituted the first defeat it had ever sustained in its thirty-three-year history. That HUAC had precipitated the repeal by its own racism made the destruction of the act all the sweeter to Wilkinson and the JACL. And the defeat was a premonition of the committee's approaching demise.[7]

CHAPTER 37

Suddenly, the Once Seemingly Indestructible HUAC Wasn't

HUAC WAS STILL alive in 1971—in every way but name. In 1969, Congress had allowed HUAC to change its name to the House Internal Security Committee (HISC), hoping by that name change to transform a grub worm into a butterfly, albeit a butterfly with only one wing (the right one). Or, to change the simile, here's Senator Sam Ervin's judgment on that occasion: "It is said a rose by any other name would smell as sweet, but a crushed gentian weed by any other name would smell as bad."[1]

The man behind this transparent name-change was Congressman Richard Ichord of Houston, Missouri, who had moved into the chairmanship of HUAC. No longer would the committee's emphasis be on exposing "un-American propaganda" meant to poison the faith of our Founding Fathers. From now on, said Ichord, the emphasis would be on "internal security." That is, HISC intended to ferret out persons and organizations eager to overthrow our elected government and establish a "totalitarian dictatorship" by using "any unlawful means." In other words, the goal of HISC was essentially the same as HUAC's—to butt into protective oversight duties that several cabinet departments, several other congressional committees, and the courts were already attending to, and to do it in ways that would surely ignore the Bill of Rights.

One of Ichord's few efforts to make HISC seem different from HUAC was to do away with the "Are you now or have you ever been a Communist" confrontation with unfriendly witnesses. In fact, this reform bow to the First Amendment was nothing but a defensive move, for one of the most embarrassing symptoms of HUAC's decay had been the regularity with which federal courts started overturning contempt citations inflicted on witnesses who refused to answer that question.

HISC's preferred method of blackening reputations—much easier than wrangling with stubborn witnesses—was to obtain and publish lists of groups that it claimed were "financing" dangerous radicals. One of Ichord's first forays of this sort was to send questionnaires to 179 colleges and universities asking for the names, sponsors, and honoraria of "all guest speakers on the campus from September 1968 to May 1970." Sifting through the responses, Ichord's committee published a list of speakers it charged with being affiliated with fourteen "subversive" organizations—their dangerous nature determined by the fact that they were either on record as opposing HUAC/HISC or had been named in testimony given to this or other committees by J. Edgar Hoover and similarly reliable witnesses. On the list were such suspicious people as John Ciardi, the poet; Muhammad Ali, the boxer; and John C. Bennett of the Union Theological Seminary. The committee's report also listed the names of the colleges and universities that refused to return the questionnaires.

Perhaps the best response would have been simply to leave it to the autopsy of humorists. But district court judge Gerhard A. Gesell barred publication of the list on the grounds that it was a blacklist. Its effect "inhibits speech on college campuses, infringes on the rights of the individuals named therein . . . without any proper legislative purpose, and is illegal to publish at public expense."[2]

Citing a House resolution asserting immunity from a court's

interference with its legislative function, Ichord's committee went ahead and distributed the list anyway.

What legislative function? Publishing the list was simply exposure for the sake of exposure—as the work of HUAC had always been. What in the world did it have to do with legislating? This was a question HUAC had never been able to answer, and HISC was now falling into the same ditch.

But more dangerous to its existence was the fact that, in floundering around seeking a reason to exist, it kept butting into the work of long-standing, powerful committees. For some time now, ghetto and campus unrest had been considered fruitful places to dig for signs of Communism, which is why several other committees—especially those run by southerners—had already staked out that territory. Indeed, the Senate Committee on Government Operations, run by Arkansas's touchy senator John McClellan, had just finished a three-year investigation into "the cause and cure" of urban rioting. Hoping to cut off scholarships and federal aid to student radicals who might be helping the rioters, McClellan's panel had subpoenaed a dozen major universities to supply the names of campus troublemakers.

And here were Ichord and his investigators tramping over the same well-trod territory with their own subpoenas. Old-timers in Congress did not take kindly to jurisdiction-grabbers.

■ HISC'S DESPERATE HAVEN: MILITARISM

Like many politicians who have never served a day in the military, Ichord was a devotee of all things militaristic, and under his chairmanship, HISC promptly became an outlet for the Cold War policies of superpatriot pundits in such places as the American Security Council (ASC).

The ASC, founded by ex–FBI agents in the mid-1950s, was the richest and most aggressively politicized organization in the private intelligence community. Claiming that its file contained more than six million entries (although if duplicates and "John Does" were subtracted, the count would probably have been no more than half that), it dominated the market of those in the business of peddling "counter-subversive" information to giant corporations worried about the loyalty of persons seeking, or holding, jobs with them.

But by the early 1970s, the right wing's old warning that sneaky Communists were trying to take over the minds of Americans—especially young Americans—had been used so often that it was wearing thin. If Communism was as terrible as Richard Nixon had always said it was, why was he now getting cozy with Communists? Why did he visit Romania in 1969 as the first president to visit a Communist country since World War II? Why did he become the first president to visit (the very Red) China in February 1972? And if the Soviet government was so untrustworthy, why did he go to Moscow that year to sign an arms treaty, declaring that it would be "the foundation for a new relationship between the two most powerful nations in the world"? What was going on?

In his biography of Nixon, Tom Wicker of the *New York Times* says that just as "the world had changed since the fifties, Nixon, watching the change, had changed too. He took office convinced, for example, that a serious American foreign policy could not 'exclude one-fourth of the human race'—China. He understood, too, that the arena was no longer bipolar, divided between Washington and Moscow, but multipolar, with Peking, Tokyo, and Western Europe able to play major roles. The U.S. would not be able again to dominate such a world, even if it wanted to.

"'Five great economic superpowers watching and challenging each other,' Nixon predicted in a July 6, 1971, speech in Kansas City, would not be 'a bad thing.' In fact, he suggested, general economic progress probably would be promoted by the competition."

Economic progress? Did this mean that the voices of international capitalists yearning for new markets abroad were beginning to mean more to him than the voices of his old pals, the Communist-hunters and the military industrialists? Whatever it meant, writes Wicker, "his abandonment of the outspoken anticommunism of his early career, which so many Americans shared,

his about-face on China after twenty years of hostility, his deal-
ings with the Soviets who, in his telling, supposedly had menaced
the U.S. for so long—such realpolitik needed more convincing
explanations, more discussion, if they were to be translated into
permanent American attitudes. Nixon, operating so much in
secrecy, was unable to function as a good teacher. . . ."[3]

And Ichord was going to use HISC to do all he could to make
sure Nixon and any like-minded successors would continue to
malfunction as teachers of the new realpolitik. To that end, he
would get significant help from ASC; its board, heavy with generals
and admirals, was supported by leading military industrialists. The
ASC advisers would even lead him into broader, swampier fields:
namely, foreign affairs. From 1970 to 1973, HISC held eleven hearings built around the testimony of sixteen defectors and escapees
from Communist countries. It began to find potential terrorists
everywhere, especially among those Communist Cubans, so close
to the border. HISC speculated that U.S. Communists might adopt
some of their tactics. No, they hadn't yet, but they *might*. In fact,
some U.S. Communists *might* be down there right now studying
those tactics. Better investigate! So in 1971 HISC went to Miami
for a hearing on Communism in Latin America. Knowing that a
little left-wing gloss would help, Ichord, no dummy, invited that
worn-out old liberal from the New Deal days, Miami congressman Claude Pepper, to preside over the hearing. (It wasn't hard
to get him to preside. He would be up for reelection the next year,
and there were 350,000 Cuban refugees, all bitterly anti–Castro-
style-Communism, living in the Miami area.) Pepper was invited
back in 1974 for a HISC hearing on the overthrow of the Allende
regime in Chile. The point of the hearing, as Frank Donner points
out, was to show that the overthrow "was really a countercoup
by a reluctant, freedom-loving military junta, summoned by an
oppressed civilian population to free it from the brutal yoke of
socialism."[4] The Chilean embassy in Washington sent copies of the
hearing to all members of Congress. But not all were impressed.
California congressman Robert L. Leggett observed with heavy
sarcasm:

I am curious as to why the Internal Security Committee, whose mandate is to inquire into internal matters, has taken the time and effort to compile a 225-page hearing record on Chile's internal problems. Dictators are not uncommon in this world—we should know, we support some of the best money can buy—but none of them have been deemed worthy of the energy and efforts of the Internal Security Committee. It appears that what we have here is a case of selective security: it does not matter how repressive, how undemocratic, or how dictatorial a government, it is OK with HISC—as long as it is not Communist.[5]

Leggett's appraisal of HISC's meandering beyond its mandate into fields that rightly belonged to other committees touched on the unforgivable sin of filching public credit. It was a sin that Ichord's gang indulged in repeatedly. "All the major HISC hearings from the very beginning," writes Donner, "involved subjects to which other committees had a more convincing jurisdictional claim."[6] The chairmen and members of these other committees were outraged by the invasions. How dare HISC hold hearings on "Attempts to Subvert the United States Armed Services," or on industrial and port security—two problems that obviously belonged to the Armed Services Committee? How dare it hold hearings, for three years, on how to improve the federal employee loyalty program—things that should be left to the Post Office and Civil Service Committee? How dare it reinvestigate the causes of prison unrest when that was already being studied by three other panels, including a House Judiciary subcommittee chaired by Robert W. Kastenmeier, Wisconsin liberal? Kastenmeier, who had been in the House long enough to justifiably feel some proprietary rights, was angry for two reasons. First, his subcommittee had spent two years, 1971 and 1972, exhaustively studying the prison problems, and he didn't want some fly-by-night HISC spooks mucking up its findings. Second, he hated HUAC/HISC enough to have voted several times to either starve it of funds or dismember it completely.

Kastenmeier, whose district encompassed Madison, the birth-place of Wisconsin's progressive movement, was among the first of the young activist members of Congress Frank recruited for his anti-HUAC drive after he got out of prison in the early 1960s. Two other congressmen were elected around that time who later could justifiably claim to have played principal roles in the suc-cessful plot to assassinate HUAC/HISC. In fact, they were among a select group who actually pulled the trigger. Fittingly, they were both from the Bay Area, which had already supplied so much to Frank's rebellion.

The first was Don Edwards, a veteran of the World War II Navy, a graduate of Stanford Law School, and wealthy (he owned the only title company in wildly growing San Jose and Santa Clara County). He was elected to Congress in 1962 and, although he was reelected by only a hair, a friendly state legislature redrew the lines of his district so that he was never in trouble again. He was one of the House's most liberal members and had the committee appointments to prove it. For example, as chairman of the Judi-ciary Committee's Civil and Constitutional Rights Subcommittee, he helped keep anti-abortion constitutional amendments from getting to the House floor. His subcommittee also conducted a careful investigation of the FBI (for one year before the war, he had been an FBI agent). And he was on a special committee to investigate the CIA. Labor and liberal organizations always scored his voting record 90 to 100 percent: he was against the Vietnam War, against building the B-1 bomber, against deregulating natural gas, and for all environmental, consumer, and worker-protection bills. Not that he was in tune with the whole of California. There was another California, a California that elected song-and-dance Republican George Murphy to the U.S. Senate in 1964 and Ronald Reagan governor in 1966. But Edwards never had to worry about that California.

Also impervious to the attacks of California's right wing was Edwards's coconspirator on the HUAC/HISC assassination team, the awesome deal-maker Phillip Burton, who was the most hard-headed and politically savvy of the House's ultraliberals.

At that time, Burton represented the 5th District, which took in the eastern half of San Francisco and had a dramatically global population—everyone from blacks to Samoans to the offspring of white pioneers to immigrants from every country around the Pacific Rim—and a large chunk of the city's poor. If ever a district was fated to be permanently Democratic, this was it.

An army veteran of World War II and the Korean War, Burton was a lawyer and a member of the California Assembly for eight years before being elected to Congress in 1964. At that time the House had only a tiny left wing. But that wing grew, and so did he, becoming one of the House's most prolific legislators, especially in pushing through major environmental advances, such as the establishment of a large redwoods park in northern California. Elected head of the Democratic Study Group in 1971, he made it the real power in the House—rounding up votes on important issues, preparing crucial amendments, and raising campaign money for candidates Burton thought could win.

Among the freshman Democrats elected in 1974 were many who would show their gratitude for Burton's support when he asked the House that year to consign HUAC to oblivion.

One other congressman played a key part in the HUAC assassination plot: Robert F. Drinan of Newton, Massachusetts. A Jesuit priest (with an LLM, 1950, from Georgetown University Law Center), Father Drinan had been dean of the Boston College Law School for four years before being elected to Congress in 1970 as an outspoken foe of the Vietnam War and of the Cold War. The times they were a-changin', and nowhere more than in the 3rd District of Massachusetts, which for twenty-eight years had been represented by one of the most hawkish members of the House Armed Services Committee, Philip J. Philbin. But the 3rd District was redrawn in such a way that Drinan's antiwar supporters put him over the top. Although Massachusetts had elected dozens of Catholics over the years (including such conservative hacks as Philbin and Speaker John McCormack), by electing Drinan it gave the House of Representatives its first Roman Catholic priest. Drinan was appointed to the Judiciary Committee, where he would team up in significant ways with Don Edwards and other liberals. He was also, at his own request, put on the newly named HISC. He meant it no good.

Radical activists, never totally absent from Catholic clergy in the United States, of course, had recently moved dramatically into the headlines via the careers of Jesuit Father Daniel Berrigan and his brother, Josephite Father Philip Berrigan, both of whom were sent to prison for their antiwar activities. J. Edgar Hoover accused their followers of plotting to kidnap presidential adviser Henry Kissinger and commit other acts of violence. Father Drinan represented a less dramatic and yet politically effective mini-revolution. That is, with his election it could be said that in terms of the Communist witch hunt, at least part of the Catholic Church had come full circle.

For, two decades earlier, some of its leaders had been among the witch hunt's most important actors. None deserved that reputation more than Francis Cardinal Spellman, who from the St. Patrick's Cathedral pulpit constantly warned that the United States was in imminent danger of "Communist conquest and annihilation," he helped launch the career of Joseph McCarthy. And Father John F. Cronin, S.S. was virtually an undercover FBI agent in the labor movement and tutored Richard Nixon in naming names when Nixon was a freshman congressman.[7]

Before reaching Congress, Drinan had made no secret of his abhorrence of HUAC/HISC. His criticisms could be found in numerous Catholic publications. But that was nothing compared to what he did to sway House members against the committee when he got to Congress in 1971.

Throughout this time, NCAHUAC had been actively talking to these renegades and their staffers, meeting to strategize on how they could finally do HUAC in—continuing the death by a thousand cuts and/or pulling off some big finale. Frank describes his friend Drinan's next achievement:

> Father Drinan was not only a priest, a dean of a law school, and a prominent Jesuit, but he was a very feisty, articulate

guy and a good civil libertarian. The first thing he did when he reached Congress and became a member of HISC was, he went to Ichord and said, "I'd like to see our files." Ichord replied, "Well, the chairman and the staff maintain those files. I'm in charge of the files. We ordinarily don't discuss them."

Drinan said, "Well, I want to see them. I'm a member. I want to see them."

Ichord said, "Well, it's unusual, but let's go." So he took Drinan to a huge room on the third floor of the old Cannon Office Building. Accompanying Drinan was Marty Michaelson, who was on his staff and later became vice-chairman of my committee to abolish HUAC/HISC. In this room there was a giant Rolodex-like apparatus, operated by a fifty-foot-long rope crank. It worked like one of those things at a dry cleaner where they push a button until your suit comes around. Only this had no electricity. This was all hand-cranked by a guy sitting down at the end. When he wanted a name, he would crank until the thing came around to the right place.

Drinan said to Ichord, "My God, how many names do you have in that file?"

Ichord: "We've got 50,000 right here."

Drinan: "Let's look at my file. Put in my name." The operator started cranking, but Ichord stopped him and said to Drinan, "No, no, no. Your name isn't here. When a member is elected to Congress, we take his file out and put it in my office, in a closet, under lock and key."

Drinan went right to the House floor, stood in the well, and offered a resolution, saying, "We've got to relieve our brother Ichord. I've discovered he has a burdensome responsibility. It's unfair to him. He has files on all of us, locked in his office, and he has to guard those files. I move that we free him from that burden and open those files to us."

Ichord turned beet red, and the members roared with laughter at his embarrassment. But the resolution carried.

"Later," says Frank, "I teamed up with Drinan at a Boston College School of Law meeting. The subject was 'Abolish HUAC from the Inside—Featuring Robert F. Drinan, and from the Outside— Featuring Frank Wilkinson.' After that, we were a speaking team on several occasions. It was very popular and much fun because here we literally had a member of HUAC out in the field organizing to get rid of it.

"A lot of things were moving toward the death of HUAC, and Drinan's talk to the House about the hidden list of congressional names contributed to it."

■ FINALLY, CONGRESS BEGINS TO REBEL

But nothing contributed so much to HUAC's death as the organization that had been so important in keeping it alive: the FBI. Over the years, HUAC had developed a patina of power from its close relationship with Hoover's agency, which in turn was saturated with power because so many in government, especially in Congress, feared what Hoover might do with the secrets he was believed to possess about their lives. As HUAC began crumbling, Hoover backed away from it, and began trying to back his troops away from the "black-bag jobs" and illegal wiretaps that had been its hallmark, and any remaining behind-the-scenes support for HUAC. But it was too late, and Hoover was beginning to dodder, and the FBI to fumble.[8] Those long targeted began to strike back, and the agency's clumsy prying into the lives of congressmen and other politicians (mainly Democrats) began to surface in front-page ways.

On April 5, 1971, Rep. Hale Boggs (D-LA), House majority leader, angrily accused the FBI of tapping his telephone and said he knew of at least three other congressmen who had been subjected to similar harassment. Of course J. Edgar Hoover denied the wiretapping, but his denials began to sound hollow two weeks later when a federal judge released documents showing the FBI had recorded four telephone conversations between Rep. John Dowdy (D-TX) and an FBI informant.

Before the month was over, Senator Edmund S. Muskie (D-ME) came up with evidence that the FBI had recently spied on Earth Day rallies, gathering data in an effort to torpedo the environmental movement. And in March, a youth-led organization called the Citizens Committee to Investigate the FBI dramatically stole documents from the FBI's Media, Pennsylvania office that proved Hoover's spies had spent many hours bugging and wiretapping black student groups and student groups for peace. The thieves were never caught, but their plunder was shared widely. A few of the more entertaining documents revealed such things as the FBI's efforts to recruit Boy Scouts as patriotic spies. Naturally, the documents made headlines across the country, for days. They were so juicy that the subcommittee run by Senator Sam Ervin didn't get the attention it deserved for revealing, in February, that the army had been doing a lot of spying on political figures (mostly Democrats, who happened to be running Congress in those days).

More and more evidence began to surface of asinine and/or illegal government prying into the lives of Americans, especially federal employees—whose dossiers already overflowed with job profiles and personality tests containing such questions as, "Do you think there is anything wrong with your sex organs?" and, "Do you think Jesus Christ was a greater man than Abraham Lincoln?" Senator Ervin uncovered a new test with more urbane questions, such as "Do you cross your legs and if so which one goes on top?"

Arthur R. Miller's *The Assault on Privacy* (1971), at that time the most authoritative survey of the scope and impact of surveillance in the United States, noted that the average adult was already the subject of ten to twenty dossiers in government and private files, many of them filled with bizarre, inaccurate, vengeful, and irrelevant data—which would never be discarded. The Civil Service Commission had files on 10 million people who had applied for jobs since 1939, plus another 1.5 million filed away as "suspected subversives." The FBI's computerized National Crime Information Center reportedly had 1.7 million personal files and 195 million sets of fingerprints. And the privacy intruders were never satisfied. The putative boss of the FBI, Attorney General John Mitchell, denounced the federal courts for denying him carte blanche wiretapping powers against anyone he considered a potential "domestic subversive"; he conceded that innocent people would be hurt in his wiretap sweep, but he said that couldn't be helped. (The rate of official wiretapping increased 100 percent between 1969 and 1970.)

The Pentagon had files on 25 million people, including 7 million who had been subjected to "security, loyalty, criminal and other types of investigations," and including especially 14,000 who were marked for detention if ever an insurrection occurred (Frank Wilkinson was among them). Military surveillance agents, many of whose files were inherited by the FBI, commonly categorized a subject as "Communist" or "non-Communist" on no more conclusive evidence than a photo taken at a rally. Robert E. Jordan III, the U.S. Army's general counsel, acknowledged that "most of it [the surveillance data] was garbage." And more and more garbage was sought. In one year, agents from the FBI and the IRS had paid fifty thousand visits to credit bureaus to get information sometimes based on nothing more solid than newspaper clips.

The State Department's Passport Office, a notorious right-wing fortress, admitted reluctantly, under questioning from reporters, that it did have a secret computerized "lookout list" of 250,000 names; when people on the list applied for a passport, the Passport Office would tip off certain "security" officials. And so it went, on and on around the bureaucracy; but, as Miller wrote, "even now only the extremities of a vast, subterranean information structure may be visible."

And beyond the bureaucracy were, of course, the faithful, rabid watchdogs of patriotism—HUAC/HISC and the SISS—each with its files crammed with the names of individuals and organizations deemed suspect, if not downright dangerous.

Most people in the United States, not paying much attention to national issues and probably convinced by the FBI's PR machine, had heard or read virtually nothing of this government spying. And another significant segment of the population did know about these civil liberty threats, but heartily endorsed, and felt much safer, under Big Brother.

On the other hand, the United States was also benefiting from one of its periodic mood swings, one of the inevitable enough-is-enough upswings. At long last, there were many, many people, especially professional people, hip to civil liberties—not only liberals, but libertarians and old-fashioned conservatives who didn't like being pushed around by the government—who were vastly offended by what was going on.

As never before in recent decades, the conduct of governmental snoops was drawing hoots and jeers and threats from a large chorus of politicians and editorial writers. Finally, it was a safe thing to do. In the past, critics of HUAC and/or Hoover had felt justifiably afraid of repercussions. But that danger evaporated entirely when, on May 2, 1972, Hoover was found dead in his Capitol Hill home. From then on, voting to kill HUAC/HISC would not risk anything more discomfiting than supernatural reprisals.

■

CONSIDERING THE MASSIVE political earthquake of 1973–74, the rendering of HUAC/HISC to rubble was so easily accomplished that it was hardly noticed. Voters were shell-shocked from Watergate and its aftermath—with nineteen individuals, including some top Nixon aides, convicted or pleading guilty to such charges as perjury, bribery, and obstruction of justice. The executive branch was cracking. After being exposed as a crook, Vice President Spiro Agnew resigned. Prodded by the certainty of impeachment if he hung around, Nixon resigned the presidency on August 8, 1974. The next day, Gerald R. Ford was sworn in to succeed him. The public was not in a forgiving mood: when Ford took office, a Gallup poll showed 71 percent of the electorate was behind him; after he gave Nixon an unconditional pardon, his popularity dropped 21 points. Michigan voters underscored their dissatisfaction by electing a Democrat to fill Ford's old Grand Rapids, Michigan seat—the first time a Democrat had won that seat since 1910. The public was sick of politicians, who were blamed not only for low morals but for the highest inflation rate since the Korean War and an unemployment rate that was heading for 7 percent. In that year's election, 62 percent of the eligible voters stayed home; the 38 percent turnout was one of the weakest in modern times. Economics as well as revulsion at Nixon's conduct contributed to the GOP's loss of forty-three House seats and four Senate seats. In the House Judiciary Committee, which served as a grand jury for considering the impeachment question, four of the eleven Republicans who vehemently defended Nixon against the impeachment charges were defeated in their bids for reelection.

At his brief inauguration ceremony, President Ford declared, "Our long national nightmare is over." He of course wasn't alluding to it, but part of that long national nightmare had been the House Un-American Activities Committee, and it too would be over in 1975. With liberals clearly in the ascendancy that election year, and much of the electorate fed up with Big Brother politics, not many conservatives were enthusiastic about voting to keep that old dog alive. As it turned out, they didn't have to choose its death. Our liberal conspirators brilliantly offered the conservatives a cover.

■ REALLY, THE FINAL DEATH OF HUAC/HISC

Many years later, Don Edwards reminisced about his long-running battle with HUAC and the part he and his rebellious colleagues had played in bringing about its death.

> In 1962 I won election to Congress by just a few hundred votes—just a hair. I stood for a number of controversial things, like wanting to get out of Vietnam and wanting to get HUAC out of Congress. It was a time when the fabric of society was being ripped and I wanted to do something about it. So when I got to Washington, I called Larry Speiser-head of the Washington ACLU office, and started plotting. There were others who felt the same way—congressmen like

Kastenmeier of Wisconsin and Father Drinan. We called ourselves "The Group," and we even hired a one-person staff. We wrote a number of books on things like the Vietnam War. They were rotten books, but they made us feel better. And we would visit the HUAC office and rustle around. It drove them crazy.

Judging from past efforts, there was no chance of getting the House to vote HUAC out of existence. But Phil Burton was chairman of the Democratic caucus, which was very powerful at that time, and in the caucus we had the votes to transfer HUAC to the Judiciary Committee. Doing that was easier for the members to swallow than killing it outright. So in the caucus we passed the motion to make the transfer and then, in the full House, we passed it into law. [This was in January 1975, right after the massive Democratic win in the elections of November 1974. With control of the House, the Democrats were in charge of the committees, their jurisdictions, and their chairs. As always, at the beginning of the Congress, the party in charge allocates these critical issues.]

I'll never forget how we got it through the caucus. Father Drinan was supposed to make the motion, but he was out in the hall talking to a reporter. So I made the motion, and I'd hardly got it out of my mouth when Phil said, just like lightning, "Movedsecondedandpassed!" *Bang*! Down came his hammer and he walked quickly out of the room.

Well, the vote in the full House transferred HUAC to the Judiciary Committee—which had a lot of good liberal and moderate Democrats and even a couple of fairly liberal Republicans—and its final destination was my Civil and Constitutional Rights Subcommittee [of the Judiciary Committee]. There it lay, never to be heard of again. It just quietly died.[9]

Esther Herst had been hired by NCAHUAC six months before to head up its Washington office, as she would do off and on for more than a decade. She was quickly up to her elbows lobbying on Capitol Hill with the caucus to figure out how to put the kibosh on HISC. She remembers the final process as pretty anticlimactic, just as Edwards described it—she says, there was "no big recorded vote or anything." It was such a sure thing, Esther says, that "my strongest personal memory is that on the morning that the caucus met (they met at noon, I think), I went to NPR [National Public Radio] headquarters . . . and did a radio interview about the abolition (as though it had happened already) with Judith Miller (then at NPR) for *All Things Considered*." And then the thing was done. Esther adds, "We partied that afternoon and evening and my line to the rest of the [NCAHUAC] folks was that it took them twenty years to abolish HUAC but I got it done in six months (since I started in D.C. that September)."[10]

It all sounds so stunningly simple. After thirty-eight years of controversy—after wrecking hundreds of lives by triggering everything from permanent unemployment to prison terms on trumped-up charges to suicides—the most hated and feared faction of Congress went out of business with neither a bang nor a whimper. It just disappeared.

One can't help but think that maybe Frank Wilkinson, who had spent the last twenty years of his life very successfully recruiting politicians and citizens to help kill the committee, would have preferred that this historic victory be celebrated by at least a few multicolored skyrockets fired into the night sky over the U.S. Capitol. Or, as a final taunt of the witch-hunters, perhaps he would have found it more satisfying if the skyrockets exploded only into a shower of red, the color HUAC hated the most.

By Kit Gage, Director,
First Amendment Foundation and NCARL

HERE END THE adventures and misadventures of Frank Wilkinson and his cohorts versus HUAC and the FBI. But what happened to Frank and the National Committee Against Repressive Legislation (NCARL—the new name of NCAHUAC) following the abolition of HUAC?

■ STOPPING S.1

About the time that the House Un-American Activities Committee was "disappeared" into the House Judiciary Subcommittee on Civil and Constitutional Rights, the NCAHUAC changed its name to the National Committee Against Repressive Legislation (NCARL). The change was timely, as in 1973 the Nixon administration drafted a criminal code that would have expanded federal jurisdiction over crimes, created a multifaceted official secrets act criminalizing release of national security-related information (like the Pentagon Papers), enhanced prosecutorial power over judges, expanded prison sentences across the board, and undermined due process protections. Fortunately, that proposal collapsed with Watergate and President Nixon's resignation.

But then, in 1975 the criminal code proposal came back. Senator John McClellan (D-AR) introduced a four-hundred-plus-page proposal, similar to that of the Nixon administration, to revise and codify the federal criminal code (Title 18). It too contained a broad variety of repressive features. This bill, named S.1 (the first bill of that session of the Senate), had broad bipartisan support, and the skids were greased for passage. Among its provisions were alterations to law that would have had devastating impacts on the fundamental rights of freedom of expression, press, assembly, and due process.

Soon after its introduction, however, news reports of some of the provisions began to surface, and NCARL began to organize across the country to oppose the bill. The committee drew on its recent coalition efforts to abolish HUAC, but expanded that outreach, as issues raised by S.1 were of concern to a wider range of organizations.[1]

Esther Herst coordinated the coalition-building from Washington from September 1974 through July 1983, trained in Chicago in the early 1970s, mentored by Dick Criley. Meanwhile Frank promoted the effort in his field work across the country. Part of that field work included Mike Honey and Martha Allen (daughter of Donna—the first D.C. office staffer), who started working for the Southern Conference Education Fund (SCEF) in 1970. This project evolved into an NCARL southern office, jointly funded by SCEF and NCARL. By August 1970 the NCARL southern office in Memphis was continuing to organize against S.1, as well as a variety of anti-racist issues. In its campaign against S.1, NCARL produced some of its best-known posters, in which the parts of the Bill of Rights and Constitution that would be affected by S.1 are depicted with slashes through them. These posters appeared all over the country following Frank's organizing campaign.

Among S.1's most egregious proposals were revisions to the federal espionage laws—including an official secrets act, as noted above; a reinstitution of the federal death penalty; criminalization of certain acts of political assembly and organizing, as well as some union strike activities; the abolition of federal parole; the creation of a sentencing guideline system that would remove judicial discretion and increase prosecutorial power; and an expansion of federal laws on obscenity.

In part as a result of the organized opposition, S.1 died at the end of 1976. But it was reintroduced, with some changes, as S.1437 in 1977, with the cosponsorship of Sen. Edward M. Kennedy (D-MA). Kennedy's support was meant to neutralize the opposition of the liberal members of the Senate, and S.1437 passed in January 1978 with only fifteen dissenting votes.

In the House Judiciary Committee it received a highly negative reception, and House members articulated a perspective that had been recommended by NCARL and the anti-S.1 coalition: an omnibus bill to revise the federal criminal code was bound to have dangerous hidden provisions; the most constitutionally responsible way to change federal law, it said, was via an incremental approach.

As a result of NCARL's leadership, no omnibus criminal law codification was ever passed, but, with the election of Ronald Reagan as president in 1980 and the increasingly conservative makeup of Congress, many of the individual provisions first proposed in S.1, including sentencing guidelines and the reinstitution of the federal death penalty, were subsequently passed into law.

In the Washington office of NCARL, Esther Herst returned to the leadership role again from August 1985 to August 1986.

■ MORE FBI AND CIA ABUSES

At about the same time the S.1 battle was raging, a more long-standing issue concerning both the CIA and the FBI was coming to a boil. As we know from previous chapters, the FBI had bugged, burglarized, and opened mail on about 432,000 supposed "subversives."

But the CIA, supposedly under the strict authority of the National Security Act of 1947, which prohibited it from spying within the United States, had also violated its strictures. In 1976, the *New York Times* reported that between 1967 and 1973 the CIA (with a knowing wink from the Johnson and Nixon administration) had collected data on 300,000 U.S. citizens—including full dossiers on some 7,200. It had lent equipment to police to spy on civil rights and antiwar groups. It had intercepted and read 250,000 letters from U.S. citizens. It had hired Cuban exiles in the United States to keep files on, picket, and harass embassies the CIA didn't like.

On the FBI front, the combination of the revelations from the Media, Pennsylvania, break-in, the abuses of the Nixon administration, and Hoover's death triggered the first-ever thorough investigations and significant detailed exposure of FBI abuses. The Senate's Church Committee (named for chair Sen. Frank Church, D-ID) and in the House the Pike Committee (named for chair Rep. Otis Pike, D-NY) held hearings and issued remarkable reports that included damning copies of FBI files.

■ CAMPAIGN FOR POLITICAL RIGHTS

Fortunately, the coalition NCARL had built to fight S.1 had created alliances that would help provide public pressure to move congressional revelations about the FBI and CIA forward.[2] In fact, this coalition created alliances that would have far-reaching impact on constitutional issues into the next century. But first, in 1977, NCARL, the Center for National Security Studies, the Institute for Policy Studies, and the ACLU formed a new coalition, the Campaign to Stop Government Spying, subsequently renamed the Campaign for Political Rights. Esther Herst served as cochair of the board of the campaign from 1977 through 1983. Comprising about sixty-five civil rights, civil liberties, peace, labor, and religious organizations, the campaign provided the grassroots muscle to support NCARL's lobbying efforts for a charter to control the domestic spying activities of the FBI and to remove the CIA from all domestic political surveillance on protected First Amendment rights activities. The charter effort failed, in part because a portion of the movement opposed passing any legislation that would recognize the authority of the FBI as a federal police force.

While failing to pass comprehensive legislation limiting the FBI, the overall prolonged national focus on FBI abuses served to stimulate the Justice Department to set out guidelines that required the FBI to have evidence of a criminal act or information that one was being planned before a judge could authorize wiretaps, searches, or the like. Known as the Levi Guidelines, for President Ford's attorney general, Edward Levi, these guidelines are the high-water mark of regulation of political spying in the twentieth century.[3] This is true not only because of their clarity, but also because this was the point at which public sentiment made clear that the kinds of abuses committed by the FBI were no longer going to be tolerated. No more "black bag" jobs; political spying was unacceptable; and Congress would see to it that this was enforced—more or less.

At roughly the same time, following the revelations from the Pike and Church committees, some of the national organizations that were subject to COINTELPRO sued the FBI, as NCARL would later. The Socialist Workers Party (SWP) and the National Lawyers Guild (NLG)—for itself and for others—sued under the relatively new Freedom of Information Act (FOIA) to find out the extent of the abuses committed by the FBI and other agencies.[4]

Over a period of seven years, at least ninety-two times, the FBI had broken into SWP offices trying to prove that it was plotting the violent overthrow of the government. But the government, according to its own records, never found a speck of evidence to indicate spying, violence, or criminality, despite the break-ins and planted informants.

The organizational underpinning of NCARL's work to control federal intelligence agencies was encapsulated in a resolution written by Professor Thomas I. Emerson and adopted at the national committee meeting of NCARL in 1983:

Given NCARL's experience as a political force and as a victim of intelligence agency abuses, we are in a unique position to begin a long-term program for the protection of the First Amendment against newly increasing attacks by the intelligence community. This program will seek the comprehensive control of those agencies, especially the FBI, through positive legislation which recognizes the legitimate intelligence needs of our country but prohibits political spying and disruption, thereby bringing the agencies within the confines of our constitutional system . . . NCARL will continue . . . to focus on immediate legislative concerns such as attempts to revise the Levi FBI Guidelines, the recent Executive Orders extending the scope of intelligence activities and increasing the volume of information classified as secret, the attacks on the FOIA, and the increasing smears of political movements which are aimed at disabling those activities and discrediting dissent.

This programmatic mandate carried NCARL through the next twenty years—and to some extent continues today.

■ RED SQUADS

As the revelations expanded to include spying by local police on dissenters, the Chicago Committee to Defend the Bill of Rights (CCDBR), the sister organization of NCARL,[5] played a leadership role in the landmark federal lawsuit—filed in 1974 by a diverse array of Chicago organizations, including the ACLU—to stop political spying by the infamous Chicago Police "Red Squad." The suit resulted in public exposure of political spying and disruption by the Chicago police over the course of several decades and a court ruling that established, for the first time, that political spying and disruption by police violates constitutional rights. After the Chicago example, Red Squad suits were filed in Seattle, San Francisco, New York, and other cities. All were resolved through settlements that restricted political spying.

NLG attorneys and sometimes ACLU attorneys were active in bringing these suits.

Dick Criley continued to direct CCDBR; Rachel Rosen assumed the position of assistant director after Esther Herst's departure for Washington in 1974. Upon Criley's retirement, Rosen became the executive director of CCDBR.

■ CHANGING TIMES AND THE CISPES

From that high-water mark during the Ford administration, things have slowly deteriorated in terms of FBI oversight and regulation. During the Carter administration, Mark Felt (later known as Deep Throat) and Edward Miller were the first high-level FBI officials ever convicted of illegal wiretapping and burglaries, but that lesson to the FBI was short-lived, as the Reagan administration, soon after taking power, pardoned the men. Also in 1981, Reagan ordered the gloves to be removed from the FBI. By 1983, his attorney general, William French Smith, announced a relaxing of the Levi Guidelines to better combat "domestic and international terrorism."[6] The changes began the transformation from fighting Communism to fighting terrorism, using the same tools. It also began the evolution toward criminalizing the advocacy of violence rather than simple culpability for criminal acts. While the Supreme Court had ruled that First Amendment activity could not be prosecuted, the executive branch was starting to butt up against that prohibition.

The first major test was what became known as the CISPES investigation in the mid-1980s. The Reagan administration was supporting an armed revolt in Nicaragua against the leftist government of the Sandinistas, and at the same time propping up the Duarte dictatorship in El Salvador. Mass opposition rose up in the United States, most popularly characterized by the group CISPES, the Committee in Support of the People of El Salvador. The FBI was swift to get involved, and using as a pretext the allegations of an FBI "operational asset," Frank Varelli, and ultra-right reports from the Young Americans Foundation, it opened an investigation into opponents of U.S. policies in El Salvador. After finding no evidence of gunrunning or other criminal acts, the FBI nonetheless expanded the investigation to fifty-two of its fifty-five regional offices, and proceeded to spy on the political activities of the opposition.

Frank Varelli didn't get paid what he thought he was due, and he blew the whistle on the operation. Activists went ballistic, including the national coalition that NCARL helped mobilize. The press had a field day. The Center for Investigative Reporting and then the Center for Constitutional Rights promptly sued under the Freedom of Information Act, and traced the misguided venture through the files it obtained. Following activists' demands and to quiet the press, Congress held hearings in which it called the new FBI director, William Sessions, on the carpet. Sessions promised it wouldn't happen again, and a few FBI agents were punished lightly—mostly by early retirements. But the message NCARL and other groups were getting out—fairly successfully—was that the FBI should not be investigating First Amendment activity, and that was the message the FBI was repeating to Congress in 1987.[7]

All this time, Frank was still traveling the country, typically more than a hundred days a year, speaking out on the connections between the investigation against CISPES and the investigations of the Cold War. I was now director of the Washington office, continuing to expand the coalition work begun by Esther Herst, Linn Shapiro, and others, and writing a monthly national letter urging targeted lobbying in defense of the right to dissent and related civil liberties issues.

One of the other NCARL projects at the time was opposition to the use of covert operations by the U.S. government. NCARL's concern was about the core deniability of the practice. Covert operations are generally the opposite of public U.S. policy (for example, that we don't mess with other countries' elections!). They defy public oversight and tend to stymie congressional oversight. I wrote and distributed "At War with Peace, U.S. Covert Operations" as a short public education pamphlet about this sordid and relatively unknown topic, its legislative and regulatory authorization and limitations. As part of this project, NCARL worked with disgruntled former CIA and other agents unhappy about the abuses.[8]

■ LOUIS FREEH, RUBY RIDGE, WACO, AND THE RIGHT GETS IT

After a quick succession of FBI directors, President Clinton's appointment up from the ranks of Louis Freeh as FBI director was greeted with public hope that the FBI would finally get things right. It didn't last long. Right-wing separatist groups were in the resurgence, and law enforcement began to target them. First in Ruby Ridge in 1992 and then in Waco in April 1993, police standoffs with families (broadly defined) holed up in their homes became bloody messes. Randy Weaver's family was the first target, with his wife and a son falling victim in a standoff with police at his mountain cabin near Ruby Ridge, Idaho. Then came David Koresh and his followers from the Branch Davidians. Attorney General Janet Reno had been just days in office when she was told that Koresh was abusing children. Under pressure from the FBI and the Bureau of Alcohol, Tobacco, and Firearms, she authorized a bulldozer and fire attack on the compound. It burned to the ground with most of the women and children still inside.

A public uproar followed these two over-the-top law enforcement reactions. At a Senate hearing investigating Ruby Ridge, four FBI sharpshooters took the Fifth (noted wryly by followers of HUAC). The FBI was found to have changed the so-called rules of engagement to allow snipers to shoot any adult male outside the cabin, either on site or back in Washington.[9]

From the NCARL perspective, the cumulative impact on the Right of this overreaching on the part of federal law enforcement was remarkable. For virtually the first time, people on the Right were talking with us about law-enforcement abuses, and some were expressing sympathy for the people spied on during the FBI investigation of CISPES and similar groups. It was a watershed moment and resulted in an expansion of the coalition of concerned civil liberties activists. Now NCARL and the ACLU could call on Gun Owners of America, the CATO Institute, the American Conservative Union, and others on the right to meet and discuss how to limit these kinds of abuses. The cross-connections, called variously the Left-Right Coalition or Strange Bedfellows, while not rock solid, continues today. It is a critical change of tactics: a coalition that has no issues in common except the fight to defend the right to dissent is a ready advocacy group no matter who controls Congress and the presidency.

■ FRANK AS EDUCATOR

As you know by now, Frank Wilkinson is an inveterate organizer and educator. Starting in the late 1980s, his education program became codified in an unusual way. The U.S. Department of Education—still not exactly a bastion of radicalism—invited Frank to come to Wake Forest University in Winston-Salem, North Carolina, to speak to fifty teachers, one from each state, all winners of a competition, to discuss civil liberties and civil rights. He was allotted two days to focus on civil liberties as he knew it—the FBI versus the First Amendment. He was a smashing success with the group and soon began getting invitations to speak to teachers all over the country—Colorado, Oklahoma, Nebraska, and Arkansas. After federal funds dried up, the American Bar Association picked up the program as law-related education.

One great story out of many: In 1990 Frank spoke in Okla-homa to thirty-five competitively selected teachers brought in from all over Oklahoma for a three-day session sponsored by the Oklahoma Bar Association. The day before he met the teachers, he got nervous; he had received the teachers' résumés, and every teacher had listed, in addition to their schools and grades taught, the name of their Baptist church. How could this old religious skeptic relate to such obviously religious people?

He woke up the next morning with an old Methodist hymn running through his head: "He Leadeth Me, O Blessed Thought." He kept trying to go back to sleep, but the hymn kept waking him up. And so he started his speech with an apology—"You know, I'm not sure that I can relate to you people. You're all such religious people and I'm really not active in religion at all. But I was brought up in a very wonderful Methodist background, and for a time I thought about becoming a Methodist minister. Last night I had this dream full of that old hymn, 'He Leadeth Me, O Blessed Thought.' I just couldn't get it out of my mind. So I guess no matter how religious I think I am or not, once you're a Methodist, you're a Methodist.'" Well, says Frank, "they just opened up to me. They accepted me just the way I described myself."

The long love affair had begun. Three months later the teachers brought him back to Oklahoma to speak to each of their classes. He kept his talks to the point—the FBI and the First Amendment. Word got around, and he started speaking all over the state. On one visit he spoke to forty-two groups in six days. He was a First Amendment evangelist. In 1995 his total audience, mostly in Oklahoma, was 460 teachers and 14,000 high school and middle school students. Then Oklahoma press associations began inviting him. Then bar associations. Ponca City, "this little town in the middle of nowhere," as Frank puts it, made him its guest of honor because one of its junior high students wrote a paper for Oklahoma History Week on "The Frank Wilkinson Story: The FBI Versus the First Amendment." NBC's *Today Show* sent a crew to film the occasion.

Frank also often traveled, of course, to San Francisco, Boston, and New York, where the witch hunt era had been best controlled and he had the closest allies. At Yale Law School a standing-room-only crowd heard his lecture "Revisiting *Wilkinson v. United States,*" a commentary on his Supreme Court battle. The much-beloved and now deceased American University Law School constitutional law professor Burt Wechsler had first met Frank in Gary, Indiana, when Frank came in his raincoat in the winter to help organize those beleaguered labor activists. In the 1990s Wechsler, on his own nickel, would bring Frank as a surprise guest to tell his constitutional law students the story of *Wilkinson v. United States* firsthand.

■ FBI FIRST AMENDMENT PROTECTION ACT

NCARL began to develop a petition to Congress to seek both to eliminate legislative vestiges of the Cold War (the Smith Act, the McCarran Act, etc.) and to more clearly, legislatively, limit the FBI to investigating people based on some evidence of criminal activity. Petition initiators UCLA law professor Carol Goldberg Ambrose, Yale Law School's Thomas I. Emerson—a top First Amendment scholar—and Harvard's Vern Countryman headlined the outreach to constitutional law professors, collecting about a hundred notables to begin the call. One of Frank Wilkinson's favorite modes of outreach, it harked back to HUAC days. Using this unimpeachable core, NCARL then reached out to historians, writers and artists, and librarians. More than five hundred law professors eventually signed, as did hundreds in each of the other categories. The petitions were sent to members of Congress so that they could see the names of people they respected in their districts.

A year or so after the petition began circulating, Representatives Don Edwards (D-CA, key in pocketing HUAC) and John Conyers (D-MI) took on the challenge to match the petition with legislation. Their bill, the FBI First Amendment Protection Act, H.R. 50, was introduced in the early 1990s and reintroduced over several sessions of Congress. It succeeded in obtaining significant support from members of the House Judiciary Committee and eventually almost one hundred cosponsors, including members of the House Judiciary Committee. Toward the end of 1994, Congressmen Edwards and Conyers succeeded in inserting a sentence into the omnibus crime bill prohibiting the FBI from terrorism investigations based only on First Amendment activity. The government "may not initiate or continue an investigation . . . unless the existing facts reasonably indicate that the target knowingly and intentionally has engaged, is engaged, or will engage in a violation of federal criminal law." The provision stayed, and the bill passed on September 1, 1994.

At the end of 1994 Goldberg Ambrose, Wechsler, and I met with high-level Justice Department officials to seek the support of the Clinton administration for the full H.R. 50. After a friendly and

encouraging November meeting, in January the Clinton administration introduced its new crime bill. In that bill, not only was
there no H.R. 50 language, but the new Edwards-Conyers amendment was excised, with a page of explanation from the FBI that
the provision "imposes an unprecedented and impractical burden
on law enforcement concerning the initiation and continuation
of criminal investigations under 18 USC 2339A."[10]

■ OKLAHOMA CITY BOMBING

In April 1995, the Oklahoma City Federal Building was bombed
and destroyed. After initial reports that the culprits were Arabs,
investigators settled on domestic terrorists, and two white men
were arrested in short order. That horrible attack, as all such attacks
do, spurred Congress on to pass legislation related in some way
to terrorism. The Clinton bill fit the need. It passed in the Senate
quickly, though a coalition mobilized with the help of NCARL
tried to slow the bill down in the House. One of the problems
was a new "material support for terrorism" provision that would
charge people with crimes for providing training or supplies, even
if entirely unrelated to any criminal acts, to people connected to
government-listed terrorist organizations. This could criminal-
ize (and later would prove to include) purely charitable activity
for noncombatants. The other main concern was a proposal to
set up a special deportation court that would have allowed the
use of secret evidence in deportations. In addition to the obvious
unfairness to deportees, who would not see the evidence against
them, the government also could not assess the accuracy of the
information if it never saw the light of day. The Left-Right Coalition did succeed in slowing down the bill, and got some minor
modifications made before passage.[11]

Following passage of the Antiterrorism Act, NCARL and
other groups who understood the implications for politically
active immigrants, joined together in the summer of 1996 to form
the National Coalition to Protect Political Freedom (NCPPF). It
opposed both the use of secret evidence in deportation proceedings

and codification of the expanded material support for terrorism provision. The coalition combined most of the national Muslim and Arab American groups, as well as many immigrant-rights, ethnic-rights, and civil liberties groups. Shortly after its inception, the NCARL Washington office became the coordinating center for NCPPF; this arrangement continues to date.[12]

When the government began to use secret evidence in deportations without bothering to set up the secret evidence court, NCPPF began to roll. It publicized the use of secret evidence, helped connect the national network to local organizations to educate people about the implications, helped obtain good lawyers for the individuals facing secret evidence, and met with the Justice Department to express concern about its use. About two dozen men ultimately faced deportation proceedings in which the government used secret evidence to deny their bond, the result of which is that many of them spent three years in jail accused of no crime but deportability. With the combination of legal, organizing, media, and Washington pressure, NCPPF helped get the government to stop using secret evidence in almost all the cases, which resulted in some wonderful court decisions opposing the use of secret evidence. Another measure of our success was the statement made by George W. Bush in the presidential debates with Al Gore that Bush opposed the use of secret evidence—which immediately reverberated throughout the Arab American community across the United States.

We wanted to bring a challenge to the material support provision of the law that we felt was so good we were almost sure it would win. The Humanitarian Law Project (HLP) had what we all thought was a fabulous case and, with the help of some lawyers expert in this area, brought suit on the material support provision. HLP wanted the government to tell them in advance that it would be legal to print and give out pamphlets with only the text of the UN Declaration of Human Rights on it—nothing else. The kicker was that they wanted to distribute the pamphlets to members of a group listed by the State Department as "terrorist" under the Antiterrorism Act provisions.

Although these pamphlets merely spelled out basic rights and had no value on the market to be sold for guns or anything else, the HLP in *HLP v. Reno* lost the main part of the case in court. The court did agree that the part of the law prohibiting people from providing "training" support to these groups was "vague" and thus unenforceable. When you lose a case as "good" as *HLP v. Reno*, it shows how quickly the courts change based on one small provision of a large bill. It would be a precursor to the massive changes brought by the USA Patriot Act and other executive branch practices post–9/11.[13]

Frank Wilkinson passed on the national directorship of NCARL and the First Amendment Foundation (NCARL's charitable sister organization) to me in Washington, D.C. (I was also coordinator and president of NCPPF, resulting in a crisis of acronyms.) Wilkinson continued as educational director in Los Angeles.

At around the same time, a bipartisan group of House Judiciary Committee members introduced the Secret Evidence Repeal Act. With little qualification, the bill would have prohibited the government from using secret evidence in deportation-related proceedings. This bill ended up with a huge number of cosponsors, got a very favorable hearing in the House, and reportedly had the support of President Bush just up to September 2001.[14]

But then came 9/11.

■ 9/11

Within hours of the attacks on the Pentagon and the World Trade Center, I and other longtime civil liberties activists were planning strategies to anticipate the next over-the-top legislation coming to Congress. At the meetings that followed, we succeeded in organizing a huge press conference convening a hundred groups on all sides of the political spectrum, urging the president and Congress to act carefully in enacting any new legislation responsive to the horrible 9/11 attacks. To say our admonitions went unheeded is a gross understatement.

The USA Patriot Act was introduced a couple of weeks after 9/11—the same day, in fact, we held that huge press conference. Despite some behind-the-scenes negotiations in the Senate, and a remarkable House committee markup, a bill very close to the one first introduced became law. At that eight-hour House committee meeting, about twenty amendments were offered making substantial due process improvements to the act. The amendments all passed unanimously (even though the House Judiciary was—and still is—very disparate politically). This careful amendment process was vitiated when the House Republican leadership, completely contrary to normal procedure, ignored the committee-modified bill and substituted the original for a final vote by the full House. That was one angry House committee when their bill was buried. The substitute House bill then passed overwhelmingly on the floor.[15]

The nonlegislative activities were as bad—or worse. About fifteen hundred people were rounded up in lockups in and near New York City immediately following 9/11. They were held without charges, and mostly allowed no calls to lawyers or visits. The prisoners were in a black hole. Only slowly were they released, deported, and, in a tiny number of cases, charged with any crime. None were charged with crimes of any terrorist nature.

The Justice Department modified the domestic crime guidelines (not the foreign counterintelligence guidelines, as one would expect) to allow law enforcement to monitor anyone—without even a hint that they might be involved in criminal activity. Noncitizens and citizens alike who were of Arab or South Asian ethnicity or were Muslim were called in to talk to the FBI. Dissenters were called traitors by Attorney General John Ashcroft. It was a horrible time in general, and a horrible time for civil liberties in particular.

As the United States went to war first in Afghanistan and then in Iraq, people from the battlefield and elsewhere were detained. They were then held in lockups in those countries, or moved to third countries in secret, and some were then brought to Guantanamo for indefinite detention. Some of these people in all of these places have been tortured and, in a few cases, killed in captivity while being interrogated. These procedures have almost all been conducted in secret, with the names of the detained and the reason for their detention kept from their families and the public at large. U.S. citizens Jose Padilla and Yasser Hamdi were detained in the United States. Even for these citizens, the United States created a third kind of legal system—separate from domestic constitutional law and from international law including the Geneva Conventions—to try to subvert the core of habeas corpus (the right to challenge detention). Hamdi and Padilla's cases ended up before the U.S. Supreme Court. All these changes are still reverberating in the courts.

Groups including the Center for Constitutional Rights, Amnesty International, and Human Rights Watch have strongly condemned these procedures and challenged them in court. And the good news is that they are beginning to make legal headway.

Partly in response to feelings of futility on a federal legislative level, a movement gradually started to build across the country. The Bill of Rights Defense Committee passed a resolution to uphold the Bill of Rights locally, even if it seemed in peril nationally. City by county by state, jurisdictions passed similar resolutions.[16] The ACLU kicked in its resources to help, and NCARL helped organize the first national conference of these activists and national experts in October 2003. We worked to broaden the coalition, connect the activists to the best resources for expertise in these complicated areas of law, and expand the reach of the movement. The changes to law and policy are remarkably comprehensive.

In the days of HUAC, the FBI was regularly engaged in illegal break-ins, "black bag" jobs, wiretapping, and the like. Today the barriers have been lifted: wiretapping and searches can be performed without any evidence at all that the subject has or may have committed a criminal or violent act. The predicate (initiating activity) is simply membership or association with a group. So in some ways we're back to the days of HUAC—but the break-ins are legitimated. The fight against terrorism is real and very serious. But the tactics are, in significant ways, both wrong-headed and damaging to our constitutional rights. Our task today is to get our government to target terrorism accurately and pointedly, not with a broad brush against ethnicity and dissent.

■ BACK TO FRANK'S STORY

Now that Frank's mostly back home in Los Angeles these days, some in that city finally decided that anyone who had once made so many screaming headlines in the local papers should be given his due. And what is more appropriate for a boy who had grown up in Hollywood than a tribute on the stage? And so it came to pass that in June 2003, eighty-eight-year-old Frank and his wife, Donna, were celebrated at the opening of the musical *Chavez Ravine* at the Mark Taper Forum. The documentary musical, performed by the Latino group Culture Clash, tells the story of Chavez Ravine: the community that was first razed to build integrated housing—the project that was killed when Frank was Red-baited so long ago—and that now holds Dodger Stadium.

The *L.A. Times*, which had so lambasted Frank back in 1952, called the play "a fascinating urban chronicle." Musician Ry Cooder took the Chavez Ravine story, interviewed Frank at length, included Frank's clash with HUAC, and, with other musicians from *Chavez Ravine*, made it into a CD entitled *Chavez Ravine*.[17]

Then there was the more somber tribute to Frank at the USC Fisher Gallery's sculpture garden, commemorating the First Amendment and the many victims of the McCarthy era. There, among the names of the Hollywood Ten and others, is, of course, that of Frank Wilkinson.

"When I'm talking to students," says Frank,

> I always bring up some of the seeming victories I've been part of and the overturning of those victories later on. You know, we did abolish the Un-American Activities Committee, we did repeal the concentration camp law, we did repeal the Subversive Activities Control Board, or at least weaken it. We stopped the worst parts of the criminal code. We've

done a lot of things. Yet take the Un-American Committee: It officially dies January 11, 1975. But exactly five years later, the Republicans took over the Senate and South Carolina's Strom Thurmond became chair of the Judiciary Committee and presided over the creation of a subcommittee modeled after HUAC.[18] This subcommittee was HUAC all over again, but this time encouraged by the patriots of the upper chamber to indulge in such nonsense as watching the press for signs of Soviet terrorism influence in the country and trying to decide if Jane Fonda and Tom Hayden were terrorist agents. I tell students that such revivals go with a Jefferson quote: "The price of freedom is eternal vigilance."

■ PREFACE

1. Most of the quotes and detail on Frank Wilkinson's life come from author interviews and an insightful and remarkably detailed UCLA oral history by Dale Treleven, director of the UCLA Oral History Project.
2. Swanberg, *Luce and His Empire*, 341.
3. ibid., 473.
4. ibid., 311.
5. ibid., 79.
6. E. Thomas, *Robert Kennedy*, 379.
7. Gentry, *J. Edgar Hoover*, 462.
8. ibid., 721–722.
9. Breuer, *J. Edgar Hoover and His G-Men*, 224.

■ CHAPTER 1

1. British Broadcasting Corporation, *The Un-Americans*," Producer Archie Baron.
2. Gentry, *J. Edgar Hoover*, 78–79.
3. ibid., 202.
4. Demaris, *The Director*, 74–75.
5. Gentry, 107.
6. Donner, *The Age of Surveillance*, 144.

7. Morgan, *FDR*, 484. Other FDR biographers say that the president called in Secretary of State Cordell Hull, asked for his approval and got it emphatically: "Go ahead and investigate the hell out of those cocksuckers."

8. ibid., 578–9.

9. Gentry, 321.

10. McCullough, *Truman*, 673.

11. Donovan, *Conflict and Crisis*, 283.

12. Offner, *Another Such Victory*, 358.

13. ibid., 354.

14. ibid., 211.

15. Mitchell, *Tricky Dick and the Pink Lady*, 85.

16. Morgan, *Reds*, 304.

17. McCullough, 552.

18. Morgan, op cit, 305.

19. Mitchell, op cit, 86.

20. Sherrill, *Why They Call It Politics*, 960.

21. Sanders, *Cold War on the Campus, 1946–1964*, 153.

22. McCullough, 553.

▪ CHAPTER 2

1. Barber, *Presidential Character*, 250–253.

2. Barson, *Better Dead than Red*, introduction.

3. Shirer, *Nightmare Years: 1930–1940*, 172.

4. Friedrich, *City of Nets*, 381, 384, 385.

5. Severo and Milford, *The Wages of War*, 330–332.

6. ibid.

7. Schlesinger, *Robert Kennedy and His Times*, 733.

8. Powers, *Not Without Honor*, 245.

9. Barnet, *The Rocket's Red Glare*, 303.

10. Faulk, *The Uncensored John Henry Faulk*, 169.

▪ CHAPTER 3

1. Mitchell, *The Campaign of the Century*, 358.

2. ibid., 49.

3. ibid., 61.

4. ibid., 540.

5. Morris, *Richard Milhous Nixon*, 14.

6. McWilliams, *The Education of Carey McWilliams*, 45.

▪ CHAPTER 4

1. Cohen, *When the Old Left Was Young*, 119.

2. ibid., 23.

3. ibid., 108.

4. ibid., 118.

5. Salmond, *A Southern Rebel*, 141. Responding to a *Literary Digest* poll in 1935, about 81 percent of 65,000 college students said they would not fight for the United States abroad, and 16.5 percent said they would not fight even if the United States were invaded.

6. Unlike Wilkinson, Lambert was working his way through UCLA and was a good student. On graduation, he became a Rhodes scholar, went into law, and eventually was made head of the Association of Trial Lawyers of America.

■ CHAPTER 5

1. Which shows what Frank missed by not traveling around his hometown. During the Great Depression, eating out of garbage cans was not unknown in Los Angeles. A history-making meal of that sort occurred in 1933, in the alley behind Dr. Francis Townsend's home in Long Beach. It's said that when he looked out a back window and saw women eating out of garbage cans in the alley, he began to scream and curse. Not at them, but at a nation that would allow people to become so poor. Out of that experience came the famed Townsend Plan, which proposed that every American over the age of sixty should receive $200 a month, if they promised to spend it within thirty days. Thousands of Townsend Clubs sprang up across the country. Some believe the plan's popularity helped push President Roosevelt into creating his Social Security legislation.

2. The inflation of prices since then probably makes a ten-cent meal sound like a fairy tale, but they were available all during the Depression. On page 348 of Morris Bartel Schnapper's *American Labor: A Pictorial Social History* (Public Affairs Press, 1979) you will find a photo of Bob's Quick Lunch, in some unnamed city, with a very large menu painted on its outside front. All but two of the seventeen items cost ten cents or five cents. The two exceptions, costing fifteen cents, were ham and eggs and bacon and eggs. It offered "meals" for ten cents, hot cakes and coffee for five cents, corned beef hash for ten cents, etc.

3. Wilkinson UCLA Oral History, 338–341.

4. If nothing else, Maxwell Street turned out some pretty tough guys. Perhaps its most celebrated alumnus was Barney Ross (born Barnet Rosofsky), who was forced to leave school and earn his way when his father was murdered by robbers and his brothers and sisters were sent to an orphanage. He won championship titles in three weight divisions, and ranked behind only Joe Louis and Henry Armstrong as the preeminent boxer of the 1930s.

5. Trachoma is a chronic, contagious form of conjunctivitis, which can impair sight.

6. Wilkinson UCLA Oral History, 475.

7. ibid., 478–479.

8. ibid., 592–595.

9. Kennedy, *The Rise and Fall of the Great Powers*, 323.

10. ibid., 323. He was certainly right about that, and it wasn't happening so "gradually." The population was being educated at an unprecedented pace. The number of graduate engineers rose from 47,000 in 1928 to 289,000 in 1941.

▪ CHAPTER 6

1. McWilliams, *The Education of Carey McWilliams*, 82–83.

▪ CHAPTER 7

1. Frank's college friend, Gil Harrison, was in Washington in those days, and he head become fanatically anti-Communist. When he sensed that Frank might be moving in that direction, he protested the move. Frank notes:

> Whenever I came to Washington and called him, Gil would break what he was doing and we'd go out for lunch and talk. But he was giving me a harder and harder time. I was not able to, or didn't want to, discuss what my politics were at that time, but he was implying that I was associating with Communists or that I was in fact a Communist myself, and he was telling me how terrible Communists were. It was Gil that first gave me George Orwell's *1984* to read. He said, "You read this and you'll know what I'm talking about." And I'm telling Gilbert, "Well, when I was in Russia, I didn't see it that way." It became quite a strain. I remember Gilbert attacking me, walking along the streets of Washington with him just attacking me in the strongest possible way. When I'd leave him, I was just exhausted and hurt emotionally, but my love for the guy continued.

   But the political strain on the friendship eventually broke it.
2. Many years later, the film surfaced in someone's garage and Frank arranged with the USC film department to have it saved. While the dialogue uncomfortably reflects the overt paternalism common in the period, it nonetheless provides an amazing documentary visual archive of the slums of Los Angeles of the 1940s.

▪ CHAPTER 8

1. Lewy, *The Cause That Failed*, 62.
2. Sherwood, *Roosevelt and Hopkins*, 128.
3. Shaw and Pryce, *World Almanac of the Soviet Union from 1905 to the Present*.
4. Barson, *Better Dead than Red*, 24.
5. Barson and Heller, *Red Scared!*, 43–44.
6. Barson, op cit., 46.
7. Frank left the party years after the shocking revelations about Stalin's gulags, when many in the United States would quit. It's not clear why he didn't join the masses who left after those revelations, unless it was because he was so enmeshed in maintaining his right in the United States to belong that it mattered less to him what Stalin had done in far-off Russia. Frank says he finally left for First Amendment reasons—because the Communist Party USA tried to outlaw and silence the Ku Klux Klan and the American Nazi Party. This was sort of an ideological graveyard gesture. "When I joined the party," says

Frank, "it had 100,000 members. When I quit, it had about 5,000 members—and many of them were FBI informers," including the only other remaining man in his group in L.A. So, in effect, he was quitting a dead party. The KKK and Nazi party were equally dead. And so was J. Edgar Hoover. And HUAC was breathing its last. So who was left to notice, much less care, about Frank's departure?

8. British Broadcasting Corporation, *The Un-Americans*, Part One, Producer Archie Baron.

9. ibid.

10. Healey and Isserman, *Dorothy Healey Remembers*, 152–153.

11. ibid., 228.

12. ibid., 229.

13. ibid., 237.

■ CHAPTER 9

1. Brodie, *Richard Nixon*, 171.

2. Having learned how to deal with political lunacy on the local level, Roybal moved up to Congress in 1965, where he was one of three members of Mexican-American descent and one of its most liberal members.

3. Keane, *Fritz B. Burns and the Development of Los Angeles*, 174.

4. Cuff, *The Provisional City*, 291.

5. Prior to this, as a teacher who had received many awards for her work, Jean had been groomed to become president for the very prestigious academic sorority, Delta Kappa Gamma; but it got cold feet after her firing and expelled her.

    The tenure laws gave her a couple of years to stay on the job while she fought back against the firing. In the 1990s, interviewed for Griffin Fariello's *Memories of the American Inquistion*, Jean told her part of her ordeal:

    I remember when my principal was down at the board of eduction for a meeting, other principals would come to her and ask, "What's it like having a Communist on your staff? What does she look like?" As though I had a tail and horns. My principal was a very loyal and good friend and a believer in civil liberties. In the last stages, when they had decided they were going to fire me but they had to wait so many months to let it take effect, they said I should work in the files to keep me away from the children. [A Califiornia Superior Court judge had upheld her firing by saying she had been "sowing the dragon seeds of treason in the classroom."]

    The funny thing was that I was teaching in a school for delinquent girls on the east side of Los Angeles. It was a great job and I loved it, but not many people wanted to deal with these tough customers. So my principal said, "No, Jean's my best teacher, and I'm not going to give her up until I have to, so I'll keep her in the classroom."

    I found some letters from the girls at the school. These were mostly Mexican-American kids, and there's a certain style in their writing. They don't know how to spell, but express themselves they did. One of them offered to go down and beat the shit out of the board of education, which I thought was the best offer I'd had. [Fariello, *Red Scare*, 467–8.]

6. *Los Angeles Herald*, September 30, 1952.
7. Cuff.
8. Keane, 182.
9. *Los Angeles Times*, May 18, 2003.

 CHAPTER 11

1. Wilkinson clipping book 1961–64, 7.

■ CHAPTER 12

1. Donner, *The Age of Surveillance*, 61.
2. Kutler, *The American Inquisition*, 153.
3. Navasky, *Naming Names*, 31.
4. Kutler, op cit, 155.
5. ibid., 152.
6. ibid., 57.
7. ibid., 164.
8. Bailey, "Progressive Lawyers," 53.
9. Healey and Isserman, *Dorothy Healey Remembers*, 142.
10. ibid., 195.
11. ibid., 139.

■ CHAPTER 13

1. Jo Wilkinson, letter to author, 2005, 3.
2. Gellhorn, *The States and Subversion*, 28.
3. Norris, *Racing for the Bomb*, 268, 516.
4. Gellhorn, op cit, 44.

■ CHAPTER 14

1. Theoharis, *Beyond the Hiss Case*, 132.
2. Bailey, "Progressive Lawyers," 130.
3. ibid., 146.
4. ibid., 139.
5. ibid., 139.
6. ibid., 172.
7. ibid., 172. See also, Donner, *The Age of Surveillance*, 149–150.

■ CHAPTER 15

1. Bailey, "Progressive Lawyers," 156.
2. ibid., 173.

■ CHAPTER 16

1. He was dean of Brown University, 1903–1911, president of Amherst College, 1912–1923, chairman of the Experimental College, University of Wisconsin, 1927–1932, founder of the San Francisco School of Social Studies, on the national board of the American Civil Liberties Union, 1927–1963, and from 1960 until his death in 1964, cofounder with Frank and others of the National Committee to Abolish the House Un-American Activities Committee.
2. Such was the glacial movement of the majority members of the U.S. Supreme Court in this field that it wasn't until 1977—thirty years after the Hollywood Ten went to prison for their silence—that the Court, in *Wooley v. Maynard*, ruled that the First Amendment protects the right to refrain from speaking about one's political beliefs as well as the right to speak, the two being complementary components of the broad concept of individual freedom of mind.
3. Alexander Meiklejohn testimony before Senate Judiciary Subcommittee on Constitutional Rights, 1955.
4. Jo Wilkinson, letter to author, 3–5.
5. In litigation against the FBI, Wilkinson, the First Amendment Foun-dation, NCARL, and attorneys for the case were prohibited from using this witness's name by federal judge A. Wallace Tashima, at the behest of the FBI and under threat of contempt of court. We will honor that order here, as her name is irrelevant to the story.

■ CHAPTER 17

1. Gentry, *J. Edgar Hoover*, 233, 438. FBI files forced open by the Freedom of Information Act show that Ernst reported to Hoover the private conversations he had with such enemies of the FBI as I. F. Stone. The files included many letters from Ernst to Hoover and his top aides. Those addressed to "My dear Edgar . . . for your eyes alone" expressed such sentiments as "You are a grand guy and I am in your army." And, " . . . a lot of people think I am a stooge for you which I take as a high compliment."
2. Navasky, *Naming Names*, 54.
3. McWilliams, *The Education of Carey McWilliams*, 161.
4. Navasky, 326–327.
5. It's believable that the Hungarian Freedom Fighters' "media event" had some encouragement from our government, as you can see from the following:

> According to National Security Council records, Frank Wisner, chief of CIA's clandestine operations, began large-scale programs designed to bring thousands of anti-Communist exiles to the United States. . . . including some groups with clear ties to extreme nationalist and Fascist organizations in Europe. The agency simultaneously funneled millions of dollars into advertising and staged media events inside the United States during the same period. . . .
>
> Tens of thousands of Eastern European refugees emigrated to the United States throughout the late 1940s and 1950s. . . . Just as any

large group of humans contains some criminals, so, too, did this emigration. The difference this time was that of the criminals who did come, many were experienced right-wing political activists who were highly organized and blessed with the patronage of the CIA.... [and] began to take on a distinct life and authority of their own during the cold war, particularly inside America's large Eastern European immigrant communities.... [Simpson, *Blowback*, 9–10.]

∎ CHAPTER 18

1. Cook, *The Nightmare Decade*, 321.
2. ibid, 384.
3. Sherrill, *Gothic Politics in the Deep South*, 211. It was one of history's ironies that long after he sounded these alarms about the threat of Communism, and after the death of J. Edgar Hoover—who covered up for Eastland—FBI records showed that one of the senator's staff aides had passed information to the Soviet Union for years before being detected [Ungar, Sanford J. *The FBI: An Uncensored Look Behind the Walls* (Atlantic Little, Brown, 1975), 117.]
4. Navasky, *Naming Names*, 14.
5. Packer, *Ex-Communist Witnesses*, 203.
6. Salmond, *A Southern Rebel*, 236.
7. ibid., 240.
8. ibid., 243.
9. ibid., 244–246.
10. Sherrill, op cit, 198.

∎ CHAPTER 19

1. Zilg, *Dupont*, 316.
2. Gentry, *J. Edgar Hoover*, 204.
3. Zilg, 296.
4. ibid., 297.
5. ibid., 296.

∎ CHAPTER 20

1. And they were impressively successful. Six years after *Brown*, not a single school had been integrated in the Deep South, and ten years after *Brown*, 98 percent of the schools in that region were still segregated.
2. Fosl, *Subversive Southerner*, 177.
3. ibid., 202–203.
4. ibid., 230.
5. Jo Wilkinson, letter to author, 10–12.

∎ CHAPTER 21

1. Nossiter, *Of Long Memory*, 90.
2. ibid., 103.

3. Things move very slowly in the South. In 1994, a mere thirty-one years after the murder, Mississippi, having entered an entirely different era, finally got around to hauling Beckwith back into court for a third trial, this time with a conviction.

4. Sherrill, *Gothic Politics in the Deep South*, 54–5.

5. "Hard-core" was one of the favored words of the witch-hunters. Being a Communist was bad, but being a "hard-core" Communist was intolerable. It is safe to say that not once, in all the years of the Cold War, was anyone ever called a "soft-core" Communist.

■ CHAPTER 22

1. Just in case some readers still believe the FBI supported the civil rights movement, as portrayed in the film *Mississippi Burning*: in the 1960s, Hoover continued to use his power to wiretap in unprecedented ways and particularly to try to destroy the civil rights movement.

   Effective blackmailing, of course, depends on letting the victim know the danger of not playing along with the blackmailer. That's why Hoover was always eager to tell Attorney General Robert Kennedy or President John F. Kennedy what he knew about the president's extramarital dalliances. In fact, that's how Hoover got Robert Kennedy's permission to install electronic listening devices in Martin Luther King Jr.'s hotel rooms. Previously, Bobby had steadfastly refused, but in October 1963, there were newspaper stories about a high-priced brothel being run on Capitol Hill. One of the call girls working part-time in the brothel was Ellen Rometsch, a beautiful East German suspected of being a spy. She was also among the women who dallied in the White House, and Hoover of course knew about it. When the Senate Rules Committee got ready to hold closed-door hearings on the allegations, Robert Kennedy met with Hoover and asked him not to disclose what he knew. Later that day, Hoover persuaded the committee to drop the Rometsch scandal. And Bobby promptly approved the bugging of King.

2. It would be the conclusion of the most disputed, drawn-out, loftily absurd death penalty case in California history. Chessman, who had been in and out of prison since he was sixteen, was not a killer, but he was a sadistic rapist. Over a period of eleven years Chessman had been scheduled for execution nine times. Thanks to a legal-political-publicity battle, he had been spared eight times. Manuscripts he smuggled out of prison were turned into books that made him an international cause célèbre. World figures as diverse as Albert Schweitzer and Brigitte Bardot sent telegrams to California governor Pat Brown, asking for mercy for Chessman.

3. Brown and Adler, *Public Justice, Private Mercy*, 49.

4. HUAC, *Operation Abolition*.

5. Powers, *Not Without Honor*, 307.

6. Even the city's rich, with their attitude of *noblesse oblige*, contributed to the city's ambiance of tolerance. True, Harry Bridges, as head of the longshoreman's union, was perhaps considered an ideological devil by many of San Francisco's

business leaders, but even that crowd credited him with bringing a kind of stability to one of the city's most crucial arenas, the docks. And anyway, if he was a devil, he was *their* devil, and a lot of natives were justifiably angered to see him on TV being forcibly ejected from city hall even before the hearings began.

7. Mandel, *Saying No to Power*, 365.
8. Billy Boy parody, *Sing Out!*, 1:4, 16.
9. Angus Cameron, mentioned above as having been "identified," in fact had a very solid if somewhat contentious reputation in the book world—editor-in-chief and vice president of the upscale publishing house Little, Brown and Company—before being forced to resign because the slander-for-sale magazine *Counterattack* had "identified" him as a Communist.
10. HUAC pamphlet, October 10, 1962, 1476.
11. Vincent Hallinan, son of an impoverished Irish immigrant family, was without question the most colorful and most radical lawyer ever to take on the San Francisco establishment. Eight times he ended up in fistfights with opposing lawyers; Hallinan called it "settling out of court." Once he was sent to prison for contempt of court because of his aggressive defense of Harry Bridges, whom the government was trying to deport as a Communist. In prison, Hallinan led other inmates in a successful strike to integrate the cafeteria

∎ CHAPTER 23

1. *Watkins v. United States.* 360 U.S. 109, 111 (1959).
2. Mason, *The Supreme Court from Taft to Warren*, 3.
3. *Jencks v. United States.* 353 U.S. 657 (1957).
4. *Barenblatt v. United States.* 360 U.S. 109, 79 S. Ct. 1081 (1959).
5. Wagman, *The Supreme Court*, 149.
6. Brant, *The Bill of Rights*, 467.

∎ CHAPTER 24

1. Gentry, *J. Edgar Hoover*, 411, and Theoharis, notes to author.
2. Berman, *Frontier* magazine, April 1961, 5–7.
3. Mason, *The Supreme Court from Taft to Warren*, 160–161.
4. Kutler, *The American Inquisition*, 154.
5. Demaris, *The Director*, 119.
6. Reppetto, *American Mafia*, 213; Gentry, 334–335.
7. Halberstam, *The Fifties*, 421.
8. Bickel, *The Morality of Consent*, 200.
9. Knight, *The Life of the Law*, 240.
10. Lewis, *Make No Law*, 200.
11. ibid., 190.
12. Wagman, *The Supreme Court*, 179.
13. ibid.
14. Sherrill, *Governing America*, 148.

15. ibid., 385. Their enmity was of long standing. In 1940, a year after Frankfurter was named to the Court, he and Black crossed opinions in a way that permanently set them at odds. This was in *Bridges v. California*, which covered cases involving the *Los Angeles Times* and Harry Bridges, the always contentious head of the West Coast longshoremen's union. Although the *Times* looked upon Bridges as a Communist and Bridges considered the *Times* fascist, at the moment they were allied in fighting contempt convictions for having made critical statements about pending cases (the *Times* in three editorials, Bridges in a telegram to the U.S. secretary of labor). Both claimed First Amendment protection and asked the Supreme Court to set aside their convictions.

Frankfurter, who voted against the defendants, based much of his argument on British common law. He considered the First Amendment—and the entire Constitution—as a natural development out of English traditions. Black, in arguing for the defendants, saw the First Amendment as something distinctly new and American, and his response was to tell Frankfurter: "Our Constitution and Bill of Rights [have given] far more security to the people of the United States with respect to freedom of religion, conscience, expression, assembly, petition and press than the people of Great Britain had ever enjoyed. It is a prized American privilege to speak one's mind, although not always in good taste, on all public institutions." (Lewis, 98–100.) Frankfurter never forgave him for that.

16. Halberstam, 412, and Sherrill, *Why They Call It Politics*, 385.
17. *New York Post*, February 28, 1961.
18. Murray Kempton, *New York Post*, February 28, 1961.

■ CHAPTER 25

1. Later, when Kerr caved in to FBI demands, Hoover probably thought better of him. In the 1970s, despite faculty protests, Kerr surrendered lists of student organizations in the antiwar movement to the FBI. But his most shameful capitulation to the right wing came just a few years later, in 1964, when UC Berkeley's students launched their Free Speech Movement, a protest against the university's restrictions on political activities. When students took over Sproul Hall, Kerr—who was quoted as saying 49 percent of the protesters were Communists or fellow travelers—called in the Oakland police, considered the most brutal force in northern California. The cops made the press and religious observers leave the building, put paper over the windows, locked the doors, and began beating the hell out of the eight hundred or so students left inside. Jackie Goldberg, beaten so badly she had trouble walking for several weeks, recalls, "They would grab you by the neck or by the hair or by the heels, and drag you down the stairs, your head hitting the cement or the marble." Of course, this brutality at Berkeley only inspired and expanded student antiwar and civil rights activities there and on other campuses (Schultz and Schultz, *The Price of Dissent*, 289).

2. *San Francisco Chronicle*, March 23, 1961.

■ CHAPTER 26

1. Jo Wilkinson, letter to author, 2005, 8.
2. ibid., 7.

■ CHAPTER 27

1. Roberts, *The Brother*, 437.
2. Theoharis, *Chasing Spies*, 136.
3. Jo Wilkinson, letter to author, 2005, 16.
4. *Los Angeles Examiner Herald*, January 25, 1962.

■ CHAPTER 28

1. Father Mallette quote about how good Criley was. *Chicago Daily News*, February 23, 1966.
2. *Chicago Tribune*, March 2, 1985, and Swearingen, *FBI Secrets*, 32, 38.
3. Criley was also indispensable, decades later, at a time of the committee's triumph. A federal court ordered the FBI to hand over to Frank its entire record of harassing him. As mentioned earlier, that came to 132,000 pages. With large sections blacked out by the FBI and much of the rest full of ellipses and bureaucratic jibberish, making sense of it all would have been comparable to deciphering the Rosetta Stone. Frank didn't try; he passed the whole thing on to Criley, who succeeded. One of the results was the book *The FBI v. The First Amendment*, a concise, award-winning history of the running battle between Frank's NCAHUAC and the FBI.
4. Jo Wilkinson, letter to author, 2005, 16.
5. Four years later, Dorothy Healey received an impressive 86,149 votes in an effort to become Los Angeles County tax assessor. She financed her campaign by selling two buttons, one saying, "Vote for Dorothy Healey for a radical alternative," the other saying, "Vote for Dorothy Healey. Vote Communist." She started out charging fifty cents a button. But the Communist button became so popular she started charging a dollar for it. "By this time," she recalls, "I had become a kind of local institution, and I think I got the votes of a number of people who had simply stopped thinking of me only as a Communist and instead voted for me as Dorothy Healey, the local troublemaker." (Healey and Isserman, *Dorothy Healey Remembers*, 195).
6. Schultz and Schultz, *The Price of Dissent*, 54.

■ CHAPTER 29

1. *New Yorker*, March 19, 1996, and *Los Angeles Times*, March 6, 1964.
2. *New York Times*, April 6, 1966.
3. *Daily Utah Chronicle*, November 6, 1963.
4. ibid., 153, 168.
5. Schultz and Schultz, *It Did Happen Here*, 276.
6. Criley, *The FBI v. The First Amendment*, 62.
7. *Wall Street Journal*, August 6, 1963.

■ CHAPTER 30

1. Jo Wilkinson, letter to author, 2005, 1.
2. ibid., 9.
3. ibid., 9–10.
4. ibid., 6.
5. ibid., 19.
6. ibid., 4–5
7. ibid., 12.
8. Fariello, *Red Scare*, 468.

■ CHAPTER 31

1. Gentry, *J. Edgar Hoover*, 604.
2. Schultz and Schultz, *The Price of Dissent*, 278.
3. ibid., 282.
4. *Washington Post*, January 6, 1963.
5. Schultz and Schultz, op cit, 283, 286, 287.
6. *Charleston Gazette*, December 8, 1964.
7. *Washington Post*, December 8, 1964.
8. Ybarra, *Washington Gone Crazy*, 462.
9. *Washington Post*, December 6, 1964.
10. O'Connor, O'Connor, and Bowler, *Harvey and Jessie*, 232, 233, 244.
11. *Harpers*, November 1966.
12. Bentley, ed., *Thirty Years of Treason*, xvii.
13. Brinkley, *The End of Reform*, 141.
14. Gentry, 241–42.
15. Carr, *The House Un-American Activities Committee*, 216.
16. ibid., 222.
17. Olmstead, *Red Spy Queen*, 183.
18. ibid., 138.
19. Morris, *Richard Milhous Nixon*, 494.

■ CHAPTER 32

1. Kaiser, *1968 in America*, 111.
2. ibid., 233.
3. ibid., 148.
4. West, *HUAC's Chicago Defeat, 1965–66*, 55–6.
5. James H. Pfister was chairman of the Louisiana legislature's Un-American Activities Committee.
6. Kinoy, *Rights on Trial*, 299–300.
7. *Chicago Daily News*, May 29, 1965.
8. *Chicago American*, May 27, 1965.
9. *Toledo Blade*, June 1965.
10. Walker, *In Defense of American Liberties*, 265.
11. *Stamler v. Willis* 415 F. 2nd 1365 (7th Cir., 1969).
12. Kinoy, 301.

■ CHAPTER 33

1. *San Francisco Examiner,* August 5 and 6, 1966
2. *Washington Post,* August 20, 1966
3. *Nation,* September 5, 1966.
4. Kinoy, *Rights on Trial,* 304–6
5. *New York Times,* August 22, 1966.
6. *San Francisco Chronicle,* August 15, 1966.
7. *Milwaukee Journal,* August 19, 1966.
8. *St. Louis Post Dispatch,* August 18, 1966.
9. *Boston Globe,* November 14, 1966.
10. *Providence Journal,* August 29, 1966.
11. *Washington Post,* September 16, 1966.
12. *Detroit News,* September 15, 1966.
13. *Saturday Evening Post,* September 24, 1966.
14. *Commonweal,* September 2, 166, No. 20.

■ CHAPTER 34

1. Perlstein, *Before the Storm,* 110–118.
2. Caro, *Master of the Senate,* 303.
3. Dugger, *The Politician,* 36.
4. Sherrill, *The Accidental President,* 232, 233.
5. Kinoy, *Rights on Trial,* 259.
6. ibid., 263.
7. Burnham, *Above the Law,* 48–52.
8. *Capital Times,* Madison, WI, 1962.
9. *Congressional Record,* February 1963.
10. Perhaps more enlightening was Congressman Ryan's box score for HUAC in 1961, quoted in a reprint from the Citizens Committee to Preserve American Freedoms in Los Angeles; in Wilkinson clips 1961–1964:

    Total bills introduced in House: 9,480
    Average number referred to committees other than HUAC: 497
    Total referred to HUAC: 27
    Less duplicated bills (identical bills introduced by various
        congressmen): 16
    Less bills contained in omnibus bill referred to HUAC: 5
    Less similar bills referred to other committees: 3
    Less bills referred to HUAC but under jurisdiction of other
        committees: 0
    Bills exclusively and properly referred to HUAC: 0

11. Rep. Henry B. Gonzalez, letter to constituents, from updated Wilkinson clips 1961–64.
12. Herblock cartoon, *Washington Post,* March 1, 1963.

■ CHAPTER 35

1. Daniel, ed., *America's Century*, 295.
2. HUAC, "Guerrilla Warfare Advocates in the United States" May 1968.
3. *Pittsburgh Post-Gazette*, 1968. Updated from Wilkinson clips, 1968.
4. *Louisville Courier-Journal*, May 8, 1968.
5. Kaiser, *1968 in America*, 243.
6. ibid., 192.

■ CHAPTER 36

1. *Communist Party v. Control Board* 367 USI (1961).
2. *Albertson v. SACB* 382 U.S. 70 (1965).
3. *Oakland Tribune*, November 16, 1965.
4. *Nation's Business*, October 1967, Vol. 55, 42.
5. *Wall Street Journal*, December 26, 1967.
6. Smith, *Democracy on Trial*, 118.
7. *Akron Law Journal*, Vol. No. 296–97.

■ CHAPTER 37

1. *Akron Law Journal*, 289.
2. Donner, *The Age of Surveillance*, 391.
3. Wicker, *One of Us*, 659, 662.
4. Donner, 401.
5. *Congressional Record*, July 24, 1974, 24831.
6. Donner, 391.
7. Cook, *The Nightmare Decade*, 145.
8. Theoharis, *Chasing Spies*, 241.
9. Don Edwards, James Dempsey, conversation with the author, February 2005.
10. Esther Herst, memo to Kit Gage, May 2005.

■ EPILOGUE

1. Most of the S.1 story is told through Esther Herst's recounting in a memo to Kit Gage, May 2005.
2. The Campaign for Political Rights story is also Esther Herst's, from the May 2005 memo.
3. "Guidelines on Domestic Security Investigation," U.S. Department of Justice, Attorney General Edward Levi, 1976.
4. *Socialist Workers Party v. Attorney General* 419 U. S. 1314 (1974). *National Lawyers Guild v. Attorney General et al.* 77 CIV.0999 (CLB). "FBI Admits Bid to Disrupt Lawyers Guild," *New York Times*, October 13, 1989.
5. Rachel Rosen DeGolia memo to Kit Gage, May 2005, regarding the role of CCDBR in the Red Squad suits.
6. Attorney General Guidelines on Racketeering, Criminal Enterprise and Domestic Security/Terrorism Investigations, Attorney General William French Smith, March 7, 1983 (Reprinted in 32 Crim. L. Rep (BNA) 3087 (1983). In force until 1989.

7. www.publiceye.org and Gelbspan, *Break-ins, Death Threats and the FBI, 7–11*.

8. "At War with Peace, U.S. Covert Operations," published by NCARL, 1990, 8 pages. It is still available from NCARL. NCARL helped form the Covert Operations Working Group. Such well-known disgruntled former CIA employees as David MacMichael and Ralph McGehee were important members of the working group.

9. *New York Times*, September 13, 1995.

10. *Congressional Record*, January 10, 1995, S2525.

11. Antiterrorism & Effective Death Penalty Act, P.L. 104–132.

12. www.ncppf.org.

13. *HLP v. Reno*, 352 F 3d 382 (9th Cir. 2003).

14. Secret Evidence Repeal Act, H.R. 2121. Sponsored by Tom Campbell (R-CN) and David Benoir (D-MI).

15. USA Patriot Act, P.L. 107-56.

16. www.bordc.org and www.aclu.org

17. Ry Cooder, "Don't Call Me Red," *Chavez Ravine*, Nonesuch #79877–2.

18. It was called the Senate Subcommittee on Internal Security and Terrorism—terrorism was just starting to supplant Communism as the main named threat—and it lasted until Democrats reclaimed the Senate in 1986.

Adams, John G. *Without Precedent: The Story of the Death of McCarthyism*. New York: W.W. Norton, 1983.

Aronson, James. *The Press and the Cold War*. New York: Monthly Review Press, 1970.

Bailey, Percival Roberts. "Progressive Lawyers: A History of the National Lawyers Guild, 1936–1958." PhD thesis. New Brunswick, NJ: Rutgers College, 1979.

Barber, James David. *Presidential Character: Predicting Performance in the White House*. Upper Saddle River, NJ: Prentice Hall, 1985.

Barnet, Richard J. *The Rocket's Red Glare*. New York: Simon and Schuster, 1990.

Barson, Michael. *Better Dead than Red: A Nostalgic Look at the Golden Years of Russiaphobia, Red-baiting, and Other Commie Madness*. New York: Hyperion, 1992.

———, and Steven Heller. *Red Scared! The Commie Menace in Propaganda and Popular Culture*. San Francisco: Chronicle Books, 2001.

Bennett, David H. *The Party of Fear: From Nativist Movements to the New Right in American History.* New York: Vintage Books, 1990.

Bentley, Eric, ed. *Thirty Years of Treason: Excerpts from Hearings before the House Committee on Un-American Activities, 1938–1968.* New York: Thunder's Mouth Press/Nation Books, 2002.

Berman, Daniel Mason. "The Supreme Court Decides Against Freedom." *Frontier* magazine, April 1961.

Bickel, Alexander. *The Morality of Consent.* New Haven, CT: Yale University Press, 1977.

Blackstock, Nelson. *COINTELPRO: The FBI's Secret War on Political Freedom.* New York: Anchor Foundation, 1975.

Branch, Taylor. *Pillar of Fire: America in the King Years 1963–65.* New York: Simon & Schuster, 1998.

Brant, Irving. *The Bill of Rights: Its Origin and Meaning.* Indianapolis: Bobbs-Merrill Co., 1965.

Breuer, William B. *J. Edgar Hoover and His G-Men.* New York: Praeger, 1995.

Brinkley, Alan. *The End of Reform: New Deal Liberalism in Recession and War.* New York: Vintage Books, 1996.

———. *Voices of Protest: Huey Long, Father Coughlin and the Great Depression.* New York: Alfred A. Knopf, 1982.

Brodie, Fawn. *Richard Nixon: The Shaping of His Character.* Cambridge, MA: Harvard U. Press, 1983.

Brown, Edmund G., and Dick Adler. *Public Justice, Private Mercy: A Governor's Education on Death Row.* New York: Grove Press, 1989.

Burnham, David. *Above the Law: Secret Deals, Political Fixes, and Other Misadventures of the U.S. Department of Justice.* New York: Scribner, 1996.

Canon of Professional Ethics, p. 15. See: www.abanet.org/cpr/ethics/mcpr.pdf.

Carlton, Don E. *Red Scare: Right-wing Hysteria, Fifties Fanaticism and Their Legacy in Texas.* Austin, TX: Texas Monthly Press, 1985.

Caro, Robert A. *Master of the Senate: The Years of Lyndon Johnson.* New York: Knopf, 2002.

Carr, Robert K. *The House Un-American Activities Committee, 1945–1950.* Ithaca, NY: Cornell University Press, 1952.

Cohen, Robert. *When the Old Left Was Young: Student Radicals and America's First Mass Student Movement, 1929–1941.* New York: Oxford University Press, 1993.

Cohn, Roy, and Sidney Zion. *Autobiography of Roy Cohn.* Secaucus, NJ: Lyle Stuart, 1988.

Colby, Gerard. *DuPont: Behind the Nylon Curtain.* Englewood Cliffs, NJ: Prentice-Hall, 1974.

Cook, Fred J. *The Nightmare Decade: The Life and Times of Senator Joe McCarthy.* New York: Random House, 1971.

Criley, Richard. *The FBI v. The First Amendment.* Los Angeles, CA: First Amendment Foundation, 1990.

Cuff, Dana. *The Provisional City: Los Angeles Stories of Architecture and Urbanism.* Cambridge, MA: MIT Press, 2000.

Daniel, Clifton, ed. *America's Century.* New York: Dorling Kindersley Publishing, 2000.

Davis, Kenneth F. *FDR: The War President 1940–1943.* New York: Random House, 2000.

Demaris, Ovid. *The Director: An Oral Biography of J. Edgar Hoover.* New York: Harper's Magazine Press, 1975.

Dinnerstein, Leonard. *Anti-Semitism in America.* New York: Oxford University Press, 1994.

Donner, Frank. *The Age of Surveillance: The Aims and Methods of America's Political Intelligence System.* New York: Vintage Books, 1981.

Donovan, Robert J. *Conflict and Crisis: The Presidency of Harry S. Truman 1945–1948.* Columbia, MO: University of Missouri Press, 1996.

Dugger, Ronnie. *The Politician: The Life and Times of Lyndon Johnson.* New York, W.W. Norton, 1982.

Fanebust, Wayne. *Echoes of November: The Life and Times of Senator R. F. Pettigrew of South Dakota.* Freeman, SD: Pine Hill Press, Inc., 1997.

Fariello, Griffin. *Red Scare: Memories of the American Inquisition*. New York: Avon Books, 1995.

Faulk, John Henry. *The Uncensored John Henry Faulk*. Austin, TX: Texas Monthly Press, 1985.

Fosl, Catherine. *Subversive Southerner: Anne Braden and the Struggle for Racial Justice in the Cold War South*. New York: Palgrave Macmillan, 2002.

Friedrich, Otto. *City of Nets: A Portrait of Hollywood in the 1940s*. New York: Harper & Row, 1986.

Gabler, Neal. *Winchell: Gossip, Power and the Culture of Celebrity*. New York: Vintage Books, 1994.

Galbraith, John Kenneth. *A Life in Our Times: Memoirs*. Boston: Houghton Mifflin, 1981.

Gelbspan, Ross. *Break-ins, Death Threats and the FBI: The Covert War against the Central America Movement*. Boston: South End Press, 1991.

Gellhorn, Walter. *Security, Loyalty and Science*. Ithaca, New York: Cornell University Press, 1950.

———. *The States and Subversion*. Westport, CT: Greenwood Press, 1976.

Gentry, Curt. *J. Edgar Hoover: The Man and the Secrets*. New York: W.W. Norton, 1991.

Goodwin, Richard N. *Remembering America: A Voice from the Sixties*. Boston: Little, Brown, 1988.

Green, Mark, and Robert Massie, eds., *The Big Business Reader*. New York: Pilgrim Press, 1980.

Halberstam, David. *The Best and the Brightest*. New York: Random House, 1992.

———. *The Fifties*. New York: Villard Books, 1993.

Hallinan, Vincent. *A Lion in Court*. New York: G. P. Putnam's Sons, 1963.

Healey, Dorothy, and Maurice Isserman. *Dorothy Healey Remembers: A Life in the American Communist Party*. New York: Oxford University Press, 1990.

Heckscher, August. *Woodrow Wilson: A Biography*. New York: Charles Scribner's Sons, 1991.

Herrmann, Dorothy. *Helen Keller: A Life*. New York: Alfred A. Knopf, 1998.

Heymann, C. David. *RFK: A Candid Biography of Robert F. Kennedy*. New York: Dutton, 1998.

Johnson, George. *Architects of Fear: Conspiracy Theories and Paranoia in American Politics*. Los Angeles: Tarcher Press, 1983.

Kaiser, Charles. *1968 in America: Music, Politics, Chaos, Counterculture, and the Shaping of a Generation*. New York: Weidenfeld & Nicholson, 1988.

Keane, James Thomas. *Fritz B. Burns and the Development of Los Angeles: The Biography of a Community Developer and Philanthropist*. Los Angeles: The Historic Society of Southern California, 2001.

Kennedy, Paul. *The Rise and Fall of the Great Powers: Economic Change and Military Conflict from 1500 to 2000*. New York: Random House, 1987.

Kessner, Thomas. *The Golden Door: Italian and Jewish Immigrant Mobility in New York City, 1880–1915*. New York: Oxford University Press, 1977.

Kinoy, Arthur. *Rights on Trial: The Odyssey of a People's Lawyer*. Cambridge, MA: Harvard University Press, 1983.

Klurfeld, Herman. *Behind the Lines: The World of Drew Pearson*. Englewood Cliffs, NJ: Prentice-Hall, 1968.

Knight, Alfred H. *The Life of the Law: The People and Cases that Have Shaped Our Society, from King Alfred to Rodney King*. New York: Crown Publishers, 1996.

Kutler, Stanley I. *Abuse of Power*. New York: The Free Press, 1997.

———. *The American Inquisition: Justice and Injustice in the Cold War*. New York: Hill & Wang, 1982.

Landau, Saul. *The Dangerous Doctrine: National Security and U.S. Foreign Policy*. Boulder, CO: Westview Press, 1988.

Lewis, Anthony. *Make No Law: The Sullivan Case and the First Amendment*. New York: Random House, 1991.

Lewy, Guenter. *The Cause That Failed: Communism in American Political Life*. New York: Oxford University Press, 1990.

Lichtenstein, Nelson, et al. *Who Built America? Working People and the Nation's Economy, Politics, Culture, and Society (Vol. Two, 1877 to the Present)*. New York: Pantheon Books, 1992.

Lingeman, Richard. *Theodore Dreiser: An American Journey*. New York, John Wiley & Sons, 1993.

Lowenthal, Max. *The Federal Bureau of Investigation*. Westport, CT: Greenwood Publishing Group, 1950.

Lukas, J. Anthony. *Nightmare: The Underside of the Nixon Years*. New York: Viking, 1973.

Mandel, William. *Saying No to Power: Autobiography of a Twentieth Century Activist and Thinker*. Berkeley, CA: Creative Arts, 1999.

Mason, Alpheus Thomas. *The Supreme Court from Taft to Warren*. Baton Rouge, LA: Louisiana State University Press, 1968.

Matusow, Harvey. *False Witness*. New York: Cameron & Kahn, 1955.

McCullough, David. *Truman*. New York: Simon & Schuster, 1993.

McGrath, John S., and James J. Delmont. *Floyd B. Olsen, 1891–1936*. McGrath and Delmont, 1937.

McElvaine, Robert S. *The Great Depression: America 1929–1941*. Westport, CT: Three Rivers Press, 1993.

McWilliams, Carey. *California: The Great Exception*. Berkeley and Los Angeles: University of California Press, 1999.

———. *The Education of Carey McWilliams*. New York: Simon & Schuster, 1978.

———. *Factories in the Field: The Story of Migratory Farm Labor in California*. Berkeley and Los Angeles: University of California Press, 1966.

Meagher, Sylvia. *Accessories after the Fact: The Warren Commission, The Authorities and the Report*. New York: Vintage Books, 1992.

Miller, Arthur R. *The Assault on Privacy*. New York: Signet Books, 1972.

Mitchell, Greg. *The Campaign of the Century: Upton Sinclair's Race for Governor of California and the Birth of Media Politics*. New York: Random House, 1992.

———. *Tricky Dick and the Pink Lady: Richard Nixon vs. Helen Gahagan Douglas—Sexual Politics and the Red Scare, 1950.* New York: Random House, 1998.

Morgan, Ted. *FDR: A Biography.* New York: Simon & Schuster, 1985.

———. *Reds: McCarthyism in Twentieth-Century America.* New York: Random House, 2003.

Morris, Roger. *Richard Milhous Nixon: The Rise of an American Politician.* New York: Henry Holt, 1991.

Navasky, Victor. *Naming Names.* New York: Viking Press, 1980.

Norris, Robert S. *Racing for the Bomb: General Leslie R. Groves, the Manhattan Project's Indispensable Man.* Hanover, NH: Steerforth, 2003.

Nossiter, Adam. *Of Long Memory: Mississippi and the Murder of Medgar Evers.* Cambridge, MA: Da Capo Press, 2002.

O'Connor, Jessie Lloyd, Harvey O'Connor, and Susan M. Bowler. *Harvey and Jessie: A Couple of Radicals.* Philadelphia: Temple University Press, 1988.

Offner, Arnold A. *Another Such Victory: President Truman and the Cold War, 1945–1953.* Palo Alto, CA: Stanford University Press, 2002.

Ollestad, Norman. *Inside the FBI.* New York: Lancer Books, 1968.

Olmsted, Kathryn S. *Red Spy Queen: A Biography of Elizabeth Bentley.* Chapel Hill, NC: University of North Carolina Press, 2002.

Oney, Steve. *And the Dead Shall Rise: The Murder of Mary Phagan and the Lynching of Leo Frank.* New York: Pantheon Books, 2003.

O'Reilly, Kenneth. *Hoover and the Un-Americans: The FBI, HUAC, and the Red Menace.* Philadelphia: Temple University Press, 1983.

Packer, Herbert L. *Ex-Communist Witnesses.* Stanford, CA: Stanford University Press, 1962.

Pearson, Drew, and Tyler Abell. *Diaries [of Drew Pearson, Vol. I]: 1949–1959.* New York: Holt, Rinehart and Winston, 1974.

Perlstein, Rick. *Before the Storm: Barry Goldwater and the Unmaking of the American Consensus.* New York: Hill & Wang, 2001.

Pipes, Richard. *A Concise History of the Russian Revolution.* New York: Vintage Books, 1996.

Powers, Richard Gid. *Not Without Honor: The History of American Anticommunism.* New York: The Free Press, 1995.

Reeves, Richard. *President Nixon: Alone in the White House.* New York: Simon & Schuster, 2001.

Renshaw, Patrick. *The Wobblies: The Story of Syndicalism in the United States.* Garden City, NY: Doubleday Anchor, 1967.

Reppetto, Thomas. *American Mafia: A History of Its Rise to Power.* New York: John MacRae Books, 2004.

Roberts, Sam. *The Brother: The Untold Story of Atomic Spy David Greenglass and How He Sent His Sister, Ethel Rosenberg, to the Electric Chair.* New York: Random House, 2001.

Russell, Francis. *The Shadow of Blooming Grove: Warren G. Harding and His Times.* New York: McGraw-Hill, 1968.

Sachar, Howard M. *A History of the Jews in America.* New York: Vintage Books, 1993.

Salmond, John A. *The Conscience of a Lawyer: Clifford J. Durr and American Civil Liberites.* Tuscaloosa, AL: University of Alabama , 1990.

———. *A Southern Rebel: The Life and Times of Aubrey Willis Williams, 1890–1965.* Chapel Hill, NC: University of North Carolina Press, 1983.

Sanders, Jane. *Cold War on the Campus: Academic Freedom at the University of Washington, 1946–1964.* Seattle, WA: University of Washington Press, 1979.

Shindler, Colin. *Hollywood in Crisis: Cinema and American Society, 1929–39.* New York: Routledge, 1996.

Schlesinger, Arthur. *Robert Kennedy and His Times.* Boston: Houghton Mifflin, 1978.

Schultz, Bud and Ruth. *It Did Happen Here: Recollections of Political Repression in America.* Berkeley, CA: University of California Press, 1989.

——. *The Price of Dissent: Testimonies to Political Repression in America*. Berkeley, CA: University of California Press, 2001.

Severo, Richard, and Lewis Milford. *The Wages of War: When America's Soldiers Come Home—From Valley Forge to Vietnam*. New York: Simon & Schuster, 1989.

Shaw, Warren, and David Pryce. *World Almanac of the Soviet Union from 1905 to the Present*. New York: Pharos Books, 1990.

Sherrill, Robert. *The Accidental President*. New York: Grossman, 1967.

——. *Gothic Politics in the Deep South*. New York: Ballantine Books, 1968.

——. *Governing America: An Introduction*. New York: Harcourt Brace Jovanovich, 1978.

——. *Why They Call It Politics: A Guide to America's Government*. New York: Harcourt College Publishers, 2000.

Sherwood, Robert E. *Roosevelt and Hopkins*. New York: Enigma Books, 2001.

Shirer, William L. *Nightmare Years: 1930–1940*. Edinburgh, Scotland: Birlinn, 2002.

Simpson, Christopher. *Blowback: America's Recruitment of Nazis and Its Effects on the Cold War*. New York: Grove Press, 1988.

Smith, John Chabot. *Alger Hiss: The True Story*. New York: Holt, Rinehart and Winston, 1976.

Smith, Sally Bedell. *Grace and Power: The Private World of the Kennedy White House*. New York: Random House, 2004.

Smith, Page. *Democracy on Trial: The Japanese American Evacuation and Relocation in World War II*. New York: Simon & Schuster, 1995.

Starr, Kevin. *Inventing the Dream: California through the Progressive Era*. New York: Oxford University Press, 1985.

Summers, Anthony. *Official and Confidential: The Secret Life of J. Edgar Hoover*. New York: G. P. Putnam's Sons, 1993.

Swanberg, W. A. *Luce and His Empire*. New York: Charles Scribner's Sons, 1972.

Swearingen, M. Wesley. *FBI Secrets, An Agents Exposé*. Boston: South End Press, 1995.

Tanenhaus, Sam. *Whittaker Chambers: A Biography*. New York: Modern Library, 1998.

Theoharis, Athan, ed. *Beyond the Hiss Case: The FBI, Congress, and the Cold War*. Philadelphia, PA: Temple University Press, 1982.

———. *Chasing Spies: How the FBI Failed in Counter-intelligence but Promoted the Politics of McCarthyism in the Cold War Years*. Chicago: Ivan R. Dee, 2002.

———. *Spying on Americans: Political Surveillance from Hoover to the Huston Plan*. Philadelphia: Temple University Press, 1978.

Thomas, Dana. *Media Moguls*. New York: Putnam, 1981.

Thomas, Evan. *Robert Kennedy: His Life*. New York: Simon & Schuster, 2000.

Unger, Robert. *The Union Station Massacre: The Original Sin of J. Edgar Hoover's FBI*. Kansas City, MO: Andrews McMeel Publishers, 1997.

Wagman, Robert J. *The Supreme Court: A Citizen's Guide*. New York: Pharos Books, 1993.

Walker, Samuel. *In Defense of American Liberties: A History of the ACLU*. New York: Oxford University Press, 1990.

Weintraub, Stanley. *MacArthur's War: Korea and the Undoing of an American Hero*. New York: The Free Press, 2000.

West, James. "HUAC's Political Defeat," *Political Affairs*. New York, 1965.

Wicker, Tom. *One of Us: Richard Nixon and the American Dream*. New York: Random House, 1991.

Wilkinson, Frank. *Akron Law Review*. Akron, OH: University of Akron, Reprint 1974.

———. "Revisiting the McCarthy Era, Looking at *Wilkinson v. the United States* in Light of *Wilkinson v. the Federal Bureau of Investigation*." *Loyola Law Review*. Spring 2000, Vol. 33, No. 2, 681.

Wise, David. *Molehunt: The Secret Search for Traitors that Shattered the CIA*. New York: Random House, 1992.

———. *Nightmover: How Aldrich Ames Sold the CIA to the KGB for $4.6 Million*. New York: HarperCollins, 1995.

———. *Spy: The Inside Story of How the FBI's Robert Hanssen Betrayed America*. New York: Random House, 2002.

Wofford, Harris. *Of Kennedys and Kings: Making Sense of the Sixties*. New York: Farrar Straus Giroux, 1980.

Ybarra, Michael J. *Washington Gone Crazy: Senator Pat McCarran and the Great American Communist Hunt*. Hanover, NH: Steerforth Press, 2004.

Young, Brigadier Peter, ed. *World Almanac of WWII*. New York: Pharos Books, 1981.

Youngdale, James M., ed. *Third Party Footprints: An Anthology from Writings and Speeches of Midwest Radicals*. Minneapolis, MN: Ross & Haines, 1966.

Zilg, Gerard Colby. *Dupont: Behind the Nylon Curtain*. Englewood Cliffs, NJ: Prentice-Hall, 1974.

■ INTERVIEWS

British Broadcasting Corporation, *The Un-Americans*: "*Frank Wilkinson—The Campaigner*." Producer Archie Baron, 1992.

Frank Wilkinson Oral History, UCLA Oral History Program, Dale Trelevan, Director. December 15, 1984–September 5, 1992. 6 vol. © Regents of the University of California.

HUAC, *Operation Abolition*, 1960, Narrated and Ed. by Fulton Lewis, 3rd.

Interviews by author with Frank Wilkinson, fall 2002

Life Magazine, "The Bill of Rights," Fall Special 1991, Vol. 14, No. 13, 63.

Public Broadcasting Service, *Frontline*, "Inside the FBI: The Price of Freedom." August 11, 1997.

Public Broadcasting Service, *Frontline*, on HUAC, February 1993.

ACKNOWLEDGMENTS

ONLY "CHARACTERS" ARE fun to write about, so I'm indebted to Frank Wilkinson for being what he is: a brilliant, self-centered, stubborn, charming, feisty character, through and through. Essential guidance for the writing of this book came from six hefty volumes of recollections drawn from Wilkinson over a period of eight years by Dale E. Treleven, director of the UCLA Oral History Program. I also interviewed Wilkinson. Essential help came from Loeb and Loeb, the Los Angeles law firm that, with the ACLU of Southern California, forced the FBI to turn over zillions of records showing how it tried to ruin Wilkinson's life (for a while it did a pretty good job of it).

Much of the pleasure of working on this biography came from reading, and cribbing from, the many splendid histories and biographies spawned by the Age of Crazed Anti-Communism. Among the dozens I could mention gratefully were those written or compiled with special flair by Curt Gentry, Frank J. Donner, Victor Navasky, Ovid Demaris, Eric Bentley, James Aronson, Christopher Simpson, Michael J. Ybarra, Robert K. Carr, Michael Barson, Athan Theoharis, Griffin Fariello, and Kenneth O'Reilly.

I was also lucky enough to have an editor, Kit Gage, who was a walking encyclopedia of this era.

—Robert Sherrill

•

WE LIED IN the book. From the very beginning. Third word. *Felon*. Frank Wilkinson was not a convicted felon. He was convicted of 2 U.S.C. 192, the *misdemeanor* of refusing to answer a question posed by either house of Congress or by a committee within it. Punishable by a fine of not more than $1,000 and imprisonment of not more than twelve months. But you can't call Frank a First Amendment Misdemeanant, because when you read the part of the book in which his time in prison is described, you tell us if it doesn't seem like he was the worst kind of felon. That's how he was treated, anyway. We all liked the title—except for Frank. But he got a whole book about him, and didn't have a say in any bit of it. So "First Amendment Felon" stuck.

The First Amendment Foundation was formed in 1985 as a sister nonprofit organization to NCARL, which started out life in 1960 as the National Committee to Abolish HUAC. Frank helped start both groups.

The Foundation, which initiated this project, is enormously grateful to the Open Society Institute, which welcomed and funded it, and for its patience while the book took shape.

The Foundation also greatly appreciates the detailed assesment of the book by Athan Theoharis and Ken O'Reilly, both of whom are world experts on most of these issues. Ally Bolin did a valiant job of the first editing. Katie Roberts, assistant director at the Foundation, was essential as a reader, untangler of computer messes you don't even want to hear about, and all-around supporter. Esther Herst, Mike Honey, and Rachel Rosen DeGolia graciously dug through files and memories and helped guide me through the epilogue.

I join Bob in thanking Dale Treleven and the UCLA Oral History Program for first downloading Frank's life onto the printed page. By reminding Frank that he had already told the whole story to Dale, and parts of the story to thousands of his advocates and fans across the country, we were able to convince him that the story and its lessons deserved a shorter and more portable telling.

Carl Bromley and Ruth Baldwin of Nation Books have been enthusiastic and patient to the end, and our agent, Frances Goldin, persevered in connecting us to Nation Books, while appreciating the value of this story.

I hope that—as it did for me—your reading of this book leads you to discover more about the rise of the Red Scare and the Cold War, the evolution of the FBI, and the remarkable characters, for good and ill, that populate this history and deepen our understanding of the present. After you've finished reading, grab the bibliography and head out!

As with all books, a decent chunk of this book ended up on the cutting-room floor. What got cut mostly wasn't Frank's story, but additional material about the FBI, Hoover, HUAC, Alger Hiss, etc. Fortunately, the best of the cuts are up on the First Amendment Foundation Web site for your perusal (www.firstamend.org), as is more information about how to schedule a book tour to your area that can also include a reading and stories of other targets of HUAC and/or the FBI, and dissenters who prevailed.

Visit us.

KIT GAGE, DIRECTOR,
FIRST AMENDMENT FOUNDATION AND NCARL